The Bouschor Family
of the Upper Peninsula

The Bouschor Family
of the Upper Peninsula:

The Ancestors

Aaron N. Bouschor

BARQUE
POINT PRESS

Published 2024

ISBN-13: 979-8-9868807-3-0 (Hardcover)
ISBN-13: 979-8-9868807-4-7 (Paperback)

Library of Congress Control Number: 2024923575

Book cover design by Rica Graphics

Barque Point Press, LLC
330 E Mountain Vista Pl
Tucson, AZ 85704

www.barquepointpress.com

In Memory of Simon & Harriette

Table of Contents

Table of Contents

Table of Contents

List of Illustrations

List of Illustrations

Acknowledgments

This book could not have been written without the assistance of numerous friends, relatives, and organizations along the way. The following individuals who contributed to the content of this work deserve to be recognized by name.

My sincere thanks to David and Gloria Bouschor of Duluth. Dave and Gloria graciously hosted me at their home on multiple visits to Duluth over the years and were unsparing with their time and conversation. A special thanks goes to their daughter Denise Bouschor who invited me to a 2017 family reunion in Red Lodge, Montana, and first introduced me to her wonderful extended family. Several of the photographs in this and the planned second volume are thanks to David and Gloria sharing them with me.

The late Robert Leslie Bouschor and his wife, Denise, of Marquette, Michigan, were incredibly generous with their time and records. I was fortunate to have spent the better part of a day with Robert before his passing and listened to him share numerous stories of life on the Bouschor homestead. Denise has been a good friend in subsequent years and welcomed me on my visits to Marquette. I can thank Denise as well for sharing a number of documents and artifacts that greatly enhanced my understanding of the Bouschor family history.

Mary Bouschor of New York was another enthusiastic and helpful collaborator. She shared countless pictures and documents that helped make this book what it is today. Mary was always glad to help with identifying unknown figures in photographs and responded to my numerous questions and inquiries with enthusiasm. Thanks to Mary, I know vastly more about the Nels Bouschor branch of the family and his descendants than I otherwise would have.

The Schoolcraft County Historical Society has been an invaluable resource for researching the Bouschor family along with Manistique and Schoolcraft County at large. Society President Larry Peterson kindly worked with me to locate and scan records

on a pair of visits, and he shared some of his vast knowledge of the county and its inhabitants. Larry is an outstanding writer and historian as well, and anyone interested in Manistique and Schoolcraft County history would be well served to seek out his articles in Manistique's *Pioneer-Tribune* and his 2020 book *The Hiawatha Anthology*. Beginning during the pandemic, the Historical Society also made its monthly meetings accessible worldwide via Zoom, and it's been a pleasure getting to know the organization's leadership over the years. As of this writing, the Society is hard at work on expanding the museum so it can make its vast holdings of artifacts, photographs, and other exhibits available to the public.

Brenda Tibbetts of Garden, Michigan, kindly spent an afternoon with me at the Garden Peninsula Historical Society's museum in downtown Garden and shared records and photographs related to the Bouschor and Gray families. Moreover, Brenda's work leading the Historical Society's Facebook page sets the standard for ensuring generations of Garden Peninsula descendants can share memories and stories about the Peninsula and its inhabitants.

Laurie Jasmin and the Thompson Township Advisory Committee do a phenomenal job preserving and sharing the history of Thompson Village and the greater Township. I had the pleasure of meeting with Laurie in May 2024, and she gave me a tour of the Thompson Township Town Hall and its historical records. We can thank Laurie and the Committee for the interpretive plaques gracing the lakeshore at Thompson Village today and for ensuring the Township's voluminous records are available worldwide via the Upper Peninsula Digital Network.

My gratitude to Bruce and Judy Woodburn of Thompson Township for their knowledge and passion about the Barque Point homestead. I spent the better part of a day in May 2024 with Bruce and Judy, sharing knowledge about the area's history and its inhabitants. They kindly led me on a tour of the old homestead grounds, pointed out many remains of the Bouschor family legacy, and shared their thoughts on where many of the homestead's structures were once located. A subsequent visit later in the week included a walk along the original road that once brought the Bouschor family and visitors to the homestead. Bruce and Judy's lovely home overlooks Lake Michigan on the southern shore of Barque Point and feels as close as you could get to what life must have been like in the pioneer days when only a handful of families called the Barque Point area home. Their love of the Point and deep appreciation for its historical legacy is unparalleled, and the Bouschor family and the Garden Peninsula at large couldn't ask for better custodians.

My thanks to Bill and Myra Bouschor of Curtis, Washington, for providing me over the years with several photographs and records pertaining to my grandfather, Victor Henry Bouschor, and his parents, Henry and Louisa (Dawson) Bouschor. My uncle, Jim Bouschor of Juneau, Alaska, likewise kindly shared photographs and documents pertaining to Henry and Louisa. My gratitude to my mother, Denise, and brother, Andrew, for their insights as well.

Several members of the Ancestry.com and Facebook community contributed to this work as well by sharing pictures, documents, and memories of family members. While there are too many online contributors to name individually, I want to single out Georgia Tillotson, Lisa Busch, Karen LaFond Maki, Dean Jay Elliott, Carol Brown, Bill Macy, and Adrienne Waterman.

Several libraries were of great service in making records and microfilm available for review. I want to thank the Manistique Public Library, the Stephen B. Luce Library at SUNY Maritime College, the Bayliss Public Library of Sault Ste. Marie, and the Escanaba Public Library. A special mention belongs to the Upper Peninsula Digital Network (UPLINK), a collaboration led by Northern Michigan University, Michigan Tech University, and Lake Superior State University. UPLINK works with local historical societies, libraries, and other groups to digitalize and make available one-of-a-kind records on its website. Much of this volume's content would have been impossible to research or substantiate without UPLINK's growing wealth of content.

My thanks to Madeleine Swart for her proofreading and final review of this volume. Her eagle eye caught several issues and she made suggestions that helped the flow of the text. Any remaining mistakes are entirely the fault of the author. Also, my appreciation and gratitude to Rica Graphics for the beautiful cover design and jacket layout. I couldn't ask for a better team of professionals.

Finally, my deepest gratitude and love to my wife, Jennifer. Her patience with my multiple trips to the U.P. as well as accompanying me on visits to various archives, historical sites, and libraries over the past decade was inexhaustible. While she's undoubtedly heard more stories about the Bouschor family and obscure moments from U.P. history than anyone could reasonably tolerate, she's never expressed the slightest frustration, even when well warranted.

Note on Names, Places, and Dates

At various times in their lives, the first and second generation of Bouschors went by either Bouchard or Bouschor. For consistency, I've referred to them in this volume as Bouschor, except in direct quotes from sources that utilize other versions or spellings.

Part Two, detailing the ancestors of Simon Bouschor, includes many inhabitants of France and Canada from the 1500s to the 1800s. Prior to the municipal reorganization of France on 4 March 1790 as part of the French Revolution, France was loosely organized into historical provinces during what came to be known as the Ancien Régime. The revolutionaries organized France into eighty-three departments, a bureaucratic organization that persists to this day. Each department is itself part of a region, of which there are twelve in mainland France following reform and consolidation in 2014. Individual towns and communities are known as communes and are generally the smallest organizational unit, similar to an incorporated municipality in the United States. Thus, the name of Claude Bouchard's birthplace in 1626 was Saint-Cosme-en-Vairais in the historic French province of Maine. Following nearly four centuries of municipal reorganization in France, it is known today as the commune of Saint-Cosme-en-Vairais, Sarthe department, Pays de la Loire region of France. To capture both the historic as well as current references, the text below lists Claude's birthplace as "Saint-Cosme-en-Vairais, Maine, France (Saint-Cosme-en-Vairais, Sarthe, Pays-de-la-Loire, France)."

Regarding locations in Quebec, from 1535 until 1763, the French territory in present-day Canada was known as "Canada" and sometimes referred to as "New France." Following the Treaty of Paris awarding French territory in Canada to Great Britain in 1763, the territory became known as "Quebec" or the "Province of Quebec." From 1791 until 1841, present-day Quebec was known as "Lower Canada" and from 1841 to 1867 as "Canada" or the "Province of Canada." Finally, following confederation in 1867, Quebec took on its present-day name. To avoid confusion resulting from name changes throughout these time periods, I will refer to the territory held by France from 1535 to 1763 as "Canada," said territory held by the British from 1763 to 1791 as the "Province of Canada," and the same pre-confederation territory as it existed from 1841 to 1867 as the "Province of Canada." Any references to Canada or Quebec dating from after 1867 will refer to the country as a whole and the present-day province, respectively. As names of locations changed considerably over the years, I have provided the historical name associated with the location at the time of the event together with the present-day location in parentheses. For example, at the time of Elie Bouchard's birth in 1794, his birthplace was named Carleton, Lower Canada. That same town is today known as Carleton-sur-Mer in Quebec's Gaspésie–Îles-de-la-Madeleine administrative region. To reconcile this—and to give the reader adequate information—Elie's birthplace is listed as "Carleton, Lower Canada (Carleton-sur-Mer, Gaspésie–Îles-de-la-Madeleine, Quebec)." With regard to contemporary locations in both Canada and the United States, references to the country name are omitted as the reader is assumed to be generally familiar with U.S. states and Canadian provinces.

I've employed a similar convention for ancestors who lived in the United States. If they were born when a state was still a territory, or a municipality went by another name at the time of a life event, I've listed the place name at the time of the event first, followed by the present-day location in parentheses. For example, Simon Bouschor was born on 25 December 1829 on what was then known as Michilimackinac Island in the Michigan Territory. Thus, I've listed this event as "Michilimackinac Island, Michilimackinac County, Michigan Territory (Mackinac Island, Mackinac County, Michigan)" in the text.

Francophones often have multiple given names. In some cases, the name was intended to be a compound name, such as Jean-Baptiste or Jean-Pierre. Because it is often unclear from records whether individuals with more than one given name were intended to have compound names, I've omitted hyphens for French and French-Canadian ancestors to avoid ambiguity. For example, Simon Bouschor's paternal grandfather's full name is listed as Abel François Alexis Bouchard. When it comes to names of people and locations, I've retained French spellings of names and diacritical marks whenever possible for consistency. Historically, French women do not take their husband's surname upon marriage. Thus, female Francophone ancestors and relatives detailed herein are typically referred to by their original surname.

Lastly, in setting forth dates in this volume, I've utilized the Day-Month-Year structure common to European publications. This is especially helpful in the notes and annotations where extraneous punctuation could lead to confusion.

Introduction

The history of the Bouschor family parallels the trajectory of the Upper Peninsula from the nineteenth century to the present day. Both Elie Bouchard and Simon Champagne, Simon Bouschor's father and maternal grandfather, left their homeland of Quebec in the early 1800s seeking economic opportunity through the burgeoning fur trade. Their travels in pursuit of a livelihood brought them to Mackinac Island, which emerged as a crossroads of commerce for the Great Lakes by the late 1700s. The island grew in population and importance with the establishment of John Jacob Astor's American Fur Company in the 1810s. Simon and Elie readily adapted to the island's culture, and both married Odawa Indian women whose ancestors had called Mackinac Island and the surrounding region home for generations. As the fur trade receded in importance, Simon Champagne and Elie responded to changing economic conditions and demands. Simon developed his occupation as a shipbuilder and fisherman, while Elie returned to the seas as a ship captain. Elie's family relocated to the Green Bay area for a decade in the 1830s and 1840s before he and several of the children returned to Mackinac Island following Josette Champagne Bouchard's death around 1845. Elie worked well into the 1870s, much of that time employed with the United States Revenue Cutter Service, and spent his final days on New York's Staten Island at a rest home for retired sailors.

Following in his father's footsteps, Simon Bouschor became a ship captain on the Great Lakes. Before the introduction of the railroad and the advent of the motor car, transportation by vessel was the quickest and most efficient means of moving passengers and goods around the lakes. Ship transport remains integral to the Upper Peninsula to this day, as anyone who's seen the massive ore ships pass through the Soo Locks can attest. At the same time as Simon was making his name known as a ship captain in the early 1850s, the family of his future wife, Harriette Isabella Gray, settled on the Garden Peninsula located on the Upper Peninsula's Lake Michigan coast. Isabella's family had moved from Nova Scotia to New Brunswick to Connecticut before reaching Rochester, New York in the 1840s, where her father, David, worked as a teamster on the Erie Canal, the waterway that revolutionized transportation and commerce in upstate New York and turbo-charged settlement of the upper Midwest. After a handful of years in Rochester, the family departed for South Bend, Indiana, in search of a better life before finally reaching the Upper Peninsula in the 1850s to farm their 130-plus acre homestead just outside the small town of Garden. In doing so, the Gray family participated in another livelihood crucial to the Upper Peninsula's modern history—farming.

These two industries—the land and the sea—came together through Simon and Harriette's marriage in 1854 and their establishment five years later of the Bouschor homestead on Schoolcraft County's Barque Point in 1859. While Simon gave up the risky livelihood of a seafaring captain in exchange for life on the homestead, the ideally located land allowed them to grow fruit and raise livestock while maintaining a robust fishing operation on Lake Michigan that sustained them well into the early twentieth century. The Barque Point homestead became a waypoint between the growing community of Manistique to the northeast and the established communities of Fayette and Garden village on the Garden Peninsula's western shore.

Simon's lifespan—from his birth on Mackinac Island on 25 December 1829 to his death in Manistique on 19 July 1916—dovetails with the rise and pinnacle of the Upper Peninsula's fortunes. As illustrated in the table on the following page, the Upper Peninsula's population (then consisting of only two counties—Chippewa and Michilimackinac, as depicted in the 1836 map on page 3) enumerated the year following Simon's birth numbered only 1,503. However, four years after Simon's death in 1916, some 332,626 individuals called the Upper Peninsula home. That figure represented the high-water mark for the Upper Peninsula's population.

Census Year	Upper Peninsula Population
1800	561
1810	615
1820	819
1830	1,503
1840	1,457
1850	5,745
1860	21,414
1870	43,700
1880	85,030
1890	180,608
1900	261,362
1910	325,628
1920	332,556

Upper Peninsula population from 1800 to 1920[1]

The jump from just shy of 1,500 inhabitants in 1840 to nearly 6,000 ten years later coincided with a rapid transformation in the Upper Peninsula as the discovery of iron ore, copper deposits, and vast stands of hard and softwood trees brought numerous settlers to the area seeking to capitalize on the newfound wealth. The timber resources resulted in the establishment of a handful of small sawmills that foreshadowed the mammoth operations that would come to dominate Manistique and other communities within a decade.[2]

From 1880 to 1890, the Upper Peninsula's population increased by over 112% as new residents flooded the region to partake in the boom times. However, while the supply of white pine and other softwood trees seemed insatiable, the industry's decline was already evident by the 1890s. Indeed, lumbermen like Timothy Nestor saw the writing on the wall and began to look towards northern Wisconsin and the north woods of Minnesota as the next great source of softwood timber. Within a twenty-year period, many of the timber barons had liquidated their Upper Peninsula holdings and shifted to other regions of the upper Midwest or the Pacific Coast. Those who had purchased acreage harvested what they could of the remaining pine, but soon had to pivot to hardwood operations, which were unable to be transported by water and required development of railways to bring the timber to sawmills

and distribution centers.[3] The hardwood boom itself was short-lived, and by the 1920s many operators had pulled out of the Upper Peninsula and shifted operations to the south and the Appalachian highlands.[4]

Another trend that manifested in the first two decades of the twentieth century was the aging of the Upper Peninsula's population. From 1870 to 1910, males between the ages of twenty and thirty comprised at least ten percent of the total population—unsurprising given the rough living conditions and nature of the era's available jobs. However, their segment of the population shrank considerably in the decade from 1910 to 1920 as resource-heavy industry like mining and logging declined and the population diversified.[5] Many young men—including several members of the Bouschor family—who might otherwise have stayed in the area left for other parts of the country like the Pacific Northwest, where numerous opportunities remained for those interested in logging and other extractive industries.

Community leaders in the Upper Peninsula saw trouble on the horizon long before industry and population began its gradual decline. Indeed, nearly 250 representatives from the U.P.'s various counties met on 22 April 1911 to acknowledge the economic headwinds and brainstorm new means of bringing opportunity to the region—including through the

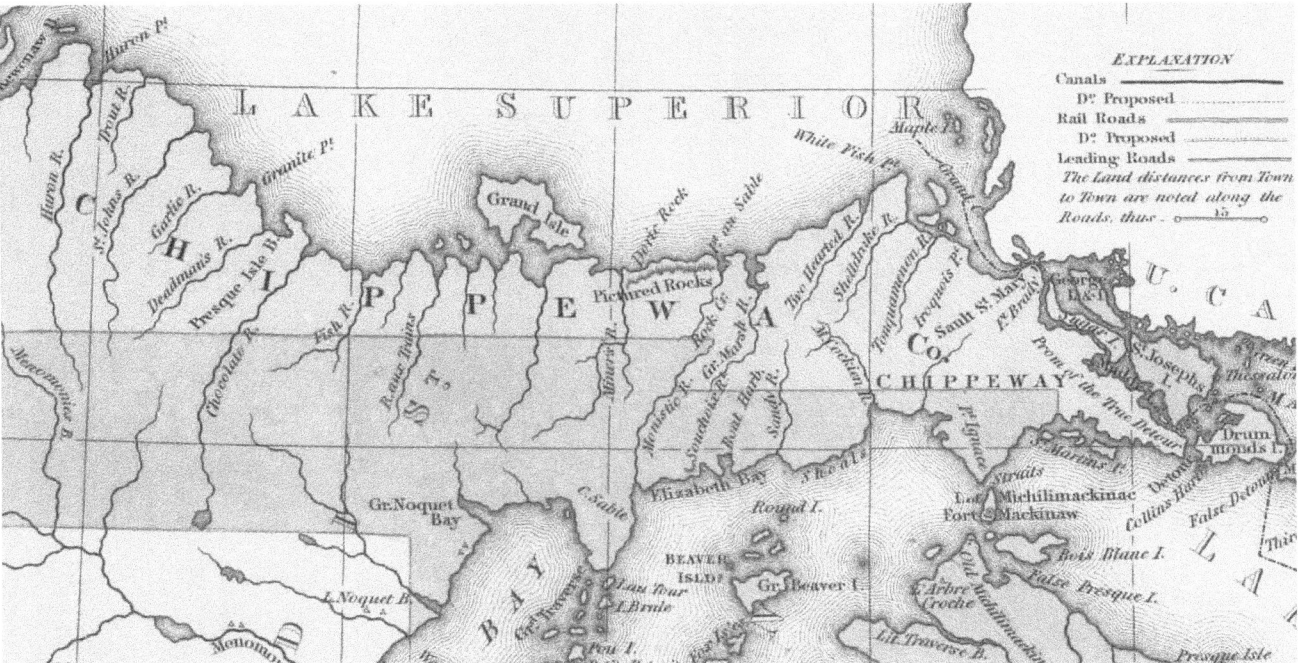

1836 Upper Peninsula Map – Seven years after Simon's birth, the U.P. was divided between Chippewa County in the north and Michilimackinac County in the south

wealth of tourist and natural recreational opportunities.[6] The decline in fortunes beginning in the 1920s coincided with a shift from the state's predominantly rural lifestyle to one increasingly urbanized. While a majority of the population lived in rural areas as of 1910, that figure dramatically shifted to 61% living in urban areas by 1920.[7] The Upper Peninsula's demographic decline can be tied to the state's shifting economic interests. World War I generated immense demand for the kind of natural resources that abounded in the Upper Peninsula, but a marked slowdown in copper and iron mining following the end of the war left many individuals unemployed. As much of the western Upper Peninsula was inhospitable to farming, families were left without a suitable form of income. They increasingly drifted south, particularly to southern Michigan, where growing industry offered stable and well-paying careers.[8]

Simon and Harriette's children and the trajectory of their lives illustrate the peak of the Upper Peninsula's fortunes in the first three decades of the twentieth century and its gradual economic decline that continues to this day. Their eldest child Ida Isabelle Bouchard Farley's two children stayed in the Manistique area and remained for the rest of their lives

until passing away in the 1960s. Several of David Bouschor's and Charles Bouschor's children moved west to Minnesota in the early years of the twentieth century, seeking new opportunities in that burgeoning state. Their descendants continue to call Minnesota home, and several have made significant contributions to the state's history in the business and legal communities.

George and Simon Junior's children perhaps represent the best example of the Upper Peninsula changing fortunes. By the early 1920s, several of their children had moved south to communities including Flint and Detroit, and often found work in the automobile industry that drew countless others from across the country and world to Michigan. Michigan's emergence at the vanguard of the automobile industry makes sense in retrospect. Southern Michigan was an epicenter of agricultural equipment manufacturing in the nineteenth century, and it likewise dominated the wagon and carriage industry with 125 companies in the industry calling it home in the 1890s. Similarly, several railroad car manufacturers were headquartered in Detroit, including the Pullman railcar company that operated a plant until 1893.[9] The abundance of raw lumber combined with access to iron ore and other

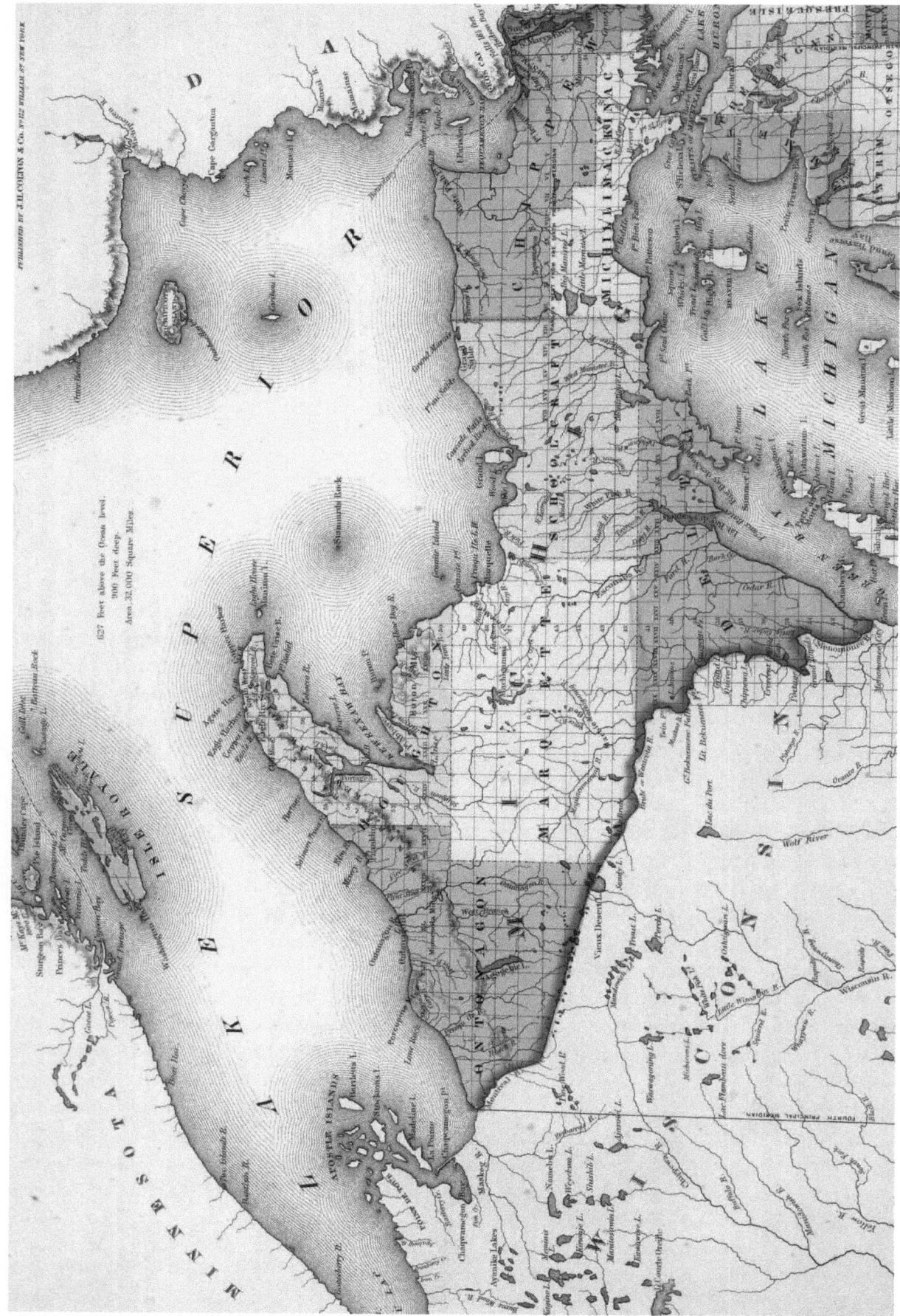

1856 Upper Peninsula Map – Three years before the Bouschor family settled at the Barque Point homestead, the Upper Peninsula now numbered seven counties, including Delta and Schoolcraft Counties

natural resources positioned Michigan for industrial success. The automobile itself took off in Michigan in 1901 when Ransom Olds developed and manufactured his first one-cylinder automobile in Detroit, followed by Henry Ford's June 1903 establishment of the Ford Motor Company in Detroit as well.[10] Flint likewise emerged as a leader in automobile production with the 1904 establishment of a factory for the Buick Motor Car Company. Buick experienced rapid growth and met with great success under the leadership of William C. Durant.[11]

Two Bouschor brothers, Henry and William, left the Upper Peninsula in their early adulthood to try their fortunes out on the West Coast. Both worked in the timber industry, a concern that previously held a prominent position in Michigan commerce for decades. With much of the harvestable timber gone by the turn of the century, the industry shifted to the Pacific Northwest.[12] The panic of 1893 further contributed to economic struggles across Schoolcraft County and the Upper Peninsula at large, and the two brothers likely sought better opportunity out west, where vast forests remained largely unexploited at the time. After years spent in Canada and moving up and down the Pacific coast, both Henry and William found their way to the Puget Sound region of Washington state. Similarly, Anna Olive Bouschor's daughter, Norma Pierce Taber, grew up in northern Wisconsin on Lake Superior and later moved out west to Central Washington state, where

she passed away in 1967.

Mary May Bouschor's four children all stayed in the Upper Peninsula, but the family left the Manistique area for opportunities in other parts of the state, such as the lumber milling community of Munising on Lake Superior and various points on the eastern Upper Peninsula, including Sault Ste. Marie. While the youngest of the Bouschor siblings, Nelson Burton "Nels" Bouschor, stayed in Manistique, his son Cletus James Bouschor went to the East Coast during World War II and ended up staying in New York the rest of his life after meeting his future wife in the mid-1940s.

The Upper Peninsula's population stagnated and declined by nearly 30,000 people between 1920 and 1970, as illustrated in Table 2 below. Although it enjoyed a brief rise in the 1970s, the decline continued in the years following 1980 and has fallen steadily. As of the 2020 U.S. Census, the Upper Peninsula numbers fewer individuals than lived there in the first decade of the twentieth century. Some counties were hit harder than others, with Luce County experiencing a 19.4% decline from 2010 to 2020 while Ontonagon and Gogebic Counties experienced a 14% and 12% decline, respectively.[13] Absent a reversal in fortune in the area's industrial and commercial landscape, the population is likely to fall below 300,000 for the first time in well over a century.

Census Year	Upper Peninsula Population
1920	332,556
1930	318,685
1940	323,544
1950	302,256
1960	303,054
1970	302,892
1980	320,272
1990	313,915
2000	317,676
2010	311,361
2020	301,608

Upper Peninsula population from 1920 to 2020[14]

The population decline is unsurprising considering the region's evolving economic challenges. While Michigan faced an overall unemployment rate of 6.9% in 1960, the Upper Peninsula suffered from unemployment nearly three times as high in parts. The continued decline in production from the great copper and iron ranges of the western Upper Peninsula didn't help, despite the efforts of many to devise solutions for the region's faltering economy.[15] Even the iconic Mackinac Bridge—construction of which began in 1954 and was formally completed in November 1957—failed to transform the region's economy, despite easing a major bottleneck for access from the Lower Peninsula and ramping up development of amenities and services for tourists.[16] Between the 1950 and 1960 U.S. Censuses, sixty-one percent of adults between the ages of twenty and twenty-four left the upper Great Lakes. In 1960 alone, unemployment stood at thirty percent.[17]

Historians Willis F. Dunbar and George S. May observed that efforts to develop new industry in the Great Lakes met with mixed results in reducing unemployment. While many mid-century leaders and members of the business community sought to capitalize on the area's natural beauty to combat stubborn unemployment and economic stagnation, success was limited at best. By the 1980s, all but three of the Upper Peninsula's counties experienced declining populations, much of that driven by young people who left for better economic opportunities despite the area's undeniable beauty and unique character.[18]

Manistique and Schoolcraft County—two locations frequently associated with the Bouschor family in the Upper Peninsula—witnessed similar trends. Table 3 below details the progression of Schoolcraft County and Manistique's population from 1880 through the most recent U.S. Census in 2020:

Census Year	Schoolcraft County Population	Manistique Population
1880	1,575	693
1890	5,818	2,940
1900	7,889	4,126
1910	8,681	4,722
1920	9,977	6,380
1930	8,451	5,198
1940	9,524	5,399
1950	9,148	5,086
1960	8,953	4,875
1970	8,226	4,324
1980	8,575	3,962
1990	8,302	3,456
2000	8,903	3,583
2010	8,485	3,097
2020	8,047	2,828

Schoolcraft County and Manistique Population from 1880 to 2020[19]

A review of the population trajectory for Manistique and Schoolcraft County over the 140-year period mirrors that of the Upper Peninsula at large. Both county and city experienced rapid growth from 1880 to 1920, culminating in population totals

of 9,977 and 6,380, respectively. While Schoolcraft County and Manistique's populations held relatively stable through the 1950s, they both witnessed an overall decline. Several members of the Bouschor family, including George Wallace and Simon Joseph

Bouschor, were amongst the net 1,182 individuals who departed from Manistique between 1920 and 1930. Overall, the decline in population from 1920 to 2020 for Schoolcraft County has been less dramatic than that of Manistique—1,930 or 19.3% versus 3,552 or 55.7%.

Nonetheless, population estimates in the wake of the COVID-19 pandemic and its great upheaval suggest a rebound in Manistique and Schoolcraft County's fortunes. The U.S. Census Bureau's 1 June 2022 population estimate for Schoolcraft County put its population at 8,188 (a 139-person increase).[20] It remains to be seen whether remote-work flexibility or a greater demographic realignment countrywide are behind these trends.

By the third and fourth generations of Simon and Harriette's descendants, only a dwindling handful called the Upper Peninsula home. As a result of the diaspora described above, Bouschor descendants span the entire country, with significant numbers found in Minnesota, Washington state, New York, Arizona, and as far away as Alaska. While their lives have diverged, the common thread of our Upper Peninsula legacy is the tie that binds us all.

The Bouschor Family and Military Service

Service in the armed forces was another theme for the descendants of Simon and Harriette. The family was no stranger to public and military service. Simon's younger brother, Eli Bouchard Junior, fought for the Union Army during the Civil War and died on a Virginia battlefield in 1864, while their brother Edward A. Bouchard served in the Union Navy. Simon and Harriette's son-in-law Alexander Daignault served in Michigan's Volunteer Infantry during the Spanish-American War. During the early 1910s, Simon and Harriette's son William Edward was an officer in the nascent Oregon Naval Militia, serving as assistant engineer and ordinance officer.

Several descendants and spouses of descendants fought in World War I, including Erich A. Blank (husband of Mildred I. Bouschor), William McCall (husband of Mary M. Bouschor), and Raymond J.

Bouschor, all serving in the Army. George F. Bouschor served in the Navy. Kenneth W. Matheson (first husband of Eva Grey Bouschor) flew fighter planes over Europe during World War I as part of the U.S. Army Aviation Section. Brothers Aldred S. Bouschor and Harvey H. Bouschor likewise served in the Army Aviation Section. They were amongst the 135,485 soldiers and sailors from Michigan who served during that global conflict.[21] Eva Grey Bouschor's second husband, Roy H. Cromley, was also a musician with the Michigan National Guard.

World War II involved an even greater number of Bouschor descendants who served with great distinction in various theaters of the war. Oral H. Bouschor, George W. Craig (husband of Helen J. Havlichek), Robert P. Smith (husband of Joan B. Matheson), David B. Thornton (husband of Julie Anne Cromley), Archibald C. Fletcher (husband of Joanne M. Croson), and Claude E. Daniels served in the Army during World War II. Charles F. Bouschor was an Army Dental Corps officer in the Pacific Theater. Orville P. Taber, Robert Lloyd Bouschor, Joseph W. Bouschor, Elson W. Carberry (first husband of Dorothy H. Daniels), and Cletus J. Bouschor served in the Navy. Daniel H. Havlichek and Milford H. Carr both served in the U.S. Army Air Corps, while Edward L. Havlichek, Maxine Havlichek Brown, Gordon Samuel Brown (husband of Maxine Havlichek), and Victor H. Bouschor served in the Marine Corps. Earl R. Carr served during World War II with the Coast Guard. David J. McCall (grandson of David Eli Bouschor) also served in the Armed Forces during World War II. Brothers Victor and Joseph Bouschor were present at Pearl Harbor on 7 December 1941 when the Japanese launched their sneak attack that kicked off America's involvement. Many other family members contributed to the war effort via the USO and other service organizations on the home front.

Other Bouschor family descendants served during the Korean War, the Vietnam War, and later conflicts, as well as fulfilling vital functions as members of the armed forces during peacetime. Any omission by name herein is unintentional, and the author plans to highlight individual service in the forthcoming volume detailing the lives of Bouschor family descendants.

The Bouschor Family's Native American Ancestry

All descendants of Simon and Harriette Bouschor have Native American ancestry by virtue of their relationship to Simon's mother, Josette Champagne Bouchard. Josette was one-half Odawa (also known as Ottawa) Indian via her mother, Marguerite Champagne. Josette received payments from the U.S. government via the 1836 Treaty of Washington by virtue of her and her three eldest children's Native American heritage as mixed-blood descendants.[22] These payments had great ramifications for Elie, Josette, and their descendants. Shortly after Josette and her children received their treaty payments, the family relocated from Mackinac Island to Green Bay in what was then Wisconsin Territory and spent the next decade in the rapidly growing port city. It's believed that Simon's $305.89 treaty payment allowed him to purchase the Barque Point homestead in the late 1850s.

The 1860 U.S. Census lists Simon as being an Indian male and records his and Harriette's three children as "mulatto."[23] In later census records towards the turn of the twentieth century, references to the family's Indian heritage all but disappear. For example, both the 1880 and 1900 U.S. Censuses list all members of the family as white.[24] This phenomenon was common across the country for those with Indian ancestry owing to societal attitudes and the emphasis on "whiteness" as paramount to advancement in American society. Historian Anne F. Hyde observed in *Born of Lakes and Plains*, her 2022 study of mixed-blood society and its impact on American history, that families with Indian or other minority heritage took great pains to downplay their heritage out of concern about backlash from racist and nativist elements in society. "To protect their children and histories, they hid, they passed, they traveled, and they denied family stories," Hyde wrote.[25]

Only in more recent years has acknowledging Indian ancestry become socially acceptable in the United States—even desirable in many cases. In recent years, a descendant of Simon and Harriette, Bernard Bouschor of Sault Ste. Marie, even served as chairman of the Sault Tribe of Chippewa Indians.

Organization

The impetus for writing this history of the Bouschor family began at an early age. As long as I can remember, my parents and grandparents had grown used to correcting the spelling and pronunciation of our name. Anyone who's been blessed with it can likely sympathize. While genealogy interested me in my youth, it wasn't until the late 2000s that I took up research of our family history in earnest. Over the ensuing years, I uncovered a wealth of information and met many people along the way who've helped shed light on certain facts or contributed to my understanding of our heritage.

In researching and writing this book, the uniqueness of the Bouschor surname proved to be a boon. Chances are anyone carrying the name is somehow related to the Bouschors of Barque Point. This book will focus on the ancestors of Simon and Harriette Bouschor. A future volume will discuss Simon and Harriette's descendants. Other family members descended from Elie and Josette Bouchard subsequently adopted the Bouschor surname, namely several of Remi Bouchard's descendants. Their stories are ample material for a future volume. No disrespect is intended by excluding their coverage in this present work.

This volume is divided into four parts. Part One provides an overview of locations throughout northern Michigan that were home to Bouschor family descendants over the years. Part One is intended to give the reader a brief history and orientation for each location. A central theme of this volume is the integration of the Bouschor family into Upper Peninsula life. Certain places, like Barque Point and Manistique, are indelibly linked to the family, and our Bouschor ancestors left a mark and influence on these communities that endures to this day.

Part Two discusses the lives of Simon and Harriette Gray Bouschor. As Simon and Harriette are the pivotal individuals for this entire study, devoting a section solely to their lives and influence is appropriate. After all, it was Simon and Harriette who first adopted the unique Bouschor surname in the late 1800s after years of living as Bouchards. Their lives dovetail with some of the most important years of the Upper Peninsula's history, and both witnessed extraordinary changes in the United States, having lived from the pre-Civil War era through the dawn of flight in the early years of the twentieth century.

Parts Three and Four detail the ancestors of Simon Bouschor and Harriette Isabella Gray, respectively. I have limited the overview to five generations of ancestors. Simon's storied history stretches all the way back to sixteenth-century France while Harriette's features ancestors spanning Nova Scotia to the Isle of Man. Five generations is sufficient to cover the early settlers of New France and, in some cases, detail the lives of those who still lived in France in the sixteenth and seventeen centuries. It is difficult to find reliable records going back any further, and trying to do so often relies on speculation at best. The reader will notice the information about Harriette's ancestors is far less detailed than that about Simon's. French-Canadians and the Catholic Church from the time of settlement in New France were prodigious recordkeepers. Their meticulous recordkeeping significantly aided the work of countless genealogists and historians alike. Many of Harriette's ancestors, including nearly all her paternal ancestors, are unknown at present. The author hopes additional information will come forward that will allow this section to be updated.

Simon and Harriette's ancestors are numbered using the *Ahnentafel* system. Thus, Simon is designated as number 1, while his parents, Elie Bouchard and Josette Champagne, are designated as numbers 2 and 3, respectively. Simon's grandparents are designated as numbers 4 through 7, and so on. In a similar fashion, Harriette is designated as individual number 1 in Part Four of this volume detailing her family. Harriette's parents, grandparents, and subsequent ancestors each receive a sequential number.

In researching and writing this history, I originally intended it to be a single volume covering two to three generations of Simon and Harriette's descendants in addition to their ancestors. As my research progressed and I discovered more and more material, I recognized a single volume would exceed the bounds of what could reasonably be printed. In the interest of cost and convenience to the reader, I split this work into two volumes.

As such, a future volume will detail the lives of three generations' worth of Simon and Harriette's descendants. As eleven of their thirteen children survived to adulthood, Simon and Harriette have many descendants. Each has a unique story, and I'll attempt to provide an overview of each of their lives. Some descendants have a great deal of information about their lives and pursuits. For example, George Leslie Bouschor's twenty-plus year service as Schoolcraft County Clerk and Register of Deeds made him a prominent figure in the Manistique community. This combined with outstanding newspaper archive coverage of the *Escanaba Daily Press*, the *Manistique Pioneer-Tribune*, and other regional periodicals made for an abundant amount of information at the author's disposal. In contrast, other descendants have all too few details, likely owing to an earlier death or a paucity of information available about their lives. No disrespect is intended where one family member's biography is shorter than that of another.

I have no doubt that more details will come to light in the future. Already, resources like the Upper Peninsula Digital Network—an online database coordinated by the Upper Peninsula's three universities and hosting thousands of records from organizations across the Upper Peninsula—have made historical research easier than ever. Nonetheless, countless records, photographs, and artifacts remain in public and private collections awaiting discovery.

It is my sincere hope that interest in this volume will inspire demand for a second edition that can incorporate feedback gathered from other family members throughout the world. Readers with additional information, records, or photographs are encouraged to contact the author.

Notes

1   Russell M. Magnaghi, *Understanding Two Centuries of Census Data of Michigan's Upper Peninsula* (Marquette, MI: Belle Fontaine Press, 2007), 1, Northern Michigan University.

2   Theodore J. Karamanski, *Deep Woods Frontier: A History of Logging in Northern Michigan* (Detroit: Wayne State University Press, 1989), 26.

3   Karamanski, *Deep Woods Frontier*, 141-44, 175.

4   Karamanski, *Deep Woods Frontier*, 205.

5   Karamanski, *Deep Woods Frontier*, 216-217.

6   Willis F. Dunbar and George S. May, *Michigan: A History of the Wolverine State*, 3rd Ed. (Grand Rapids: Wm. B. Eerdmans Publishing Co., 1995), 380.

7   Dunbar and May, *Michigan*, 482.

8   Dunbar and May, *Michigan*, 502-03.

9   Dunbar and May, *Michigan*, 396, 402, 413.

10 Dunbar and May, *Michigan*, 423, 431

11 Dunbar and May, *Michigan*, 436-37.

12 Dunbar and May, *Michigan*, 340.

13 Michael Broadway and John Broadway, "The UP at a Crossroads: Beyond the 2020 Census Results," Rural Insights, 15 December 2021, https://ruralinsights.org/content/the-up-at-a-crossroads-beyond-the-2020-census-results/.

14 Magnaghi, *Understanding Two Centuries of Census Data of Michigan's Upper Peninsula*; 1 Broadway and Broadway, "The UP at a Crossroads."

15 Dunbar and May, *Michigan*, 554-55.

16 Dunbar and May, *Michigan*, 556.

17 Karamanski, *Deep Woods Frontier*, 259.

18 Dunbar and May, *Michigan*, 643.

19 1880 Census to 2020 Census, U.S. Census Bureau, https://www.census.gov/en.html.

20 "QuickFacts, Schoolcraft County, Michigan; United States," U.S. Census Bureau, accessed 13 March 2024, https://www.census.gov/quickfacts/fact/table/schoolcraftcountymichigan,US/PST045223.

21 Dunbar and May, *Michigan*, 461.

22 1836 Mixed-Blood Census Register, Ottawa and Chippewas of Michigan Treaty of March 28, 1836, Transcribed by Larry M. Wyckoff, http://sites.rootsweb.com/~mimacki2/annuities/1836mb.pdf.

23 1860 U.S. Census, Delta Township, Delta County, Michigan, population schedule, p. 134, dwelling 1282, family 867, lines 37-39, Simon and Harriet Bouchard.

24 1880 U.S. Census, Hiawatha Township, Schoolcraft County, Michigan, population schedule, enumeration district 37, p. 15, dwelling 153, family 153, lines 32-42, Simon and H.E. Bouchard; 1900 U.S. Census, Thompson Township, Schoolcraft County, Michigan, population schedule, enumeration district 168, sheet 10B, dwelling 174, family 177, lines 73-78, Simon & Harriet Bouschor.

25 Anne F. Hyde, *Born of Lakes and Plains: Mixed-Descent Peoples and the Making of the American West* (New York: W.W. Norton & Co., 2022), 328.

Part One

The Bouschor Family and Michigan's Upper Peninsula

The history of the Bouschor family is inextricably linked to Michigan's Upper Peninsula. From Simon Bouschor's birth on Mackinac Island in 1829 through the present day, Bouschor family descendants have called the Upper Peninsula home for close to 200 years. The goal of this section is to place the family's history in the context of the Upper Peninsula, and to give readers an appreciation for the area's rich and unique history. Thus, it will track the family's progression from Mackinac Island in the early nineteenth century, to the Garden Peninsula in the 1850s, to the Barque Point homestead in 1859, and then onward to the village of Thompson and the city of Manistique in the latter part of the 1800s and early 1900s. While many family members remained in Manistique and the rest of the Upper Peninsula after the region's heyday in the early twentieth century, other descendants of Simon and Harriette fanned out across all corners of the country, including Alaska, California, and Florida.

This section is not intended to be a comprehensive history of the Upper Peninsula. Those interested in learning more would be wise to seek out Russell M. Magnaghi's *Upper Peninsula of Michigan: A History*. Similarly, Willis F. Dunbar and George S. May's *Michigan: A History of the Wolverine State* provides a thorough introduction to the history of Michigan at large.

Mackinac Island

The Bouschor family's Upper Peninsula legacy began in the 1820s when Quebecois fur trader Elie Bouchard (1794–1879) arrived on Mackinac Island to begin the next phase of his life. Located in the northeast corner of Lake Huron east of the Straits of Mackinac, Mackinac Island is just over four square miles in land area and comprises multiple settlements, historic sites, and well-preserved natural areas. The historical region known as Michilimackinac comprised not only the namesake island, but also the territory surrounding the Straits of Mackinac, including present-day St. Ignace and Mackinaw City.[1] Herein, the use of the term "Michilimackinac" will refer to the entire region while "Mackinac Island" will be used to denote the island itself to avoid confusion.

Known in Ojibwa as *mishimikinaak* or *michilimakinak*, generally meaning "Great Turtle," the area received the name Michilimackinac from the French after they settled in the area in the 1700s.[2] Bacqueville de la Potherie, an eighteenth-century chronicler of New France, offered the following alternative explanation for the name's origin:

> Michilimakinak, according to the old men, is the place where Michapous sojourned longest. There is a mountain on the shore of the lake which has the shape of a hare; they believe that this was the place of his abode, and they call this mountain Michapous. It is there, as they say, that he showed men how to make fishing-nets, and where he placed the most fish. There is an island, two leagues from the shore, which is very lofty; they say that he left there some spirits, whom they call Imakinagos. As the inhabitants of this island are large and strong, this island has taken its name from those spirits; and it is called Michilimakinak, as who should say Micha-Imakinak – for in the Outaoüak language micha means "great," "stout," and "much." This place is a strait, which separates Lake Huron from Méchéygan, otherwise "Lake of the Illinois."[3]

However, de la Potherie's explanation is by no means definitive. Other historians have taken the position that the name means Big or Great Turtle. This includes historian Virgil J. Vogel, who endorsed A. F. Chamberlain's 1902 conclusion: "The place-name Mackinac (Mackinaw) would represent an Ojibwa (or closely related dialect) makinák ('tur-

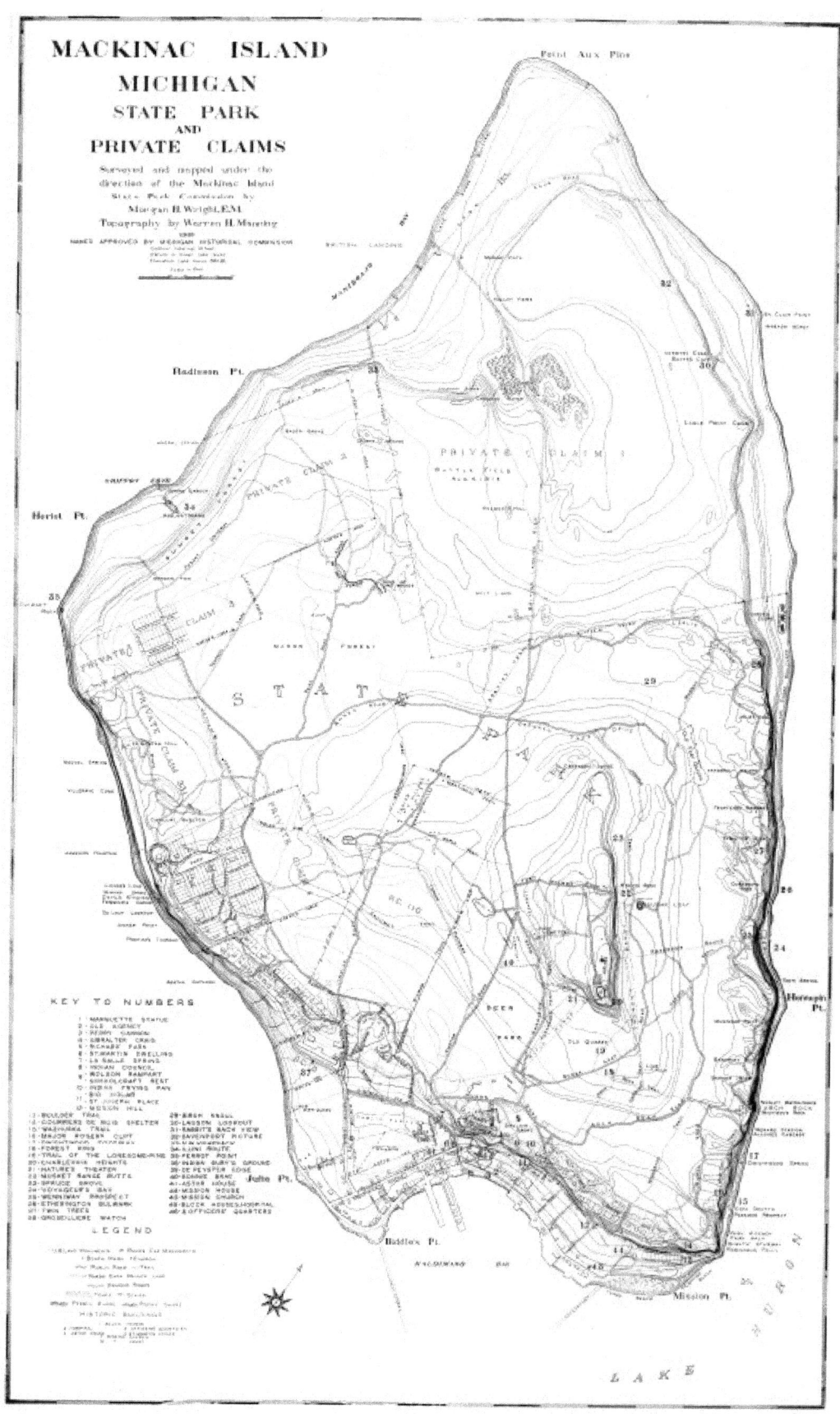

Mackinac Island in 1913 – The parcel designated as "Private Claim 2" previously belonged to Simon Champagne

tle'), but the word is said to be really a shortened form of Michilimackinác, a corruption of mitchi mackinác ('big turtle')."[4]

While Elie and his future father-in-law, Simon Champagne, were relatively recent inhabitants of Michilimackinac Island, the Odawa (or Ottawa) ancestors of Simon Bouschor's mother called the island home for generations. One of the Odawa on the island, a woman named Te Pi Ma Guain, married Simon Champagne and took the French name Marguerite. Simon and Marguerite had several children, and their daughter Josette Champagne married Elie Bouchard in 1828 and gave birth the following year to Simon Bouschor. For a detailed discussion of the Odawa people and Indian life at Michilimackinac, see the entry below on Te Pi Ma Guain beginning at page 112.

The Michilimackinac region came under French control with the arrival of French-Catholic Jesuit missionaries. Early missionaries included Father Claude Dablon, who established a short-lived mission on Michilimackinac Island in 1670, and, a year later, Jacques Marquette. Father Marquette founded a mission strategically located near both Huron and Odawa villages at present-day St. Ignace.[5] Owing to the region's strategic importance, the French established a military post, Fort de Buade, at St. Ignace in 1690 that lasted until approximately 1697.[6] Michilimackinac remained in French hands until the region and Fort Michilimackinac fell under British control following French surrender on 8 September 1760 during the conflict later known as the French and Indian War.[7] It took another year before British troops occupied Fort Michilimackinac following the French withdrawal in 1760.[8]

Michilimackinac would ping-pong between French, British, and American control over the next fifty years. Despite the area coming under British rule in 1760, the British remained sensitive to the inhabitants' French heritage, and they passed the Quebec Act in 1774 that guaranteed religious liberty to Roman Catholics, as well as application of French civil law.[9] Even more monumental to the development of Mackinac Island was the relocation of Fort Michilimackinac from its longstanding location on the southern shore of the Straits of Mackinac dating from 1715 (near present-day Mackinaw City) to a high bluff on the island's south side beginning in 1779 and largely completed by 1781. Along with the fort, many residences and Ste. Anne's Church were relocated from the south side of the Straits and rebuilt on Mackinac Island.[10] While the British acknowledged Mackinac Island to be the sovereign possession of the Ojibwa Indians, a council with eight chiefs representing different bands of Indians in 1780 resulted in a 12 May 1791 deed that gave the territory to the British in exchange for payment to the Ojibwa.[11]

British control over the new fort was short-lived. The 3 September 1783 treaty resolving the Revolutionary War awarded control over the future area of Michigan and Mackinac Island to the United States. Nonetheless, both the fort and the island remained garrisoned with British troops until Jay's Treaty of 1794 resolved outstanding questions over control of the Great Lakes. On 1 September 1796, the British withdrew, and Major Henry Burbeck led 110 American soldiers into the fort.[12] Within three years of the British withdrawal, Simon Bouschor's maternal grandfather, Simon Champagne, arrived on the island from Montréal, Quebec, and made it his home for the rest of his life.

Formal possession of and authority over Mackinac Island by the United States government *vis-à-vis* the tribes came into realization with the 1795 Treaty of Greenville. The treaty ended the Northwest Indian War and resulted in the cession of Mackinac Island by the signing tribes—including representatives of the Odawa and Chippewa—to the United States in exchange for goods and various annuity payments.[13] The terms of the treaty expressly included "The post of Michilimackinac, and all the land on the island on which that post stands, and the main land adjacent, of which the Indian title has been extinguished by gifts or grants to the French or English governments."[14] The townsite located on the island's southeast end was known as the Borough of Michilimackinac until 1847 and as the Village of Mackinac beginning the following year.[15] Many of the island's French and Indian population lived in the western and inner part of the village, where domiciles were constructed from cedar posts with moss chinking and cedar bark roofs.[16] U.S. Superintendent of Indian Affairs Thomas L. McKenney visited Mackinac Island in 1826 describes the island's houses as being small structures constructed from logs and "most of them covered with bark, and nearly all are going to decay" with the exception of the structures owned by the American Fur Company.[17]

At the beginning of the nineteenth century, Mackinac Island was a hub for the voyageurs, who engaged in fur trading and commerce throughout the Great Lakes region.[18] Since the seventeenth century, Michilimackinac had served as a rendezvous point for French fur traders working a territory that extended hundreds of miles away.[19] Even during the years of British control, the region's fur traders remained largely French.[20] Despite the formal British withdrawal from the fort in 1796, the British continued to exercise great control over the day-to-day affairs of the island, particularly regarding the fur trade. Heavy marine traffic to and from Mackinac Island in the late 1790s and early 1800s included many Frenchmen and Indians. Father Jean Dilhet observed in 1804 that "There is a great influx of merchants, hired men, and Indians. For three months nothing else is seen but the coming and going of canoes, or Frenchmen and Indians arriving in canoes and many leaving."[21]

The British-dominated North West Company

An 1813 engraving of Michilimackinac Village by Richard Dillon and Thomas Hall

Photograph of Mackinac Island's village in the late nineteenth century – The spire of Saint Anne's Catholic Church is visible at the far left

headquartered in Montreal controlled much of the region's fur trade until 1806, when its owners organized the Michilimackinac Company (also known as the Mackinac Company).[22] Nonetheless, the United States attempted to break the British hegemony by establishing a government "factory" on Michilimackinac Island in 1808 and sold goods at cost to the area's Indians.[23]

A larger threat to British dominance was John Jacob Astor. Astor established Mackinac Island as the headquarters for his American Fur Company in 1808, transforming the island into a trading hub for the northern Great Lakes. Astor allocated fifty thousand dollars for construction of the American Fur Company's headquarters and other buildings, and millions of dollars in merchandise passed through the island each year. Many traders left Mackinac Island in fall laden with numerous items intended for trade. The traders would set up shop at a designated post and trade goods for furs brought in by Indians over the course of the winter. The headquarters was where French voyageurs deposited furs collected from their travels. While traders could earn a good deal of money over the course of the trading season, life on Mackinac Island enticed them to spend it quickly upon their return in spring. While Astor's enterprise was soon interrupted by the War of 1812, the American Fur Company nonetheless emerged as the dominant commercial force on the island.[24]

Many of the voyageurs were French-Canadian, including Elie Bouchard and his future father-in-law, Simon Champagne, both of whom were drawn to the island by the fur trade. When Congress eliminated the government-sponsored "factories" in 1822, Astor's American Fur Company established a near-monopoly over the fur trade in the northern Great Lakes. Boatmen—the lowest-level position in the fur trade industry and likely the role fulfilled by both Elie and Simon—were paid poorly. A boatman employed by the American Fur Company received an average of $83 in compensation, but boatmen were required to purchase their own supplies.[25] Astor liked to hire French-Canadian voyageurs as he found them less independent and more likely to follow orders than their American counterparts.[26]

Conflict over the Great Lakes region and control over its vast natural resources was one cause of the War of 1812 between the United States and the United Kingdom. As one of the few garrison forts in the region and a critical hub for trade and commerce, Mackinac Island stood in the crosshairs of the conflict. The American forces were unprepared, and British forces landed on the northwest cove of the island on 17 July 1812 and make rapid progress south towards Fort Michilimackinac. The fort's American commander saw they stood no chance of defending the fort against the invaders, and he surrendered the same day.[27] The British retained their hold over Mackinac Island throughout 1813 and 1814 despite supply challenges and American desire to retake the island.[28] Only with the cessation of hostilities via the 1815 Treaty of Ghent did Michilimackinac return to American control. The British withdrew on 18 July 1815, retreating to nearby Drummond Island, while American forces reoccupied the island and its namesake fort.[29]

The Treaty of Ghent awarded permanent control of Mackinac Island and its fort to the United States. On 6 April 1817, the Borough of Michilimackinac was incorporated, allowing for administration over the island and provision of basic services. By the 1820s, the island's name was permanently shortened to Mackinac Island.[30] Notwithstanding nominal British and American control over the island beginning in 1760, France and French culture dominated the region well into the 1820s. French and French-Canadians comprised most of the island's population and exerted immense social and political influence. While Mackinac Island has since diversified, the legacy of the early voyageurs and habitants lives on with names like Cadotte Avenue, French Lane, and Marquette Park.[31]

Mackinac Island was likewise central to Native and European relations throughout the years of the fur trade. In recognition of the island's importance, all Great Lakes Indian agencies were consolidated into a single agency headquartered on Mackinac Island in the early 1830s.[32] We know all too little about the day-to-day goings-on on Mackinac Island in these early years. The first newspaper in the Upper Peninsula did not emerge until the *Lake Superior News and Miners' Journal* of Copper Harbor published its debut issue on 11 July 1846.[33] For Catholic residents like the Bouchards and Champagnes, Ste. Anne's Catholic Church occupied a central role in island life. The church bell rang at six a.m., noon, and again at six in the evening for the Angelus.[34]

Elie and Josette married in 1828, and their eldest three children were born on Mackinac Island. The 1820s and 1830s was when the Great Lakes fur trade began to sunset. In its place, fishing emerged as Mackinac Island's primary resource and livelihood. The island became the processing and packaging center for lake trout and whitefish caught from surrounding waters. In 1840 alone, the island exported 4,000 barrels of fish, growing to 20,000 barrels only six years later.[35] A visitor to the island by the name of Sears observed in 1848 "two or three large boxes on wheels, hauled on the deck by tough-looking fishermen of the genuine French breed."[36] As the fur trade's importance diminished, both Simon Champagne and Elie Bouchard turned to other nautical livelihoods—namely shipbuilding, fishing, and captaining vessels on the Great Lakes. Mackinac Island's fishing industry reached its high point in the 1850s, though a decline soon ensued due to overfishing.[37]

In December 1836, amidst the island's great economic transition, the Bouchard family relocated to Green Bay, Wisconsin, where five more children were born to Elie and Josette. After Josette's death in 1845, Elie and the surviving children returned to Michigan's Upper Peninsula. Elie himself returned to Mackinac Island, where he spent the next thirty years until moving to a New York rest home for sailors shortly before his death in 1879. Simon, Edward, and Joseph became ship captains on the Great Lakes, and all the children continued to live in various parts of the Upper Peninsula and Wisconsin over the next several decades. In the 1850s, Simon Bouchard found his way to the Garden Peninsula on the Lake Michigan side of the Upper Peninsula.

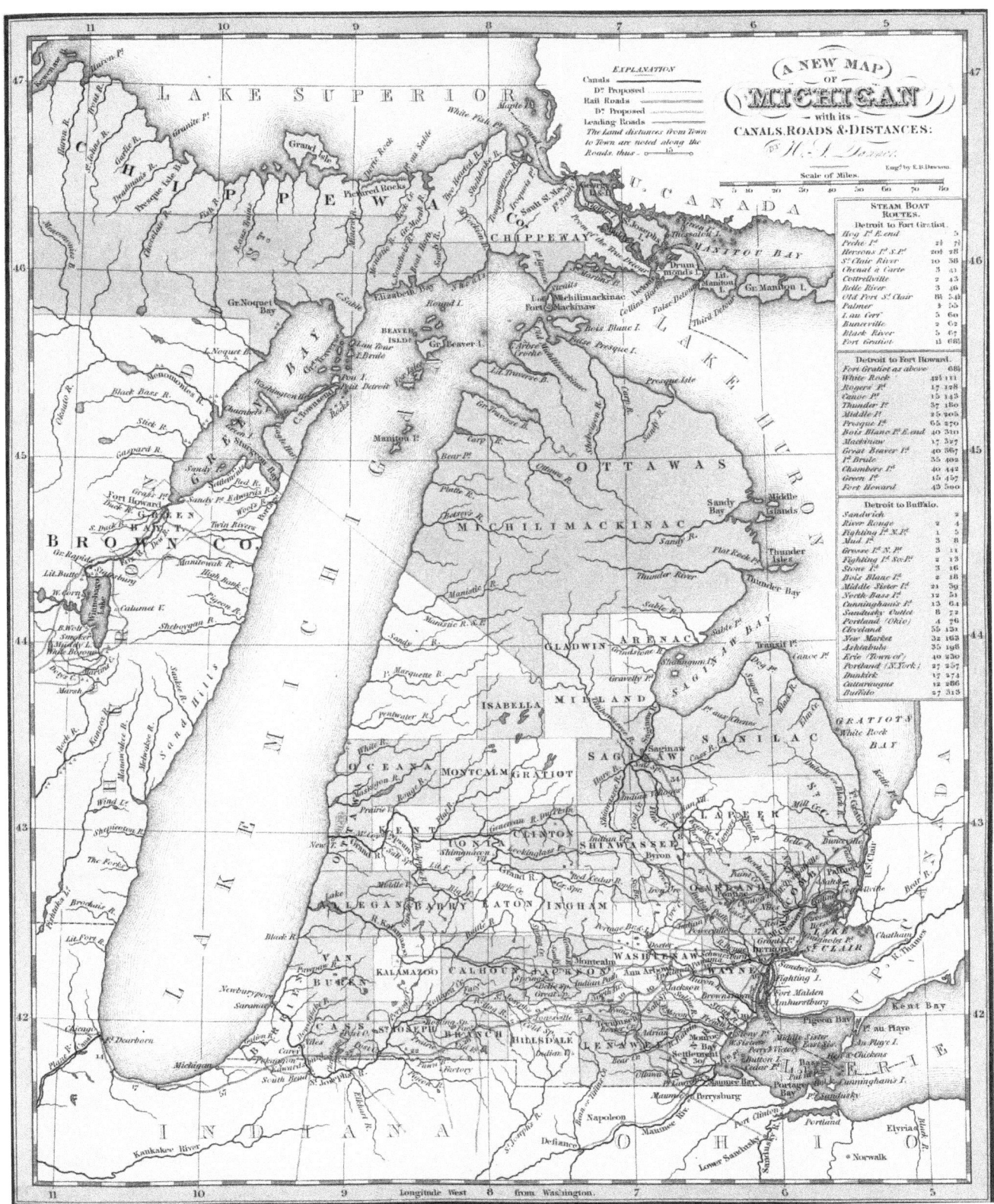

1836 Map of Michigan showing the county divisions at the time Elie and Josette Bouchard's family left Mackinac Island for Green Bay in Wisconsin Territory

Etching of an Indian camp on Mackinac Island by art historian Anna Brownell Jameson (1794–1860) from her 1837 visit to the island shortly after the Bouchard family left for Green Bay

His future wife, Harriette Isabella Gray, had spent most of her childhood there. Other descendants of Elie and Josette Bouchard continued to live on Mackinac Island.

The United States maintained Fort Mackinac until its closure in 1895, at which time the federal government transferred the fort and all other federal land on the island to the State of Michigan. The state transformed much of Mackinac Island into a state park that visitors from all over the world can experience to this day.[38]

As Mackinac Island faded in strategic and resource-oriented importance, it became a popular resort destination—culminating in the establishment of the Grand Hotel on 10 July 1887. Even by the late 1830s, Mackinac Island had emerged as a summer destination resort for travelers, with several inns and boarding houses opening to accommodate visitors.[39] The Grand Hotel remains a crowning landmark to this date, visible for miles as one approaches the island by boat. The island's clean air and climate made it attractive to visitors from around the state and country, especially for those suffering from hay fever and other ailments troubling downstate locales.[40]

Mackinac Island remains mercifully free of the motor vehicle traffic that plagues so many other tourist destinations. While the island hosts an airport with a single, 3,500-foot runway, most visitors continue to arrive on Mackinac Island in the same way they have for hundreds of years—via watercraft. Every day, high-speed ferries crisscross the Straits of Mackinac from St. Ignace and Mackinaw City, bringing residents and visitors alike to and from the mainland.

No trip to the Upper Peninsula is complete without a pilgrimage to Mackinac Island. For Bouschor descendants, it is all the more awe-inspiring knowing the island is the place our ancestors first called home in Michigan.

Delta County, the Garden Peninsula, and the Village of Garden

Generations of Bouschor and Gray family descendants have called the Garden Peninsula home. Bordered by the Big Bay de Noc to the west and the open waters of Lake Michigan to the east, the Garden Peninsula is twenty-two miles long from north to south and plunges into Lake Michigan. The entire peninsula was once covered by old-growth forests that were heavily logged in the second half of the nineteenth century for use in developing charcoal fuel to power the Jackson Iron Company's kilns in Fayette.[41]

The region's Native American population inhabited the Garden Peninsula and area around the Bays de Noc for over 5,000 years. When Father Jacques Marquette explored the Great Lakes in the early 1670s, he encountered the Nocquet Indians living around the Garden Peninsula. Also known as the Nokes or the Nocquettes, they were an Algonquin Indian tribe who inhabited territory stretching from present-day Green Bay all the way to the Upper Peninsula's north shore on Lake Superior.[42] Their name is believed to mean "bear foot" and, in a shortened form, gave name to the Little Bay de Noc and the Big Bay de Noc, the latter of which forms the western shore of the Garden Peninsula. While it's unclear if the Nocquet or any other tribe established a permanent settlement on the Garden Peninsula

1873 map of Delta County showing the township divisions – the Garden Peninsula is on the lower right

prior to the nineteenth century, other tribes, including the Menominee and the Potawatomi, could be found around the peninsula and the chain of islands between Fairport and the Door Peninsula. Later, a band of Indians led by Chip-pa-ny settled in the Garden Bay and were present at the time the Gray family settled on its homestead in the 1850s.[43] Close to the Gray family homestead on the south side of Garden Bay was a settlement known as "Indian Town" on Puffy Creek. Mrs. John Wesley Gray later recalled that one Indian woman would camp on the beach behind the family homestead and weave baskets.[44] The name of the Garden Peninsula, Garden Township, and the village of Garden came about when early European settlers to the area in the 1850s found Menominee Indians working fertile gardens in the area.[45]

Formerly the territory of the Chippewa Indians who lived in the area, the Garden Peninsula passed to possession and control of the United States via the 1836 Treaty of Washington with several of the region's tribes, including the Chippewa (Ojibwa) and Odawa.[46] This ceded land included much of Michigan's present-day Upper Peninsula. Michigan Territory established control over the remaining portions of the Upper Peninsula in April 1836 when the United States carved the Wisconsin Territory out of western Michigan Territory and fixed the northern boundary between the two soon-to-be states.[47] Delta County was one of the earlier counties platted in the Upper Peninsula. The legislature initially created Delta County out of Michilimackinac County as well as territory on the Upper Peninsula's western border known as Non-County Area 6 on 9 March 1843. Prior to 1843, Michilimackinac County comprised a massive swath of the Upper Peninsula from Drummond Island in the east to the Wisconsin Territory border at the west around present-day Ironwood. The newly organized Delta County ran all the way from Lac Vieux Desert along the western border with the new State of Wisconsin to the Michilimackinac County line. The state later created Menominee County out of Delta County's southwest portion on 12 March 1861 and reorganized the boundary with Schoolcraft County

to reach its present-day configuration. A series of court cases in the 1920s and 1930s resolved boundary disputes between Wisconsin and Michigan and determined control over the Potawatomi or Grand Traverse Islands—the chain of islands extending between the terminus of the Garden Peninsula and Door County in Wisconsin.[48] Prior to the 1861 reorganization of Delta and Schoolcraft Counties, the entirety of the Garden Peninsula belonged to Delta County. However, the present-day county line delineating Delta and Schoolcraft Counties bisects the Garden Peninsula west from east as shown in the maps at left and below.

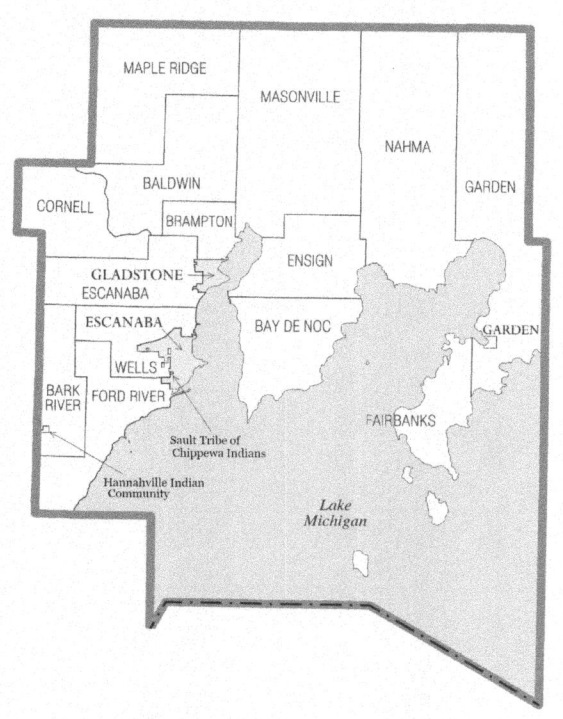

Present-day Delta County showing Garden Township and the village of Garden

European settlement of the Garden Peninsula began in earnest in the middle part of the 1800s as families from the East Coast poured into the newly opened "Northwest." The David and Isabella Gray family settled near present-day Garden Village in the mid-1850s after David Gray obtained a homestead land patent to their first tract of land in Section 18 of Township 39 North, Range 18 West

A 1926 photograph of the Gray family homestead farmhouse on the southern shore of Garden Bay

on the Garden Bay on 10 June 1856.[*] David was one of the first settlers to obtain title to land in Township 39 North, Range 18 West that covered much of the central Garden Peninsula. Other early settlers that summer included Philemon Thompson, Perry Hibbard, and Asahel Y. Bailey. A dozen years later, Frederick Conklin acquired a patent on lands in Section 18 adjacent to the Gray family homestead.[49] While much of the Upper Peninsula was ill-suited for agriculture due to the weather and sandy soil, certain areas, including much of Delta County, proved hospitable to farming, especially after removal of the timber. A claimant seeking land would typically pay the area a visit, scout a piece of suitable land (often with the assistance of a paid land locator), and then file a claim with the land office. Once the claimant had filed the necessary paperwork, the claimant would return home and prepare his family and possessions for the move to their new home.[50]

At the time the Gray family settled in Michigan, former New Yorkers comprised twenty-five percent of the state's total population, far outpacing any other group.[51] The Grays were former residents of Rochester, New York, and would have been neighbors to many New Yorkers. These included Reuben Allen, who married David and Isabella's daughter Margaret and settled near the Gray family farm on the south side of Garden Bay in approximately 1855.[52]

---

[*] The basic subdivision of land in Michigan and other western states resulted from the Ordinance of 1785 that divided territory into regions known as townships, each comprising thirty-six one-mile-square (640 acre) sections. The government numbered the sections based on their distance from the prime meridian—a longitudinal line running south from Sault Ste. Marie at 84 degrees, 22 minutes, and 24 seconds west—and a base line running east and west through the northern boundary of lower Michigan's second tier of counties. Each section was further divided into four quarters, with another four quarters embedded in each quarter. Thus, a buyer—or later, a homestead claimant—could gain title to a parcel as small as a forty-acre quarter of a quarter section. For more information on the impact of the Ordinance of 1785 on land division and ownership in Michigan, *see* Willis F. Dunbar and George S. May, *Michigan: A History of the Wolverine State*, 3rd Ed. (Grand Rapids: Wm. B. Eerdmans Publishing Co., 1995), 93, 154.

The Gray family homestead occupied the southern shore of Garden Bay. A short distance to the east lay the town of Garden—which is now the largest community and primary commercial center for the Garden Peninsula. During the Gray family's early years on the Garden Peninsula in the mid-1870s, the town of Garden consisted of approximately 150 inhabitants, with fish, potatoes, cordwood, and cedar posts comprising the town's primary exports.[53]

Prior to 1863, the entire Garden Peninsula was part of the Nahma Township—one of only two townships in all of Delta County, the other being Escanaba Township. The name Nahma came from the Ojibwa word meaning sturgeon—one of the primary fishes in Lake Michigan.[54] Shortly after the Gray family and others settled in the area, the area's residents petitioned for the establishment of a new township, which resulted in the creation of the Garden Township in 1863. This didn't last long, as Garden Township was merged with neighboring Delton Township approximately four years later in 1867, with the surviving entity known as Delton Township. The area around Garden Bay and the future village of Garden remained part of Delton Township until 10 October 1882 when Garden Township was reestablished as a standalone township. Finally, almost four years later on 13 April 1886, the village of Garden was incorporated, separating it administratively from the surrounding township of the same name.[55]

The village of Garden was home to many members of the Gray family. Philimin Thompson and his family were the first white settlers in the future townsite of Garden and arrived in 1850. Within ten years, several other families—including the Grays, Truebloods, Farleys, Conklins, and Allens—joined the Thompsons and established homesites on the south side of the bay.[56] By 1888, Garden village had established itself as the commercial center for eastern Delta County. The population underwent a rapid increase, and 60 x 140-foot village lots sold for $75 to $300. That year, Garden village numbered two sawmills, three general stores, four blacksmiths, six hotels and boarding houses, five saloons, and numerous other businesses including a photographic studio and a jewelry and watch dealer.[57]

Garden village sits on the eastern shore of the Big Bay de Noc, with a population of just over 174 residents as of the 2020 U.S. Census, down from 221 in 2010 and from a peak of nearly 500 around 1910.[58] The Garden Peninsula Historical Society maintains a museum in downtown Garden and provides a wealth of information on the area's history for visitors and researchers alike. Outside the village of Garden, the remaining portions of the Garden Peninsula in Delta County are entirely divided between Garden Township comprising the peninsula's northeastern half and Fairbanks Township comprising the southwest portion.

Harriette Gray likely spent some of her teenage years on the Gray family homestead before marrying Simon Bouschor in 1854. The young couple remained in Delta County for several years, as their eldest child, Ida Isabelle, was born in Nahma Township in January 1856 and their second child, David Eli, was born on Summer Island[†] in November 1858. Details of their whereabouts in these earlier years are largely unknown, but it's believed Simon worked as a Great Lakes ship captain for several years. Harriette eventually persuaded Simon to surrender his seafaring life, and in 1859 they settled on their future homestead at Barque Point—a homestead that would remain in the Bouschor family for over one hundred years.

---

† Summer Island is one of the Potawatomi Islands (also known as the Grand Traverse Islands) running between the Garden Peninsula and Wisconsin's Door Peninsula in the south. The islands form part of the Niagara Escarpment that also includes portions of the Garden Peninsula.

Barque Point and the Bouschor Family Homestead

Of all the locations associated with the Bouschor family, none is more storied than the family homestead located at the southern tip of Schoolcraft County, which remained in the family's hands for well over one hundred years. Barque Point lies nearly opposite the village of Garden at the eastern edge of the Garden Peninsula in rural Schoolcraft County.

Barque Point has also been called Point Aux Barques or Bark Point. An 1856 map of the Upper Peninsula and Lake Superior region denotes the landmark as "Bark Point."[59] However, the official survey of Lake Michigan completed in 1863 by the United States Lake Survey for the northern portion of Lake Michigan gives the name as Point Aux Barques.[60] Similarly, the official U.S. Geological Survey map denotes the southeast portion of the Garden Peninsula as the "Point Aux Barques Quadrangle."[61] To make matters worse, there is also a "Pointe Aux Barques" township on the other side of the state in Huron County at the tip of Michigan's Thumb. For consistency, this volume shall refer to the Bouschors' ancestral home on the Garden Peninsula as Barque Point, except when an alternate spelling is used in direct quotes from another source.

Settlement and Early Development

The Bouschor family settled on the Barque Point homestead in 1859 and are regarded as the earliest European settlers in Thompson Township.[62] Barque Point was a local landmark and was evidently used by a government survey party in the mid-1800s as a camp along the shore beneath the bluffs. During a visit to the homestead in 1894, journalist F. A. Rogers observed "large flat stones" had been placed in front of the survey crew tents.[63] At the time the Bouschor family settled on the homestead, Barque

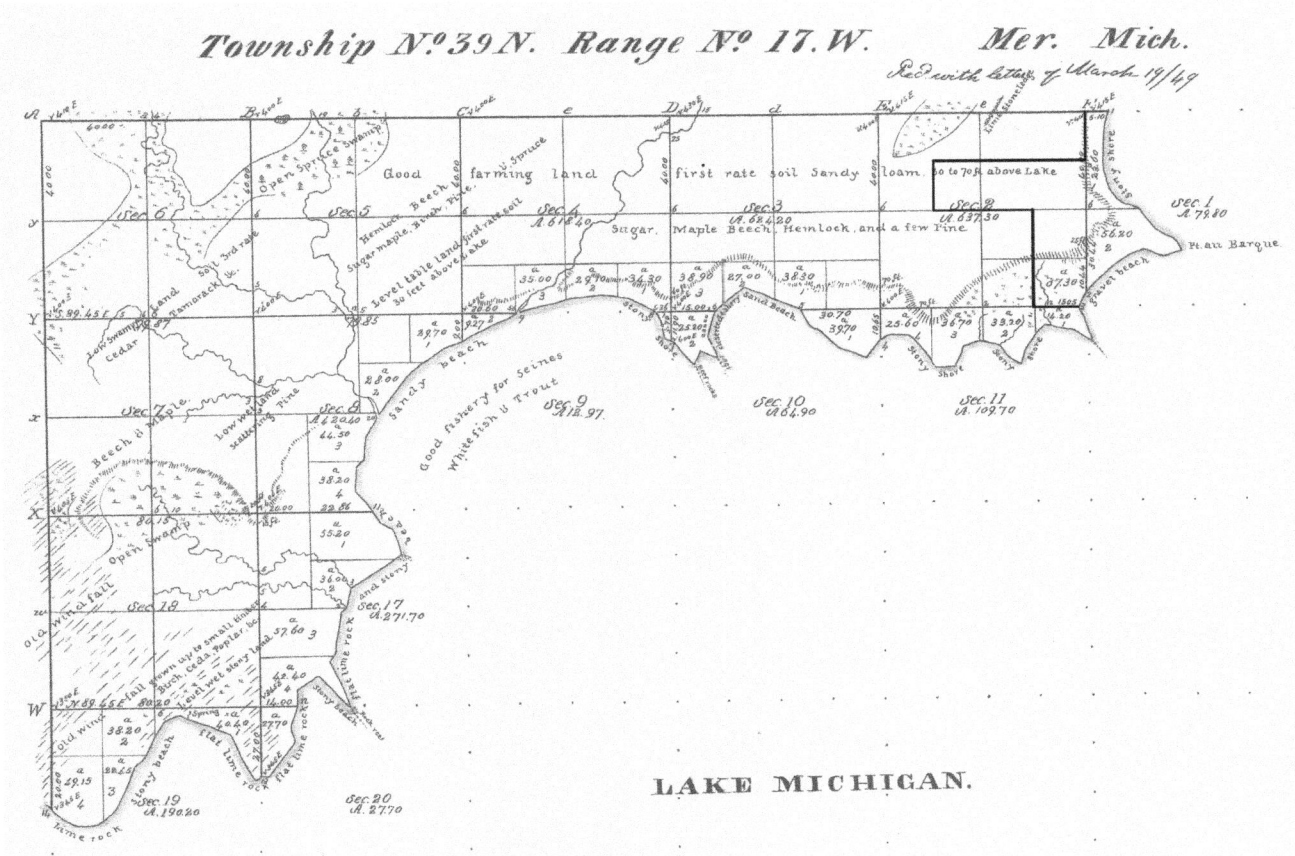

USGS survey map with the boundaries of the Barque Point homestead circa 1890 indicated by darkened line

Point and the entire Garden Peninsula fell within the boundaries of Delta County (see the 1856 map of the Upper Peninsula on page 4). For a brief period between 12 March 1861 and 17 January 1862, the Barque Point homestead and the area comprising present-day Manistique were placed into what was known as "Michigan Non-County Area 8." Finally, effective 18 January 1862, the territory comprising Michigan Non-County Area 8 merged with the rest of Schoolcraft County such that Barque Point and the eastern portion of the Garden Peninsula joined Schoolcraft County, where they remain to this day.[64] Thus, the 1860 U.S. Census lists the Bouschor family as living in Delta County's Delta Township despite their having settled on their homestead at Barque Point on the east coast of the Garden Peninsula.[65] The homestead records together with the legislature's reorganization of Delta and Schoolcraft Counties indicate that they likely lived at Barque Point as of 1860.

After residing on the Barque Point homestead for approximately three to four years, Simon initiated the process of acquiring formal title to the land under the newly-enacted Homestead Act of 1862. Simon sought a homestead claim on 18 July 1863 by paying $11.67 and filing homestead application number 32 with the Marquette Land Office on Lot 2 of Section 1 and the eastern half of the southeast quarter of Section 2, Township 39 North, Range 17 West, comprising a total of 133.5 acres.[66] In filing his application, Simon executed an affidavit averring:

> That I am the head of a family; that I am a citizen of the United States; that I have never borne arms against the government nor given aid and comfort to its enemies; that said Application No 32 is made for my exclusive benefit; and that said entry is made for the purpose of actual settlement and cultivation, and not for the use or benefit of any other person or persons whomsoever.[67]

Five years later, on 21 September 1868, Simon made payment in full on the Barque Point homestead and applied to perfect his homestead claim by filing the required affidavit averring the following:

> I, Simon Buschord [sic] having made a Homestead entry of the Lot No 2 Sec 1 & E.2 of SE/4 Section No. 2 in Township No. 39 N of Range No. 17 W subject to entry at the Land Office Marquette Michigan under the first section of the Homestead Act of May 20, 1862 do now apply to perfect my claim thereto by virtue of the first provisio [sic] to the second section of said Act; and for that purpose do solemnly swear that I am a citizen of the United States; that I have made actual settlement upon and have cultivated said land, having resided thereon since the eighteenth day of July 1863,‡ to the present time; that no part of said land has been alienated, but that I am the sole bona fide owner as an actual settler; and that I have borne true allegiance to the government of the United States.[68]

In support of Simon's homestead application, Pascal LaLonde and David Farley executed an affidavit swearing they had known Simon for five years, that his family consisted of a wife and seven children, and that he inhabited the land subject to the homestead claim.[69] The LaLonde and Farley affidavit further reflects that the Bouchard family entered and settled on the land on 18 July 1863 and constructed:

> A double (?) log house one part 20 by 20 feet and the other part 16 by 20 feet one story high, one outside room and three inside rooms—has six windows, cedar bark roof & board floors, a good stone cellar, and is a good comfortable house to live in.[70]

The LaLonde and Farley affidavit further described the homestead land by averring that Simon had:

---

‡   The family's residency from 1859 to filing of the homestead claim in 1863 is unclear. Pending enactment of the 1862 Homestead Act, the family may have squatted on the land until they were able to establish formal residency and title.

ploughed, fenced, and cultivated about 20 acres of said land, and has made the following improvements thereon, to wit: has about 35 acres fenced of the [unclear], has a barn 18 feet square, chicken house, has 20 fruit trees planted, has about 2 ½ acres of potatoes planted & about one ½ acres of corn on said [unclear] about 4 acres of oats and one acre of peas.[71]

Upon execution of Simon's 1868 affidavit and his five-dollar payment representing the balance of the homestead fees, the Marquette Land Office issued Certificate No. 5 certifying that Simon had made payment in full for the 133.5-acre Barque Point homestead.[72] Finally, on 4 November 1869, Simon received a land patent from the federal government reflecting his full title on his 133.5 acres.[73]

Fishing and Farming Activities at Barque Point

In approximately 1863 or 1864, Simon and the family cleared some of the homestead land of timber, which they sold to the Jackson Iron Company in Fayette, located south of Garden village, for use in their iron furnaces with the timber shipped around the peninsula by ship. The furnaces consumed vast amounts of wood—some forty thousand cords of wood for the average-sized plant annual—and the Jackson Iron Company constantly needed fresh supplies of hardwood to keep the furnaces operating.[74] Simon also used the cut timber to build his own fishing boats. In addition to the log cabin and boats, Simon built docks for their fishing boats.[75] As early as 1865, county records referenced Simon Bouschor's farm on Little Harbor Road.[76]

Given their proximity to the lake and the family's seafaring past, it's little surprise the Bouschors turned to fishing as a livelihood. The waters of Lake Michigan were well-stocked with lake trout and whitefish. Lake Michigan led the Great Lakes in terms of fish production, and the string of islands and shoals stretching from Washington Island

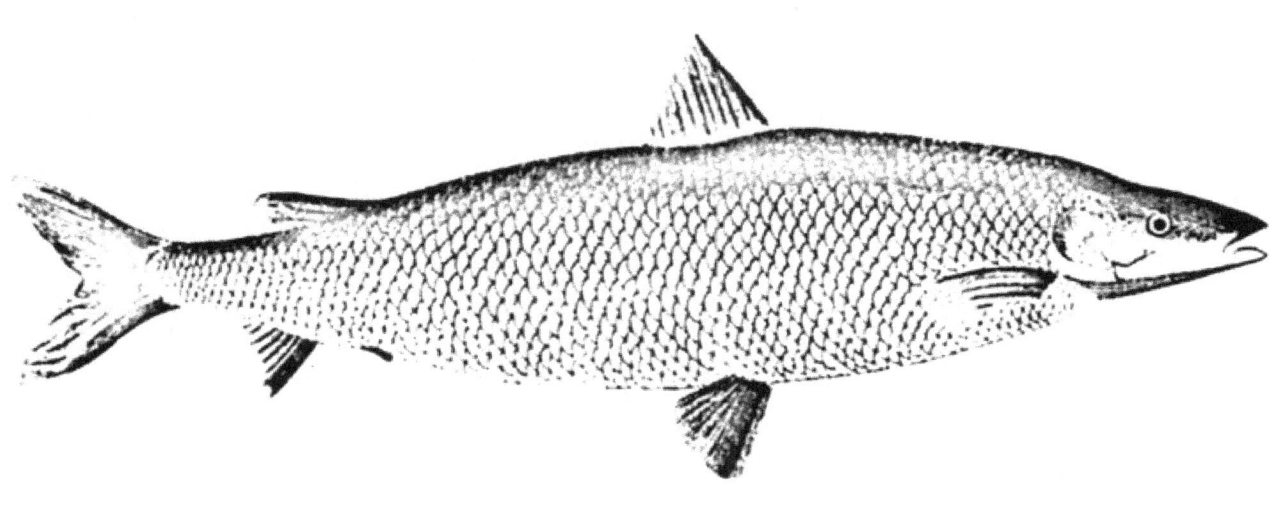

WHITE FISH of the LAKES.

Drawing of a Great Lakes whitefish from Thomas L. McKenney's 1827 work Sketches of a Tour to the Lakes

in the south to the Garden Peninsula teemed with fishing activity beginning in the mid-1800s.[77]

The most-coveted species of Great Lakes fish is the lake whitefish (*Coregonus clupeaformis*). Lake whitefish taken from the Great Lakes average two to four pounds and are typically eighteen to twenty-two inches in length.[78] In his work *Old and New Mackinac*, historian James Alvin Van Fleet records the 1842 observations of Daniel Drake, M.D., extolling the virtues of whitefish:

> a different inhabitant, of more interest than either to the dyspeptic and the gourmand, is the celebrated white-fish, which deserves to be called by its classical name, coregonus albus, which, liberally translated, signifies food of the nymphs. Its flesh, which in the cold and clear waters of the lake, organized and imbued with life, is liable but to this objection—that he who tastes it once will thenceforth be unable to relish that of any other fish.[79]

Whitefish were highly sought after on the Great Lakes, and fishermen realized their highest prices for the species. Whitefish tended to be a shallow-water species and could be caught utilizing gill nets placed near shore.[80] However, overfishing diminished their once ample numbers, and by the turn of the century the catch had considerably declined, from twelve million pounds harvested in 1880 to fewer than two million pounds in 1899.[81]

The next-most coveted fish after the whitefish was the lake trout (*Salvelinus namaycush*). In contrast to the smaller whitefish, lake trout living in the Great Lakes average between six and twelve pounds in weight and are twenty-three to twenty-nine inches in length. They became highly sought after once the whitefish numbers declined in the late 1880s.[82]

While whitefish and lake trout were the primary catches, other native species found in Lake Michigan included the lake herring (*Coregonus artedi*), also known as the cisco and quite common in the shallow waters around the Potawatomi Islands between Wisconsin and the Garden Peninsula, and the

1859 drawing of a two-masted Mackinaw boat – the workhorse of Great Lakes' fishermen

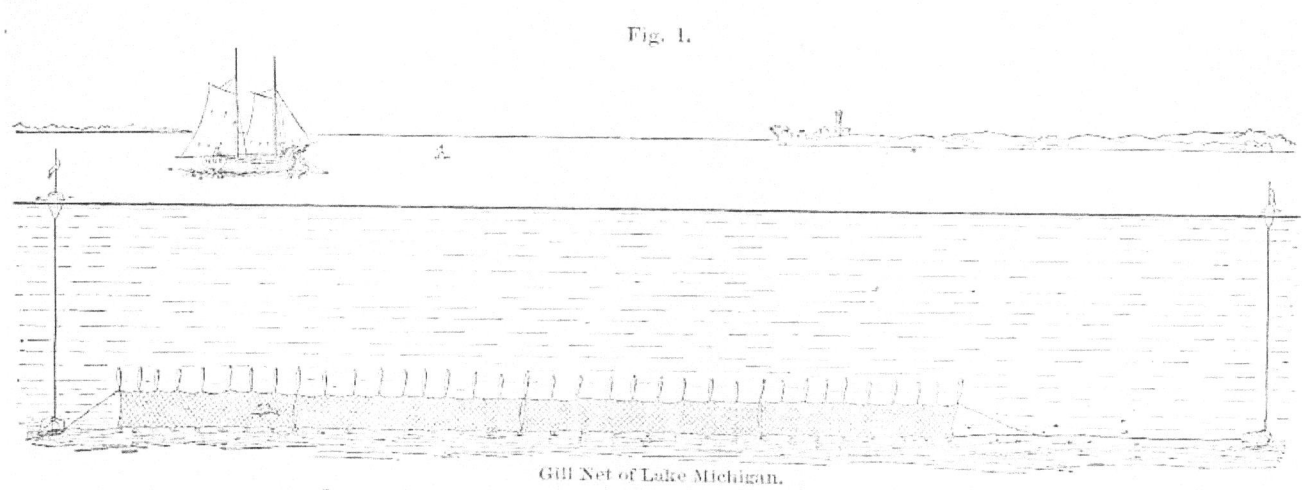

Fig. 1.

Gill Net of Lake Michigan.

Set at bottom of water, kept vertical by cedar floats.—only a few lengths of net represented.

Drawing illustrating the use of gill nets on Lake Michigan

bloater chub (*Coregonus hoyi*), which favored Lakes Michigan and Superior's underwater slopes.[83]

The Great Lakes fishermen of the nineteenth century most often used what was known as the Mackinaw boat to ply their trade. Mackinaw boats are wooden, two-masted vessels approximately twenty-five to thirty-five feet in length with flat bottoms that enable them to carry heavy loads and navigate in shallow waters.[84] The Mackinaw boat became the most popular fishing vessel on northern Lake Michigan and had largely supplanted canoes by 1850. Writer William Cullen Bryant visited Mackinac Island in 1846 and later wrote: "The Mackinaw navigators have also given their name to a boat of peculiar form, sharp at both ends, swelled at the sides, and flat-bottomed, an excellent sea-boat it must be said, as it must be to live in the wild storms that surprise the mariner on Lake Superior."[85]

Mackinaw boats were typically constructed from white pine or white cedar—both available locally in ample quantities—in an overlapping sideboard construction known as "clinker built." By the time of their heyday in the late 1800s, Mackinaw boats sported two masts with gaff-rigged sails.[86] Their versatility and relative stability and safety afforded by the simple design contributed to their popularity. In this regard, an 1874 government report on fishing in the Great Lakes made the following observations about the Mackinaw boat:

The famous "Mackinaw" of the lakes has bow and stern sharp, a great deal of sheer, the greatest beam forward of amidships and tapers with little curve to the stern. She is either schooner-rig, or with a lug-sail forward, is fairly fast, the greatest surf-boat known, and with an experienced boatman will ride out any storm, or if necessary, beach with greater safety than any other boat. She is comparatively dry, and her sharp stern prevents the shipment of water aft, when running with the sea. They have been longer and more extensively used on the upper lakes than any other boats, and with less loss of life or accident. The objection to the more general use of the Mackinaw is that her narrowness aft affords too little room for stowage. They are employed entirely with the light-rig gill-net stocks, and are usually from twenty-two to twenty-six feet in length. Lake Superior, the northern half of Lake Michigan, and a large portion of Lake Huron, are the regions where they are in general use.[87]

An undated image taken at Barque Point shown on the opposite page depicts a two-masted Mackinaw boat tied up to the dock. Simon and an unidentified man stand on the dock next to the boat, displaying an impressive fish hauled from the lake.

Fishermen like the Bouschors frequently used nets with handmade cedar floats strung along the top of the net line to hold the nets upright, while notched stones gathered from the area beaches were fastened to the bottom of the net line via rope using a slip knot. Known as gill nets, these were handmade well into the 1880s and involved around ten days of labor to knit a 300-foot net.[88] The image at the top of the opposite page illustrates how fisherman used gill nets to trap fish at the bottom of Lake Michigan. On occasion, the larger sturgeon that also inhabited Lake Michigan's waters were known to cut through the family's gill nets, wreaking havoc on their ability to catch the desired whitefish and lake trout.

The U.S. government's 1885 *Review of the Fisheries of the Great Lakes* provides a detailed survey of fishing on the Great Lakes. With regard to the area around Barque Point, the report noted:

The fisheries between Point aux Barques and Point Detour are of comparatively little importance. A few gill-net fisherman live in the section, and others from Thompson and Manistique build fishing shanties, where they remain with their boats and gill-nets during the fishing season. Some of them are provided with small setlines, which they use in connection with their gill-nets to a limited extent. The greater part of their catch is salted, though a few fish are sold fresh to the collecting boats from Manistique.[89]

The report goes on to note that in 1885, there were fourteen crews with fourteen boats and 1,400 gill-nets fishing along the area's shores, and that their total catch amounted to 19,500 pounds of fresh whitefish, 6,500 pounds of fresh trout, 153,150 pounds of salt whitefish, and 51,050 pounds of salt trout, with an aggregate yield valued at $8,647.[90] The Bouschor family and its small crew were but a

The dock and a Mackinaw boat at Barque Point. Simon Bouschor stands at the far-right with a rifle balanced on his shoulder (the remaining figures in the photograph are unidentified)

part of this larger haul.

As evidenced by the government's 1885 statistics, most fish harvested from the lakes were salted to prepare them for shipment. Salting fish involved removing the heads and splitting the fish along the back so they lay flat. The fishermen would then salt both sides of the fish and layer them in wooden kegs, one on top of the other. Adequately preserved, the catch could then be shipped south to waiting customers in places like Milwaukee and Chicago.[91]

Fishing around Barque Point suffered some by the mid-1890s due to large quantities of sawdust from the mills at Manistique and Thompson depositing on the sturgeon and whitefish feeding grounds and suffocating the grass that the species relied upon for survival.[92] Nonetheless, the Bouschor family even caught a Columbia River salmon that had been planted by the government several years earlier. The 12 May 1899 issue of the *Manistique Pioneer-Tribune* detailed that the "Bouschor boys" caught a salmon approximately four to five years old and weighing five pounds in their nets off Wiggins Point. According to the *Pioneer-Tribune*, a photographer named Lockwood "secured a fine picture of the fish," and it's possible this is the fish shown on the previous page held by an unidentified man standing next to Simon Bouschor, though the fish pictured admittedly looks larger than five pounds.[93]

While the family's "primary occupation was fishing, they also farmed grains and vegetables."[94] The 1880 U.S. Non-Population Census, detailing production of agriculture across the United States, provides a glimpse at life on the Barque Point homestead in the late 1880s. It lists Simon and Harriette's property as comprising forty acres of tilled land, two-and-a-half acres of "permanent meadows, permanent pastures, orchards, vineyards, and 150 acres of woodland and forest." In terms of agricultural production, they mowed five acres of grassland in 1879, realizing a two-ton harvest of hay, while another acre and a quarter of land produced 295 bushels of Irish potatoes. A quarter acre of Indian corn produced ten bushels of crop in 1879, and

they grew a single bushel of Canadian peas that same year. Lastly, the family devoted three quarters of an acre of land to growing apples, though the census schedule does not list them as producing any harvest that year.[95]

In terms of livestock and other animals on hand as of June 1880, the 1880 Non-Population Census lists them as owning three horses, four milk cows and five other head of cattle with three calves dropped the previous year, and thirty-six poultry that processed 100 dozen eggs the previous year. The census schedule also notes they had one sheep slaughtered in 1879 and one fleece in 1880 that produced three pounds of wool. In total, the census lists the farm itself as having a value of $400 and the livestock, $447. In terms of operating expenses, the family spent $50 building and repairing fences in 1879 and paid $120 in wages for farm labor that same year.[96]

Undated photograph of horses grazing at Barque Point

By the 1890s, around 160 acres of the homestead's total acreage were improved, with the family raising multiple cereals, roots, and tubers along with "a fine piece of buck wheat in full bloom [that] formed a lovely contrast to the eye."[97] Deer were also in abundance, as a 25 August 1894 article in the *Manistique Semi-Weekly Pioneer* describes one of the Bouschor sons taking a deer with "mammoth antlers" that yielded some 237 pounds of meat.[98]

Shipwrecks and Safety Around Barque Point

Barque Point served as both a landmark and an obstacle for the ships plying the waters of upper Lake Michigan. Barque Point's location and the shallows along the Garden Peninsula's eastern point made it a magnet for marine distress over the years. In the early part of the twentieth century, authorities made plans to construct a lighthouse on Barque Point following completion of another on St. Martin Island. They even went so far as to appropriate $3,200 for its construction. The *Evening News* of Sault Ste. Marie noted the following in 1904:

> The need of a lighthouse on Barque Point is unquestionable. Several miles off shore at this place there is a sunken island, where the water is only three or four feet deep.
>
> Mr. Bouschor states that it is necessary for steamers to use their sounding lead with the utmost caution when in the neighborhood of this point on a foggy day.[99]

Ultimately, nothing ever came of the Barque Point lighthouse, and the point remains a looming menace for marine traffic to this day.

While the Bouschor family wasn't known to lose any fishing boats or other vessels, other ships were not so fortunate. In fall of 1930, the freighter *Griffin* went aground off Barque Point. Its crew had to jettison several hundred tons of pig iron overboard to float the vessel. The following summer, Captain Ben Gallagher of Marquette worked to salvage the submerged pig iron using an electromagnet affixed to a large scow.[100] Nearly nine years later, in April 1939, the *Vernon*—a fish tug operated by Glenn Hughson—went aground between Barque Point and Wiggins Reef but was freed by the *Escanaba*, a coast guard cutter.[101]

Family Life at the Barque Point Homestead

In total, eleven of Simon and Harriette's thirteen children were born on the Barque Point homestead: George Wallace on 12 November 1859; Anna Olive on 9 November 1861; Simon Joseph on 20 January 1864; Charles Wesley on 2 April 1866; Louis Remit on 26 November 1867; Harriet Marie on 3 December 1869; Henry Archibald on 26 December 1872; Moise on 11 March 1874; William Edward on 27 May 1876; Mary May on 28 August 1879; and Nelson Burton on 6 March 1882. A photograph taken in the mid-1880s and reproduced on page 61, likely at the Barque Point homestead given the tall stands of trees in the background, depicts Simon and Harriette along with six of their thirteen children—Simon Jr., Charles, Henry, William, Mary May, and Nels.[102]

Two of Simon and Harriette Bouschor's children may still be buried on the property. Mrs. Hasell Osterhout's series of articles for the *Manistique Pioneer-Tribune* on the history of Thompson Township notes, "The site of the homestead is still marked today by two small graves in a white enclosure. The graves are those of two of the Bouschare [sic] children who died in infancy. The Bouschare's [sic] had a total of 13 children."[103] Other sources suggest the graves of Moise and Harriet Marie were moved to a family burial plot on the Gray family homestead near Garden.

By the time of Mary May's birth in 1879, the pioneer cabin built by Simon in 1859 proved to be far too small for the swelling family. Simon had earlier purchased the adjoining 143.6-acre property belonging to John Fountain, and the family relocated to a larger house located on Mr. Fountain's former property.[104] Mr. Fountain had obtained title to Lot 1 of Section 1 and the southern half of the northeast quarter and the southeast quarter of the northwest quarter of Section 2 of Township 39 North, Range 39 East via a homestead patent dated 4 November 1869—the same date Simon obtained title to his original 133.5 acres of the homestead.[105] The addition of Mr. Fountain's land doubled the homestead's overall size. Simon also acquired the land owned by Tellas and Ida Farley, where the Farley Halfway House once stood to welcome travelers heading from Manistique to Garden, Fayette, and beyond. The Farley land comprised 160 acres at the present junction of Little Harbor Road and Barque Point Trail.[106] In 1899, however, the *Manistique Pioneer-Tribune* noted that Simon and Harriette's family moved into a house formerly occupied by Joseph Kingham. It's unclear if this house was located at Barque Point or in the village of Thompson itself.[107]

Barque Point homestead – Early twentieth century

Barque Point homestead fish sheds – 1923 (Left to Right: Milo Hogarty, Anton Weber, Wilfred Farley, Louis Bouschor)

Barque Point homestead with barn in background

In the pioneer days of the 1880s, prior to the establishment of any maintained roads, the primary access to the Barque Point homestead was via the Portage Trail. Approximately fifty miles in length, the trail, established by the area's Indian population, ran from Manistique south through Thompson and Barque Point before veering west to Little Harbor and Garden, then continuing south onward to Fayette.[108] The Portage Trail was primitive at best, with one mail carrier in the 1860s describing it as a "blind trail" and "nothing like a road." Despite the trail's logistical challenges, Harriette Gray Bouschor's fifteen-year-old niece, Elizabeth Allen, took on the mail route in 1868 and brought mail by horseback from Garden village to Manistique (then called Epsport or Monistique).[109]

A present-day visitor to Barque Point can see the unmistakable path of the original trail running from just off North Barque Point Trail road, winding down a gentle slope before turning southeast towards the original homestead grounds. Mature trees line either side of the pathway and give the visitor an appreciation for what it must have been like to approach the homestead on horseback when only a handful of settlers called the area home. In his capacity as Commissioner of Highways for Hiawatha Township and, later, Thompson Township in the early 1880s, Simon was instrumental in the routing and development of Little Harbor Road that presently runs south from Highway 2 through the village of Thompson and south to Barque Point before making a sharp turn west at the Bouschor Homestead and bisecting sections 2, 3, and 4 on its way to the Schoolcraft/Delta County line.[110]

The Barque Point homestead proved to be a place of hospitality and refuge in the sparsely populated Garden Peninsula. A party given for Simon and Harriette's ten-year-old daughter, Mary May, in late 1889 counted thirty to forty of their neighbors in attendance.[111] On another occasion, an Indian man felling timber had a tree fall on him, pinning one leg such that the man had to amputate his own leg. He managed to crawl to the Bouschor homestead, where Harriette helped nurse him back to health.[112] The Garden Peninsula Historical Society's history *Our Heritage* notes that a man named Harry Hutchins would deliver mail from Manistique using the Portage Trail, and that he'd make his first stop overnight at the Bouschor homestead on Barque Point.[113] In winter, the mail carrier would make his way along via snowshoes and complete the trip to Fayette in approximately three days.[114]

Journalist F. A. Rogers of the town of Reading in Hillsdale County, Michigan, detailed a visit he made to Barque Point in the summer of 1894. Rogers offered the following description, published in Manistique's *Semi-Weekly Pioneer*:

> Art and nature being charmingly blended, the place is grandeur itself. Here is a row of beautiful trees and shrubbery clothed in verdant foliage, there is a line of gorgeous flowers sparkling in the rays of a morning sun, now a rich field of golden grain erected across the magnificent landscape, then far away to the south and eastward lies a [illegible] at once romantic and beautiful beyond description. The lofty terraces in front and in the background of the locality may easily command the wonder and admiration of all those who are fortunate to view this pleasant retreat.[115]

Rogers went on to describe the homestead and his reception: "I must not forget to mention that because of my early arrival, a repast of toast and eggs and steaming coffee should be placed before me, and while waiting in the parlor for the lady of the house to prepare the frugal meal, I fairly bathed myself in a rich store of charming [illegible] that carried me from the sunny Tropics and Oriental lands, to the far-away regions of the frozen North. A fine musical instrument and many splendid engravings adorned the walls of the room from carpet to ceiling. Good taste and refinement indeed."[116] Rogers likely praised a variety of berries growing along the lakeshore, including one he described as similar to high-bush huckleberries and another as resembling "a large, flat, red raspberry."[117]

Rogers made a second visit to Barque Point at

An unidentified figure enjoying a visit to Barque Point in the early 20th century

and the Bouschor homestead. This article offers perhaps the best contemporaneous description of life on the homestead at the turn of the century and bears quoting in full:

> On a pleasant Sunday, our host and hostess took us on a drive to Barque Point, which, were it within reach of civilization, would be seized upon by resorters on account of the beauty of its situation. It is fourteen miles through the woods southwest of Manistique, and there on a little clearing he calls his farm we found Simon Bouschor, father of the Ciscoe's captain. Forty years ago, Simon Bouschor was a lake captain, having then sailed for thirty years. His wife insisted upon his leaving his perilous life, and upon her consenting to settle wherever he might choose, he took her to that spot among the Indians and wild animals and made their home there. The nearest trading point was seventy-five miles distant. Here they had lived for forty years and reared their children. Asked if he did not get lonesome, the old man said "I get lonesome when I go to town. I never get lonesome here, where the woods are full of game."[120]

Christmas time in 1894. During this follow-up visit, Rogers noted, "At the present time Mr. Bouschor is quite busy engaged in lumbering pine, hard-maple, and birch. Some is decked away in the woods, while the balance is immediately placed at the landing along the lakeshore; he is somewhat cautious, however, in regard to advancing too rapidly, fearing the winter will not be favorable enough for business operations."[118] At the time of Rogers' visit, Simon and Harriette's two youngest children—Mary May and Nels—lived on the homestead with their parents.[119]

Nearly ten years later, newspaper editor Frank M. Johnson traveled from his home in Lowell, Michigan, in the Lower Peninsula, on a trip through Manistique and Thompson. In an article he wrote for the 15 October 1903 issue of the *Lowell Ledger*, Johnson recounted a Sunday visit to Barque Point

Indeed, the distance from Barque Point to civilization made for considerable challenges to travelers. In their early years of residence, Simon had to carry one child—believed to be George Wallace, the first born on the homestead—all the way to the Indian Lake Mission Chapel outside Manistique to be baptized. A parish priest later commented, "The little fellow was carried on the shoulders of his father through the wilderness, a distance of 17 or 18 miles."[121]

Prior to white settlement of the area, Barque Point was the site of an Indian battleground between Ojibwa and the Odawa, as evidenced by arrowheads found on the beach and lodged in trees.[122] In describing Barque Point's topography, Frank M. Johnson's article in the *Lowell Ledger* offers a detailed account of the clash:

Foundation ruins of the Bouschor family homestead at Barque Point in 2024

Pathway of the old road at Barque Point looking southeast towards the Bouschor family homestead in 2024

Next, the water for a long distance is a stretch of sandy beach, which is fringed by timber, just back of the edge of which is a high bluff at whose top is a ridge of limestone shale. Mr. Bouschor informed us that this marked the place where an Indian battle took place at least a century ago. Simon says that Chief Ossawinamakee, for whom Manistique's big hotel is named, told him the story. Before the battle of Mackinac between the British and the Americans, which was in 1814, the Menominees lived there. At one time, a young Indian for some offense was condemned to die. He was bound hand and foot and placed in a canoe when the wind was off shore, and was expected to perish. Fates ordered it otherwise, however, and the frail bark canoe carried its burden in safety to the shores of Southern Michigan, where he was rescued by the Ottawas. He induced a war party of these to return with him to give battle to the Menominees. There on the ridge at Barque Point the red foemen met. The Menominees fought from the ridge and used their dead for breastworks. After the fight, in which the Menominees were badly defeated, the dead were gathered on the ridge and covered with the stones. Many years ago, Simon's hogs in rooting among the stones uncovered a great number of human bones. His inquiry among the Indians brought out the story we have told.[123]

Disturbingly, Johnson's article ends by calling out any doubters of the "Indian story," and claiming to have an Indian arm bone dug out from the battleground. He adds, "If you do not agree that it is a hundred years old, we'll treat to peanuts."[124] One hopes the remains were returned to the tribe's descendants or reburied with the dignity they deserve.

Education and Religion at Barque Point

At one point, Barque Point had its own school— Barque Point School No. 5. According to Thompson Township historian Mrs. Hasell Osterhout, "A

A picnic at the Little Harbor school in the early 1920s — This structure is believed to be the "Bouschor School" once located on Little Harbor Road

farmer in the Barque Point area provided transportation for the students either by horse and wagon or sleigh. His horse, Jenny Lind, had traveled the route so often she needed no reins or lines for guidance. She would also stop along the route at the proper place to pick up or drop off the students."[125] Mrs. Osterhout further noted that the school was originally known as the Bouschor School and was located on Little Harbor Road before being moved to the top of the hill at Little Harbor. The photograph at right shows the Little Harbor school sometime in the early 1920s. As late as 1975, a well and spring located at the school site were still in use.[126]

Several Bouschors worshipped at St. Frederick's Catholic Church, built in approximately 1900 and located on the north side of Pine Street in the Village of Thompson. Aldred Bouschor, son of Simon Joseph and Marion (Heric) Bouschor, assisted in the construction of St. Frederick's, while Aldred's younger sister, Meta Marion Bouschor, was the first person baptized in the new church.[127] However, the Methodist church also used the Bouschor School on Little Harbor Road for Sunday school, and the church continued to use it for that purpose following the building's move to Little Harbor itself.[128] While Simon was raised Catholic, Harriette belonged to the Methodist Church and had her funeral at the Methodist church in Manistique in 1906. It's believed the couple agreed that the boys

A picnic at the Barque Point homestead in the early 1920s attended by several Bouschor family descendants

would be raised in the Catholic Church while the girls would be raised in their mother's Methodist faith.

Later Years and Present-Day Barque Point

After Harriette passed away and Simon moved to Manistique to live with his son George's family, no one lived at the Barque Point homestead. Nonetheless, it continued to be used over the years. As shown in the photograph above, family members including G. Leslie Bouschor, Nels and Marie Bouschor and their daughter Harriet, and Lewis R. Bouschor traveled to Barque Point for a picnic. In the 1930s, a group calling themselves the "Barque Point Picnic Club" made frequent use of the homestead grounds for organized weekend picnics.[129] One such gathering on Sunday, 23 July 1933, included Nels, Marie, and Cletus Bouschor, Wilfred and Emma Farley, and others who enjoyed various diversions with basket lunches served at noon and early evening.[130] Similarly, the Knights of Columbus used Barque Point for barbeques and gatherings.[131] By the 1950s, the point's pristine wilderness and location made it an ideal spot for a Boy Scouts' camp. In 1959, the Michigan Centennial Farm Association

declared the Bouschor Homestead a Centennial Farm. The Bouschor Homestead was the first farm in the Upper Peninsula to register as a Centennial Farm. At the time of this declaration, G. Leslie Bouschor, a grandson of Simon and Harriette, owned the Barque Point land.[132] In celebration of the achievement, Leslie organized a commemoration picnic at the homestead in 1959. It took place on 23 August 1959, and the Schoolcraft Historical Society even published an article in the *Escanaba Daily Press* inviting the public to attend and to bring photographs of the early days.[133] Several relatives attended, including Nels Bouschor, and Ida and Tellas Farley's children, Wilfred Farley and Bertha Farley Deemer.[134] Leslie prepared and delivered remarks on the homestead's history and the early efforts by Simon and family to cultivate the land.[135]

In commemoration of the new Centennial Farm, the Michigan Historical Commission issued a plaque memorializing its newfound status. The plaque was unveiled and the Centennial Farm dedicated during the 23 August 1959 picnic.[136] The photograph opposite from 1959 depicts Nels Bouschor and his nephew G. Leslie Bouschor holding the plaque prior to its installation at the homestead.[137] Nearly ten years later, the Michigan Historical Commission presented Leslie and Lydia Bouschor with another plaque at the U.P. State Farm on 16 August 1968 in recognition of their Centennial Farm.[138] G. Leslie's wife, Lydia Bouschor, recalled "the times we visited to pick apples and enjoy the sandy beach of Lake Michigan."[139]

In the early 1970s, Leslie sold the homestead, now comprising 760 acres, to a group of eight Battle Creek, Michigan, investors who intended to develop the land into a recreation area with multiple amenities including fishing, nature trails, and 200 camping units.[140] A 1971 newspaper article notes that the "first section of the trailer park is being completed" and observed "provisions have been contemplated to accommodate up to 5,000 units."[141] After 110 years in the Bouschor family, the homestead passed into other hands. By 1986, the former homestead was owned by the Pointe Aux Barques Land Company.[142] Ultimately, the grand redevelopment plans came to naught. While some structures were erected for the campground and multiple utility hookups for campers installed, the vast majority of the former homestead remained undeveloped until it was gradually subdivided and individual parcels were developed. Today, Barque Point and the former Bouschor homestead can be reached from Highway 2 by driving south on Little Harbor Road at Thompson Township. From there, Barque Point Trail permits access to several homes and land lots, including the core of the original Bouschor homestead occupying Barque Point. As of 2024, the core of the Bouschor homestead property, comprising 11.71 acres, continues to be owned by the Pointe Aux Barques Land Company.[143]

Nels Bouschor and G. Leslie Bouschor at the Barque Point homestead displaying the plaque granted by the Michigan Centennial Farm Association in commemoration of one-hundred years of continuous ownership by the Bouschor family

Thompson Township and the Village of Thompson

Barque Point forms the southernmost reaches of present-day Thompson Township. The village of Thompson proper, located several miles north of the Barque Point homestead, flourished as a saw-mill town around the turn of the century, and it became home to several of Simon and Harriette's children and their descendants in its heyday.

The boundaries of Thompson Township stretch from the northern portions of Schoolcraft County in the Hiawatha National Forest near Steuben, all the way to the south to just west of Point O'Keefe on the Garden Peninsula where Schoolcraft meets Delta County (see Schoolcraft County map on page 42). A township is the most basic unit of organized government in Michigan, and it comprises "an area that may or may not include some sort of municipality."[144] Thompson Township includes Barque Point and the land that comprised the Bouschor family homestead and totals over 98,000 acres.[145] The village of Thompson, however, is located at the crossroads where the east-west U.S. Highway 2 meets the north-south Michigan State Highway 149.

Thompson's history began with the 1880 construc-tion of a lumber mill in the village by the Delta Lum-ber Company.[146] Thompson's early settlers founded the township on 6 March 1882 by detaching land from the larger territory comprising Hiawatha Township.[147] Thompson Township held its first of-ficial census on 1 June 1884, under the auspices of enumerator William Thomas Kinner, and recorded a total of 537 individuals residing in the Township, with 207 living in the village of Thompson itself and the remaining 330—including the Bouschor family at Barque Point—living in the Township at large.[148] The founders of Thompson village formal-ly platted the townsite on 8 November 1888 and named the community in honor of Delta Lumber Company President E. L. Thompson.[149]

Mr. Thompson of Michigan's Lapeer County and two other men—R. B. Currier of Springfield, Mas-sachusetts, and Michigan Governor John T. Rich—had acquired vast acres of timbered land across Schoolcraft and Delta Counties that offered them ample stock for the lumbering operation.[150] Their enterprise initially paid off, as the Delta Lumber Company shipped eighteen million board feet of lumber in 1886—soon rising to around twenty-five million board feet per year by the late 1880s.[151]

Photograph of the village of Thompson in 1910

However, following the Delta Lumber Company's failure in 1893, the F&F (Frank and Friant) Company took over operations for approximately six years. Once all the area's pine was harvested, the mill switched to processing hardwood and was operated for a time by A. M. Chesbrough.[152] After sitting idle for several years, the Thompson Lumber Company restarted operations and continued until the mill's final closure in the early 1920s.[153] Other companies that made Thompson their headquarters for lumbering operations included Paulting & Chipman, Schlosser & Tighe, and Truant & Fuller.[154]

Thompson Township held its first meeting and annual election on 3 April 1882 and elected its inaugural group of officials. This inaugural group included Simon Bouschor as Commissioner of Highways and his son George Bouschor as one of four constables.[155] Over the ensuing decades, Bouschor family members held multiple positions with Thompson Township, as follows:

Name	Office and Year(s) Elected or Appointed
Simon Bouschor	Commissioner of Highways, 1882 – 1884
	Assessor, School District No. 3, 1882 – 1980
	Overseer of Highways District 4, 1889 – 1891
Harriette Bouschor	Director, School District No. 3, 1880 – 1891
George Wallace Bouschor	Constable, 1882 – 1884, 1886
	Overseer of Highways District 1, 1884
	Commissioner of Highways, 1888
	Board of Review, 1897
Oliver Adrian Pierce	Overseer of Highways District 1, 1883
	Overseer of Highways District 2, 1885, 1887 – 1888
Tellas Farley	Moderator, School District No. 3, 1882 – 1889
	Constable, 1885
	Poundmaster, 1889
Simon Joseph Bouschor	Constable, 1888 – 1889, 1891
	Board of Review, 1894 – 1895, 1903
	Supervisor, 1896 – 1897, 1899 – 1900, 1910 – 1913
	Justice of the Peace, 1903
	Clerk, 1904
	School Inspector, 1907 – 1914
David Eli Bouschor	Constable, 1890

Bouschor family office holders in Thompson Township[156]

Like the surrounding communities on the Great Lakes, Thompson also hosted active fishing operations in the late 1880s. The operation was largely controlled by a Detroit firm that established a station at Thompson in 1884.[157] As Thompson grew in importance as a community in the late 1800s, several Bouschor family members migrated north from the Barque Point homestead. Simon Joseph Bouschor's family lived in Thompson for several years, and he operated one of the village's saloons. The building housing Simon's saloon was one of three buildings owned by Henry Voisine and stood at the busiest part of town. It lasted until being destroyed by fire in April 1929.[158] During Thompson's peak years of activity in the 1890s, George Wallace Bouschor operated a livery stable in Thompson while his brother David Eli Bouschor ran a saloon (and later a major boarding house in town). Likewise, their brother-in-law Tellas Farley operated a hotel in Thompson.[159] Mary May Bouschor Daignault and her husband, Alexander Daignault, also called Thompson home in the early 1900s.[160]

At the turn of the century, Thompson Township numbered eight schools, three churches, a hospital, numerous other businesses, and a railroad line running from Thompson village to Big Spring that transported tourists in addition to timber.[161] Simon Junior's family worshipped at St. Frederick's Catholic Church, located on Pine Street just east of Bluff Street on the village's Lot No. 7. Priests who served at St. Frederick's included Fathers Geers, Cebul, and LaForest. Joseph Hoholik later moved the church building to his farm on County Road 149 near Indian Lake. Highway 2 currently passes over the site of the church, but the church sacristy has been restored and placed nearby.[162] Some 300 men worked in Thompson's sawmills cutting, then loading lumber aboard schooners to carry the lumber south to cities like Chicago.[163] Thompson was also the departure point for the infamous Christmas Tree Ship, the schooner *Rouse Simmons*, that departed Thompson village on 22 November 1912 laden with Christmas trees destined for Chicago but sank the following day in bad weather.[164]

Most timber in the Thompson region was harvested by World War I, and Thompson's mills had shut

Village of Thompson taken from a treetop in the early 1900s

down by the early 1920s. Several Bouschor families, such as those of Ida, George, Simon Junior, and Nels, moved on to the larger community of Manistique as Thompson's fortunes declined. Nonetheless, fishing continued to be a lifeline for the community after lumbering ceased to be viable.[165] One of the town's main employers after the timber industry's decline was the Thompson Fish Hatchery. The hatchery opened in 1922 and continues to produce Chinook salmon, walleye, and steelhead.[166]

The village of Thompson ceased to exist as a government body in the 1950s and has since fallen under the administration of Thompson Township. Though many of Thompson's historic buildings have succumbed to the ravages of time, destruction by fire, and substantial remodeling, the township endures, and its population exceeds 800 residents as of the 2020 U.S. Census.[167] While no school presently operates in Thompson and the post office closed for good in 1988, dozens of homes—some dating to the village's heyday, like the A. M. Chesborough house—line Thompson's remaining streets.[168] Most Thompson residents do their shopping in nearby Manistique or Escanaba, and children in the area are bused to Manistique for school.[169] Today, organizations like the Thompson Township Historical Advisory Committee help preserve Thompson's history and have made it possible for future generations to learn about the township's rich history through displays, interpretive placards, and numerous records and photographs available online.§

§   To learn more about Thompson's history and to see additional photographs visit the Thompson Township Historical Advisory Committee's Facebook page at https://www.facebook.com/Thompsonhistoricalcommittee or via the Upper Peninsula Digital Network at https://uplink.nmu.edu/islandora/object/nmu%3A69618.

Manistique and Schoolcraft County

Situated northeast of the Garden Peninsula and Thompson Township, Manistique was the longtime home of many Bouschor descendants and is the resting place of Simon and Harriette Bouschor and several of their children. Manistique is the seat of Schoolcraft County and remains the county's largest settlement by population.

Prior to the arrival of the first white settlers, the Chippewa Indians inhabited the land. The father of Antoine Ossawinamkee received a portion of what came to be Schoolcraft County following the War of 1812.[170] The Indians occupied the Manistique area for centuries before the arrival of white settlers. Father Frederic Baraga, a Slovenian-born Catholic missionary, founded a mission church on the shores of Indian Lake in 1833 and is regarded as the area's first white settler.[171] The area comprising Schoolcraft County and Manistique became part of Michigan Territory via the 1836 Treaty of Washington.[172]

Schoolcraft County underwent multiple boundary revisions following its creation on 9 March 1843.

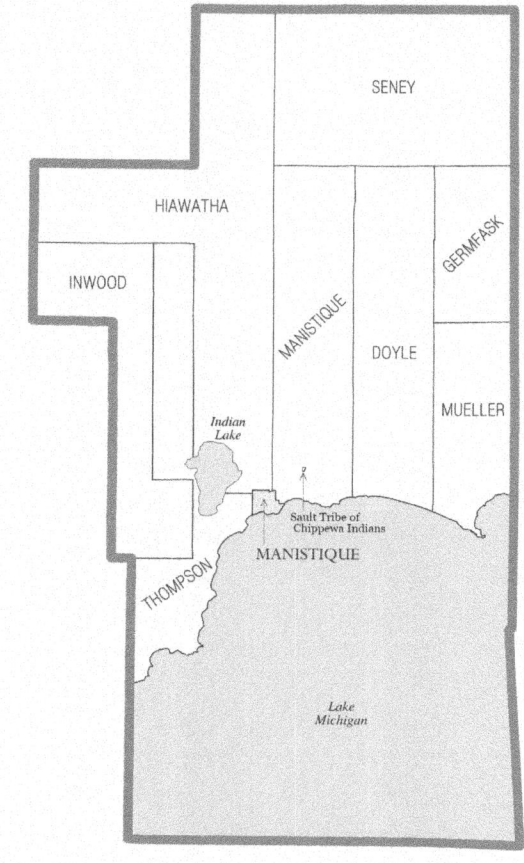

Map of Schoolcraft County showing Thompson Township, the city of Manistique, and surrounding jurisdictions

The state initially carved Schoolcraft County out of Chippewa and Michilimackinac Counties and named it after Henry Rowe Schoolcraft, an early explorer, Indian agent, and self-taught historian whose journals contain some of the earliest records of the Ojibwa and Odawa Indians living in the area.[173]

From its 1843 creation until March 1861, Schoolcraft County terminated at the boundary between Townships 41 and 42 North and did not include any portion of the Garden Peninsula or the present-day City of Manistique. Following reorganization of Delta and Schoolcraft Counties in 1861, Delta County gained some territory formerly in southwest Schoolcraft County, while the eastern portion of the Garden Peninsula (including Barque Point and the future Thompson Township) and a strip

Henry Rowe Schoolcraft: Namesake of Schoolcraft County

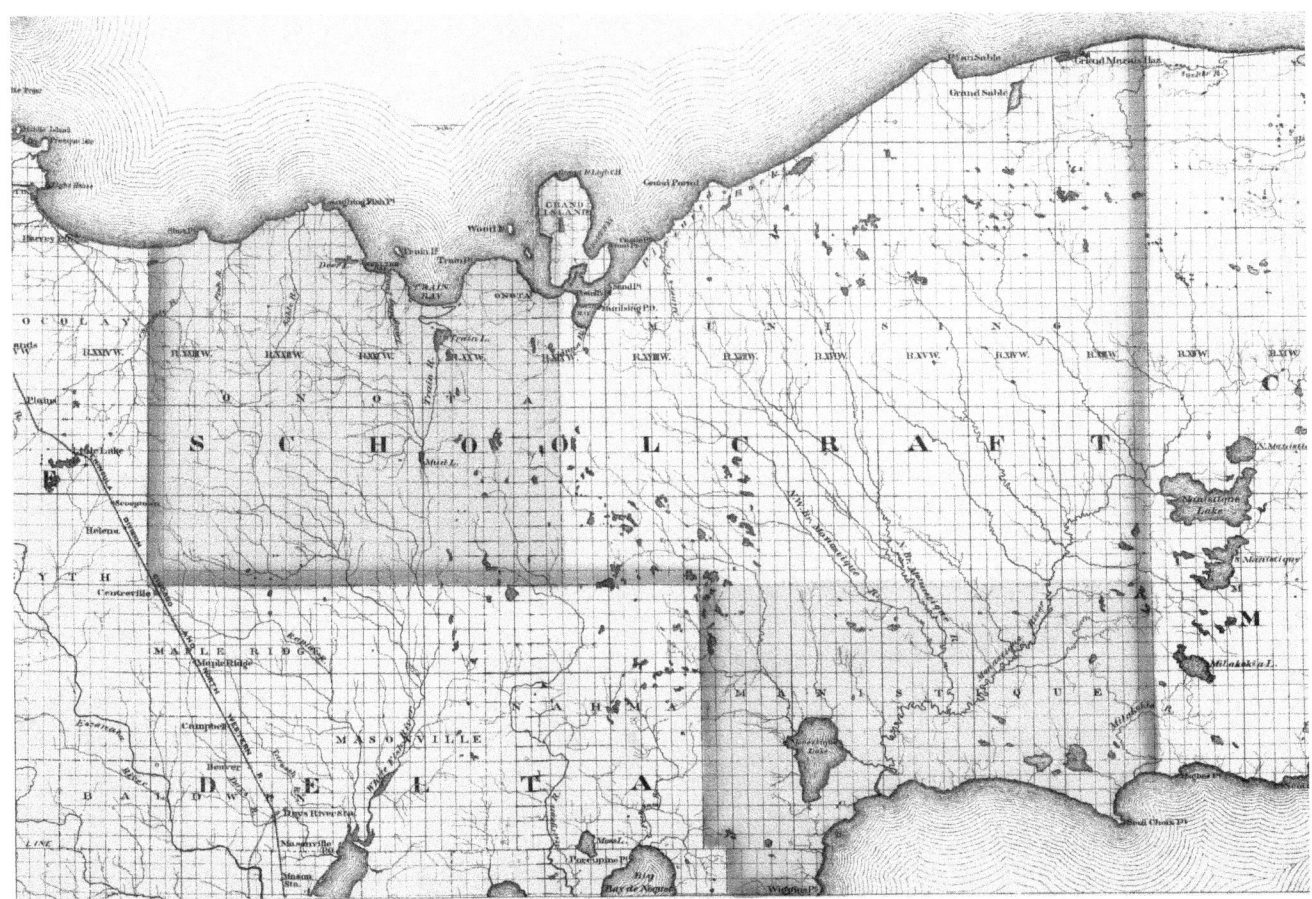

1873 map of Schoolcraft County when the county stretched from Lake Michigan to Lake Superior – The northern portion was split off as Alger County in 1885

of partial township sections lining Lake Michigan became part of Schoolcraft County. This included present-day Manistique east to the Gulliver area. The county achieved its present-day configuration on 17 March 1885 when the state formed Alger County out of Schoolcraft's northern half, reducing the county's overall size by nearly fifty percent.[174]

The Manistique River winds its way through Schoolcraft County from its headwaters near Manistique Lake in neighboring Luce County. The present-day name Manistique is a misnomer, as the river that gave rise to its name was called the Monistique River and derived its name from the Ojibwa word *monistique* meaning "river with the big bay."[175] A substitution of an "a" for the "o" engendered the spelling that persists to this day. The name is related to that of Manistee, which is given to a pair of rivers as well as a city and county on the Lower Peninsula. An early reference to Manistique in the sixteenth century gave the name as Oulamanistik.[176] Jesuit father, historian, and missionary William F. Gagnieur, S.J., opined that the name Manistique derived from "Onaman (red ochre or vermillion) and tigweia (referring to a river), because along that river are to be found in plenty the Onaman or vermillion roots. It is still called by the Indians Onamanitikong, i.e. Vermillion River."[177] In 1913, the river itself was navigable by the largest boats on the lake up to a half a mile from its mouth.[178] As with many Upper Peninsula rivers, the Manistique served as conduit for tens of thousands of fallen trees that were floated down the river from deep in the heart of the central Upper Peninsula's forests and processed at the area sawmills.

Prior to the founding of Manistique proper, a small lumber village called Epsport was situated at the mouth of the Manistique River.[179] Charles T. Harvey founded Epsport and named the community in honor of his wife's family name, Eps, in approximately 1860 when he built a dam on the Manistique River. Harvey was an engineer by training and worked on the Soo Locks at Sault Ste. Marie before coming to the Manistique area. As a result of his work in developing and completing the locks canal project, Harvey received title to 140,000 acres of Upper Peninsula land that he personally selected from a bounty of 750,000. This included land in Schoolcraft County straddling the Manistique River.[180] Harvey's dam powered a sawmill run by Spinney and Boyd, who were soon succeeded by the organizers of the Chicago Lumbering Company. Within five years of its founding, Epsport hosted a sawmill, two lumber slips, a store, a boarding house, and a scattering of dwellings.[181] A consortium of eastern investors headed by Abijah Weston and A. J. Fox purchased the Chicago Lumbering Company and both soon moved to Manistique to manage the company.[182] Simon Bouschor even played a part in Manistique's early days as he "bore the distinction of being the first mail carried [sic] from the outside world to Manistique, having carried the mail from Escanaba to Manistique over the ice."[183]

Commerce grew in the 1870s as the timber industry expanded its reach, and Epsport became the seat of Schoolcraft County on 15 June 1879, having replaced Onota, a ghost town in present-day Alger County.[184] A new sawmill was constructed in 1876 with "three gangs, a circular saw, two edgers, two trimmers, a shingle mill and a lathe mill" capable of manufacturing 10 to 20 million board feet of lumber every month.[185] Manistique soon replaced Epsport as the town name in the mid-1880s.

Manistique's early settlers established the town's first school in 1872 on present-day Arbutus Avenue, followed by the Central School in 1881.[186] Schoolcraft County even gained a newspaper when the Schoolcraft County *Pioneer*—the forerunner of today's *Pioneer-Tribune*—published its first issue on 29 April 1880. In its first editorial, the *Pioneer* set forth its principles guiding its publication, including: "The Pioneer will be the fair and truthful exponent of the advantages to be derived by a rapid and healthy development of this county and village, and will oppose all hindrances to the same. Its immense lumber interests, its agricultural advantages, it geographic position and climate will all receive the attention their merits demand."[187]

Prior to the arrival of the railroad, lake steamers served as Manistique's connection to the outside world. A vessel known as the *Express* initially served Epsport in the summer months in the early to mid-1870s, followed by the *Union*, a side-wheeler that began serving Manistique around 1876 to 1877, and the *M.C. Hawley*, which made weekly and, later, bi-weekly trips across the lake.[188] In 1881, the steamer *Van Raalte* began running a twice-weekly service from Cheboygan to Manistique called the "Brook Trout Line"; it was captained by Simon Bouschor's younger brother, Edward Albert Bouchard.[189] By the early 1900s, the railroads also ran several railroad car ferries that allowed people to board via the railcar from Frankfort on the Lower Peninsula and Kewanee and Manitowoc, Wisconsin, and travel via

Epsport founder Charles Harvey in 1854

The Arcade Saloon and Manistique's notorious Flat Iron block prior to destruction by fire in 1893

lake steamer to Manistique. Operated by the Ann Arbor Railroad's subsidiary, the Manistique and Lake Superior Railroad, it operated for over sixty years until service to Manistique ended in 1968.[190] Silas J. Perry constructed the town's first railroad, which was later purchased by the Chicago Lumbering Company and ran from Manistique north through Steuben before connecting with the Duluth, South Shore and Atlantic Railroad at Shingleton in Alger County. The new line not only connected Manistique to the outside world, it also allowed Abijah Weston's companies to access additional areas of timber unreachable from the river.[191] Known formally as the Manistique and Lake Superior Railroad, its popular nickname was "the Haywire." The Haywire operated until 1968 and was converted to a rail trail two years later.[192] Prior to the Haywire's introduction, anyone wishing to connect to the railroad had to travel via stagecoach north to Seney to catch the Detroit, Mackinac and Marquette Railroad.[193] Manistique later sat on the Minneapolis, St. Paul and Sault Ste. Marie Railroad line, better known as the Soo Line, which ran from Sault Ste. Marie to Minneapolis and reached Manistique in 1888. A depot constructed in 1921 remains in existence, though passenger trains ceased operation along the line in 1959.[194]

The 1872 purchase of the local sawmill by New Yorker Abijah Weston heralded the rise of Manistique in the late 1800s via Weston's Chicago Lumbering Company. Weston rebuilt the lumber mill, created a company store, and constructed company-owned housing across town to house the hundreds of workers and families needed to run the mill and its related enterprises.[195] Manistique functioned largely as a company town in its early days, and the Chicago Lumbering Company dominated most aspects of life well into the twentieth century. The Company not only owned expansive timber holdings in Schoolcraft County and the surrounding area, it also controlled the sawmill, the system of lumber docks at the mouth of the river, and the boats used to transport milled lumber throughout the Great Lakes region. The Chicago Lumbering Company employed about 1,000 men during its busiest times of the year and owned 375 dwelling houses, stores, and offices that it rented out to its employees and merchants in town.[196] The Company vociferously opposed the sale or consumption of alcohol in town and refused to sell or rent any of its holdings to saloonkeepers.[197] Deeds for property sold by the Chicago Lumbering Company even contained restrictions prohibiting the manufacture or sale of alcohol on the property.¶ This prohibition resulted in saloon owners like Dan Heffron seeking out property in Manistique unencumbered by the restrictions and gave rise to the infamous "flat iron block" bounded by Pearl and Water Streets (pictured on opposite page).[198]

Owing to the restrictions on the commercial sale of alcohol, many lumberjacks living in lumber camps resorted to home brew, often so noxious it would "raise a blood-blister on leather boots," in the words of historian Lewis C. Reimann.[199] While the homes and company-owned buildings were generally well-maintained and featured many of the modern conveniences like libraries and hospitals largely unavailable outside of major cities, the company owners were benevolent dictators at best and extracted long hours and loyal service from their employees in exchange for these comforts.[200]

An added feature of many lumber companies and camps was to pay lumberjacks and other workers with scripts that could only be redeemed for goods at the company store. This forced those living in the camps to redeem their wages for goods at inflated prices. This model of compensation grew increasingly unpopular until companies discontinued it due to understandable pushback from employees.[201] The company town model proved desirable by the turn of the century. Fewer lumberjacks wanted to live on their own, and many in the industry had families. A well-run company town featuring amenities and pleasant living conditions could attract a better class of workers seeking stability who may otherwise shun the work.[202]

The Chicago Lumbering Company's wholly owned subsidiary, the Weston Lumber Company, built a second mill in 1882 on the west side of the Man-

istique River. Both companies focused on milling white pine timber.[203] Weston branched out into other industries in the 1880s and 1890s, including the Weston Manufacturing Company—which operated a planning mill that produced dressed lumber, sash, and doors—and the Weston Furnace Company.[204] At their peak, the Chicago Lumbering Company and Weston Lumber Company churned out 90 million board feet of lumber each year, primarily white pine.[205] Abijah Weston was somewhat old-fashioned in that he resisted adoption of the nimble band saws that considerably reduced the amount of sawdust produced by traditional gang saws. One estimate generated by company shareholders determined the use of gang saws squandered $93,000 worth of pine that could have been salvaged through use of a band saw.[206] Through another subsidiary, the Manistique River Improvement Company, the Chicago Lumbering Company controlled the flow of logs down the Manistique River and extracted a fee from any other concerns wishing to use it.[207]

Unsurprisingly, the Chicago Lumbering Company also controlled water privileges around Manistique and had exclusive rights to fish the area. In the 1880s, a Chicago firm affiliated with the Lumbering Company operated an icehouse in Manistique along with two collection steamers, a tug, and a sailboat engaged in gill-net operations on the lake. Independent fishermen living in Manistique and Thompson built camps along the shore from Barque Point on south to fish the waters. Some of their live catch would then be sold to the Company's collection steamers.[208]

Manistique was incorporated in 1901. The town had the good fortune of being located on the Minneapolis, St. Paul and Sault Ste. Marie Railway mainline, better known as the Soo Line, and its industry at the turn of the century centered on lumber, with other entrepreneurs engaged in production of iron,

---

¶   The following is an example of the language the Chicago Lumbering Company inserted into property deeds: "It is understood and agreed between the respective parties hereto that all lands herein mentioned shall never be used by the party of the second part, its successors or assigns, for the business of manufacturing, storing or selling intoxicating liquors, whether distilled or fermented, nor for a house or place of prostitution or assignation, nor for any business or occupation prohibited or punished by the law of the land." *See* Larry Peterson, *The Hiawatha Anthology: Stories from Upper Michigan's Pioneer Past* (Self-published, 2020), 48.

Downtown Manistique in the early twentieth century looking north on Cedar Street

lime, leather, wood alcohol, and other extractive industries like fishing. In 1901, Manistique had three newspapers—the Manistique *Härold*, *Pioneer-Tribune*, and *Courier*—and boasted no fewer than six hotels: the Ossawinamkee, Hiawatha, Hotel Barnes, Trechler, Keystone, and St. James. As of 1901, approximately three-fifths of Schoolcraft County's population lived in Manistique.[209] Those on the west side of the river lived in an area known as "Indiantown" and included immigrants from Scandinavia and the British Isles who came to work in the lumber business.[210]

In addition to Abijah Weston's myriad enterprises, important businesses at the turn of the century included the White Marble Lime Company, the Federal Leather Company, the Manistique Telephone Company, and a local brewery—the Willebrand-Manistique Brewery Company.[211] These and other enterprises mushroomed at the close of the nineteenth century in response to a demand for services appurtenant to the timber industry. The White Marble Lime Company formed in 1889 out of a partnership between Abijah Weston and George Nicholson and sought to take advantage of the region's ample limestone. Nicholson constructed a

six-kiln lime plant on Maple Street in 1889 and, two years later, established an additional two-kiln plant east of town at Marblehead.[212] The White Marble Lime Company later became the Inland Lime and Stone Company and operates today as Carmeuse Lime & Stone at Port Inland in Gulliver. Nels Bouschor and Wilfred Farley both worked for the White Marble and Inland Lime and Stone Companies at different times.

In greater Schoolcraft County, numerous hastily constructed logging camps dotted the landscape and harvested timber for shipment downriver to the Manistique mills. Employees included swampers, sawyers, timber fitters, the all-important cooks, teamsters, and the river drivers who conducted the dangerous work of moving logs down the Manistique River.[213] In total, over three *billion* feet of pine alone traveled down the Manistique River from the time logging operations began in the 1850s through the decline of operations in the 1920s.[214] Commercial fishing also occupied an important role in Manistique's early years, with ships including the Coffey fleet and A. Booth and Sons operating in search of whitefish and lake trout.[215]

It was around the turn of the century that members of the Bouschor family began moving to Manistique. George Wallace Bouschor moved his family there from Thompson and operated one of the town's livery stables as early as 1901 (pictured below). George later ran a Schoolcraft County lumber camp and was involved with several other businesses. Between 1900 and 1910, George's older sister Ida and her husband, Tellas Farley, also moved to Manistique, taking up residency on Arbutus Avenue in the Lakeside District. Ida and Tellas' two children, Wilfred and Bertha, moved to Manistique around the same time and spent the rest of their lives there. Another of the Barque Point siblings, Simon Joseph, lived in Manistique for a time after leaving Thompson and before moving south to Detroit with his wife and children around 1920. The youngest of the siblings, Nelson Burton Bouschor, was a longtime Manistique resident. He and his wife, Marie Weber, moved from Thompson to Manistique in the mid-1910s and lived there for the next sixty years until passing away in the early 1970s. Other

siblings and family members who lived in greater Schoolcraft and Delta Counties undoubtedly spent time in Manistique during these years, doing business and visiting friends and family.

The influx of Bouschors to Manistique coincided with the town's rising fortunes. In 1913, the Manistique Commercial Club issued a pamphlet entitled *Manistique: The Live Wire City of Upper Michigan*. The Club stated its purpose was to "create a city which will attract outsiders by the sheer force of its advantages; a city with personality; a city that anyone would be proud to call 'home'; a city in which the drum beat of progress shall never cease." In the pamphlet, the Club boasted that Manistique had five public schools, one parochial school, and a commercial college, with the public school employing thirty-four teachers providing instruction to 1,041 grade schoolers and 209 high schoolers. The Club further noted the city's fifty streets with fifteen miles of macadam paving, and the eight miles of sewers and ten miles of water mains that resulted in

A 1905 image of the G.W. Bouschor Livery & Feed Barn located in Manistique

not a single epidemic of typhoid fever as of 1913. The town hosted no fewer than ten grange organizations and a fire department with two engines, a hose wagon, and a hook and ladder truck, in addition to a fire-fighting river tug.[216]

The Commercial Club's goal of creating a superlative city appeared to work—for a time. Manistique hit its peak population of 6,380 inhabitants in 1920. While the population hovered in the 5,000-person range for the next forty years, it steadily declined to its present population, less than half that of its 1920 peak. The decline coincided with the retreat of the timber industry in the area after the Chicago Lumbering Company harvested billions of board feet of timber from the surrounding forests. The Chicago Lumbering Company and Weston Lumber Company divested their Schoolcraft County assets in 1912 to an outfit known as the Consolidated Lumber Company that was owned and operated by William Crowe and Louis Yalomstein. The sale generated $750,000 and comprised some 160,000 acres of land still covered with millions of board feet of standing timber. At the time of the sale, the Company owned approximately seventy percent of Schoolcraft County, but it began selling off both homes and commercial real estate that had previously been leased to tenants. The Consolidated Lumber Company operated until 1926, when its remaining assets were liquidated. The Consolidated Lumber Company's demise shifted operations to hardwood loggers and brought an end to Manistique's once-prominent status as a white-pine port.[217] The last great log drive down the Manistique River took place in July 1929. Crews floated over two million feet of pine, hemlock, and hardwood—a far cry from the 100-million-plus feet of logs that regularly came down the river in the 1880s and 1890s.[218]

In the wake of the timber industry's decline, business in Schoolcraft County shifted to processing and manufacturing, although the wood industry remained central to the area's livelihood. A paper mill opened in Manistique in May 1920, similar to operations that sprang up in former logging towns like Marinette, Ontonagon, and Menominee after much of the larger stands of hard and softwood were vanquished through clearcut operations.[219] UP Paper, a successor of Manistique's original papermill, remains in operation to this day and produces kraft paper for packaging out of recycled materials.[220]

Other businesses that emerged during the 1910s and 1920s included the Brown Lumber Company, the Manistique Handle Company, the Thomas Berry Chemical Company, and the Manistique Cooperage, which operated from 1914 until 1922 on North Houghton Avenue.[221] The flood of 1920 wrought catastrophic destruction on the city when it struck in March 1920 as the result of an ice jam that caused the river to back up. Much of Manistique's west side was under water, as well as a considerable portion of the town's industrial and commercial enterprises, and the rushing waters brought about the collapse of the Waddell Lumber and Supply Company warehouse and the Goodwille Box Factory.[222] The flood struck a crippling blow to Manistique's economy, as several businesses elected not to rebuild due to the risk of future flooding.

Manistique's iconic water tower was promoted by newspaper owner and Manistique mayor Benjamin Gero and constructed in 1922.[223] The water tower remained in operation for many years, and Nels Bouschor even worked there for a time in the 1940s during his employment with the city water company. The water tower remains owned by the city and is occasionally opened to the public by the historical society.

Simon Bouschor spent his final years in Manistique after Harriette's death, having moved into the George Wallace Bouschor residence, where he passed away in 1916. As noted above, several of Simon and Harriette's children lived in Manistique, and four of them—Ida Isabelle Farley, George Wallace Bouschor, Louis Bouschor, and Nels Bouschor—passed away in Manistique. Numerous children and grandchildren likewise called Manistique home. Some became very involved in the community, like George Wallace's youngest son, George Leslie Bouschor, who served for a couple decades as Schoolcraft County Clerk and Register of Deeds and remained a prominent figure in the community. Leslie and Lydia Bouschor's two children, George Kroeger and Robert Leslie Bouschor, both attended the Manistique school system and graduated from Manistique High School.

Today, no Bouschor descendants are known to reside in Manistique, though many have made the pilgrimage back to visit over the years. Other descendants of Simon and Harriette settled in all corners of the Upper Peninsula, and several call it home to this day. Their lives and relevant details of the places they lived will be detailed in a follow-up volume chronicling the descendants of Simon and Harriette.

Manistique's famous lighthouse and east breakwater looking west towards Thompson and the Garden Peninsula

Notes

ABBREVIATIONS

BLM GLO. Bureau of Land Management, General Land Records Office, https://glorecords.blm.gov/default.aspx

EPL. Escanaba Public Library, http://www.archiveol.com/escanaba/home

FS. FamilySearch https://www.familysearch.org/en/united-states/

GB. Google Books, https://books.google.com/

NA. NewspaperArchive, https://newspaperarchive.com/

NARA. U.S. National Archives and Records Administration

NC. Newspapers.com, https://www.newspapers.com/

TTHAC. Thompson Township Historical Advisory Committee

UPDN. Upper Peninsula Digital Network, https://uplink.nmu.edu/

1   Brian Leigh Dunnigan, *A Picturesque Situation: Mackinac before Photography, 1615-1860* (Detroit: Wayne State University Press, 2008), x.
2   Virgil J. Vogel, *Indian Names in Michigan* (Ann Arbor: The University of Michigan Press, 1986), 110-12.
3   Bacqueville de la Potherie, "History of the Savage Peoples Who Are Allies of New France," in *The Indian Tribes of the Upper Mississippi Valley and Region of the Great Lakes*, ed. Emma Helen Blair (Cleveland: Arthur H. Clark Company, 1911), 1:286-87.
4   Alexander F. Chamberlain, "Algonkian Words in American English," in *Journal of American Folklore* 15 (October-December 1902), 246-47 quoted in Vogel, 111-12.
5   Willis F. Dunbar and George S. May, *Michigan: A History of the Wolverine State*, 3rd Ed. (Grand Rapids: Wm. B. Eerdmans Publishing Co., 1995), 34, 42, 59-60.
6   Dunnigan, *A Picturesque Situation*, 23.
7   Keith R. Widder, "After the Conquest: Michilimackinac, a Borderland in Transition, 1760-1763," *Michigan Historical Review* 34, no. 1 (Spring 2008): 43, https://www.jstor.org/stable/20174257; Dunbar and May, *Michigan*, 34, 42, 59-60.
8   Dunnigan, *A Picturesque Situation*, 37.
9   Dunbar and May, *Michigan*, 77.
10   Dunbar and May, *Michigan*, 82; Dunnigan, *A Picturesque Situation*, 4, 40.
11   Dunnigan, *A Picturesque Situation*, 61.
12   Dunbar and May, *Michigan*, 88, 102; Dunnigan, *A Picturesque Situation*, 41.
13   Michael Ray, "Treaty of Greenville," Encyclopedia Britannica, accessed 20 March 2023, https://www.britannica.com/event/Treaty-of-Greenville.
14   "The Treaty of Greenville 1795," 3 August 1795, The Avalon Project, Yale Law School Lillian Goldman Law Library, https://avalon.law.yale.edu/18th_century/greenvil.asp.
15   Dunnigan, *A Picturesque Situation*, x.
16   Dunnigan, *A Picturesque Situation*, 227.
17   Thomas L. McKenney, *Sketches of a Tour to the Lakes, of the Character and Customs of the Chippeway Indians, and of Incidents Connected with the Treaty of Fond Du Lac*, Baltimore: Fielding Lucas, Jr., 1827, 397, GB.
18   Kathleen Lavey. "Mackinac Island Restores its Native American History," *Lansing State Journal*, 7 March 2017, https://www.lansingstatejournal.com/story/travel/michigan/2017/03/07/restoring-mackinac-islands-native-american-history/98809484/.
19   Dunbar and May, *Michigan*, 22.
20   Dunnigan, *A Picturesque Situation*, 37.
21   Dunnigan, *A Picturesque Situation*, 78.
22   Dunbar and May, *Michigan*, 88, 111, 118.
23   Dunbar and May, *Michigan*, 88, 118.

24   Dunbar and May, *Michigan*, 141-42; James J. Strang, *Ancient and Modern Michilimackinac, Including an Account of the Controversy Between Mackinac and the Mormons*, 1854, 9, University of Michigan County Histories and Atlases; Dunnigan, *A Picturesque Situation*, 143-44; Dunnigan, *A Picturesque Situation*, 78.

25   Dunbar and May, *Michigan*, 139-41.

26   Don Bamford, *Freshwater Heritage: A History of Sail on the Great Lakes, 1670-1918* (Toronto: Natural Heritage Books, 2007), 201.

27   Dunbar and May, *Michigan*, 126.

28   Dunbar and May, *Michigan*, 134-35.

29   Dunbar and May, *Michigan*, 137.

30   Dunnigan, *A Picturesque Situation*, 164; Cathryn Lien, "A History of the Borough of Michilimackinac, City of Mackinac," *Mackinac Island Town Crier* (Mackinac Island, MI), 14 April 2017.

31   Dunbar and May, *Michigan*, 63.

32   Anne F. Hyde, *Born of Lakes and Plains: Mixed-Descent Peoples and the Making of the American West* (New York: W.W. Norton & Co., 2022), 181.

33   Dunbar and May, *Michigan*, 274.

34   Keith R. Widder, "Magdelaine LaFramboise: The First Lady of Mackinac Island," *Mackinac History IV, No. 1* (Mackinac Island: Mackinac Island State Park Commission, 2007), 7.

35   Dunnigan, *A Picturesque Situation*, 231-32.

36   Dunnigan, *A Picturesque Situation*, 232.

37   Dunnigan, *A Picturesque Situation*, 276.

38   "Fort Mackinac and the Mackinac National Park," Mackinac State Historic Parks, 22 January 2016, https://www.mackinacparks.com/fort-mackinac-and-the-mackinac-national-park/.

39   Dunnigan, *A Picturesque Situation*, 198, 275-76.

40   Dunbar and May, *Michigan*, 373.

41   Dunbar and May, *Michigan*, 363-64; Lewis C. Reimann, *When Pine Was King* (Ann Arbor: Edwards Brothers, Inc., 1952), 97.

42   Jacqueline Tatrow, "Indians of the Garden Peninsula Wey-Oh-Qua-Touk or Bays de Nocquette," in *Our Heritage: Garden Peninsula, Delta County, Michigan 1840-1980* (Michigan: Garden Peninsula Historical Society, 1982), 116.

43   Tatrow, "Indians of the Garden Peninsula," 117-18.

44   Tatrow, "Indians of the Garden Peninsula," 119.

45   Vogel, *Indian Names in Michigan*, 91.

46   Dunbar and May, *Michigan*, 146.

47   Dunbar and May, *Michigan*, 216.

48   John H. Long, ed., "Michigan: Individual County Chronologies," Michigan Atlas of Historical County Boundaries, The Newberry Library, accessed 27 November 2019, https://digital.newberry.org/ahcb/documents/MI_Individual_County_Chronologies.htm; Richard W. Welch, *County Evolution in Michigan 1790 – 1897* (Lansing, MI: Michigan Department of Education, 1972), 7, FS.

49   General Land Office Records, database, U.S. Department of the Interior, Bureau of Land Management, accessed 1 August 2021, https://glorecords.blm.gov/default.aspx.

50   Dunbar and May, *Michigan*, 165.

51   Dunbar and May, *Michigan*, 243.

52   Garden Peninsula Historical Society, "The Reuben Allen Family," in *Our Heritage: Garden Peninsula, Delta County, Michigan 1840-1980* (Michigan: Garden Peninsula Historical Society, 1982), 194.

53   *Polk's Michigan State Gazetteer and Business Directory* (Detroit: The Tribune Printing Company, 1875), 371, GB.

54   Vogel, *Indian Names in Michigan*, 109.

55   Judith Manning, "Governmental Organization," in *Our Heritage: Garden Peninsula, Delta County, Michigan 1840-1980* (Michigan: Garden Peninsula Historical Society, 1982), 83.

56   Jacqueline Tatrow, "The Settling of the Village of Garden," Jacqueline Tatrow, in *Our Heritage: Garden Peninsula, Delta County, Michigan 1840-1980* (Michigan: Garden Peninsula Historical Society, 1982), 123.

57   Tatrow, "The Settling of the Village of Garden," 138.

58   U.S. Census Bureau, "Garden village, Michigan," generated by Aaron N. Bouschor using data.census.gov, accessed 22 November 2023, https://data.census.gov/table?q=Garden%20village,%20Michigan.

59   G. W. Colton, *Lake Superior and the Northern Part of Michigan, Map, From Colton's Atlas of the World* (New York: J.H. Colton, 1856), David Rumsey Map Collection, David Rumsey Map Center, Stanford Libraries.

60   United States Lake Survey, *North End of Green Bay the Islands at the Entrance and N.W. Shore of Lake Michigan*, Map, 1863, University of Wisconsin Digitalized Collections.

61   "Point Aux Barques Quadrangle Map," United States Geological Survey, 2019, accessed 18 May 2022, https://ngmdb.

usgs.gov/ht-bin/tv_browse.pl?id=23b2c4e13c503448332bd9d5e483e714. The USGS explains that each quadrangle is usually named after the quadrangle's most prominent feature—in this case, Point Aux Barques. *See* "USGS Maps," United States Geological Survey, accessed 18 May 2022, https://pubs.usgs.gov/gip/usgsmaps/usgsmaps.html.

62   Mary L. Wermuth, *Michigan's Centennial Family Farm Heritage* (Hillsdale: Ferguson Communications, 1986), 43; "Thompson the Result of Mill Construction," *Escanaba Daily Press*, 31 March 1987, NA.

63   F. A. Rogers, "Echoes from a Steel Pen," *Manistique Semi-Weekly Pioneer*, 5 January 1895, UPDN.

64   Long, "Michigan: Individual County Chronologies"; Welch, *County Evolution in Michigan 1790 – 1897*, 7.

65   1860 U.S. Census, Delta Township, Delta County, Michigan, population schedule, p. 134, dwelling 1282, family 867, lines 37-39, Simon Bouchard.

66   Simon Bouchard Homestead Application No. 32, Marquette, MI, 18 July 1863, NARA.

67   Simon Bouchard Homestead Application Affidavit, Marquette, MI, 18 July 1863, NARA.

68   Affidavit Required of Homestead Claimants, Acts of May 20, 1862, and June 21, 1866, Marquette, MI, 21 September 1868, NARA.

69   Affidavit of Pascal LaLonde and David Farley, Proof Required Under Homestead Acts May 20, 1862, and June 21, 1866, Marquette, MI, 21 September 1868, NARA.

70   Affidavit of LaLonde and Farley, NARA.

71   Affidavit of LaLonde and Farley, NARA.

72   Homestead Certificate No. 5, Marquette, MI, 21 September 1868, NARA.

73   Simon Buschord [sic] Land Patent, Homestead Certificate No. 5, Application 32, 4 November 1869, BLM GLO.

74   G. Leslie Bouschor, Notes on the Bouschor Family and Barque Point Homestead, undated, collection of Aaron N. Bouschor; Theodore J. Karamanski, *Deep Woods Frontier: A History of Logging in Northern Michigan* (Detroit: Wayne State University Press, 1989), 87.

75   G. Leslie Bouschor, Notes on the Bouschor Family and Barque Point Homestead, undated, collection of Aaron N. Bouschor.

76   Billie Doyle, "Thanks for a Hollow House," *Pioneer-Tribune* (Manistique, MI), 22 November 1989, UPDN.

77   Trygvie Jensen, *Wooden Boats and Iron Men: History of Commercial Fishing in Northern Lake Michigan & Door County 1850 – 2005* (De Pere, WI: Paisa (Alt) Publishing Co., 2007), 8.

78   Jensen, *Wooden Boats and Iron Men*, 70.

79   James Alvin Van Fleet, *Old and New Mackinac* (Ann Arbor: Courier Steam Printing House, 1870), 159-160, GB.

80   Jensen, *Wooden Boats and Iron Men*, 71.

81   Jensen, *Wooden Boats and Iron Men*, 72.

82   Jensen, *Wooden Boats and Iron Men*, 73.

83   Jensen, *Wooden Boats and Iron Men*, 75-78.

84   Jacqueline Tatrow, "Commercial Fishing on the Waters of the Big Bay de Noc," in *Our Heritage: Garden Peninsula, Delta County, Michigan 1840-1980* (Michigan: Garden Peninsula Historical Society, 1982), 15.

85   William Cullen Bryant, *Letters of a Traveller; or, Notes of Things Seen in Europe and America* (London: Richard Bentley, 1850), 298, GB.

86   Jensen, *Wooden Boats and Iron Men*, 23-25.

87   James W. Milner, "Report on the Fisheries of the Great Lakes; and the Result of Inquiries Prosecuted in 1871 and 1872," in *Report of the Commissioner for 1872 and 1873* (Washington, D.C.: Government Printing Office, 1874), 13-14, GB.

88   Tatrow, "Commercial Fishing on the Waters of the Big Bay de Noc," 15-16.; Larry Peterson, *The Hiawatha Anthology: Stories from Upper Michigan's Pioneer Past* (Self-published, 2020), 86.

89   Smith and Snell, comps., *Review of the Fisheries of the Great Lakes in 1885*, 92.

90   Review of the Fisheries of the Great Lakes in 1885, 92.

91   Tatrow, "Commercial Fishing on the Waters of the Big Bay de Noc," 16.

92   F. A. Rogers, "A Visit to Point o' Barque," *Manistique Semi-Weekly Pioneer*, 25 August 1894, UPDN.

93   "Salmon in the Lake," *Manistique Pioneer-Tribune*, 12 May 1899, UPDN.

94   Wermuth, *Michigan's Centennial Family Farm Heritage*, 43.

95   1880 U.S. Census, Hiawatha Township, Schoolcraft County, Non-Population Schedule, enumeration district 37, p. 2, farm 1, Simon Bouchard.

96   1880 U.S. Census, Hiawatha Township, Schoolcraft County, Non-Population Schedule, enumeration district 37, p. 2, farm 1, Simon Bouchard.

97   Rogers, "A Visit to Point o' Barque."

98   Rogers, "A Visit to Point o' Barque."

99   "Lighthouse Nearly Done," *Evening News* (Sault Ste. Marie, MI), 16 June 1904, NA.

100   "Salvaged Pig Iron Being Taken Here," *Escanaba Daily Press*, 1 July 1931, UPDN.

101   "Into the Past – Ten Years Ago," *Escanaba Daily Press*, 28 April 1949, UPDN.

102   Simon & Harriette Bouschor Family, photograph, undated, collection of Aaron N. Bouschor.

103   Mrs. Hasell Osterhout, "A History of Thompson Twp. & Village of Thompson," *Manistique Pioneer-Tribune*, 5 June 1975. Note: Mrs. Osterhout's full name was Georgia A. Taylor Osterhout. However, as she authored her articles under the name, Mrs. Hasell Osterhout, the latter will be used throughout this work.

104   G. Leslie Bouschor, Notes on the Bouschor Family and Barque Point Homestead, undated, original in possession of the author. Little is known about Mr. Fountain. According to the Garden Peninsula Historical Society, "he was remembered as having beautiful wavy hair and being very handsome and charming. Also that he played the violin." See Garden Peninsula Historical Society, "The John Fountain Sr. Family," in *Our Heritage: Garden Peninsula, Delta County, Michigan 1840-1980* (Michigan: Garden Peninsula Historical Society, 1982), 225/

105   John Fountain Land Patent, Homestead Certificate No. 13, Application 33, 4 November 1869, BLM GLO.

106   Tellas Farney [sic] Land Patent, Homestead Certificate No. 1230, Application 2699, 16 February 1889, BLM GLO.

107   "Thompson," *Manistique Pioneer-Tribune*, 28 April 1899, UPDN.

108   Judith Manning, "Portage Trail," in *Our Heritage: Garden Peninsula, Delta County, Michigan 1840-1980* (Michigan: Garden Peninsula Historical Society, 1982), 50; Judith Manning, "Mail Service on the Garden Peninsula," in *Our Heritage: Garden Peninsula, Delta County, Michigan 1840-1980* (Michigan: Garden Peninsula Historical Society, 1982), 89.

109   Larry Peterson, *The Hiawatha Anthology: Stories from Upper Michigan's Pioneer Past* (Self-published, 2020), 87.

110   Thompson Township Highway Commissioner's Record, 1882-1891, TTHAC, UPDN.

111   "Upper Peninsula," *Iron Port* (Escanaba, MI), November 2, 1889, accessed 3 November 2018, EPL.

112   David Sinclair Bouschor, Sr., discussion with the author, Duluth, MN, 11 August 2018.

113   Manning, "Portage Trail," 50.

114   Manning, "Mail Service on the Garden Peninsula," 89.

115   Rogers, "A Visit to Point o' Barque."

116   Rogers, "A Visit to Point o' Barque."

117   Rogers, "A Visit to Point o' Barque."

118   Rogers, "A Visit to Point o' Barque."

119   Rogers, "A Visit to Point o' Barque."

120   Frank M. Johnson, "In the Pine Woods," *Lowell Ledger* (Lowell, MI), 15 October 1903, Kent District Library.

121   *Triple Jubilee celebration: 1833, 1883, 1933* (Manistique, MI: St. Francis de Sales Church, 1958), 17, HathiTrust.org.

122   Mrs. Hasell Osterhout, "A History of Thompson Twp. & Village of Thompson," *Manistique Pioneer-Tribune*, 23 October 1975.

123   Frank M. Johnson, "In the Pine Woods," *Lowell Ledger* (Lowell, MI), 15 October 1903, Kent District Library.

124   Johnson, "In the Pine Woods."

125   Mrs. Hasell Osterhout, "A History of Thompson Twp. & Village of Thompson," *Manistique Pioneer-Tribune*, 3 July 1975; Mrs. Hasell Osterhout, *Religious Heritage of Thompson, Michigan* (Self-published, 1970, Courtesy of Mary Bouschor.

126   Mrs. Hasell Osterhout, "A History of Thompson Twp. & Village of Thompson," *Manistique Pioneer-Tribune*, 3 July 1975.

127   Mrs. Hasell Osterhout, "A History of Thompson Twp. & Village of Thompson," *Manistique Pioneer-Tribune*, 17 July 1975.

128   Osterhout, *Religious Heritage of Thompson*.

129   "Thompson News," *Escanaba Daily Press*, 12 August 1934, NC.

130   "Picnic," *Escanaba Daily Press*, 25 July 1933, EPL.

131   "K-C Picnic Today at Barque Point," *Escanaba Daily Press*, 1 August 1937, NC.

132   Wermuth, *Michigan's Centennial Family Farm Heritage*, 43; Mrs. Hasell Osterhout, "A History of Thompson Twp. & Village of Thompson," *Manistique Pioneer-Tribune*, 5 June 1975; Florence Meron, *A History of the Township Village and People of Thompson Michigan*, Manistique School and Public Library, Unpublished Manuscript, 2003.

133   "Public Invited to Historical Picnic Sunday," *Escanaba Daily Press*, 20 August 1959, NC.

134   G. Leslie Bouschor, Notes on Bouschor Centennial Farm Commemoration, undated (approximately 1959), original in possession of the author.

135   G. Leslie Bouschor, Notes on Bouschor Centennial Farm Commemoration, undated (approximately 1959), original in possession of the author.

136   "Bouschor Heads Historical Society," *Escanaba Daily Press*, 22 May 1959, NC; "Public Invited to Historical Picnic Sunday," *Escanaba Daily Press*, August 20, 1959, NC.

137   *Nelson Burton Bouschor & George Leslie Bouschor at Barque Point, 1959, Thompson Township, Michigan*, Photograph, 1959, Courtesy of Robert Leslie Bouschor, Collection of Aaron N. Bouschor; "Centennial Farm to Be Dedicated," *Milwaukee Sentinel* (Milwaukee, WI), 15 August 1959, Schoolcraft County Historical Society.

138   "Centennial Farms: Special Program of Recognition Planned at Fair," *Escanaba Daily Press*, 6 August 1968, NA; "Manistique," *Escanaba Daily Press*, 20 August 1968, NA.

139   Wermuth, *Michigan's Centennial Family Farm Heritage*, 43.

140   "Local Men Opening Recreation Area," *Battle Creek Enquirer*, 32 February 1971, NC.

141   "Local Men Opening Recreation Area," *Battle Creek Enquirer*, 32 February 1971, NC; "Point Aux Barques Project Underway," *Manistique Pioneer-Tribune*, 4 March 1971, UPDN.

142   Wermuth, *Michigan's Centennial Family Farm Heritage*, 43.

143   Real Estate Summary Sheet Parcel 008-151-013-00, Manistique County Clerk and Register of Deeds, 21 September 2018.

144   Dunbar and May, *Michigan*, 185.

145   "Thompson Township Michigan," Thompson Township, accessed 30 December 2018, http://thompsontownshipmi.com.

146   "Thompson the Result of Mill Construction," *Escanaba Daily Press*, 31 March 1987, NA.

147   "Thompson History," Thompson Township, accessed 20 January 2019, http://thompsontownshipmi.com/wp-content/uploads/2011/06/thompson-history1.pdf.

148   First Official Census Thompson Township 1884, TTHAC, UPDN.

149   "Thompson History," Thompson Township, accessed 20 January 2019, http://thompsontownshipmi.com/wp-content/uploads/2011/06/thompson-history1.pdf; Osterhout, *Religious Heritage of Thompson*.

150   Larry Peterson, "The Early History of Thompson Township," *Pioneer-Tribune* (Manistique, MI), 20 October 2021, www.pioneertribune.com/articles/the-early-history-of-thompson-township/.

151   Peterson, "Early History of Thompson Township."

152   Peterson, "Early History of Thompson Township."

153   "Thompson the Result of Mill Construction," *Escanaba Daily Press*, 31 March 1987.

154   Gene Scott, *Michigan Shadow Towns: A Study of Vanishing and Vibrant Villages* (Self-published, 2005), 235.

155   Proceedings of 3 April 1882 Thompson Township Meeting, Thompson Township General Record, 1882-1891, TTHAC, UPDN.

156   Thompson Township Elected Officials & Officers, 1882-2020, TTHAC, UPDN.

157   Smith and Snell, comps., *Review of the Fisheries of the Great Lakes in 1885*, 91.

158   Billie Doyle, "From Fire to 'Ragtime Double,'" *Pioneer-Tribune* (Manistique, MI), 11 April 1991, UPDN.

159   Elaine Hastings, "Thompson Wasn't a Ghost Town in the 1800s," *Pioneer-Tribune* (Manistique, MI), 11 December 1997, UPDN.

160   1910 U.S. Census, Thompson Township, Schoolcraft County, Michigan, population schedule, enumeration district 244, sheet 8B, dwelling 140, family 140, lines 56-60, Alexander & Mamie M. Daniels.

161   Peterson, "Early History of Thompson Township."

162   Osterhout, *Religious Heritage of Thompson*; "St. Frederick's Catholic Church History," TTHAC, UPDN.

163   Gene Scott, *Michigan Shadow Towns*, 235.

164   Jack Orr, *Lumberjacks & River Pearls: Memories of Manistique* (Manistique: Pioneer-Tribune, 1979), 16-17.

165   Gene Scott, *Michigan Shadow Towns*, 235.

166   "Attractions," Thompson Township, Michigan, accessed 23 June 2024, https://www.thompsontownshipmi.com/township-info/attractions/.

167   U.S. Census Bureau, "Thompson Township, Schoolcraft County, Michigan," accessed 27 May 2024, https://data.census.gov/all?q=Thompson%20township,%20Schoolcraft%20County,%20Michigan.

168   Gene Scott, *Michigan Shadow Towns*, 236.

169   Hastings, "Thompson Wasn't a Ghost Town in the 1800s."

170   M. Vonciel LeDuc, *Manistique* (Charleston, SC: Arcadia Publishing, 2009), 7.

171   Manistique Centennial Inc., *Manistique Centennial Official Souvenir Book* (Manistique, MI: Manistique Centennial Inc., 1960).

172   Dunbar and May, *Michigan*, 146.

173   Long, "Michigan: Individual County Chronologies"; Welch, *County Evolution in Michigan 1790 – 1897*, 14.

174   Long, "Michigan: Individual County Chronologies"; Welch, *County Evolution in Michigan 1790 – 1897*, 14.

175   Manistique Harold, *A Souvenir of Manistique Michigan* (Manistique, MI: Manistique Harold, 1901), 2, Reprint, Manistique, MI: Schoolcraft County Historical Society, 2005.

176   Vogel, *Indian Names in Michigan*, 126-27.

177   Rev. William F. Gagnieur, S.J., "Indian Place Names in the Upper Peninsula and Their Interpretation," in *Michigan History Magazine* (Lansing: Michigan Historical Commission, 1918), 2:550-51, GB.

178   Manistique Commercial Club, *Manistique: The Live Wire City of Upper Michigan* (Manistique, MI: Manistique Commercial Club, 1913).

179   R. L. Polk & Co., Comp, *Polk's Michigan State Gazetteer and Business Directory* (Detroit: The Tribune Printing Company, 1875), 344, HT.

180   LeDuc, *Manistique*, 7; Dunbar and May, *Michigan*, 261.

181   Schoolcraft County Historical Society, *Historic Tour of Manistique* (Manistique, MI: Schoolcraft County Historical Society, n.d.), 1; Manistique Centennial Inc., *Manistique Centennial Official Souvenir Book*.

182   Mrs. E. W. Miller, "History of Manistique is Linked with Indian Lore," *Daily Mining Journal* (Marquette, MI), 7 May 1927, UPDN.

183   "Aged Resident Died Wednesday," *Manistique Pioneer-Tribune*, 21 July 1916.

184   150th Anniversary of the City of Manistique, 111th Cong., 2nd sess., Congressional Record 156, pt. 8: 10446, https://www.govinfo.gov/content/pkg/CRECB-2010-pt8/pdf/CRECB-2010-pt8.pdf; Manistique Centennial Inc., *Manistique Centennial Official Souvenir Book*.

185   Manistique Centennial Inc., *Manistique Centennial Official Souvenir Book*.

186   Miller, "History of Manistique is Linked with Indian Lore."

187   Miller, "History of Manistique is Linked with Indian Lore."

188   LeDuc, *Manistique*, 8; Miller, "History of Manistique is Linked with Indian Lore.".

189   "Lake Steamers Play Part in City Development," *Escanaba Daily Press*, 29 June 1938, NA.

190   LeDuc, *Manistique*, 51-52.

191   Manistique Centennial Inc., *Manistique Centennial Official Souvenir Book*; LeDuc, *Manistique*, 50.

192   Hugh A. Hornstein, *The Haywire: A Brief History of the Manistique and Lake Superior Railroad* (East Lansing, MI: Michigan State University Press, 2005).

193   LeDuc, *Manistique*, 9.

194   "Schoolcraft County, City of Manistique, Soo Line Railroad," Michigan Genealogy Trails, accessed 26 December 2020, http://genealogytrails.com/mich/schoolcraft/soolinedepot.html.

195   Larry Peterson, *The Hiawatha Anthology: Stories from Upper Michigan's Pioneer Past* (Self-published, 2020), 78.

196   Manistique Centennial Inc., *Manistique Centennial Official Souvenir Book*.

197   Manistique Centennial Inc., *Manistique Centennial Official Souvenir Book*; LeDuc, *Manistique*, 8.

198   Peterson, *Hiawatha Anthology*, 47-48, 52.

199   Reimann, *When Pine Was King*, 88.

200   Dunbar and May, *Michigan*, 361.

201   Reimann, *When Pine Was King*, 67-68.

202   Karamanski, *Deep Woods Frontier*, 210-211.

203   Manistique Centennial Inc., *Manistique Centennial Official Souvenir Book*.

204   Manistique Centennial Inc., *Manistique Centennial Official Souvenir Book*.

205   LeDuc, *Manistique*, 8, 14.

206   Karamanski, *Deep Woods Frontier*, 81.

207   LeDuc, *Manistique*, 9.

208   Hugh M. Smith and Merwin-Marie Snell, comps., *Review of the Fisheries of the Great Lakes in 1885* (Washington, D.C.: Government Printing Office, 1890), 91, GB.

209   Manistique Harold, *Souvenir of Manistique Michigan*, 4; LeDuc, *Manistique*, 69.

210   LeDuc, *Manistique*, 8.

211   Manistique Harold, *Souvenir of Manistique Michigan*, 4.

212   LeDuc, *Manistique*, 41; "George Nicholson – White Marble Lime Co. (1889-1928)," Schoolcraft County Historical Society, 7 March 2016, https://schs.cityofmanistique.org/george-nicholson-white-marble-lime-co-1889-1928/.

213   LeDuc, *Manistique*, 34-36.

214   Peterson, *Hiawatha Anthology*, 92.

215   LeDuc, *Manistique*, 19.

216   Manistique Commercial Club, *Manistique: The Live Wire City of Upper Michigan*.

217   LeDuc, *Manistique*, 39, 48, 69; Karamanski, *Deep Woods Frontier*, 156.

218   Peterson, *Hiawatha Anthology*, 91-92.

219   Karamanski, *Deep Woods Frontier*, 224; "Manistique Pulp and Paper Company," Michigan Genealogy Trails, accessed 29 October 2022, http://genealogytrails.com/mich/schoolcraft/pulppm.html.

220   "About Us," *UP Paper*, accessed 29 October 2022, https://uppaperllc.com/about-us/.

221   LeDuc, *Manistique*, 44-47.

222   LeDuc, *Manistique*, 59-63.

223   Haley Schoengart, "Tour the UP: How Manistique Came to Be," *Wood TV 8*, 14 May 2022, https://www.woodtv.com/news/michigan/tour-the-up-how-manistique-came-to-be/.

Part Two
Simon Bouschor & Harriette Isabella Gray Bouschor

Simon Bouschor

Born: 25 December 1829 on Michilimackinac Island, Michilimackinac County, Michigan Territory (Mackinac Island, Mackinac County, Michigan)
Died: 19 July 1916 in Manistique, Schoolcraft County, Michigan

Harriette Isabella Gray Bouschor

Born: 9 December 1839 in Hartford, Hartford County, Connecticut
Died: 18 December 1906 in Manistique, Schoolcraft County, Michigan

Simon Bouschor, the eldest child of Elie Bouchard and Josette Champagne Bouchard, was born on Christmas Day, 25 December 1829, on what was then known as Michilimackinac Island in the Michigan Territory (present-day Mackinac Island in Mackinac County).[1] Elie Bouchard was a ship carpenter and ship captain. Josette Champagne was the daughter of a fellow ship carpenter, Simon Champagne, and an Odawa Indian woman named Te Pi Ma Guain (later baptized as Marguerite Champagne). Simon was presumably named in honor of his maternal grandfather, Simon Champagne. At the time of Simon's birth, his surname was Bouchard.[2]

The 1836 Mixed-Blood Census Register, created as part of the 28 March 1836 Treaty of Washington between the United States and the Odawa and Chippewa Tribes, reflects that Simon and his younger brothers, Eli and Remi, received a $305.89 allotment by virtue of being one-quarter Odawa Indian. The Mixed-Blood Census noted the Odawa and Chippewa Tribes were "desirous of making provisions for their half-breed relatives" and limited receipt to those "of Indian descent and actually resident within the boundaries described in the first article of this treaty."[3] Simon's parents held this payment in trust for him until he reached adulthood.[4] Near the end of his life, Simon executed an affidavit attesting that he received an allotment in 1836 by virtue of being an Odawa Tribe descendant.[5]

Simon Bouschor in 1892 taken at the Kimball Studio in Manistique

Though Simon could neither read nor write, he spoke both French and Chippewa fluently in addition to English.[6] An 1883 article in Escanaba's *Iron Port* newspaper referenced "Semo Osa-win-ema-ka" and noted, "It is the euphonious name of a Chippewa chief, still living, and means, as translated for us by Simon Bouchard, yellow thunder."[7] It's likely that Simon's mother, Josette Champagne

Bouchard, taught her children Chippewa prior to her death in approximately 1845 when Simon was fifteen years old.

The early U.S. Census records do not include details on household family members. Typically, they only list the head of household by name, then identify the remaining members of the household by age range and gender. The 1830 U.S. Census for Mackinac Island lists one member of the "Eloi Bouchard" household as being a male under five years of age.[8] It is reasonable to assume this was Simon, as he was in his first year of life in 1830.

Around 1836, Elie and Josette's family relocated to Green Bay in Brown County, Wisconsin. The family reached Green Bay Harbor on 15 December 1836, three days before Simon's seventh birthday.[9] While the federal and Wisconsin Territorial censuses only list the head of household by name, they do give us some insight into Simon's whereabouts in his youth. The 1838 Wisconsin Territorial Census lists the six-member family as living in Green Bay's Astor neighborhood.[10] Similarly, the 1840 U.S. Census reflects that Elie Bouchard had six children by this point—five boys and a girl—living in Brown County, Wisconsin.[11] Simon is almost certainly one of the male children listed as being between nine and ten years old at the time.[12]

By 1842, the now nine-member Bouchard family lived in Green Bay's South Ward.[13] Simon would have been around twelve years old at the time of the 1842 Wisconsin Territorial Census. Four years later, the family still lived in Green Bay, although it is unknown whether sixteen-year-old Simon still lived amongst them, as the 1846 Wisconsin Territorial Census lists six males in the household when Elie and Josette had seven sons.[14] After Josette's death in approximately 1845 or 1846, the family scattered. Some family members, including Elie, returned to Mackinac Island. Like his younger brother Edward, Simon took to the sea at a young age. His obituary in the *Manistique Pioneer-Tribune* notes, "He spent much of his life as a sailor. He started sailing as a cabin boy at the age of ten years and for years was captain of the vessel."[15] A cabin boy, also

known as a ship's boy, was a young lad who assisted the cook and the captain with odd tasks around the ship. The cabin boy was often the victim of many a practical joke inflicted by the crew.[16] The author has been unable to locate any reference to Simon in the 1850 census records, and he is not listed as living in his father's household.[17] In all likelihood, Simon was away at sea during the 1850 census. An 1894 article in Manistique's *Semi-Weekly Pioneer* noted Simon "sailed the Lake for thirty-five seasons," suggesting that if he started sailing at the age of ten, he retired from seafaring around the age of forty-six, in approximately 1875.[18] Simon eventually made his way to Delta County and the Garden Peninsula.

Marriage and Family

Simon married Harriette Isabella Gray on 6 July or 8 July 1854 on Washington Island just over the

Harriette Isabella Gray Bouschor by H. I. Anderson of Manistique taken between 1899 and 1903

state line in Door County, Wisconsin.[19] Harriette was born on 9 December 1839 to David and Isabella (Kinread) Gray in Hartford, Connecticut.[20] By the early 1840s, the family had moved to Rochester, New York, as Harriette's younger brother Charles Wesley Gray was born there in approximately 1842. Her father, David, worked on the Erie Canal, and they lived there through 1850, as the 1850 census reflects David being employed as a teamster.[21]

Simon was twenty-four years old and Harriette only fourteen at the time of their 1854 marriage. Simon and Harriette may have spent several years living on or around the Potawatomi (also known as Grand Traverse) Islands stretching between the Garden Peninsula and Michigan's Door Peninsula, as their two eldest children were born in Delta County, the second of whom—David Eli Bouschor—is believed to have been born on Summer Island. St. Martin Island, a densely forested island located off the southern tip of the Garden Peninsula, was home to several fishermen who tried to make a living off the surrounding waters in the mid-nineteenth century.

Simon and Harriette had thirteen children, eleven of whom survived to adulthood:

1.1 **Ida Isabelle Bouchard** – Born 30 January 1856 in Nahma Township, Delta County, Michigan[*22]

1.2 **David Eli Bouschor** – Born 25 November 1858 on Summer Island, Delta County, Michigan[23]

1.3 **George Wallace Bouschor** – Born 12 November 1859 at Barque Point, Thompson Township, Schoolcraft County, Michigan[24]

1.4 **Anna Olive Bouschor** – Born 9 November 1861 at Barque Point, Thompson Township, Schoolcraft County, Michigan[25]

1.5 **Simon Joseph Bouschor** – Born 20 January 1864 at Barque Point, Thompson Township, Schoolcraft County, Michigan[26]

1.6 **Charles Wesley Bouschor** – Born 2 April 1866 at Barque Point, Thompson Township, Schoolcraft County, Michigan[27]

1.7 **Louis Remit Bouschor** – Born 26 November 1867 at Barque Point, Thompson Township, Schoolcraft County, Michigan[28]

1.8 **Harriet Marie Bouschor** – Born 3 December 1869 at Barque Point, Thompson Township, Schoolcraft County, Michigan[29]

1.9 **Henry Archibald Bouschor** – Born 26 December 1872 at Barque Point, Thompson Township, Schoolcraft County, Michigan[30]

1.10 **Moise Bouschor** – Born 31 March 1875 at Barque Point, Thompson Township, Schoolcraft County, Michigan[31]

1.11 **William Edward Bouschor** – Born 27 May 1876 at Barque Point, Thompson Township, Schoolcraft County, Michigan[32]

1.12 **Mary May Bouschor** – Born 28 October 1879 at Barque Point, Thompson Township, Schoolcraft County, Michigan[33]

1.13 **Nelson Burton Bouschor** – Born 6 March 1882 at Barque Point, Thompson Township, Schoolcraft County, Michigan[34]

---

* At the time of Ida Isabelle's birth in 1856, Nahma Township comprised not only the area of present-day Nahma, but much of the Garden Peninsula including the present-day village of Garden and Garden Township (see the 1873 map of Delta County on page "1873 map of Delta County showing the township divisions – the Garden Peninsula is on the lower right" on page 19 for an illustration of Nahma's boundaries). It's possible Ida was born on or around the Gray family homestead or at another location on the Garden Peninsula before the Bouschor family moved to Barque Point. Also note that Ida Isabelle married before the family began using the Bouschor surname, and her surname is given as "Bouchard" on the record of her 1877 marriage to Tellas Farley. As such, she is listed under the name Bouchard.

Simon and Harriette later settled at Barque Point in Schoolcraft County in 1859 before the government had surveyed the territory.[35] They are believed to be the earliest settlers of European descent in what is now known as Thompson Township.[36] Harriette feared for Simon's life as a sailor due to the grave danger inherent to the profession then, as now. Simon agreed with Harriette that in exchange for giving up his seafaring career, they could acquire land far out in what was then the wilderness. Harriette's fear was understandable, given that only a few years earlier, in 1850, 431 lives were lost at sea on the Great Lakes.[37] To make the payments necessary to secure his claim to the homestead, Simon used the fund settled on him in 1836 owing to his one-quarter Odawa Indian heritage and held in trust by his parents.[38] Around 1863, the family cut timber from the homestead land and shipped it via boat to Fayette, where it was sold to the Jackson Iron Company for use in their furnaces.[39]

An undated photograph of Simon and Harriette Bouschor

As discussed in greater detail in the previous chapter, Simon filed a homestead claim in 1863 on the Barque Point land. The land patent file reflects that they entered and settled on the land on 18 July 1863 and constructed: "A double (?) log house one part 20 by 20 feet and the other part 16 by 20 feet one story high, one outside room and three inside rooms."[40] Simon made payment in full on the Barque Point homestead on 21 September 1868, and on 4 November 1868, Simon received a land patent from the federal government reflecting his full title on the Barque Point land.[41] The property would remain in the Bouschor family for over one hundred years. In his early pioneer days on the Garden Peninsula, Simon carried the first mail to Manistique, bringing it over the frozen lake from Escanaba.[42]

The 1860 U.S. Census lists the family as still living in Delta County's Delta Township. However, Delta County included the entirety of the Garden Peninsula prior to the 1862 revision of the county lines, and it is almost certain the family lived on the Barque Point homestead during the enumeration of the 1860 U.S. Census. Simon Bouchard is listed as a thirty-one-year-old Indian male working

as a fisherman with a $150 personal estate value. Also living in the household were twenty-one-year-old Harriette and their three young children, four-year-old Ida Isabella, two-year-old David Eli, and eight-month-old George Wallace. All three of the children are listed as "mulatto" under the color column. An eight-year-old child named Edward Burk is also referenced as living in the household.[43] Nothing else is known about Edward or his whereabouts after 1860. No record in the 1870 U.S. Census could be found for Simon and Harriette or their family, but the census records for the Upper Peninsula that year appear to be incomplete.

Simon was one of the first commercial fisherman working in the area, as described in greater detail in Part One. Florence Meron's manuscript *A History of the Township Village and People of Thompson Michigan* recounts life in Thompson during the nineteenth century, and she observed the following about the fishing industry: "Fish packaging in the pioneer days: Do not cut the stomach, cut the back at rib cage, draw entrails, salt and place in a barrel, leave until brine comes up – then seal."[44]

Simon could be a man of strong opinion. The Bouschors engaged in horse trading at the Barque Point homestead and hosted many visitors and business clients. One such visitor knew Simon to be a staunch Republican owing to his admiration for Lincoln and the northern cause in the Civil War. Following Democratic candidate Grover Cleveland's return to power after defeating sitting president Benjamin Harrison in the 1892 election, Simon's guest resolved to have some fun at Simon's expense. As they were finishing dinner one evening, their guest rose to leave and moved towards the door. As he made his exit, he exclaimed, "Hooray for Cleveland!" Simon responded by picking up the dinner table, dishes and all, and hurling it at the visitor.[45]

Life at Barque Point in the 1880s and 1890s

The 1880 U.S. Census enumerated in June 1880 lists the fifty-year-old Simon's occupation as farmer.[46]

Simon had given the seafaring life up for good the previous year.[47] The 1880 Non-Population Schedule Census lists the farm as comprising forty acres of tilled land with an overall value of $400 and livestock worth $447.[48] While the 1880 census lists the family as living in Hiawatha Township, the township covered a large swath of territory stretching across Schoolcraft County, and Thompson Township wasn't established for another two years, when it was detached from Hiawatha Township on 6 March 1882.[49] The census reflects that Simon could neither read nor write, although Harriette could.[50] Also living in the household were nine of Simon and Harriette's thirteen children, ranging from their twenty-two-year-old son David Eli to their seven-month-old daughter Mary.[51] David and George are both listed as being farmers and presumably worked on the family farm, while Annie, Simon

The Simon and Harriette Bouschor family in the 1880s — Back row (left to right): George Wallace, Harriette, Charles Wesley, Simon; Front row (left to right): Henry Archibald, William Edward, Mary May, Nelson Burton

Junior, Charley, and twelve-year-old Louis are all listed as working "at home." It's reasonable to assume the Bouschor family followed the common rural life practice of having the children contribute to the household, even at young ages. Interestingly, none of the children are listed as having "attended school within the census year," suggesting that any education they received was likely done at home or at the small school building on Little Harbor Road known as the "Bouschor School." That school was later moved to Little Harbor southwest of Barque Point and used by the Methodist Church as a schoolhouse and for the Methodist Sunday School.[52] Given Harriette could read and write, it's reasonable to assume she tended to any education the children received.

Some of their neighbors at the tail end of the nineteenth century included Simon's thirty-five-year-old younger brother, Oliver Raphael Bouchard, Oliver's wife, Josephine Beaudoin Bouchard, and their seven-year-old daughter, Anna May Bouchard.[53] It is believed that Oliver and his family lived at Barque Point for a time, possibly on Simon and Harriette's homestead or an adjacent parcel of land. Oliver's occupation is listed as "laborer," and, as the 1880 U.S. Census Non-Population Schedule lists the Bouchard farm as paying $120 in wages for farm labor in 1879, it is tempting to consider that Oliver may have worked on Simon and Harriette's homestead farm during this time.[54] Another neighbor was a forty-nine-year-old man named S. R. Page, whose occupation is listed as "explorer" on the census record.[55]

The 1880 U.S. Census is the last census where the family uses the Bouchard name. The Bouschor family Bible contains the recorded list of births and deaths in the family and was likely completed by Harriette.[†] Up through William Edward's 1876 birth, the children are all listed as having the Bouchard surname. Mary May, born in October 1879 was the first child anointed with the Bouschor variation. It is likely the family began using the Bouschor surname in the late 1870s. Several explanations have

been offered for this name change, one being that Simon and another brother kept getting their mail mixed up and Simon wished to change his surname to distinguish it from that of his siblings.[56] Another explanation, offered by Robert Leslie Bouschor, is that because Simon could neither read or write, he was instructed when he settled in Schoolcraft County to find a schoolteacher or someone else who could write, to spell the family name as it sounds. With the final "d" in Bouchard being silent in the French pronunciation, the scribe came up with Bouschor.[57] This interpretation is supported by the notes of G. Leslie Bouschor, who wrote: "The name Bouschor pronounced Bush-shore, was taken from [sic] name Bouchard which is pronounced Bouschor Bush-shore."[58]

Harriette Gray Bouschor (between 1888 and 1891)

Prior to the 1882 detachment of Thompson Township from Hiawatha Township, Simon served as a Commissioner of Highways for Hiawatha Township. The Proceedings of Highway Commissioners maintained by Thompson Township includes cop-

---

† The family Bible was an 1859 gift to Harriette Isabella Bouschor from her mother, Isabella Kinread Gray, per an inscription.

ies of Simon's reports from 1880 and 1881 created by Simon in his capacity as Commissioner of Highways. The reports dated 28 July 1880, 21 June 1881, 11 July 1881, 13 July 1881, 13 August 1881, and 3 September 1881 detail Simon's effort to oversee the routing and establishment of a roadway from Manistique to Thompson village across present-day U.S. Highway 2 and then running south through Thompson Township to Barque Point and west to the Delta County line.[59]

In the mid-1880s, Simon became embroiled in a lawsuit that went all the way to the Michigan Supreme Court. In *Coon v. Bouchard*, the Court recounted that William Olmsted loaned Simon $600 in 1877, due for repayment by November 10, 1877.[60] Charles D. Coon, the complainant holding the mortgage assigned by Mr. Olmsted, claimed that Simon still owed $470.73 with interest on the note. Simon maintained that he'd satisfied the debt. The Court summarized Simon's defense as follows:

> Defendants also claim that in 1881 Olmstead requested Bouchard to catch fish for him at the mouth of the Manistique, for which work Olmstead agreed to pay Bouchard $2.50 a package, Olmsted furnished the empty packages and salt; that under this arrangement Bouchard earned and had coming to him from Olmstead over $650 for work and labor. Defendant also claims that he lost quite a considerable sum of money by reason of Olmsted failing to come for the fish caught by him, and to furnish salt as agreed, so that many of the fish caught became spoiled and worthless.[61]

Both Simon and his son George testified in Simon's defense, but the Supreme Court upheld the trial court's finding that Simon owed the complainant $375.63 with interest from the lower court's 1886 decree.[62]

Around 1884, Simon purchased an adjacent parcel of land belonging to John Fountain and comprising approximately one hundred acres.[63] John Fountain obtained title to the Fountain land in 1869, which is located to the north and northeast of the Barque Point homestead and stretched from the Lake Michigan shoreline east along Little Harbor Road immediately north of the Farley homestead.[64] With the family numbering thirteen, the cabin had grown too small, and they relocated to the Fountain residence on their newly acquired land.[65]

Various newspapers in the 1880s and 1890s reference Simon's goings-on in the community. A 17 February 1885 issue of Escanaba's *Iron Port* noted Simon was quite sick.[66] On 28 September 1886, Simon was in Garden village. In October 1886, Simon paid a visit to Manistique, as reflected in the 29 October 1886 issue of Manistique's *Semi-Weekly Pioneer*.[67] Two years later, in September 1888, he paid a visit to the *Iron Port* newspaper's Escanaba office.[68]

In summer 1894 and again that Christmas, the Bouschor family hosted Reading, Michigan journalist F. A. Rogers at the homestead for a pair of visits described in greater detail in the previous chapter. Simon evidently had some medical acumen as well, for Rogers noted, "when I was sorely disabled with many complications he promptly came to my relief after having been given up by some of the most pretentious medical practitioners of this country; and I heartily endorse and cheerfully recommend his medical skill to those who wish to employ his services."‡[69] Harriette traveled from Barque Point to Thompson in January 1898.[70] The 28 January 1899 edition of the *Iron Port* notes Simon's visit to Escanaba that week, while the 26 May 1899 issue of the *Manistique Pioneer-Tribune* recounts Simon's visit to Manistique for several days calling upon friends and relatives.[71]

As Simon was a fisherman, the closed fishing season law implemented in 1899 affected Simon's family by

---

‡ One example of Simon's medical care was his recipe for "Grandpa Bouschor's Black Salve," a treatment that was later passed down to his son George Wallace Bouschor and family. The Black Salve recipe calls for seven teaspoons of red lead and one cup of olive oil (from a Bouschor family recipe book courtesy of Denise S. Bouschor). The author cannot speak to the efficacy of the treatment.

A family photograph likely taken in the early 1900s, possibly in the residence formerly belonging to the Kingham family — Simon and Harriette sit in front; In back from left to right are Ida Isabelle (Bouchard) Farley, Nelson Burton Bouschor, Mary May (Bouschor) Daniels, Alexander Daniels, and Anna Olive (Bouschor) Smith

limiting access only to certain tug fishing concerns. While the article is unclear whether it is referring to Simon or one of his children, the 11 November 1899 issue of Escanaba's *Iron Port* newspaper states, "It is said that F. N. Clark, superintendent of the Northville hatchery, turned down a sailboat fisherman of the name of Bouscher who wanted a license to continue fishing on the same terms as those granted the tug fishermen. Bouscher has decided to continue fishing and if arrested will make his case a test of the law."[72]

Around April 1899, Simon, Harriette, and any children still living at home moved into a house previously occupied by Joseph Kingham.[73] The *Manistique Pioneer-Tribune* does not reference whether the former Kingham residence was in the vicinity

of the Barque Point homestead or further up Little Harbor Road in Thompson village. Schoolcraft County records reflect that a marriage license was issued on 30 April 1892 to twenty-six-year-old England-born merchant Joseph H. Kingham and nineteen-year-old Mary (Marion) Stark, both of Manistique.[74] The Kinghams were related to the Bouschors through Marion Stark Kingham, who was the daughter of Margaret Elizabeth Allen— daughter of Harriette's older sister Margaret Elizabeth Gray Allen. Schoolcraft County birth records reflect the birth of daughter Ruth E. Kingham on 28 August 1892 to Joseph and Marion Kingham of Manistique.[75] It's unclear when Joseph and Marion moved from Manistique to Thompson, but on 18 June 1895, a son, Gordon Kingham, was born to them at Thompson, and two years later, on 26

July 1897, they welcomed a daughter while living at Thompson.[76] The 1900 U.S. Census lists Joseph and Marion Kingham as living with four children under the age of ten in Thompson Township, Schoolcraft County, Michigan.[77] The Kingham family later relocated to western Montana, and Joseph passed away in Missoula in 1945.[78]

Simon and Harriette and the Thompson Township Community

Both Simon and Harriette held elected and appointed offices following Thompson Township's founding on 6 March 1882. At Thompson Township's inaugural meeting on 3 April 1882, Simon won election as Thompson's first Commissioner of Highways, having secured fifty-eight votes to Gilbert Olson's thirty-four.[79] Simon took his oath of office the following day and executed his Highway Commissioner's Bond and Oath of Office on 13 April 1882, naming Alvin Carpenter and John Stark, both of Thompson, as his sureties.[80] The Thompson Township Register of Electors reflects that Simon was registered to vote as of 25 October 1882.[81] Immediately prior to his election, in his capacity as Commissioner of Highways for Thompson Township, Simon filed a 25 March 1882 report as Highway Commissioner, likely in a holdover capacity from his previous service with Hiawatha Township. Following his formal election in April 1882, he filed his Highway Commissioner reports on 9 September, 3 October, and 28 October 1882 detailing his work on roadways within the township.[82] An undated inventory of tools for the Commissioner of Highways included the following: two 5/8 chains, one double wooden block, one single iron, 200 feet of rope, two shovels, and three axes.[83]

Simon won reelection to another one-year term as Commissioner of Highways on 2 April 1883 with fifty-eight votes to thirty-one for Frank Rivers and swore his oath of office on 4 April, naming John Stark and Joseph Walsh his sureties three days later.[84] He completed a report to the township on 16 June 1883 regarding highway work and attested that no damages were due to any impacted landowners.[85] He was reelected without opposition the following

7 April 1884 for an additional one-year term, swearing his oath the next day before Township Clerk John Stark and naming Peter Johansson his surety the following week.[86] In his final year-long term as Commissioner of Highways, he submitted his last report to the township on 3 January 1885 discussing the extension of a road east of 9 Mile Lake Road.[87]

After a two-year gap, Simon ran again for Commissioner of Highways at the Thompson Township annual meeting and election on 4 April 1887 but came in third with forty-eight votes. Finishing ahead of him with sixty-two votes was his son George Wallace Bouschor, who ultimately lost the race when the tied vote was determined by lots, handing the race to Lemuel Rice.[88] However, Simon won election unopposed for a one-year term as the newly created Overseer of Highways for District No. 4 on 1 April 1889 to replace previous overseer Peter Hibbert, and Simon swore his oath of office on 6 April 1889 in the presence of Township Clerk George H. Williams.[89] He was reelected without opposition to another one-year term on 1 April 1890 and swore his oath of office on 9 April 1890.[90]

Simon also served as Assessor for Thompson Township's School District No. 3, having been appointed on 11 January 1882 and reappointed to three-year terms on 1 September 1884 and 5 September 1887.[91] Harriette Bouschor likewise held positions with the education system in Thompson Township. She was appointed to a two-year term as Director of School District No. 3 on 6 September 1880 and subsequently reappointed to three-year terms as Director on 4 September 1882, 7 September 1885, and 3 September 1888.[92] This again indicates she provided education for the younger Bouschor children and likely others in the vicinity of Barque Point.

The 1900s and Death of Harriette

The 1900 U.S. Census—the first to use the Bouschor surname—shows Simon and Harriette still residing in Thompson Township, presumably in the former Joseph Kingham residence. At seventy and sixty years old, respectively, Simon and Harriette

Ida Isabelle Bouchard Farley, Mary Jane Clark Bouschor, and Simon Bouschor at Harriette's grave in Manistique's Lakeview Cemetery, likely in the year following her burial in December 1906

Simon on a visit to his brother Edward Albert Bouchard at the latter's office in Cheboygan, Michigan

had been married for over forty years by this time. Three of the couple's children—Louis, Mary May (also known as Mamie), and Nelson—still lived with them, as well as a five-year-old adopted son named Russel. Very little is known about Russel, and he is not listed as living with any family member in future census records. No occupation is given for Simon and Harriette; presumably, both were retired by this time while Louis and Nelson worked as fishermen.[93] One interesting note is that Simon and the family are referenced as living in a rented home. Their eldest son, David Eli, and his family, however, are listed as living nearby and as being the owners of a farm and home.[94] It's possible Simon conveyed the homestead to David, and Simon and Harriette continued to live on it in another dwelling. The property remained in the family, as their grandson Leslie owned the property into the 1970s.

Two other relatives living near the Barque Point homestead at the turn of the century were John Champine and his mother, Mary Champagne. John's father and Mary's husband, John Baptiste Champagne, was Simon's uncle, being the younger half-brother of Josette Champagne Bouchard. John Champine worked as a laborer at a sawmill.[95]

In late October 1904, Harriette paid a visit to the Lakeside home of George and Mary Jane Bouschor in Manistique.[96] In March 1906, Simon and Harriette hosted a get-together at their house in Thompson in honor of a visit by their son and daughter-in-law Charles and Lillie Bouschor of Duluth. Multiple guests attended, including several Bouschor family members. Given Harriette's death a couple months later, this may have been an opportunity for the family to say goodbye.[97]

Harriette died at the age of sixty-seven in Manistique at the home of her daughter Ida Isabella (Bouchard) Farley on 18 December 1906, as the result of a "left sided apoplexy." Her death certificate likewise revealed she'd been suffering from "senile changes" for the last two years of her life.[98] It's likely she moved to Manistique for the comfort of being cared for by family and to be closer to medical care than the remote Barque Point. Her funeral was

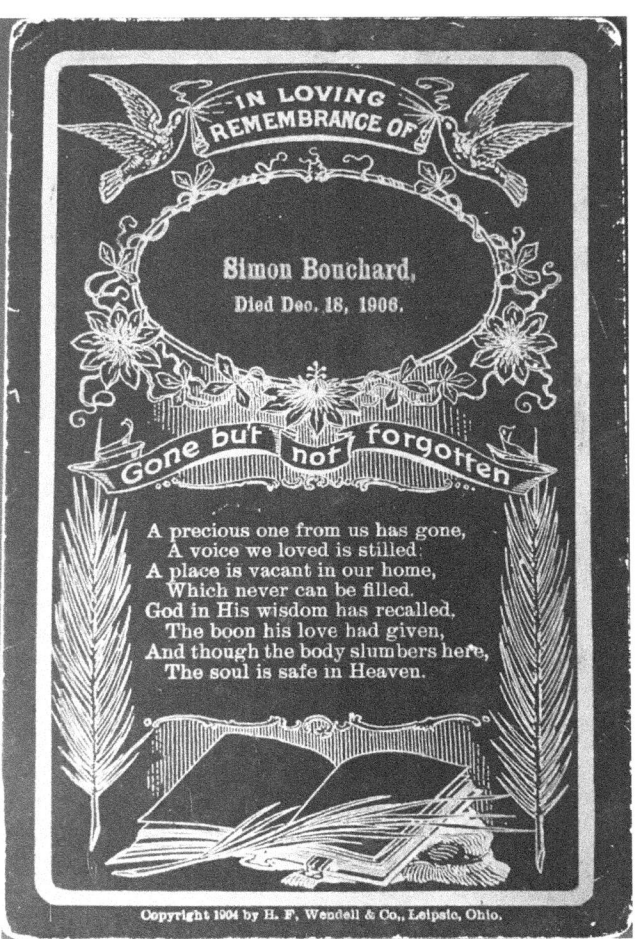

Harriette's 1906 memorial card

held at Manistique's Methodist Church on 22 December 1906 with Reverend Edmonds officiating. All her living children, save for William and Henry, who lived out west, attended her funeral. Others in attendance included Simon's younger brother Edward Albert Bouchard of Cheboygan, Michigan, and his wife, Carrie Bouchard.[99]

Harriette's obituary in the 21 December 1906 Manistique *Pioneer-Tribune* included the following:

> She and Mr Bouschor resided at Barque Point for the past forty-seven years—long before Manistique was founded and were conversant with the hardships of pioneer life. Their latch string was always out, and hundreds of friends remember the cordial and hearty reception given them by this estimable couple when they called at their

home. The deceased was universally respected for her many noble traits of character.[100]

The family had a memorial card made by the H. F. Wendell & Company business of Leipsic, Ohio, featuring the name "Simon Bouchard" and Harriette's date of death, along with a short poem (reproduced on the previous page).[101] She was buried on 21 December 1906 in Manistique's Lakeview Cemetery.[102] Her grave would form the core of the Bouschor family plot. A photograph taken of the family plot shortly after Harriette's burial shows her daughter Ida Isabella Farley, daughter-in-law Mary Jane Bouschor, and Simon standing around the grave. Ida and Mary Jane hold black umbrellas while Simon stands to the right holding a cane and wearing a dark hat. The newly installed Bouschor family monument stands at the center of the picture.

Simon Bouschor in the 1910s, Manistique

Simon Bouschor's Final Years

After Harriette's death on 18 December 1906, Simon moved into town and lived with his son George's family in Manistique. The 1910 U.S. Census lists the eighty-year-old Simon living in Manistique and being retired.[103] Interestingly, the census shows him living at the 630 Arbutus Avenue residence of Edward and Ellen Hogarty rather than the nearby address of his son George Wallace's family and refers to him as "father in law." That said, the dwelling and family number on the census schedule is listed as 47 and 53 with both numbers crossed out—these being the numbers corresponding to his daughter Ida's family on the same census schedule page, who also lived on Arbutus Avenue at the time.[104] It's known that Milo Hogarty was a good friend of Simon's, and it's possible he was visiting the Hogarty family at the time the census was enumerated on 2 May 1910, as Edward Hogarty was Milo's younger brother.

Simon remained active in his final years. He served as a pallbearer at the 9 March 1907 funeral of his cousin John B. Champine's wife, Mary Anne (Vallier) Champine, at Manistique's Saint Francis de Sales Catholic Church.[105] In September 1909, he trav-

eled to Bayfield, Wisconsin, as on September 5 his picture was taken there along with his son David, granddaughter Elsie, and great-grandchildren Oral and Mildred.[106] That October, Simon paid a visit to Cheboygan, Michigan, where his younger brother Edward Albert Bouchard lived and worked. The *Cheboygan Democrat* noted, "Capt. E.A. Bouchard was pleasantly surprised Sunday morning on answering a ring at his door bell to see his brother Simon of Thompson, Mich. Mr. Bouchard is 81 years of age but is hale and hearty and active as many men half that age." He made another visit the following year in 1912.[107] Simon began to suffer from health problems as he reached the final years of his life. In June 1913, he suffered a stroke.[108] The *Washburn Times* of Washburn, Wisconsin, went so far as to note, "Mr. Bouchor [sic] suffered a stroke of paralysis last Friday, and owing to his advanced age there is little hope of recovery. Mr. Bouchor visited in Bayfield last summer and was very proud of the fact that he was the oldest lake captain then living, being 85 years of age. A large circle of friends who met the captain will regret to learn of his affliction."[109]

Nonetheless, he evidently rallied and survived another three years in Manistique. In early 1915, Simon even made a final visit to the Bayfield, Wisconsin home of his daughter Annie Bouschor Smith and stayed several weeks at her family's home.[110] An undated snapshot taken of Simon, likely from the 1910s (reproduced above), shows him sitting on a chair or crate on the lawn of the 701 Michigan

Avenue home holding a cane in his right hand and wearing his dark suit with a sailor's cap.[111]

Simon died at George's 701 Michigan Avenue residence around seven o'clock in the evening on Wednesday, 19 July 1916, at the advanced age of eighty-six as the result of a cerebral hemorrhage.[112] According to the *Manistique Pioneer-Tribune*, "Mr. Bouschor was up and about all day Wednesday but was suddenly taken with a weak spell in evening and when a doctor was summoned it was apparent that death was near."[113] Another obituary in Sault Ste. Marie's *Evening News* reflected that after Harriette's death, "the aged man made his home with his son, George, in this city, and was frequently seen on our streets, being unusually active for a man of his age."[114]

The family held Simon's funeral at Saint Francis de Sales Catholic Church on Saturday, 22 July 1916, in a service officiated by Reverend B. J. P. Schevers. He was buried later that day in Manistique's Lakeview Cemetery in the Bouschor family plot, next to Harriette's grave.[115]

Notes

ABBREVIATIONS

AC. Ancestry.com, https://www.ancestry.com/

BCL. Brown County Library

BLM GLO. General Land Records Office, https://glorecords.blm.gov/default.aspx

CA. Chronicling America, Library of Congress, https://chroniclingamerica.loc.gov/

DMN. Digital Michigan Newspapers, Clarke Historical Library, https://digmichnews.cmich.edu/

EPL. Escanaba Public Library, http://www.archiveol.com/escanaba/home

FS. FamilySearch.org, https://www.familysearch.org/en/united-states/

MHS. Minnesota Historical Society

MSPL. Manistique School & Public Library

NA. NewspaperArchive, https://newspaperarchive.com/

NARA. U.S. National Archives and Records Administration

NC. Newspapers.com, https://www.newspapers.com/

TTHAC. Thompson Township Historical Advisory Committee

UPDN. Upper Peninsula Digital Network, https://uplink.nmu.edu/

1   Certificate of Death for Simon Bouschor, Filed 21 July 1916, Reg. No. 35, State of Michigan, Michigan Department of State – Division of Vital Statistics; "Aged Resident Died Wednesday," *Manistique Pioneer-Tribune*, 21 July 1916; Letter from G. Leslie Bouschor to Dorothy Gray Follo, 22 July 1964, Courtesy of Robert Leslie Bouschor, Collection of Aaron N. Bouschor.

2   1836 Mixed-Blood Census Register, Transcribed and Compiled by Larry M. Wyckoff, http://sites.rootsweb.com/~mi-macki2/annuities/1836mb.pdf.

3   1836 Mixed-Blood Census Register, Transcribed and Compiled by Larry M. Wyckoff, http://sites.rootsweb.com/~mi-macki2/annuities/1836mb.pdf.

4   Florence Meron, *A History of the Township Village and People of Thompson Michigan*, Unpublished Manuscript, 2003, MSPL.

5   Affidavit of Simon Bouschor, 14 August 1911, State of Michigan, Schoolcraft County, Courtesy of Robert Leslie Bouschor, Collection of Aaron N. Bouschor.

6   F. A. Rogers, "A Visit to Point o' Barque," *Manistique Semi-Weekly Pioneer*, 25 August 1894, UPDN.

7   "Our Neighbors – Manistique Pioneer," *Iron Port* (Escanaba, MI), 6 January 1883, EPL.

8   1830 U.S. Census, Mackinac Island, Michilimackinac County, Michigan, population schedule, p. 200, Eloi Bouchard, AC.

9   Meron, *History of the Township Village and People of Thompson Michigan*.

10   1838 Wisconsin Territorial Census, Astor, Brown County, Wisconsin, Elie Bouchou [sic], BCL.

11   1840 U.S. Census, Brown County, Wisconsin, population schedule, Eli Bouchard.

12   1840 U.S. Census, Brown County, Wisconsin, population schedule, Eli Bouchard.

13   1842 Wisconsin Territorial Census, Brown County, Wisconsin, Elie Bouchard, BCL.

14   1846 Wisconsin Territorial Census, Brown County, Wisconsin, Elie Bouchard, BCL.

15   "Aged Resident Died Wednesday," *Manistique Pioneer-Tribune*, 21 July 1916.

16   Theodore J. Karamanski, *Schooner Passage: Sailing Ships and the Lake Michigan Frontier* (Detroit: Wayne State University

Press, 2000), 121-22.

17   1850 U.S. Census, Mackinac Island, Michilimackinac County, Michigan, population schedule, p. 480, dwelling 546, family 564, line 20, Helie Bouchard.

18   Rogers, "A Visit to Point o' Barque."

19   "A Pioneer Dies," *Manistique Pioneer-Tribune*, 21 December 1906, MSPL; "Aged Resident Died Wednesday," *Manistique Pioneer-Tribune*, 21 July 1916; Bouschor Family Bible, "Marriages, Births, and Deaths," *New Testament* (American Bible Society, 1851). Please note that no definitive record exists of Simon and Harriette's marriage. Other sources suggest they married in Nahma or another location in Delta County, Michigan. *See*, e.g., Letter from G. Leslie Bouschor to Dorothy Gray Follo, 22 July 1964, Courtesy of Robert Leslie Bouschor, Collection of Aaron N. Bouschor.

20   Certificate of Death for Mrs. Simon Bouschor, Filed 22 December 1906, Reg. No. 58, State of Michigan, Michigan Department of State – Division of Vital Statistics; Certificate of Death for William Edward Bouschor, Filed 25 August 1948, State File No. 22316, Reg. No. 14, State of Washington, Washington State Department of Health, Division of Vital Statistics; Record of Birth for Nelson B. Bouschor, Recorded 7 June 1883, Record No. 50, Return of Births in the County of Schoolcraft for the Year Ending December 31st, A.D. 1882, Michigan Department of Vital Records, FS. Harriette is variously called "Harriet" or "Harriette" in records. For consistency, she will be referred to as "Harriette" throughout this volume.

21   1850 U.S. Census, City of Rochester, Monroe County, New York, population schedule, p. 332, dwelling 253, family 284, line 20-21, David & Isabella Gray.

22   Certificate of Death for Ida I. Farley, Filed 8 September 1914, Reg. No. 49, State of Michigan, Michigan Department of State – Division of Vital Statistics, AC; "Passed Away," *Manistique Pioneer-Tribune*, 21 August 1914, MSPL.

23   Certificate of Death for David Eli Bouschor, Filed 16 August 1924, Reg. Dist. No. 18-24, No. 29, State of Minnesota, Division of Vital Statistics, MHS; Record of Marriage for David E. Bouschor and Ida Belle Roberts, Recorded 24 January 1885, Record No. 772, Return of Marriages in the County of Delta for the Year Ending December 31st, A.D. 1885, Michigan Department of Community Health, Division for Vital Records and Health Statistics, AC.

24   Certificate of Death for George W. Bouschor, Filed 24 June 1923, State File No. 175 149, Reg. No. 5, State of Michigan, Michigan Department of Health, Division of Vital Statistics, AC; "George Bouschor Summoned Beyond," *Manistique Pioneer-Tribune*, 25 January 1923, MSPL.

25   Record of Marriage for Annie O. Bouschor and Oliver A. Pierce, Recorded 13 September 1882, Record No. 36, Return of Marriages in the County of Schoolcraft for the Year Ending December 31st, A.D. 1882, Michigan Department of Community Health, Division for Vital Records and Health Statistics, AC; "Mrs. Thos. Smith Died Friday Evening," *Bayfield County Press* (Bayfield, WI), 17 November 1916, Wisconsin Historical Society.

26   Certificate of Death for Simon J. Bouschor, Filed 25 September 1931, State File No. 149266, Reg. No. 10870, State of Michigan, Michigan Department of Health, Division of Vital Statistics, AC; "Aged Pioneer Dies in Detroit," *Escanaba Daily Press*, 25 September 1931, NC.

27   Certificate of Death for Charles Wesley Bouschor, Filed 21 April 1931, Reg. No. 371, State of Minnesota, Division of Vital Statistics, MHS; "Pioneer Railroad Man Dies in Accident," *Proctor Journal* (Proctor, MN), 24 April 1931, MHS.

28   Certificate of Death for Louis Bouschor, Filed 25 February 1929, State File No. 175 571, Reg. No. 9, State of Michigan, Michigan Department of Health, Division of Vital Statistics, AC; "Death Claims One More Co. Resident," *Manistique Pioneer-Tribune*, 28 February 1929, NC.

29   Bouschor Family Bible, "Marriages, Births, and Deaths," *New Testament* (American Bible Society, 1851); Record of Death for Harriet Buscher, Recorded 22 June 1874, Record No. 12, Return of Deaths in the County of Schoolcraft for the Year Ending December 31st, A.D. 1873, State of Michigan, Michigan Department of Community Health, Division for Vital Records and Health Statistics, AC.

30   Certificate of Death for Henry Archibald Bouschor, Filed 6 February 1937, Record No. 16, Reg. No. 14, State of Washington, Washington State Board of Health – Bureau of Vital Statistics; "Henry Bouschor Taken By Death," *Port Angeles Evening News* (Port Angeles, WA), 5 February 1937, Clallam County Genealogical Society.

31   Record of Birth for Moses Bouchard, Recorded 9 June 1875, Record No. 35, Return of Births in the County of Schoolcraft for the Year Ending December 31st, A.D. 1874, State of Michigan, Michigan Secretary of State, Department of Vital Records, AC; Bouschor Family Bible, "Marriages, Births, and Deaths," *New Testament* (American Bible Society, 1851).

32   Certificate of Birth (Delayed Registration) for William Edward Bouschor, Recorded 12 November 1943, Michigan Department of Health, Bureau of Records and Statistics, Schoolcraft County Clerk.

33   Record of Birth for Mary Jane Bouchard, Record No. 3, Recorded 30 September 1880, Return of Births in the County of Schoolcraft for the Year Ending December 31, 1879, State of Michigan, Michigan Department of Vital Statistics, FS; "Obituary – Mrs. A. Daniels," *Evening News* (Sault Ste. Marie, MI), 9 June 1939, NC. Note: The Schoolcraft County birth record for Mary May Bouschor lists her given name as "Mary Jane" Bouchard. This is the only instance where the middle name Jane is used.

34   Record of Birth for Nelson B. Bouschor, Recorded 7 June 1883, Record No. 50, Return of Births in the County of Schoolcraft for the Year Ending December 31st, A.D. 1882, State of Michigan, Michigan Department of Vital Records, FS; "Obituaries – Nelson Bouschor," *Manistique Pioneer-Tribune*, 13 September 1973, UPDN.

35   Mary L. Wermuth, *Michigan's Centennial Family Farm Heritage* (Hillsdale: Ferguson Communications, 1986), 43; G. Leslie Bouschor, Notes on the Bouschor Family and Barque Point Homestead, undated, Courtesy of Robert Leslie Bouschor, Collection of Aaron N. Bouschor; "History Picnic Planned Sunday," *Escanaba Daily Press*, 19 August 1959, NC; "Aged Resident Died Wednesday," *Manistique Pioneer-Tribune*, 21 July 1916.

36   Meron, *A History of the Township Village and People of Thompson Michigan*; "Thompson the Result of Mill Construction," *Escanaba Daily Press*, 31 March 1987, NA.

37   Robert Leslie Bouschor, discussion with the author, Marquette, Michigan, 23 September 2018; Frank M. Johnson, "In the Pine Woods," *Lowell Ledger* (Lowell, MI), 15 October 1903, Kent District Library; Karamanski, *Schooner Passage*, 189.

38   Robert Leslie Bouschor, discussion with the author, Marquette, Michigan, 23 September 2018.

39   G. Leslie Bouschor, Notes on the Bouschor Family and Barque Point Homestead, undated, Courtesy of Robert Leslie Bouschor, Collection of Aaron N. Bouschor.

40   Affidavit of Pascal LaLonde and David Farley, Proof Required Under Homestead Acts May 20, 1862, and June 21, 1866, Marquette, MI, 21 September 1868, NARA.

41   Homestead Certificate No. 5, Marquette, MI, 21 September 1868, NARA; Simon Buschord [sic] Land Patent, Homestead Certificate No. 5, Application 32, 4 November 1869, BLM GLO.

42   "Aged Pioneer Resident Died Wednesday," *Manistique Pioneer-Tribune*, 18 July 1916.

43   1860 U.S. Census, Delta Township, Delta County, Michigan, population schedule, p. 134, dwelling 1282, family 867, lines 37-39, Simon and Harriet Bouchard.

44   Mrs. Hasell Osterhout, "A History of Thompson Twp. & Village of Thompson," *Manistique Pioneer-Tribune*, 5 June 1975; Florence Meron, *A History of the Township Village and People of Thompson Michigan*, MSPL, Unpublished Manuscript, 2003.

45   Robert Leslie Bouschor, discussion with the author, Marquette, MI, 23 September 2018.

46   1880 U.S. Census, Hiawatha Township, Schoolcraft County, Michigan, population schedule, enumeration district 37, p. 15, dwelling 153, family 153, lines 32-42, Simon and H.E. Bouchard.

47   "Aged Pioneer Resident Died Wednesday," *Manistique Pioneer-Tribune*, 18 July 1916.

48   1880 U.S. Census, Hiawatha Township, Schoolcraft County, Non-Population Schedule, enumeration district 37, p. 2, farm 1, Simon Bouchard.

49   Larry Peterson, "The Early History of Thompson Township," *Pioneer-Tribune* (Manistique, MI), 20 October 2021.

50   1880 U.S. Census, Hiawatha Township, Schoolcraft County, Michigan, population schedule, enumeration district 37, p. 15, dwelling 153, family 153, lines 32-42, Simon and H.E. Bouchard.

51   1880 U.S. Census, Hiawatha Township, Schoolcraft County, Michigan, population schedule, enumeration district 37, p. 15, dwelling 153, family 153, lines 32-42, Simon and H.E. Bouchard.

52   Mrs. Hasell Osterhout, *Religious Heritage of Thompson, Michigan*, 1970, unpublished manuscript courtesy of Mary Bouschor.

53   1880 U.S. Census, Hiawatha Township, Schoolcraft County, Michigan, population schedule, enumeration district 37, p. 15, dwelling 153, family 153, lines 32-42, Simon and H.E. Bouchard.

54   1880 U.S. Census, Hiawatha Township, Schoolcraft County, Non-Population Schedule, enumeration district 37, p. 2, farm 1, Simon Bouchard.

55   1880 U.S. Census, Hiawatha Township, Schoolcraft County, Michigan, population schedule, enumeration district 37, p. 15, dwelling 154, family 154, line 43, S. R. Page.

56   David Sinclair Bouschor, discussion with the author, Red Lodge, MT, July 2017.

57   Robert Leslie Bouschor, discussion with the author, Marquette, MI, 23 September 2018.

58   Bouschor, Notes on the Bouschor Family and Barque Point Homestead.

59   28 July 1880, 21 June 1881, 11 July 1881, 13 July 1881, 13 August 1881, and 3 September 1881 Proceedings of Highway Commissioners, Thompson Township Highway Commissioner's Record, 1882-1891, TTHAC, UPDN.

60   *Coon v. Bouchard*, 74 Mich. 486 (1889), GB.

61   *Coon v. Bouchard*, 74 Mich. at 489.

62   *Coon v. Bouchard*, 74 Mich. at 491.

63   Bouschor, Notes on the Bouschor Family and Barque Point Homestead.

64   John Fontain [sic] (Marquette, MI), homestead patent no. 13; "Land Patent Search," digital images, *General Land Office Records* (https://glorecords.blm.gov/search/default.aspx : accessed 2 February 2019).

65   Bouschor, Notes on the Bouschor Family and Barque Point Homestead.

66   "Our Neighbors – Manistique Pioneer," *Iron Port* (Escanaba, MI), 17 February 1883, EPL.

67 *The Delta* (Escanaba, MI), 1 October 1886, EPL; "Personals," *Semi-Weekly Pioneer* (Manistique, MI), 29 October 1886, UPDN

68 "Personal," *Iron Port* (Escanaba, MI), 15 September 1888, EPL.

69 Rogers, "A Visit to Point o' Barque."

70 "Thompson Pickings," *Manistique Pioneer-Tribune*, 21 January 1898, UPDN.

71 "Social and Personal," *Iron Port* (Escanaba, MI), 28 January 1899, EPL; "Personal," *Manistique Pioneer-Tribune*, 26 May 1899, UPDN.

72 "Abandon Fishing," *Iron Port* (Escanaba, MI), 11 November 1899, EPL.

73 "Thompson," *Manistique Pioneer-Tribune*, 28 April 1899, UPDN.

74 Record of Marriage for Joseph H. Kingham and Mary Stark, 30 April 1892, Record No. 23, Return of Marriages in the County of Schoolcraft for the Quarter Ending June 30 A.D. 1892, Michigan Secretary of State, Department of Vital Records, FS.

75 Record of Birth for Ruth E. Kingham, Recorded 8 June 1893, Record No. 55, Return of Births in the County of Schoolcraft for the Year Ending December 31, A.D. 1892, Michigan Secretary of State, Department of Vital Records, FS.

76 Record of Birth for Gordon Kingham, Recorded 12 May 1896, Record No. 411, Return of Births in the County of Schoolcraft for the Year Ending December 31, A.D. 1895, Michigan Secretary of State, Department of Vital Records, FS; Record of Birth for Norine Kingham, Recorded 7 July 1398, Record No. 21, Return of Births in the County of Schoolcraft for the Year Ending December 31, A.D. 1897, Michigan Secretary of State, Department of Vital Records, FS.

77 1900 U.S. Census, Thompson Township, Schoolcraft County, Michigan, population schedule, enumeration district 168, sheet 8, dwelling 134, family 135, lines 68-73, Joseph & Marion Kingham.

78 Record for Joseph Kingham, 11 September 1945, Montana Death Index, 1860-2007, FS.

79 Proceedings of 3 April 1882 Thompson Township Meeting, Thompson Township General Record, 1882-1891, TTHAC, UPDN.

80 1882 Highway Commissioner's Bond and Oath of Office for Simon Bouchard, Thompson Township Highway Commissioner's Record, 1882-1891, TTHAC, UPDN.

81 Thompson Township Register of Electors, 1882-1909, TTHAC, UPDN.

82 25 March 1882, 9 September 1882, 3 October 1882, and 28 October 1882 Proceedings of Highway Commissioners, Thompson Township Highway Commissioner's Record, 1882-1891, TTHAC, UPDN.

83 Memoranda – Inventory of Tools Reported by Commissioner, Thompson Township Highway Commissioner's Record, 1882-1891, TTHAC, UPDN.

84 Proceedings of 2 April 1883 Thompson Township Meeting, Thompson Township General Record, 1882-1891, TTHAC, UPDN; 1883 Highway Commissioner's Bond and Oath of Office for Simon Bouchard, Thompson Township Highway Commissioner's Record, 1882-1891, TTHAC, UPDN.

85 16 June 1883 Proceedings of Highway Commissioners, Thompson Township Highway Commissioner's Record, 1882-1891, TTHAC, UPDN.

86 Proceedings of 7 April 1884 Thompson Township Meeting, Thompson Township General Record, 1882-1891, TTHAC, UPDN; 1884 Highway Commissioner's Bond and Oath of Office for Simon Bouchard, Thompson Township Highway Commissioner's Record, 1882-1891, TTHAC, UPDN.

87 24 May 1884 and 3 January 1885 Proceedings of Highway Commissioners, Thompson Township Highway Commissioner's Record, 1882-1891, TTHAC, UPDN.

88 Proceedings of 4 April 1887 Thompson Township Meeting, Thompson Township General Record, 1882-1891, TTHAC, UPDN.

89 Proceedings of 1 April 1889 Thompson Township Meeting, Thompson Township General Record, 1882-1891, TTHAC, UPDN; 6 April 1889 Highway Overseer Oath of Office for Simon Bouschor, Thompson Township Highway Commissioner's Record, 1882-1891, TTHAC, UPDN.

90 Proceedings of 1 April 1890 Thompson Township Meeting, Thompson Township General Record, 1882-1891, TTHAC, UPDN; 9 April 1890 Highway Overseer Oath of Office for Simon Bouschor, Thompson Township Highway Commissioner's Record, 1882-1891, TTHAC, UPDN.

91 Register of School Officers and Term of Office, Thompson Township General Record, 1882-1891, TTHAC, UPDN.

92 Register of School Officers and Term of Office, Thompson Township General Record, 1882-1891, TTHAC, UPDN.

93 1900 U.S. Census, Thompson Township, Schoolcraft County, Michigan, population schedule, enumeration district 168, sheet 10B, dwelling 174, family 177, lines 73-78, Simon & Harriet Bouschor.

94 1900 U.S. Census, Thompson Township, Schoolcraft County, Michigan, population schedule, enumeration district 168, sheet 10B, dwelling 171, family 174, lines 59-62, David Bouschor.

95 1900 U.S. Census, Thompson Township, Schoolcraft County, Michigan, population schedule, enumeration district

168, sheet 10B, dwelling 176, family 179, lines 84-85, John Champine.

96   "Manistique News in Brief," *Evening News* (Sault Ste. Marie, MI), 28 October 1904, GB.

97   "Thompson Items," *Manistique Pioneer-Tribune*, 30 March 1906, UPDN.

98   Certificate of Death for Mrs. Simon Bouschor, Filed 22 December 1906, Reg. No. 58, State of Michigan, Michigan Department of State – Division of Vital Statistics; "A Pioneer Dies," *Pioneer-Tribune* (Manistique, MI), 21 December 1906, MSPL.

99   "A Pioneer Dies," *Manistique Pioneer-Tribune*, 21 December 1906, MSPL; "Brevities," *Manistique Pioneer-Tribune*, 28 December 1906, UPDN; *Cheboygan Democrat* (Cheboygan, MI), 4 January 1907, DMN.

100   "A Pioneer Dies," *Pioneer-Tribune* (Manistique, MI), 21 December 1906, MSPL.

101   Memorial Card for Mrs. Simon Bouchard, 18 December 1906, AC.

102   Death Certificate for Mrs. Simon Bouschor [Harriette Bouschor], Filed 22 December 1906, Register No. 58, Michigan Department of State – Division of Vital Statistics, AC; Aaron N. Bouschor, *Harriette I. Bouschor Headstone*, 4 September 2017, photograph, personal collection.

103   1910 U.S. Census, Manistique City, Schoolcraft County, Michigan, population schedule, enumeration district 242, sheet 14A, dwelling 262, family 279, line 4, Simon Bouschor.

104   1910 U.S. Census, Manistique City, Schoolcraft County, Michigan, population schedule, enumeration district 242, sheet 3A, dwelling 47, family 53, lines 31-35, Tellas & Ida I. Farley.

105   "Death of Mrs. Shampine," *Manistique Pioneer-Tribune*, 15 March 1907, UPDN.

106   *Elsie M. Bouschor Family*, photograph 1909, Courtesy of Adrienne Liebenberg, AC.

107   "Local Lore," *Cheboygan Democrat*, 15 October 1909, DMN; "Local News," *Cheboygan Democrat*, 20 June 1913, DMN.

108   "Local News," *Cheboygan Democrat*, 20 June 1913, DMN.

109   "County News – Bayfield," *Washburn Times* (Washburn, WI), 26 June 1913, CA.

110   "County News – Bayfield," *Washburn Times* (Washburn, WI), 27 July 1916, CA.

111   *Simon Bouschor*, photograph, undated (possible 1910), Courtesy of Robert Leslie Bouschor, Collection of Aaron N. Bouschor.

112   Certificate of Death for Simon Bouschor, Filed 21 July 1916, Reg. No. 35, State of Michigan, Michigan Department of State – Division of Vital Statistics.

113   "Aged Resident Has Passed Away," *Manistique Pioneer-Tribune*, 20 July 1916.

114   "Pioneer Resident Dead," *Evening News* (Sault Ste. Marie, MI), 21 July 1916, GB.

115   "Pioneer Resident Dead," *Evening News* (Sault Ste. Marie, MI), 21 July 1916, GB; "Aged Resident Died Wednesday," *Manistique Pioneer-Tribune*, 21 July 1916; Certificate of Death for Simon Bouschor, Filed 21 July 1916, Reg. No. 35, State of Michigan, Michigan Department of State – Division of Vital Statistics; Aaron N. Bouschor, *Simon Bouschor Headstone*, photograph, 7 September 2017.

Part Three
Ancestors of Simon Bouschor

Generation 1 – Simon Bouschor

1. **Simon BOUSCHOR**, son of Elie A. BOUCHARD and Josette CHAMPAGNE, b. Michilimackinac Island, Michilimackinac County, Michigan Territory, 25 December 1829; m. Harriette Isabella Gray, St. Martin Island, Delta County, Michigan, 6 July 1854; d. Manistique, Schoolcraft County, Michigan, 19 July 1916.

Generation 2 – Parents of Simon Bouschor

2. **Elie A. BOUCHARD**, son of Abel François Alexis BOUCHARD and Agathe Blanche LeBLANC, b. Carleton, Lower Canada, 13 September 1794; m. Josette Champagne, Michilimackinac Island, Michilimackinac County, Michigan Territory, 2 December 1828; d. Staten Island, Richmond County, New York, 25 October 1879.

3. **Josette CHAMPAGNE**, daughter of Simon CHAMPAGNE and Te Pi Ma GUAIN (Marguerite CHAMPAGNE), b. Michilimackinac Island, Wayne County, Michigan Territory, approximately 1812; m. Elie Bouchard, Michilimackinac Island, Michilimackinac County, Michigan Territory, 2 December 1828; d. Green Bay, Brown County, Wisconsin, approximately 1845-46.

Generation 3 – Grandparents of Simon Bouschor

4. **Abel François Alexis BOUCHARD**, son of Louis BOUCHARD and Marie Françoise DUFOUR, b. Petite-Rivière, Province of Quebec, 23 August 1767, m. Agathe Blanche LeBlanc, Carleton, Province of Quebec, 17 May 1790; d. Saint-Roch, Province of Canada, 6 February 1833.

5. **Agathe Blanche LeBLANC**, daughter of Pierre LeBLANC and Marie DUGAS, b. Tracadigash, Province of Quebec, approximately 1768-70; m. Abel François Alexis Bouchard, Carleton, Province of Quebec, 17 May 1790; d. Saint-Roch, Lower Canada, 19 December 1854.

6. **Simon CHAMPAGNE**, son of Nicolas François MARMOTTE dit Champagne and Marie Geneviève BISSONNETTE, b. Montreal, Province of Quebec, 21 March 1765; m. (1) Te Pi Ma Guain, Michilimackinac Island, Michilimackinac County, Michigan Territory, 14 December 1822; m. (2) Françoise Bevien, 6 June 1834; d. Mackinac Island, Mackinac County, Michigan, 10 Dec. 1852.

7. **Te Pi Ma GUAIN (Marguerite CHAMPAGNE)**, daughter of unknown parents, b. Michilimackinac Island, Province of Quebec, approximately 1780; m. Simon Champagne, Michilimackinac Island, Michilimackinac County, Michigan Territory, Michigan, 14 December 1822; d. Wisconsin, approximately 1850.

Generation 4 – Great-Grandparents of Simon Bouschor

8. **Louis BOUCHARD**, son of Antoine BOUCHARD and Marie Madeleine SIMARD, b. Petite-Rivière, Canada, 17 May 1729; m. Marie Françoise Dufour, Petite-Rivière, Canada, 14 November 1757, d. Petite-Rivière, Province of Quebec, 16 November 1780.

9. **Marie Françoise DUFOUR**, daughter of Bonaventure DUFOUR and Elisabeth TREMBLAY, b. Baie-Saint-Paul, Canada, 27 December 1739; m. Louis Bouchard, Petite-Rivière, Canada, 14 November 1757; d. Petite-Rivière, Lower Canada, 12 June 1815.

10. **Pierre Benjamin LeBLANC**, son of René LeBLANC Fils and Marguerite THIBAULT, b. Grand-Pré, Acadia, January-February 1740; m. Marie Dugas, Carleton, Province of Quebec, approximately 1760; d. Carleton, Lower Canada, 25 February 1805.

11. **Marie DUGAS**, daughter of Charles DUGAS and Anne Suzanne LeBLANC, b. Grand-Pré, Acadia, approximately 1740; m. Pierre Benjamin LeBlanc, approximately 1760; d. Carleton, Lower Canada, 2 July 1839.

12. **Nicolas Noël MARMOTTE dit Champagne**, son of Claude MARMOTTE dit Champagne and Nicole GARAUDEL, b. Monthois, Champagne, France, 25 December 1727; m. Genevieve Bissonnette, Montreal, Canada, 9 January 1758; d. Montreal, Province of Quebec, 18 June 1774.

13. **Marie Geneviève BISSONNETTE**, daughter of Louis BISSONNETTE and Marie Geneviève BINET, b. Beauport, Canada, 26 February 1732; m. Nicolas Marmotte Champagne, Montreal, Canada, 9 January 1758; d. Montreal, Province of Quebec, 16 February 1790.

14. – 15. **UNKNOWN** (Maternal Great-Grandparents of Simon Bouchard)

Generation 5 – Great-Great-Grandparents of Simon Bouschor

16. **Antoine BOUCHARD**, son of Claude BOUCHARD and Nicole Louise GAGNE, b. Sainte-Anne-de-Beaupré, Canada, 15 October 1682; m. Marie Madeleine Simard, Baie-Saint-Paul, Canada, 20 November 1704; d. Petite-Rivière, Province of Quebec, 24 June 1759.

17. **Marie Madeleine SIMARD dit Lombrette**, daughter of Noel SIMARD and Marie Madeleine RACINE, b. Baie-Saint-Paul, Canada, 19 January 1689; d. Antoine Bouchard, Baie-Saint-Paul, Canada, 20 November 1704; d. Petite-Rivière, Province of Quebec, 20 February 1769.

18. **Bonaventure DUFOUR**, son of Gabriel Robert DUFOUR and Louise GAGNÉ, b. Sainte-Anne-de-Beaupré, Canada, approximately 1706; m. Elisabeth Tremblay, Petite-Rivière, Canada, 8 November 1734; d. Petite-Rivière, Province of Quebec, 14 April 1783.

19. **Marie Elisabeth TREMBLAY**, daughter of Louis TREMBLAY and Françoise MOREL, b. Baie-Saint-Paul, Canada, 4 March 1715; m. Bonaventure Dufour, Petite-Rivière, Canada, 8 November 1734; d. Petite-Rivière, Province of Quebec, 15 May 1799.

20. **René LeBLANC Fils**, son of René LeBLANC Père and Anne BOURGEOIS, b. Port-Royal, Acadia, approximately 1684; m. (1) Elisabeth Melanson, Grand-Pré, Acadia, 30 July 1709; m. (2) Marguerite Thibault, Port-Royal, Acadia, 26 November 1720; d. Philadelphia, Philadelphia County, Province of Pennsylvania, 6 February 1758.

21. **Marguerite THIBAULT**, daughter of Pierre THIBAULT and Jeanne COMEAU, b. Port-Royal, Acadia, 19 October 1704; m. René Leblanc Fils, Port-Royal, Acadia, 26 November 1720; d. approximately 1750.

22. **Charles DUGAS**, son of Joseph DUGAS and Marguerite RICHARD, b. Grand-Pré, Acadia, 10 December 1711; m. Anne Suzanne LeBlanc, Grand-Pré, Acadia, 7 January 1739; d. Carleton, Lower Canada, 25 January 1801.

23. **Anne Suzanne LeBLANC**, daughter of Pierre LeBLANC and Françoise LANDRY, b. Grand-Pré, Acadia, 16 March 1718; m. Charles Dugas, Grand-Pré, Acadia, 7 January 1739; d. Tracadigash, Province of Canada, 15 April 1776.

24. **Claude MARMOTTE dit Champagne**, son of son of Gerard MARMOTTE and Poncette GUERI, b. Monthois, Champagne, France, approximately 1700; m. Nicole Garaudel, Contreuve, Champagne, France, 7 January 1727; d. Unknown.

25. **Nicole GARAUDEL**, daughter of Nicolas GARAUDEL and Marguerite GUILLOT, b. Monthois, Champagne, France, approximately 1705; m. Claude Marmotte dit Champagne, Contreuve, Champagne, France, 7 January 1727; d. Unknown.

26. **Louis BISSONNETTE**, son of Jean BISSONNETTE and Marie Charlotte DAVENNE, b. Saint-Michel-de-Bellechasse, Canada, 28 May 1706; m. (1) Marie Geneviève Binet, Beauport, Canada, 9 August 1729; m. (2) Marie Anne Langevin, Montreal, Canada, 16 August 1746; d. Lachine, Canada, 15 May 1760.

27. **Marie Geneviève BINET**, daughter of Nicolas BINET and Geneviève BRISSON dit DuTilly, b. Beauport, Canada, 12 January 1707; m. Louis Bissonnette, Beauport, Canada, 9 August 1729; d. Lachine, Canada, 12 May 1745.

28 – 31. **UNKNOWN** (Maternal Great-Great-Grandparents of Simon Bouschor)

Generation 6 – Great-Great-Great-Grandparents of Simon Bouschor

32. **Claude BOUCHARD**, son of Jacques BOUCHARD and Noelle TOUSCHARD, b. Saint-Cosme-en-Vairais, Maine, France, approximately 1626; m. Louise Gagne, Quebec, Canada, 25 May 1654; d. Petite-Rivière, Canada, 25 November 1699.

33. **Louise GAGNE**, daughter of Louis GAGNE and Marie MICHEL, b. Igé, Perche, France, 21 January 1642; m. Claude Bouchard, Quebec, Canada, 25 May 1654; d. Petite-Rivière, Canada, 27 April 1721.

34. Noel SIMARD dit Lombrette, son of Pierre SIMARD and Suzanne DURAND, b. Angoulême, Angoumois, France, approximately 1637; m. Marie Madeleine Racine, Quebec, Canada, 22 November 1661; d. Baie-Saint-Paul, Canada, 24 July 1715.

35. Marie Madeleine RACINE, daughter of Etienne RACINE and Marguerite MARTIN dit L'Ecossais, b. Quebec, Canada, 25 July 1646; m. Noel Simard, Quebec, Canada, 22 November 1661; d. Baie-Saint-Paul, Canada, 3 December 1746.

36. Gabriel Robert DUFOUR, son of François DUFOUR and Françoise MORIN, b. Lisieux, Normandy, France, approximately 1669; m. (1) Anne Migneron, Canada, 1 May 1694; m. (2) Louise Gagne, Baie-Saint-Paul, Canada, 23 August 1707; d. Saint-Joachim, Canada, 26 June 1720.

37. Louise GAGNE, daughter of Ignace GAGNE and Barbe DODIER, b. Petite-Rivière, Canada, 20 September 1683; m. (1) Gabriel Robert Dufour, Baie-Saint-Paul, Canada, 23 August 1707; m. (2) Jean Baptiste Boily, Baie-Saint-Paul, Canada, 30 October 1726; d. Baie-Saint-Paul, Canada, 24 September 1747.

38. Louis TREMBLAY, son of Pierre TREMBLAY and Ozanne Jeanne ACHON, b. Château-Richer, Canada, 29 September 1667; m. (1) Marie Perron, L'Ange-Gardien, Canada, 27 November 1691; m. (2) Françoise Morel, Sainte-Anne-de-Beaupré, Canada, 19 November 1706; m. (3) Marie Letartre, L'Ange-Gardien, Canada, 26 August 1716; m. (4) Madeleine Marquis, Quebec City, Canada, 29 July 1727; d. Unknown.

39. Françoise MOREL, daughter of Guillaume MOREL and Catherine PELLETIER, b. Sainte-Anne-de-Beaupré, Canada, 16 October 1680; m. Louis Trembley, Sainte-Anne-de-Beaupré, Canada, 19 November 1706; d. Baie-Saint-Paul, Canada, 3 May 1715.

40. René LeBLANC Père, son of Daniel LeBLANC and Françoise GAUDET, b. Port-Royal, Acadia, approximately 1657; m. Anne Bourgeois, Port-Royal, Acadia, approximately 1678; d. Grand-Pré, Acadia, 3 January 1734.

41. Anne BOURGEOIS, daughter of Jacques BOURGEOIS and Jeanne TRAHAN, b. Port-Royal, Acadia, approximately 1661; m. René LeBlanc Père, Port-Royal, Acadia, approximately 1678; d. Grand-Pré, Acadia, 28 December 1747.

42. Pierre THIBAULT, son of Mathurin THIBAULT and Perrine MORAN, b. Saint-Malo, Brittany, France, approximately 1675; m. Jeanne Comeau, Port-Royal, Acadia, 26 November 1703; d. Unknown.

43. Jeanne COMEAU, daughter of Pierre COMEAU and Jeanne BOURG, b. Port-Royal, Acadia, approximately 1682; m. Pierre Thibault, Port-Royal, Acadia, 26 November 1703; d. Grand-Pré, Acadia, 12 July 1737.

44. Joseph DUGAS, son of Abraham DUGAS Fils and Jeanne GUILBAUT, b. Port-Royal, Acadia, approximately 1689; m. Marguerite Richard, Grand-Pré, Acadia, 12 January 1711; d. Louisbourg, Acadia, 4 September 1733.

45. Marguerite RICHARD, daughter of Pierre Jean RICHARD and Marguerite Marie LANDRY, b. Port-Royal, Acadia, approximately 1690; m. (1) Joseph Dugas, Grand-Pré, Acadia, 12 January 1711; m. (2) Charles de Saint Étienne de la Tour, Louisbourg, Acadia, 13 January 1736; d. Grand-Pré, Acadia, 15 September 1746.

46. Pierre LeBLANC, son of Antoine LeBLANC and Marie BOURGEOIS, b. Rivière-Aux-Canards, Acadia, approximately 1685; m. Françoise Landry, Grand-Pré, Acadia, 16 February 1711; d. Montreal, Province of Quebec, 22 October 1769.

47. Françoise LANDRY, daughter of Antoine LANDRY and Anne Marie THIBODEAU, b. Grand-Pré, Acadia, approximately 1693; m. Pierre LeBlanc, Grand-Pré, Acadia, 16 February 1711; d. Lavaltrie, Province of Quebec, 3 October 1767.

48. Gerard MARMOTTE, son of unknown parents, b. Contreuve, Champagne, France, approximately 1670; m. Poncette Gueri, unknown location and date; d. Unknown.

49. Poncette GUERI, daughter of unknown parents, b. France, approximately 1675, m. Gerard Marmotte, unknown location and date; d. Unknown.

50. Nicolas GARAUDEL, son of unknown parents, b. France, approximately 1675, m. Marguerite Guillot, unknown location and date; d. Unknown.

51. Marguerite GUILLOT, daughter of unknown parents, b. France, approximately 1680; m. Nicolas Garaudel, unknown location and date; d. Unknown.

52. Jean BISSONNETTE, son of Pierre BISSONNETTE and Marie D'ALLON, b. Quebec, Canada, 24 July 1669; m. Marie Charlotte Davenne, La Durantaye, Quebec, approximately 1692; d. Quebec, Canada, 15 May 1715.

53. Marie Charlotte DAVENNE, daughter of Charles DAVENNE and Marie DeNOYON, b. L'Ancienne-Lorette, Canada, 13 April 1676; m. Jean Bissonnette, La Durantaye, Quebec, approximately 1692; d. Quebec, Canada, 20 October 1707.

54. Nicolas BINET, son of René BINET and Catherine BOURGEOIS, b. Quebec, Canada, 11 February 1671; m. Geneviève Brisson dit DuTilly, L'Ange-Gardien, Canada, 12 November 1697; d. Beauport, Canada, 29 July 1753.

55. Geneviève BRISSON dit DuTilly, daughter of René BRISSON and Anne VEZINA, b. Quebec, Canada, 27 February 1678; m. Nicolas Binet, L'Ange-Gardien, Canada, 12 November 1697; d. Beauport, Canada, 3 March 1758.

56 – 63. UNKNOWN (Maternal Great-Great-Great-Grandparents of Simon Bouschor)

Ancestors of Simon Bouschor

Louis Bouchard
Born: 17 May 1729
Petite-Rivière, Canada
Died: 16 November 1780
Petite-Rivière, Province of Quebec

Marie Françoise Dufour
Born: 27 December 1739
Baie-Saint-Paul, Canada
Died: 12 June 1815
Petite-Rivière, Lower Canada

Pierre Benjamin LeBlanc
Born: January-February 1740
Grand-Pré, Acadia
Died: 25 February 1805
Carleton, Lower Canada

Marie Dugas
Born: Approximately 1740
Grand-Pré, Acadia
Died: 2 July 1839
Carleton, Lower Canada

Nicolas Noël Marmotte dit Champagne
Born: 25 December 1727
Monthois, Champagne, France
Died: 18 June 1774
Montreal, Province of Quebec

Marie Geneviève Bissonnette
Born: 26 February 1732
Beauport, Canada
Died: 16 February 1790
Montreal, Province of Quebec

Unknown
Great-grandfather of Simon Bouschor

Unknown
Great-Grandmother of Simon Bouschor

Grandparents

Abel François Alexis Bouchard
Born: 23 August 1767
Petite-Rivière, Province of Quebec
Died: 6 February 1833
Saint-Roch, Lower Canada

Agathe Blanche LeBlanc
Born: Approximately 1768-1770
Tracadigash, Province of Quebec
Died: 19 December 1854
Saint-Roch, Province of Canada

Simon Champagne
Born: 21 March 1765
Montreal, Province of Quebec
Died: 10 May 1852
Mackinac Island, Mackinac County, Michigan

**Te Pi Ma Guain
(Marguerite Champagne)**
Born: Approximately 1780
Michilimackinac Island,
Province of Quebec
Died: Approximately 1850
Wisconsin

Parents

Elie A. Bouchard
Born: 13 September 1794
Carleton, Lower Canada
Died: 25 October 1879
Staten Island, Richmond
County, New York

Josette Champagne
Born: Approximately 1812
Michilimackinac Island,
Territory of Michigan
Died: Approximately 1845-46
Green Bay, Brown County,
Wisconsin

Simon Bouschor
Born: 25 December 1829
Mackinac Island,
Michilimackinac County,
Michigan Territory
Died: 19 July 1916
Manistique, Schoolcraft
County, Michigan

Parents of Simon Bouschor

2.   Elie A. Bouchard

Born: 13 September 1794 in Carleton, Lower Canada (Carleton-sur-Mer, Gaspésie–Îles-de-la-Madeleine, Quebec, Canada)

Died: 25 October 1879 in Staten Island, Richmond County, New York

3.   Josette Champagne

Born: Approximately 1812 on Michilimackinac Island, Wayne County, Michigan Territory (Mackinac Island, Mackinac County, Michigan)

Died: Approximately 1845–46 in Green Bay, Brown County, Wisconsin Territory (Green Bay, Brown County, Wisconsin)

Early Life in Lower Canada

Elie A. Bouchard was born the morning of 13 September 1794, in Carleton, Lower Canada (present-day Carleton-sur-Mer, Gaspésie–Îles-de-la-Madeleine, Quebec, Canada),[*] to parents Abel François Alexis Bouchard and Agathe Blanche LeBlanc. He was baptized the same day in the Restigouche parish by Father Joseph Mauthrin Bourg. Elie's godparents were Louis Lanfierre and his maternal aunt, Théotiste LeBlanc.[1] The following section concerning Abel François Alexis Bouchard and Agathe Blanche LeBlanc provides additional information on the history and settlement of Carleton and the Bay de Chaleur.

Elie likely moved with his family west to Saint-Roch, Lower Canada (present-day Saint-Roch-de-l'Achigan, Quebec), northeast of Montreal, before he was four years old as his younger sister Marie Constance Bouchard was born in Saint-Roch in June 1798.

If Elie's application for admission to Sailors' Snug Harbor in his final years is accurate, he first went to sea sometime around 1813, at the age of eighteen or nineteen.[2] While containing some inaccuracies, the most detailed account of Elie's life comes from Perry F. Powers' multivolume 1912 work, *A History of Northern Michigan and Its People*. The following passage regarding Elie comes from an entry focusing on his fourth child, Edward Albert Bouchard:

> The father [Elie] was a native of Nova Scotia, and came to the United States in 1822. He was a ship carpenter and owned and sailed vessels on the Atlantic Ocean. On one occasion he had a cargo which the Nova Scotia authorities suspected him of smuggling into their country, and they seized his vessel at night. But Captain Eli Bouchard was not a man who would submit to an injustice tamely. He recaptured his vessel, took it to Quebec, and in that city sold both it and its cargo. He then went to Nantucket, Massachusetts, and shipped from there on a whaling voyage to the Arctic Ocean. The vessel in which he shipped was wrecked off the coast of Labrador, and all the members of the crew except Captain Bouchard and one other lost their lives. After wandering about for five days, in which he and his companion

---

[*]   Elie's 1877 admission record to the Sailors' Snug Harbor rest home for retired sailors lists his place of birth as "Bay de Chaleur," which is also known as the Baie-des-Chaleurs. The "Baie" separates Quebec's Gaspé Peninsula from New Brunswick. The town of Carleton, Lower Canada (present-day Carleton-sur-Mer, Gaspésie–Îles-de-la-Madeleine, Quebec, Canada), lies on the Bay de Chaleur's north shore. *See* "Names of Persons Admitted and Died in the Sailors Snug Harbor from Sept 24th to Dec 14th 1877," *Reports to the Trustees, 1867 - 1878*, SC-0016-III-A-2, Page 364, Sailors' Snug Harbor Records, 1757-2008, SC-0016, Stephen B. Luce Library, https://sunymaritimearchives.libraryhost.com/repositories/2/archival_objects/1900.

suffered great hardships, they arrived at a fort, where their needs were supplied. They then enlisted at Hudson Bay in the service of the British North American Fur Company, and during the next five years worked for it as voyagers, trading with the Indians. In this experience they had many thrilling adventures. On leaving the service of the fur company the two wanderers went to Sault Ste. Marie by way of the north shore of Lake Superior, and from there to Mackinac Island. Here they found the schooner Supply in course of construction and completed it, after which Captain Bouchard was appointed master of the schooner. It was at this time that he was married to Miss Josetti [sic] Champagne, a native of the island. She died at Green Bay, Wisconsin, in 1845, having, during her married life, became the mother of seven children, four of whom are living. In 1836, while sailing the schooner Supply, Captain Eli Bouchard discovered Spectacle reef, and two years later Whaleback reef, in Green Bay. He passed about thirty years in the government revenue service as pilot on the Erie, the Ingham and

the Issi Tousey and died in 1878 on Long Island, New York, while on a visit to one of his brothers.[3]

The Hudson Bay Company records confirm Elie's term of employment with the Company. A one-year servant's contract dated 15 July 1824 and pictured opposite reflects that Elie agreed to work in the District of Athabasca out of the Hudson Bay's York Factory located on the southern shore of Hudson Bay.[4] The contract stipulated the Company would pay Elie twenty-four pounds per year for his service as a *gouvernail* or steersman. Elie signed the servant's contract with an "x" indicating he was unable to write. If Elie worked in the District of Athabasca, this suggests he traveled deep into the Canadian frontier in present-day northern Saskatchewan and Alberta.

Incorporated in 1670 after a fruitful season of fur trapping in the Hudson Bay region, the Hudson Bay Company had an enormous impact on the Great Lakes region and North America at large. The Company maintained hundreds of posts and camps fanned out across the north, with French and Indian voyageurs paddling goods and items across

The Hudson Bay Company's York Factory outpost in 1853

Elie Bouchard's 1824 servant's contract with the Hudson Bay Company

the region's numerous rivers and lakes. By the late eighteenth century, the Hudson Bay Company vied with its bitter rival, the North West Company, for control of the Great Lakes fur trade. Three years prior to Elie's term of employment, the Hudson Bay Company had merged with the North West Company to form a conglomerate with a near-monopoly on the fur trade in the Great Lakes region.[5] The Hudson Bay Company established York Factory in 1684 and designated it as headquarters for the Company's Northern Department in 1810.[6]

Elie evidently successfully completed his year-long term of service with the Hudson Bay Company, as the reverse side of his servant's contract has "Free 1825" written across it in red ink.[7]

Life on Michilimackinac Island

Perry F. Powers' *A History of Northern Michigan and Its People* indicates that Elie left the fur trade in approximately 1828 and made his way to Sault Ste. Marie before settling on Mackinac Island, then known as Michilimackinac Island. As stated above, Powers notes that shortly thereafter, Elie became master of the schooner *Supply*.

Mackinac Island and the Great Lakes region enjoyed a robust maritime tradition at the time of Elie's arrival. The Indians who inhabited the region utilized carefully crafted canoes to ply the waters and travel long distances. The early European explorers to the region, including the French Jesuits, followed the lead of the native inhabitants and likewise employed canoes as they explored the coastline and rivers of the Great Lakes area. Sail-powered travel began with the arrival of French explorer La Salle's sailing vessel *Le Griffon*, which reached the waters of Michilimackinac Island around 27 August 1679 before traveling onwards to the present-day Green Bay area. The French controlled the waters around Michilimackinac Island until the conclusion of the French and Indian War resulted in transfer of sovereignty to Great Britain in 1763. Until 1788, the English prohibited private ownership of all ships on the Great Lakes, and any transportation of goods, supplies, or passengers was limited to the Crown's

vessels.[8] However, once the English repealed that restriction, maritime commerce and private industry flourished on the lakes. Some 2,000 sailing ships were registered on the Great Lakes in 1870—most of them schooners.[9]

Mackinac Island soon became a center of shipbuilding on the Great Lakes. These were vessels fashioned by hand by carpenters like Elie's father-in-law, Simon Champagne. The tools of shipwrights included several different types of adzes, augurs, caulking irons and mallets, chisels, saws, planes, and clamps as well as gauges and dividers to measure and mark the components.[10] The entire process involved countless hours of manual labor regardless of the vessel's size. Shipbuilding was a common occupation for sailors during the offseason from around December through April when navigation on the Great Lakes was closed due to inclement weather and ice.[11]

As discussed in Part One, Mackinac Island in the 1820s and 1830s was a thriving pioneer community and "a hub of fur-trading and commerce in the summers."[12] It witnessed some of the most important moments in Michigan's history. Historical texts give us an idea of life on Mackinac Island in the 1820s and 1830s. While the island was steeped in the fur trade beginning in the 1700s, fishing emerged as the dominant industry in the 1830s but would soon be overtaken by tourism, as Mackinac Island became a favorite destination of visitors and those seeking the benefits of its healthy breezes and water.[13] Alexis de Tocqueville visited Mackinac Island in 1831 and recorded his observations on the island's unique populace.[14] It's possible Elie and Josette saw or even met with the Frenchman on his travels through the Great Lakes region.

Marriage and Family

Thirty-four-year-old Elie married Josette Champagne in a 2 December 1828 ceremony on Mackinac Island officiated by Justice of the Peace John Drew.[15] Little definitive information is known about Josette. She was born in approximately 1812 on Mackinac Island in the Michigan Territory, the daughter of Simon Champagne and an Odawa Indian woman named Te Pi Ma Guain (also known as Marguerite). At the time of her marriage to Elie, Josette was approximately sixteen years old. She gave birth to her first child, Simon, just over one year later in December 1829. Additional information on Josette's Odawa ancestors will be discussed in the following section on her mother, Marguerite Champagne.

Elie and Josette had eight children—seven boys and one daughter, as follows:

i. **Simon Bouchard (a.k.a. Simon Bouschor)**, b. Michilimackinac Island, Michilimackinac County, Michigan Territory, 25 December 1829; m. Harriette Isabella Gray, Washington Island, Door County, Wisconsin, 6 July 1854; d. Manistique, Schoolcraft County, Michigan, 19 July 1916[16]

ii. **Eli Bouchard Jr.,** b. Michilimackinac Island, Michilimackinac County, Michigan Territory, February 1832; m. Justine Lancour, approximately 1857; d. Front Royal, Warren County, Virginia (Battle of Guard Hill), 16 August 1864[17]

iii. **Remi Bouchard**, b. Michilimackinac Island, Michilimackinac County, Michigan Territory, 5 September 1832; m. Philomene M. Boucher, Mackinac Island, Mackinac County, Michigan, approximately 1858; d. Naubinway, Mackinac County, Michigan, 23 March 1911[18]

iv. **Edward Albert Bouchard**, b. Green Bay, Brown County, Wisconsin Territory (born aboard the schooner Supply), 15 December 1836; m. (1) Mary E. Taylor, Mackinac Island, Mackinac County, Michigan, 9 May 1859; m. (2) Julienne Metivier, Cheboygan, Cheboygan County, Michigan, 15 January 1880; m. (3) Carrie A. King, Cheboygan, Cheboygan County, Michigan, 24 January 1900; d. Cheboygan, Cheboygan County, Michigan, 15 May 1915[19]

v. **Mary Olive Bouchard**, b. Green Bay, Brown County, Wisconsin Territory, 27 October 1838; m. Louis Preville, approximately 1863–64; d. Shorewood, Milwaukee County, Wisconsin, 17 January 1927[20]

vi. **Alexis Bouchard**, b. Green Bay, Brown County, Wisconsin Territory, 7 June 1840; d. Unknown[21]

vii. **Joseph Florimond Bouchard**, b. Green Bay, Brown County, Wisconsin Territory, 18 May 1842; m. Eliza Gereaux, Unknown; d. Green Bay, Brown County, Wisconsin, 9 August 1882[22]

viii. **Raphael Olivier Bouchard (a.k.a. Oliver R. Bouchard)**, b. Green Bay, Brown County, Wisconsin Territory, 3 February 1844; m. Josephine Beaudoin, Garden Bay, Delta County, Michigan, 13 February 1866; d. Linnton, Multnomah County, Oregon, 12 June 1916[23]

The 1830 U.S. Census reflects that Elie lived on Mackinac Island near the residence of his father-in-law, Simon Champagne. Also living in the residence was a woman between twenty and thirty (likely Josette), a child under the age of five (likely Simon), and another unknown male between the ages of fifteen and twenty.[24] Two more children, Eli Junior and Remi, were born while the family lived on Mackinac Island.

Life as a Great Lakes Sailor and Captain of the Schooner Supply

As noted above, Elie became master of the schooner *Supply* soon after his arrival on Michilimackinac Island. A schooner's most common configuration on the Great Lakes was a two-masted vessel comprising an after-mast rigged with gaff mail sail, gaff topsail, and staysail, along with a shorter foremast that could be rigged in different combinations that dictated the specific type of schooner.[25] The schooner depicted on the following page, the *J.V. Taylor*, is an example of the two-masted schooners common to the Great Lakes. Sailing ships were the workhorse of the Great Lakes during the nineteenth century. In 1860, 1,122 ships plied the waters, while twenty years later the number of sailing ships hit a peak of 1,855.[26] Variants on the schooner included the scow schooner—typically two-masted and designed with a shallow draft to carry the maximum amount of cargo; the canaller schooner—stubby, with a shallow draft and, as the name suggests, intended to pass through narrow canals to reach the Great Lakes; and the Baltimore clipper—another two-masted schooner often modified with a retractable centerboard to allow for greater stability on the open waters of the lakes.[27]

In addition to carrying settlers, merchants, goods, and equipment from the East Coast and between ports on the Great Lakes, schooners served an invaluable role in the export of resources from the growing Midwest. These resources included grain, wheat, and even iron ore from ports like Escanaba.[28] Even more important to the Upper Peninsula and towns like Manistique and Thompson, schooners carried millions of board feet of timber from the Upper Peninsula forests and sawmills south to cities like Milwaukee, Chicago, Detroit, and beyond. It's believed the first load of lumber shipped on the Great Lakes was a timber shipment from St. Joseph, Michigan, to Chicago in 1833. The lumber trade moved north as foresters cleared available timber on Michigan's Lower Peninsula and in Wisconsin. By the latter half of the nineteenth century, operations had moved further north, and ports all along the Upper Peninsula's southern shore benefited from schooner traffic. In turn, those schooners returned to the Upper Peninsula harbor towns laden with grain and goods from the cities.[29] By the end of the 1890s, rail transportation began to overtake sailing ships as the primary means of moving lumber and other goods around the Great Lakes area. Coupled with advancements in steamship technology, these developments spelled the end of the schooners' heyday on the lakes.[30]

Although a handful of sailors were born and raised

The Great Lakes Schooner J.V. Taylor *in a two-mast configuration – The* J.V. Taylor *was launched in 1867 at Chicago and sailed for some sixty years through 1928*

in the Great Lakes area, many, like Elie, came from the East Coast and had experience with saltwater sailing before making the transition to the freshwater lakes.[31] Many sailors came from Norway, along with sailors from Sweden, Ireland, Germany, and America (though the latter were more apt to prefer work on steamships than sailing vessels).[32] Due to the close of navigation on the Great Lakes from 1 December through the end of April, many sailors migrated back and forth between the Lakes and the East Coast, finding work when available between the two bodies of water.[33]

Life on a schooner was cramped, cold, and often wet. While the ship's master and mate enjoyed relative comfort in their deckhouse quarters, up to five sailors shared the crew's quarters in the forecastle below deck. Danger lurked everywhere, whether in the form of inclement weather or the risk of falling from aloft while repairing a sail. During the era when Elie sailed the Great Lakes, there was little in the way of navigational aids or reliable maps like we have today. Lighthouses were non-existent until the latter half of the nineteenth century, and in 1850 alone, 431 lives were lost on the Great Lakes. A full survey of Lake Michigan by the United States Lake Survey wasn't completed until 1874. Until then, sailors had to mostly rely on their own knowledge of lake hazards and wisdom passed down from one seaman to another.[34]

Sailors enjoyed little downtime with the ship's ever-present maintenance demands and other tasks—not that the forecastle quarters made for an altogether pleasant place to relax. Sailors entered into what were known as article agreements with the ship's master. These were contracts that set forth the compensation, duties, and destination of the voyage. During the 1870s and 1880s, a schooner sailor could expect to receive around $1.25 per day for their services aboard the ship, although this could increase during foul-weather seasons. Another key member of any ship's crew was the cook, whose skills in the kitchen could make a world of difference between a lousy voyage and a tolerable one. The cook was busy from before the break of dawn until after nightfall, preparing breakfast, lunch, and dinner, as well as simple meals for the crew on watch during the night.[35] A nineteenth-century ship captain's life was far from glamorous, and a captain working in 1836 could expect to receive $600 to $800 (approximately $19,000 to $25,000 in 2022, adjusted for inflation) for the entire sailing season.[36]

Presbyterian Minister William M. Ferry commissioned the *Supply* to replace an earlier vessel, the *Aurora*.[37] Minister Ferry had established a Protestant mission on Mackinac Island in the 1820s and built a mission house towards the east end of Haldimand Bay in 1825 that exists to this day and is operated by the Mackinac Island State Park.[38] In addition to serving the needs of the mission, the *Supply* also transported goods and merchandise for multiple businesses, including Astor's American Fur Company.[39] The *Supply* evidently ran into trouble early in its career while owned by the Mackinac Island mission and captained by one Captain Campbell. Historian J. B. Mansfield noted that in November 1832 the *Supply*:

> Was wrecked in the month of November, this year, by getting ashore on a bar at or near Gorse island, where she bilged and sunk. Her cargo, consisting of supplies, was saved, except 150 barrels of salt. A short time prior to her loss she was driven ashore on the Canada side of Lake Huron, and was with difficulty rescued. She had on board a quantity of furs, which were saved in a damaged condition. The cause of her troubles, which were several that season, was attributed to the inefficiency of the crew, who had but little or no experience.[40]

The *Supply* reentered service, and nearly two years later Mackinac Island Indian agent Henry Rowe Schoolcraft observed the *Supply* leaving Mackinac Island's harbor on 4 April 1834, bound on "her first trip to Detroit, with a fine west wind, carrying our recent guests from St. Mary's."[41] In November 1834, the *Supply* transported Minister Ferry, his family, and sixteen other settlers to the new community of Grand Haven, Michigan, located on the western shore of the Lower Peninsula.[42] Although it's unrecorded who captained the *Supply* on these voyages, one wonders if Elie replaced the hapless Captain Campbell after he had beached the ship on the Gorse Island sandbar.

It is unknown how the *Supply* was rigged, as the author was unable to locate a specific description or pictures of the ship. One reference gives its tonnage as forty-four tons.[43] Most scow schooners were under one hundred tons, so it's possible the *Supply* was a scow schooner. The fate of the *Supply* is unknown after the Bouchard family relocated to the Green Bay, Wisconsin Territory area in December 1836, but subsequent events suggest that Elie relinquished the captaincy of the *Supply* and it returned to service on Mackinac Island and the eastern shore of Lake Michigan. The family of Deacon Dame and one Louis Miller arrived on Mackinac Island aboard the *Supply* in September 1841.[44] An advertisement in the 6 June 1855 issue of the *Grand River Times* of Grand Haven, Michigan, references the *Supply* making regular runs between the ports of St. Joseph and Grand Traverse. The advertisement notes, "The *Supply* has recently been re-fitted, and is in all respects all that is desirable for the comfort of passengers and speedy transportation of freight." The advertisement was run by the Ferry & Sons company of Grand Haven, suggesting the ship remained in possession of the Ferry family who founded the mission on Mackinac Island and later relocated to Grand Haven in 1834.[45] The original *Supply* may have sunk during an 1869 storm near Manitou Island outside Traverse City while carrying a load of 300,000 bricks.[46] However, a government report references a "Scow Supply" as being "driven ashore south of the pier" while trying to enter Kenosha Harbor during a gale in May 1876.[47] This *Supply* was likely a successor vessel bearing the same name. It capsized during a squall on 3 July 1890 offshore of Yuba, Michigan, on the East Arm of Grand Traverse Bay midway between Traverse City and Elk Rapids.[48]

Move to Green Bay and Death of Josette

In 1836, Josette Bouchard received $1,812.50 by virtue of her one-half Odawa ancestry per the terms of the 1836 Treaty of Washington settling financial payments upon the mixed-blood descendants of the Odawa and Chippewa Indians living in northern Michigan.[49] The financial payments were part of the 1836 treaty that resulted in the Odawa and Chippewa ceding sixteen million acres of land throughout northern Michigan to the United States (depicted on the opposite page).[50] The family likewise received $305.89 for each of their three eldest children—Simon, Eli Junior, and Remi—to be held in trust until each child was of age.[51] Elie invested Josette's $1,812.50 settlement in the building of rafts and a tug. Captain Bouchard, as he became known, used the tug to sail the Great Lakes. The family ultimately decided to move from Mackinac Island to Green Bay in what was then the Territory of Wisconsin in late 1836 after eight years of marriage and life on Mackinac Island.[52] It was as they were pulling into Green Bay's harbor that Josette gave birth to their fourth child, Edward Albert Bouchard, on 15 December 1836.[53] Elie commanded the schooner *Supply* at the time of his son's birth, and they reached Green Bay just before the close of the navigation season.[54]

It's not known exactly why Elie and Josette chose to relocate to Green Bay. Elie's younger brother, Édouard Benjamin Bouchard—or Edward Beouchard as he was later known during his years in America—lived in the southwest corner of Wisconsin Territory in Iowa County's Mineral Point. According to Edward's 17 May 1837 naturalization petition filed in Iowa County, Wisconsin Territory, Edward arrived in Wisconsin Territory's Prairie du Chien on 16 August 1822 after leaving French Canada earlier that month.[55] Edward prospected for lead in southwestern Wisconsin and northwestern Illinois in the 1820s, fought in the Blackhawk War of 1832, returned to mining in Iowa County, Wisconsin, joined the Colonel Collins regiment of the Illinois Volunteers in 1847 to fight in the Mexican-American War, then settled in Mineral Point, where he remained until his death on 22 March 1881.[56]

Green Bay featured a natural port and connection to Wisconsin's interior via the Fox River. As early

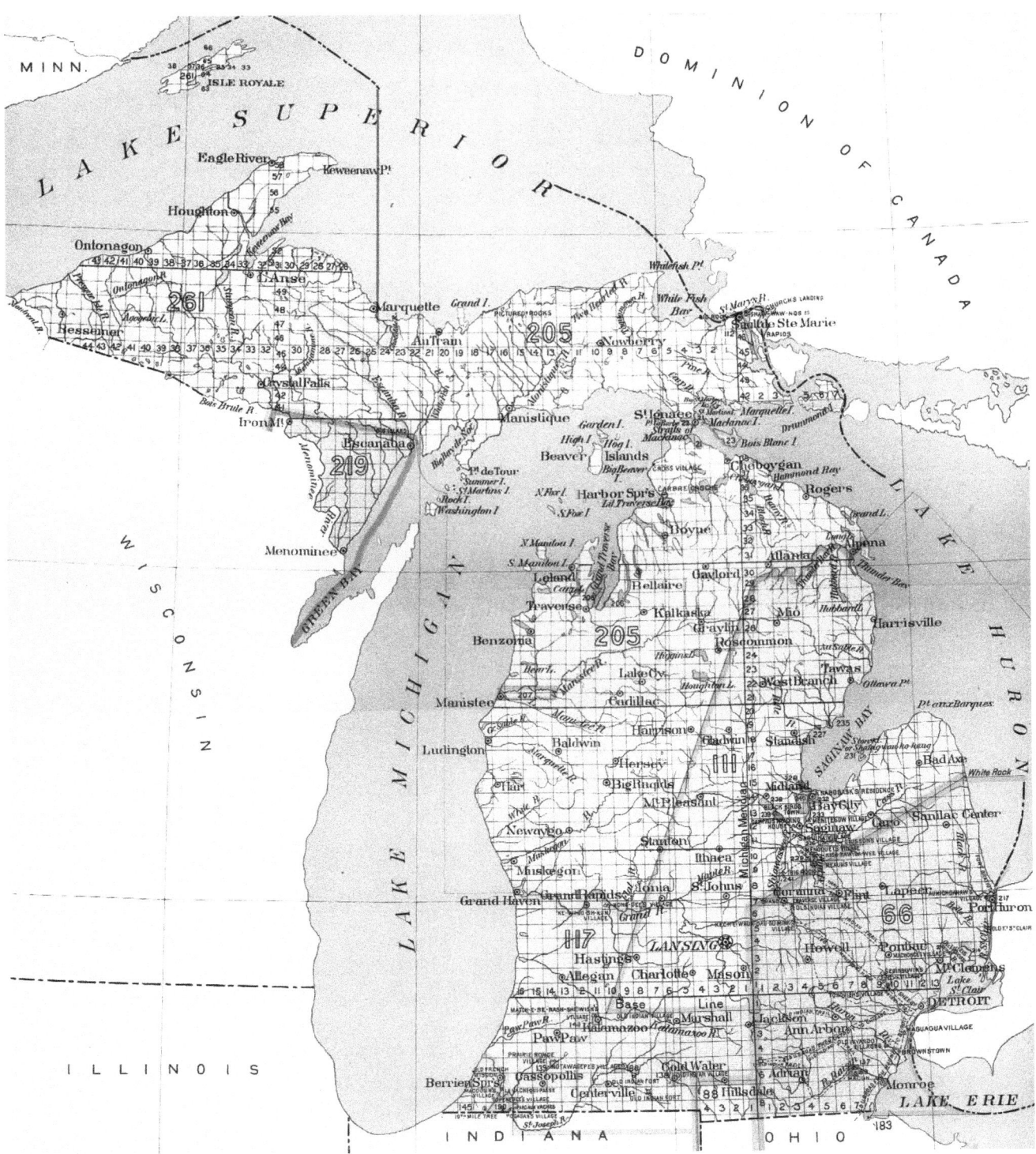

1890s map of Michigan depicting territory ceded to the United States via treaties with Indian tribes — The territory in the Upper and Lower Peninsulas denoted by the number 205 was ceded via the 1836 Treaty of Washington that provided payments to Josette Bouchard and her three eldest children by virtue of their Odawa heritage

as the 1820s, it vied with Chicago to emerge as the major port on Lake Michigan.[57] While Chicago ultimately claimed that mantle, Green Bay continued to grow in importance through the 1820s and into the 1830s. At the time of the Bouchard family's arrival in Green Bay in December 1836, the community consisted of two independent towns—Astor and Navarino. Agents of the legendary businessman John Jacob Astor founded the town of Astor in 1835.[58] Astor merged with the neighboring village of Navarino in January 1838 to form Green Bay.[59] A 2 December 1901 lecture by Fannie C. Last to the Green Bay Historic Society paints an impression of life in Green Bay when Elie and Josette arrived in 1836:

> The little village of Astor . . . contained not more than some half dozen houses, built mostly of logs, small in size and destitute of paint. . . . A long, low, log building occupied the spot where the water works plant now stands. A little lower down the river Judge Arndt kept a small inn, its latch string invitingly out, and just beside it a store where the varied wants of the rural population were supplied. In the beginning of 1835 these few buildings comprised nearly the whole of Astor, but with the completion of the new building, the tide of prosperity turned from the north and houses and shops and churches sprang up on all sides.[60]

The 1893 book *Historic Green Bay* likewise gives us an idea of boomtown-like atmosphere permeating the Green Bay area in the mid-1830s:

> During the summers of 1835 and 1836 excitement rose to fever heat, every steamer and schooner bringing settlers; speculators also crowded in, who purchased land at government prices, which they sold to later comers for treble the amount. Moneyed men from Detroit and other cities invested heavily, the sales in four days alone reaching

the sum of seventy-five thousand dollars.[61]

It's possible the hysteria and opportunity described above drew Elie and Josette to the burgeoning Green Bay settlement.

The federal and territorial census records from 1838 to 1846 give us an idea of the Bouchard family's life in Green Bay. The Bouchard family first appears in the 1838 Wisconsin Territorial Census, which lists them as living in Astor and comprising five males and one female.[62] This makes sense, as they had four sons before Mary Olive's birth on 27 October 1838. The 1840 U.S. Census references Elie and Josette as living in Green Bay. Nearly every record after this point reflects the anglicization of Elie's name as Eli. The 1840 U.S. Census references three boys under the age of five, two boys between the ages of five and ten, and one girl between the ages of ten and fifteen as living in the home. By 1840, Elie and Josette had six children—Simon, Eli Junior, Remi, Edward Albert, Mary Olive, and Alexis. In total, Josette gave birth to four children in Green Bay—Mary Olive in 1838, Alexis in 1840, Joseph Florimond in 1842, and Raphael Oliver[†] in 1844. Of the household's eight total family members, the 1840 U.S. Census further notes that one person was employed in "navigation of the ocean" (this almost certainly being Elie), and that two members of the household over twenty could not read and write (likewise indicating Elie and Josette).[63]

The 1842 Wisconsin Territorial Census reflects that the Bouchard family lived in Green Bay's South Ward and comprised seven males and two females.[64] Joseph Florimond Bouchard, the seventh child and sixth son of Elie and Josette, born on 18 May 1842, was likely the newest member of the family. The last Wisconsin Territorial Census referencing the Bouchard family is from 1846, when they are listed as living in Green Bay and comprising six males and three females.[65] As they had seven sons, it's possible Alexis Bouchard passed away prior to 1846 and that Simon left home for work. Given Elie and Josette

---

[†]   Although referred to as Raphael Olivier Bouchard in his baptismal record, he evidently preferred to be known by his anglicized middle name, Oliver, as his death certificate, censuses, and other records refer to him as Oliver R. Bouchard.

only had one daughter, the identity of the third female member of the family listed in the 1846 Territorial Census is unknown. It's possible Josette's mother, Te Pi Ma Guain, also known as Marguerite Champagne, lived with them, as the 1850 U.S. Census reflects her as living in Green Bay with her son-in-law and daughter, Augustine Rousseau and Margaret Louise Champagne Rousseau.[66]

Newspaper articles and public records from the 1840s fill in additional details regarding Elie's life in Green Bay. On a lighthearted note, Elie published a notice in the 24 and 31 December 1842 issues of the *Green Bay Republican* that a "spotted red and white Cow with the tail cut off" and her calf strayed into his enclosure, and requesting the owner "prove property, pay charges, and take them away."[67] It's unknown whether the true owner ever recovered his livestock. Elie was also involved in the community of Green Bay. On 23 March 1844, the Democratic Whig party of Green Bay appointed Elie to a five-member committee to determine suitable nominees for public office, and the party further nominated Elie for the office of Overseer of Highways.[68] Ten days later, on Election Day, 2 April 1844, Eli edged out Democrat Alvah Holmes fifty to forty-six votes for election to one of three Overseer of Highways positions.[69]

Elie evidently encountered financial trouble in his early years in Green Bay. In August 1840, Brown County Sheriff Charles Tullar published a notice in the *Wisconsin Enquirer* that he'd executed a writ issued by the Brown County Clerk of the District Court taking "all the right, title, interest, and estate which the said Bouchard may have had on the 27th day of November, A. D. 1839, in and to lot No. eleven, in block number forty-four in the town of Astor" and announced its sale at public auction at Green Bay's Astor House on 8 October 1840.[70] One wonders if this parcel of land was of the type described in *Historic Green Bay*—property purchased by a speculator at government prices and resold at a higher value to unwitting settlers. The Astor House referenced in Sheriff Tullar's sale notice was a hotel constructed by Mr. Astor in 1837 at the cost of $20,000 and that endured until it burned to the ground in 1857.[71]

In other Wisconsin property dealings, on 2 March 1843, Elie and Josette executed a warranty deed conveying the northeast quarter of the southwest quarter of Section 26, Township 15 North, Range 17 East in the Green Bay Land District to Raphael St. Marie of Fond du Lac, Wisconsin.[72] This forty-acre parcel of land is located south of Lake Winnebago in Fond du Lac County, Wisconsin. Elie obtained a patent for the same parcel of land three years later.[73] It's not known whether Elie and his family lived on or developed the Fond du Lac parcel before conveying it to Mr. St. Marie.

Josette died in approximately 1845 or 1846 in Green Bay. It's believed Josette was buried next to her mother, Marguerite Champagne, also known as Te Pi Ma Guain, at the Old Holy Cross Cemetery in Bay Settlement north of Green Bay.[74] Although the 1846 Wisconsin Territorial Census shows the Bouchard family as still living in Green Bay, the author could find no record of them in the 1847 Wisconsin Territorial Census.

Family after Death of Josette; Return to Mackinac Island and Revenue Cutter Service

After Josette's death, the remaining members of the family went into diaspora. Simon, Eli Junior, Edward Albert, and Joseph Florimond all followed their father in the seafaring life.[75] Edward Albert later recalled that after losing his mother at the age of nine, "I was a boy ten years old when I started out as a forecastle boy; the next years I was 'Royal Boy' and proudly climbed the dizzy heights of the mats in my care of the sails; gradually I ascended the ladder to become captain."[76] Simon likewise started his nautical career around the age of ten as a cabin boy.[77]

The following chart provides an overview of where each child who lived to adulthood resided over the remaining years of their lives, as reflected in U.S. Census records from 1840 through 1920:

91

Year	Simon	Eli	Remi	Edward	Mary	Joseph	Oliver
1840	Green Bay, WI	Green Bay, WI	Green Bay, WI	Green Bay, WI	Green Bay, WI	N/A	N/A
1850	N/A	Mackinac Island, MI	Mackinac Island, MI	N/A	N/A	N/A	N/A
1860	Delta, MI	Mackinac Island MI	Mackinac Island, MI	Mackinac Island, MI	Delta, MI	Delta, MI	Mackinac Island, MI
1870	N/A	N/A	Mackinac Island, MI	Mackinac Island, MI	Marquette, MI	N/A	Inverness, MI
1880	Barque Point, MI	N/A	Manistique, MI	Cheboygan, MI	Breitung, MI	Green Bay, WI	Hiawatha, MI
1900	Barque Point, MI	N/A	Garfield, MI	Cheboygan, MI	Iron Mountain, MI	N/A	Cheboygan, MI
1910	Manistique, MI	N/A	Garfield, MI	Cheboygan, MI	Appleton, WI	N/A	Garfield, MI
1920	N/A	N/A	N/A	N/A	Shorewood, WI	N/A	N/A

Residences of Elie and Josette Bouchard's children from 1840 through 1920

Following Josette's death, Elie returned to Mackinac Island. The island had changed since the time

E. A. BOUCHARD.

Captain Edward Albert Bouchard – Fourth child of Elie and Josette and younger brother of Simon Bouschor

they left in 1836, with fishing on the decline and the island increasingly catering to a diverse array of visitors. The 1850 U.S. Census lists the fifty-six-year-old Elie as living on Mackinac Island and working as a ship carpenter while owning real estate valued at $1,000.[78] The census record reflects him as living in the home of Joseph Philpots. It's unclear where most of Elie's children lived at the time. As noted above, Simon and Edward had already started their seafaring lives at an early age and may have been traveling the waters of the Great Lakes at the time of the census. His eighteen-year-old second son, Eli Bouchard, lived in Michilimackinac County (likely on Mackinac Island given that the names of several of his neighbors were known island residents) with the Noel Leveille family and worked as a fisherman.[79] A seventeen-year-old Rene Bouchard is also reflected as living on Mackinac Island with the Narcise Lecuyer family and is likely Elie's third son, Remi Bouchard.[80] The other children remain elusive in the 1850 U.S. Census records, though given the age of the younger children, most undoubtedly lived with other family members.

Eli Junior and Edward were involved in the infamous expulsion of the Strangite Mormons from Beaver Island in early July 1856. James J. Strang, a New York-born attorney, had established a breakaway Mormon community on Beaver Island after the 1844 death of Joseph Smith and proceeded to have himself crowned "King of Heaven and Earth" in a coronation ceremony held on 8 July 1850 on the island.[81] Following the 16 June 1856 shooting of Strang, numerous outsiders invaded Beaver Island and forcibly evicted anywhere from 515 to as many as 2,500 of Strang's followers from the island.[82] The year before his death, Edward recalled his involvement to the *Detroit Free Press*, saying:

It was one morning early in August, 1856, that our party embarked from [Mackinac Island] in four schooners, the Corline, Madeline, Ocean and Friendship.

My brother Eli, afterwards lieutenant in the civil war, assumed command of our party, Captain McKinley remaining behind on the Corline. We approached quietly from the rear of the village, and took possession before the other three boats had made their landing.

There was no resistance. We far outnumbered the Mormon men. They surrendered at once and we took them to McKinley's deck, where we set guards about them. We left the women in the homes to pack their belongings.[83]

Edward went on to note that they transported the captives to Racine, Wisconsin. While the expulsion of the Beaver Island Mormons is today viewed as a shameful chapter in Michigan's history, it's clear it was a point of pride at the time, as Edward's 1915 obituary likewise references the incident.[84]

Perry F. Powers' biographical sketch of Elie reflects that later in life he spent a considerable number of years in the government revenue service as pilot on the USRC *Erie*, the USRC *Ingham*, and the USRC *Isaac Toucey*.[85] The purpose of the revenue cutter service was to collect revenue via import tariffs on behalf of the federal government and to combat smuggling.[86] The USRC *Erie* was a revenue cutter schooner launched in 1833. Originally stationed at Presque Isle in Erie, Pennsylvania, it later replaced the USRC *Benjamin Rush* in service on the Great Lakes until being sold in 1849.[87]

Next, the USRC *Ingham*—named for former Pennsylvania congressman Samuel D. Ingham—was a 115-ton Harrison-class topsail schooner specifically designed for lighter draft work on the Great Lakes. The *Ingham* entered service in 1849, assigned to Erie, Pennsylvania, before being transferred to Detroit in April 1851. She ultimately served in the revenue cutter service until her sale on 24 September 1856.[88]

Lastly, the USRC *Isaac Toucey*—named for James Buchanan's Secretary of the Navy and also known simply as the *Toucey*—was a fifty-ton schooner launched in June or July 1857 and initially stationed at Mackinac Island until ordered east in 1861. She served eight additional years in the revenue service based out of Boston, Massachusetts; Castine, Maine; and New Haven, Connecticut, before being sold at New Haven on 21 June 1869.[89] If Mr. Powers' assertion that Elie piloted all three cutters is correct, it's conceivable his career on the Great Lakes spanned from the 1840s until some point in the 1860s.

The 1860s and Impact of the Civil War

Despite a diligent search, the author could not locate any record for Elie Bouchard in the 1860 U.S. Census. It's possible he was actively working in the revenue cutter service on the Great Lakes by this point and was not recorded in any census record. Two of Elie's children and their families lived on Mackinac Island in 1860. His second son, Eli Junior, Eli's wife, Justine, and their two children—Eli Oliver and George William—lived in Holmes Township on Mackinac Island. Also living in the Eli Bouchard Junior household was Elie's youngest child, Oliver Raphael Bouchard, along with two others—Charles St. Andrew and Elizabeth McGulpin. Oliver worked as a fishing hand, likely helping his older brother.[90] Next, Elie's third son, Remi Bouchard, and Remi's wife, Philomene, lived with their five-month-old son, Joseph, in Holmes Township, where Remi fished for a living.[91] Lastly, Elie's fourth son, Edward, and Edward's wife, Mary, likewise lived in Holmes Township, where twenty-two-year-old Edward also worked as a fisherman.[92]

Brothers Remi Bouchard and Simon Bouschor

As to the whereabouts of Elie's other children in 1860, Simon and Harriette had recently settled at the Barque Point homestead then in Delta County, Michigan, while Elie's only daughter, Mary Olive, and her younger brother Joseph Florimond both lived in the Delta Township, Delta County residence of fisherman Abner Cady.[93] While the 1860 U.S. Census doesn't paint a clear picture of exactly where Mary Olive and Florimond Joseph lived in Delta Township, by 1870 the Cady family is reflected as living on St. Martin Island near the residences of the Reuben Allen and George Gray families, so it's possible they lived on the island as well ten years earlier.[94]

The Civil War played a fateful role in Elie's family, as it did for many families across Michigan and the country at large. Approximately 90,000 men served in the Union Army and Navy during the war.[95] In the war's first year, 1,475 men from Michigan volunteered.[96] These included Elie's sons Edward and

Eli Junior—the former in the U.S. Navy and the latter as a member of Company K of the Seventh Michigan Cavalry. Eli Junior was one of nearly 15,000 soldiers from Michigan who lost their lives in the Civil War. Eli enlisted at Mackinac Island on 31 March 1864 for a three-year term and was mustered into service with the Seventh Cavalry on 29 April 1864. His service was all too brief, as he went missing in action during the Battle of Front Royal (also known as the Battle of Guard Hill) in Warren County, Virginia, only a few months later on 16 August 1864. According to the *Record of Michigan Volunteers in the Civil War, 1861-1865*, on 16 August the Seventh Michigan Cavalry was "engaged in action at Front Royal, charging a whole brigade of rebel cavalry, completely routing it and capturing 100 prisoners with a large number of horses and arms." Eli's body was never recovered, and he was presumed to have been killed in combat during the skirmish.[97]

It's unknown when Elie learned of his son's death, but exactly one week after Eli Junior went missing, Elie appeared before Mackinac Island Justice of the Peace Bela Chapman and executed a warranty deed conveying a 1,485-square-foot parcel of land "confirmed to Benson & Laroche" on Mackinac Island to Joseph Wilmette for $150. The deed describes the parcel as "beginning on Main Street between this lot and lot confirmed to Dr. David Mitchell, thence south 64 degrees east 130 feet to the north west corner of a lot confirmed to Trottier and Lapoint, then south 27 degrees 45 minutes west 73 feet to the south west corner of a lot confirmed to Trottier and Lapoint, then north 64 degrees west 130 to the Main Street thence north 27 degrees 45 minutes east to the place of beginning."[98] The Mackinac County property records do not reveal when or from whom Elie came into possession of this property. Aaron Greeley's 1810 *Plan of the Town and Harbour of Michilimacinac* [sic], which depicts ownership of the parcels comprising the core of the village of Mackinac, does show Parcel No. 701 confirmed to "Bison & Laroche" on the southeast side of Market Street (roughly corresponding to present-day 1151 Market Street at the corner of Market and Cadotte Avenue) and adjacent to parcels confirmed to Dr.

David Mitchell and Trottier & Lapointe. A portion of Greeley's 1810 *Plan* showing Parcel No. 701 is reproduced on the next page.[99]

Despite the 1864 property sale, by 1870 Elie still lived on Mackinac Island in Holmes Township. At the age of seventy-six, he lived with his son Edward A. Bouchard's family.[100] Both father and son worked as sailors, according to the 1870 U.S. Census. The exact residence of the Edward A. Bouchard family is unclear, but the Mackinac County property records reflect that on 22 October 1870, Charles Wachter conveyed a parcel of land on Mackinac Island described as: "Beginning at the corner of Water Street and a lane running from the shore of Lake Huron to the Road leading from the Village of Mackinac to A. R. Davenport's farm so called thence running westwardly along said lane eighty feet thence east-wardly forty five feet thence southwardly eighty feet to Water Street thence westwardly forty five feet to the place of beginning."[101] Edward and his wife, Mary, later sold said parcel of land on 18 February 1873 to John McNeal for $170.[102]

Final Years and Retirement and Death on Staten Island

Elie retired from service at sea as a captain at the age of eighty-one in 1875 after sixty-four cumulative years on the water, including fifty spent sailing under the United States flag. Ten of those years were with the Coast Survey Revenue Cutter Service, while the remaining fifty-four were with various merchant ships.[103] Elie was living in Detroit at the time of his retirement, and he had spent about three years living at the Marine Hospital in Detroit

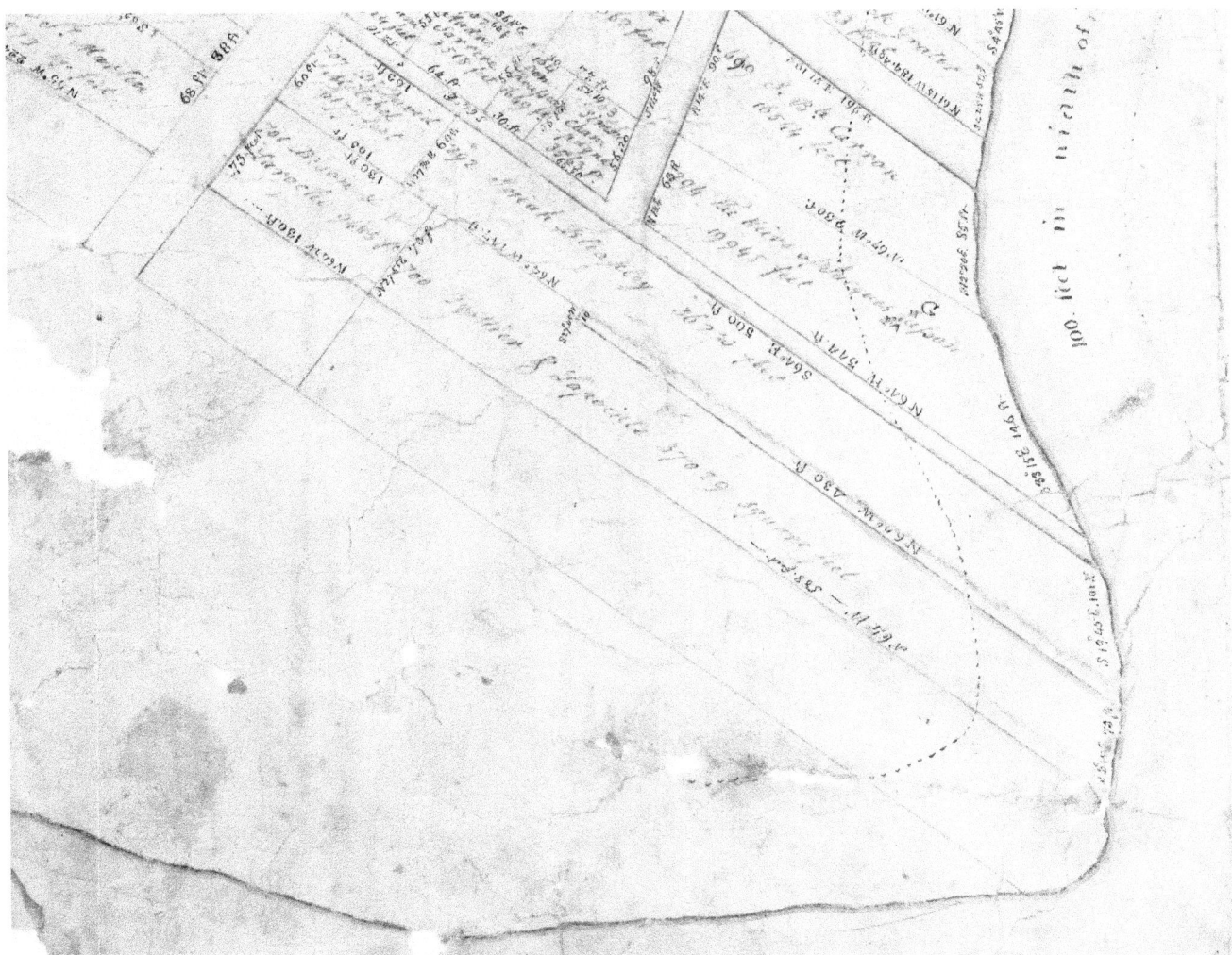

Snippet of 1810 survey of Mackinac Island village showing a parcel previous owned by Elie Bouchard (Parcel 701)

as of late 1877.[104] The Marine Hospital Service was created by Congress in 1798, and it provided for a series of hospitals intended to care for ailing sailors around the country who would otherwise be unable to afford or access such care.[105] Detroit's forty-bed Marine Hospital opened in 1855 and stood at the southwest corner of East Jefferson and Mount Elliott Avenues until a new facility was constructed in 1930. The previous building was used as an immigration detention facility until being torn down in the 1960s.[106]

Elie applied for admission to Sailors' Snug Harbor—a rest home for retired sailors on the north shore of Staten Island—on 27 August 1877.[107] A bequest of the 1 June 1801 will of wealthy Manhattan farmer Robert Richard Randall provided for the establishment of Sailors' Snug Harbor as a retirement home for "aged, decrepit, and worn out" sailors. Although the trustees initially planned to locate the institution on the island of Manhattan, the island's urbanization made them reconsider, and in May 1831 they purchased a 130-acre farm on Staten Island for $10,000 with plans to construct a facility to accommodate 200 retired seamen.[108] Randall's will provided that a trust of eight individuals—including New York City's mayor, two senior ministers, and the head of New York's prestigious Marine Society—govern the Harbor.[109] Finally, over thirty-two years after the death of its founder, Sailors' Snug Harbor opened to its first thirty-seven residents—or inmates, as they were known at the time.[110] Sailors' Snug looked out over the water separating Staten Island from New Jersey, and many a resident over the years could watch the ships pass by and be reminded of his many years spent at sea. Many sailors of foreign birth came to spend their final days at Sailors' Snug Harbor, as a man could gain admission if he'd sailed at least five years under the flag of the United States.[111] The Harbor eventually grew to comprise fifty-five major structures, including its own power plant, church, cemetery, hospital and sanitarium, and theatre.[112] In operation for nearly 150 years, Sailors' Snug Harbor grew over the decades and served as a residence for hundreds of retired sailors until its closure in 1976 and relocation to North Carolina as a retirement home.[113]

According to his application, Elie's last place of residence was Detroit, and he mostly sailed from the ports of Mackinac and Detroit. Elie's Application for Admission bore an embossed seal from the Port of Detroit Collector of Customs, and two Detroit residents, George Jerome and George H. Hopkins, vouched for Elie.[114] A Detroit city directory for 1873–74 names George Jerome as the Collector of Customs while George H. Hopkins is listed as an attorney and military secretary of the State of Michigan.[115] The trustees and governor of Sailors' Snug Harbor granted Elie's request for admission on 9 October 1877 by reason of "old age."[116] An engraving printed in a January 1873 issue of *Harper's Monthly* and reproduced at right depicts an applicant with paperwork in hand approaching Governor Thomas Melville to sign the logbook memorializing his admission.[117] Elie undoubtedly went through a similar ritual on his day of admission when he became an inmate of Sailors' Snug Harbor.

Despite spending sixty-four years at sea—a good many of those as a ship captain—Elie's application averred that he had no means of support. This was by no means unique amongst sailors. The spendthrift habits of sailors when they reached shore after long stretches at sea often left them destitute by the time the next voyage called. Elie was one of many residents who came to Sailors' Snug Harbor at the twilight of their lives with little in the way of material goods to show for a lifetime of service.

While the Application for Admission states that Elie brought no clothes, letters, or other papers with him to the retirement home, Dr. Stephen Van Rensselaer Bogert examined him and found him to be in good health considering his age.[118] His application further pledged "strict and willing compliance with [the Regulations of the Institution]" and that in consideration of being provided with food, clothing, a comfortable home, and other privileges, Elie would "readily and cheerfully perform such labor and service in and about the Institution and Farm as may be required of me by the Governor, without expecting or claiming any other reward or renumeration therefor."[119]

ADMISSION OF AN OLD SAILOR TO THE HARBOR.

1873 Harper's Monthly engraving depicting a retired sailor seeking admission to Sailors' Snug

ONE OF THE SLEEPING-ROOMS.

1873 Harper's Monthly engraving illustrating the shared sleeping quarters of the "inmates"

Once admitted to Sailors' Snug Harbor, Elie and his fellow inmates no longer had to worry about providing for themselves. Randall's bequest and the revenue generated by property around Washington Square Park held in trust allowed them to live out their remaining days in relative comfort. Food, clothing, shelter, medical care, and assistance with the day-to-day challenges of life were all provided by the Harbor. Nonetheless, the inmates were subject to strict rules of conduct, including the possession or consumption of intoxicating spirits. This prohibition led to no small amount of strife amongst the many sailors accustomed to imbibing throughout their long lives. An iron fence erected around the establishment's perimeter in 1842 and mandatory attendance at religious services were efforts to combat the scourge of drunkenness—with mixed results.[120]

The 1867 appointment of Thomas Melville as Governor of Sailors' Snug Harbor ushered in a new era that lasted until his early death in 1884 at the age of fifty-five. The number of residents had reached 600 by 1876, and within four years, three additional dormitories were constructed behind the three existing buildings.[121] Governor Melville implemented a system of demerits known as "taboos." An inmate risked receiving a taboo for violating one of the Harbor's rules. If an inmate accumulated enough taboos, he could be subject to restrictions on his movements outside the institution, withholding of tobacco, or—in extreme cases—expulsion from the Harbor. Governor Melville was not altogether popular amongst the residents and a handful even brought complaints forward to the trustees.[122] The Sailors' Snug Harbor Register page for Elie does not reflect the presence of any taboos incurred during his time in residence.

A retiree's day at Sailors' Snug Harbor officially began with the seven o'clock breakfast time, although many were up well before then, being accustomed to early hours during their lives at sea.[123] An 1874 entry from Governor Melville's Quarterly Reports to the Board of Trustees gives a flavor of life at the Harbor. Included is a handwritten sample menu for one week for the inmates. By way of example, the following is the allowance provided to the inmates on Wednesday:

> Breakfast – 5/8 oz coffee, ¾ oz sugar, ¾ oz butter, 2 oz crushed wheat
> Dinner – corned beef, cabbage, beets, potatoes, bread
> Supper – ¼ oz tea, ¾ oz sugar, ¾ oz butter, 4 oz stewed prunes, bread

A treat on Sunday featured currants and pudding with dinner.[124] Inmates lived in large, light-filled dormitory rooms with three to four men to a room.[125] During the day, they had the option of several activities, including reading the ample materials found in the reading room, visiting with fellow inmates, listening to music, visiting the nearby village of New Brighton, or even traveling to Manhattan via the ferry. Many inmates earned extra money by weaving baskets and rugs and selling them for extra money to purchase tobacco and other luxuries.[126] During Elie's two-plus years at Sailors' Snug Harbor, Governor Melville's older brother, novelist Herman Melville, was a frequent visitor to the Harbor.[127] It's unknown whether he crossed paths with Elie.

Elie passed away on 25 October 1879 after two years and sixteen days at Sailors' Snug Harbor due to paralysis of the heart, as certified by Resident Physician S. V. R. Bogert.[128] Elie had the permission of Sailors' Snug Harbor to attend Catholic Mass, and he was found dead on 25 October in the Catholic church in the adjacent village of New Brighton on Staten Island.[129] Church attendance during Elie's time was compulsory, although residents who did not wish to attend either the Episcopalian or Presbyterian services that took place on-site were excused to attend church in town—provided they returned in time for Sunday's roll call.[130] The fact that 25 October 1879 was a Saturday suggests Elie was attending services or simply visiting the church of his own volition. Dr. Theodore Walser held an inquest under the authority of Staten Island Coroner John J. Van Rensselaer at the church on 25 October and issued a determination, under the oath of six jurors, that Elie had died at the church due to paralysis of the heart.[131] The church where Elie passed was likely St. Peter's Catholic Church, which opened in 1844 but was destroyed in a fire in the 1890s. A successor structure opened in 1903 and remains in service to this day at 53 St. Marks Place in Staten Island's St. George neighborhood.[132] St. Peter's Church is approximately one mile from the Sailors' Snug Harbor home.

Elie was buried in Grave No. 1, Plot 3, Row 6 in the Sailors' Snug Harbor Cemetery in New Brighton on Staten Island.[133] However, following his death, his son Edward A. Bouchard wrote a letter to Governor Melville.[134] In his letter written from Cheboygan, Michigan, Edward wrote:

> Haveing hurd of my father's death Capt Eli Bouchard on Oct 25 can we his children git his remains to bury them at Green Bay Wisconsin by his wife and our mother. If you will give me the required information and about what it would cost to express the remains to Detroit Michigan.[135]

Edward was evidently unsuccessful in his efforts, as all evidence points towards Elie as being buried in the Sailors' Snug Harbor Cemetery on Staten Island. We do not have Governor Melville's reply to Edward's letter, but given that Elie was likely buried shortly after his death and Edward's letter didn't reach Governor Melville until several months later, exhumation and transit of his remains may have been impracticable by that point. Today, the Sailors' Snug Harbor Cemetery is unmaintained and closed to visitors, with most headstones removed years ago to prevent vandalism and theft. A group of historians and enthusiasts are working to restore the cemetery and reopen it to visitors and descendants. The Trustees of Sailors' Snug Harbor Foundation donated the cemetery to the New York City Parks Department in June 2024 with the aim "to preserve and ensure accessibility to the site for future generations."[136] This action raises hope that the burial ground will soon be reopened to the public.

Notes

ABBREVIATIONS

AC. Ancestry.com, https://www.ancestry.com/

BCL. Brown County Library (Green Bay, Wisconsin)

BLM GLO. Bureau of Land Management, General Land Records Office, https://glorecords.blm.gov/default.aspx

CA. Chronicling America, Library of Congress, https://chroniclingamerica.loc.gov/

DMN. Digital Michigan Newspapers, Clarke Historical Library, Central Michigan University, https://digmichnews.cmich.edu/

FS. FamilySearch https://www.familysearch.org/en/united-states/

GB. Google Books, https://books.google.com/

HT. HathiTrust, https://www.hathitrust.org/

NARA. U.S. National Archives and Records Administration

SBLL. Stephen B. Luce Library, SUNY Maritime College, https://www.sunymaritime.edu/library

1   Elie Bouchard Baptismal Record, 13 September 1794, Record No. 605393, Drouin Institute, GenealogyQuebec.com.
2   Application for Admittance to the Sailors' Snug Harbor – Eli Bouchard," 9 October 1877, Sub-Series A: Files, 1869-2005, Sailors' Snug Harbor Records, 1757-2008, SC-0016, SBLL.
3   Powers, Perry F, *A History of Northern Michigan and Its People* (Chicago, Lewis Publishing Company, 1912), 3:1005-06, GB.
4   Hudson Bay Company Servant's Contract for Elie Bouchard, 15 July 1824, HBCA A.32-22 fo. 36; "Servants' Contracts (1780-ca. 1926)," Hudson Bay Company Archives, Archives of Manitoba.
5   Anne F. Hyde, *Born of Lakes and Plains: Mixed-Descent Peoples and the Making of the American West* (New York: W.W. Norton & Co., 2022), 23, 46-47, 88.
6   "York Factory," Hudson Bay Company, accessed 10 April 2024, https://www.hbcheritage.ca/places/forts-posts/york-factory.
7   Hudson Bay Company Servant's Contract for Elie Bouchard, 15 July 1824, HBCA A.32-22 fo. 36; "Servants' Contracts (1780-ca. 1926)," Hudson Bay Company Archives, Archives of Manitoba.
8   Don Bamford, *Freshwater Heritage: A History of Sail on the Great Lakes, 1670-1918* (Toronto: Natural Heritage Books, 2007), 45.
9   Bamford, *Freshwater Heritage*, 172.
10   Bamford, *Freshwater Heritage*, 141-43.
11   Theodore J. Karamanski, *Schooner Passage: Sailing Ships and the Lake Michigan Frontier* (Detroit: Wayne State University Press, 2000), 86.
12   Kathleen Lavey, "Mackinac Island Restores its Native American History," *Lansing State Journal*, 7 March 2017, https://www.lansingstatejournal.com/story/travel/michigan/2017/03/07/restoring-mackinac-islands-native-american-history/98809484/.
13   Brian Leigh Dunnigan, *A Picturesque Situation: Mackinac before Photography, 1615-1860* (Detroit: Wayne State University Press, 2008), 198, 231-32.
14   Alexis de Tocqueville, *Democracy in America* (New York: Library of America, 2004), 885, GB.
15   Marriage Record of Elvi [sic] Bouchard to Josette Champagne, 2 December 1828, Mackinac County, Michigan, County Marriages, 1822-1940, AC.
16   Certificate of Death for Simon Bouschor, 19 July 1916, Reg. No. 35, State of Michigan, Michigan Department of State – Division of Vital Statistics; Bouschor Family Bible, "Marriages, Births, and Deaths," *New Testament* (American Bible Society, 1851).
17   1836 Mixed-Blood Census Register, Transcribed and Compiled by Larry M. Wyckoff, http://sites.rootsweb.com/~mi-macki2/annuities/1836mb.pdf; 1860 U.S. Census, Holmes Township, Michilimackinac County, Michigan, population

schedule, p. 87, dwelling 939, family 546, line 1, Eli Bouchard; George H. Turner, comp., *Record of Service of Michigan Volunteers in the Civil War, 1861–1865* (Kalamazoo: Ihling Bros. & Everard, 1909), 37:22, HT.

18   1836 Mixed-Blood Census Register, Transcribed and Compiled by Larry M. Wyckoff, http://sites.rootsweb.com/~mi-macki2/annuities/1836mb.pdf; 1900 U.S. Census, Naubinway, Mackinac County, Michigan, population schedule, enumeration district 96, sheet 1A, dwelling 4, family 4, lines 13-14, Ramey & Philamon Bouchar; "Ramie Bouchor," *Find A Grave*, indexed database (http://www.findagrave.com : accessed 31 July 2021), Garfield Township Cemetery, Naubinway, Michigan, Memorial No. 8838074; Certificate of Death for Rayme Bouchor, 25 March 1911, Reg. No. 5, State of Michigan, Department of State-Division of Vital Statistics; "State News Items," *Bay City Daily Tribune* (Bay City, MI) 5 April 1911, GenealogyBank.com. Note: Remi's headstone lists his date of birth as 5 September 1832 while his death certificate gives it as 1 October 1833. I have used the date on his headstone in this text as it conforms with other secondary sources.

19   Certificate of Death for Edward A. Bouchard, 17 May 1916, Reg. No. 29, State of Michigan, Department of State - Division of Vital Statistics, AC; Powers, *History of Northern Michigan and Its People*, 3:1005; Powers, *History of Northern Michigan and Its People*, 3:1008; Record of Marriage for Edward A. Bouchard and Julienne C. Metivier, Recorded 24 January 1880, Record No. 6, Return of Marriages in the County of Cheboygan for the Year Ending December 31st, A.D. 1880, State of Michigan, Department of Community Health, Division of Vital Records and Health Statistics, AC; Record of Marriage for Edward A. Bouchard and Carrie A. King, 24 January 1900, Record No. 141, Returns of Marriage in the County of Cheboygan for the Quarter Ending March 31st A.D. 1900, State of Michigan, Department of Community Health, Division of Vital Records and Health Statistics, AC.

20   Baptismal Record for Mary Olive Bouchard, 28 October 1838, File 1832-1843, Page 42, Diocese of Green Bay Archives, Courtesy of Georgia Tillotson; 1900 U.S. Census, Iron Mountain, Dickinson County, Michigan, population schedule, enumeration district 61, sheet 8B, dwelling 114, family 117, line 74-74, Louis & Marie O. Preville; Certificate of Death for Mary Preville, Filed 17 January 1927, Reg. No. 2, State of Wisconsin, Department of Health - Bureau of Vital Statistics, Milwaukee County Register of Deeds.

21   Baptismal Record for Alexis Bouchard, 7 June 1840, File 1832-1843, Page 58, Diocese of Green Bay Archives, Courtesy of Georgia Tillotson.

22   Baptismal Record for Florimond Joseph Bouchard, 19 May 1842, File 1832-1843, Page 89, Diocese of Green Bay Archives, Courtesy of Georgia Tillotson; "Death of Capt. Bouchard," *Green Bay Press-Gazette*, 10 August 1882, Newspapers.com.

23   Baptismal Record for Raphael Oliver Bouchard, 3 February 1844, File 1842-1844, Page 124, Diocese of Green Bay Archives, Courtesy of Georgia Tillotson; Record of Marriage for Oliver R. Bouchard and Josephine Beaudoin, 13 February 1866, AC; Standard Certificate of Death for Oliver R. Bouchard, Filed 14 June 1916, Reg. No. 61, Portland, Oregon, Bureau of Vital Statistics, Oregon State Archives.

24   1830 U.S. Census, Michilimackinac County, Michigan, population schedule, p. 200, Eloi Bouchard.

25   Bamford, *Freshwater Heritage*, 175-76.

26   Karamanski, *Schooner Passage*, 22.

27   Karamanski, *Schooner Passage*, 28-32.

28   Karamanski, *Schooner Passage*, 59-63.

29   Karamanski, *Schooner Passage*, 65-67, 72.

30   Karamanski, *Schooner Passage*, 73.

31   Karamanski, *Schooner Passage*, 78-79.

32   Karamanski, *Schooner Passage*, 82-84.

33   Karamanski, *Schooner Passage*, 85.

34   Karamanski, *Schooner Passage*, 91, 93-95, 189, 192.

35   Karamanski, *Schooner Passage*, 104-07.

36   Bamford, *Freshwater Heritage*, 182.

37   Keith R. Widder, *Battle for the Soul: Métis Children Encounter Evangelical Protestants at Mackinaw Mission, 1823 – 1837* (East Lansing: Michigan State University Press, 1999), n.p., GB.

38   "Mission Church," Mackinac State Historic Parks, 12 February 2021, https://www.mackinacparks.com/historic-mission-church/.

39   Keith R. Widder, *Battle for the Soul: Métis Children Encounter Evangelical Protestants at Mackinaw Mission, 1823 – 1837* (East Lansing: Michigan State University Press), n.p., GB.

40   J. B. Mansfield, *History of the Great Lakes* (Chicago: J. H. Beers & Co., 1899), 1:618, GB.

41   Henry R. Schoolcraft, *Personal Memoirs of a Residence of Thirty Years with the Indian Tribes on the American Frontiers* (Philadelphia: Lippincott, Grambo and Co., 1851), 472, GB.

42   Karamanski, *Schooner Passage*, 45.

43   Pioneer Society of the State of Michigan, *Report of the Pioneer Society of the State of Michigan* (Lansing: W. S. George &

Co., 1884), 6:394, GB.

44   Ruth Craker, "Singing Sands," *Leelanau Enterprise* (Leland, MI), 1 September 1938, DMN.

45   "The Fast Sailing Schooner Supply," *Grand River Times* (Grand Haven, MI), 6 June 1855, CA.

46   "Traverse City," *Grand Traverse Herald* (Traverse City, MI), 2 December 1869, DMN; Eric Freedman, *Michigan Free: Your Comprehensive Guide to Free Travel, Recreation, & Entertainment Opportunities* (Ann Arbor: University of Michigan Press, 1993), 7, GB.

47   United States Army Signal Corps, *Annual Report of the Chief Signal-Office to the Secretary of War for the Year 1876* (Washington, D.C.: Government Printing Office, 1876), 377, GB.

48   "The Grand Traverse Region – Yuba," *Grand Traverse Herald* (Traverse City, MI), 10 July 1890, DMN.

49   1836 Mixed-Blood Census Register, Ottawa and Chippewas of Michigan Treaty of March 28, 1836, Transcribed by Larry M. Wyckoff, http://sites.rootsweb.com/~mimacki2/annuities/1836mb.pdf.

50   Lynn Armitage, "Mackinac Island Finally Telling Native Side of History," *Indian Country Today*, 30 March 2017, https://newsmaven.io/indiancountrytoday/archive/mackinac-island-finally-telling-native-side-of-history-5UI0AK-2BCEm4JEcvJu8ppA/.

51   1836 Mixed-Blood Census Register, Ottawa and Chippewas of Michigan Treaty of March 28, 1836, Transcribed by Larry M. Wyckoff, http://sites.rootsweb.com/~mimacki2/annuities/1836mb.pdf; Florence Meron, *A History of the Township Village and People of Thompson Michigan*, Manistique School and Public Library, Unpublished Manuscript, 2003.

52   Meron, *History of the Township Village and People of Thompson Michigan*.

53   Meron, *History of the Township Village and People of Thompson Michigan*.

54   Powers, *History of Northern Michigan and Its People*, 3:1005.

55   Naturalization Record of Edward Beouchard, Page 72-73, 17 May 1837, District Court of Iowa County, Territory of Wisconsin, FS.

56   "Obituary – Edward D. Beouchard," *Iowa County Democrat* (Mineral Point, IA), 25 March 1881, CA.

57   Karamanski, *Schooner Passage*, 57.

58   "National Register of Historic Places Inventory Nomination Form – Astor Historic Village," Received 26 June 1979, United States Department of the Interior, National Park Service, https://npgallery.nps.gov/NRHP/GetAsset/1869e7ff-201b-4cc3-92de-d2e24c2fa573.

59   Fannie C. Last, "The Astor House," *Green Bay Historical Bulletin* 3.6, November-December 1927, 1-10, GB.

60   Last, "The Astor House."

61   Ella Hoes Neville, Sarah Greene Martin, and Deborah Beaumont Martin, *Historic Green Bay* (Self Published: Green Bay, WI, 1893), 258, Library of Congress.

62   1838 Wisconsin Territorial Census, Astor, Brown County, Wisconsin Territory, Eli Bouchou [sic], BCL.

63   1840 U.S. Census, Brown County, Wisconsin Territory, population schedule, Eli Bouchard, AC.

64   1842 Wisconsin Territorial Census, South Ward, Green Bay, Brown County, Wisconsin, Eli Bouchard, BCL.

65   1846 Wisconsin Territorial Census, Green Bay, Brown County, Wisconsin Territory, Eli Bouchard, BCL.

66   1850 U.S. census, Green Bay (District No. 12), Brown County, Wisconsin, population schedule, p. 51, family 417, line 41, Margaret Shampan [sic], AC.

67   "Stray," *Green Bay Republican* (Green Bay, WI), 24 December 1842; "Stray," *Green Bay Republican*, 31 December 1842.

68   "Democratic Whig Nominations," *Green Bay Republican*, 26 March 1844.

69   "Green Bay Township," *Green Bay Republican*, 9 April 1844.

70   "Sheriff's Sale," *Wisconsin Enquirer* (Madison, WI), 16 September 1840.

71   "Green Bay History," City of Green Bay, accessed 1 February 2019, http://www.ci.green-bay.wi.us/history/1800s.html.

72   Eli Bouchard to Raphael St. Marie Warranty Deed, 2 March 1843.

73   Eli Bouchard Land Patent, homestead Certificate No. 2622, 1 September 1849, BLM GLO.

74   Powers, *A History of Northern Michigan and Its People*, 1005-06; E.A. Bouchard to Thomas Melville, 5 January 1879 [sic], *SUNY Maritime College Maritime Digital Collections*, https://maritimedigitalcollections.com/Detail/objects/5191.

75   Meron, *History of the Township Village and People of Thompson Michigan*.

76   Meron, *History of the Township Village and People of Thompson Michigan*.

77   "Aged Resident Died Wednesday," *Manistique Pioneer-Tribune*, 21 July 1916.

78   1850 U.S. Census, Michilimackinac County, Michigan, population schedule, p. 480, dwelling 546, family 564, line 20, Helie Bouchard, AC.

79   1850 U.S. Census, Michilimackinac County, Michigan, population schedule, p. 460, dwelling 410, family 418, line 37, Eli Bouchard, AC.

80   1850 U.S. Census, Michilimackinac County, Michigan, population schedule, p. 471, dwelling 462, family 472, line 18, Rene Bouchard, AC.

81   Miles Harvey, *The King of Confidence* (New York: Little, Brown and Company, 2020), 120-126.

82   Harvey, *King of Confidence*, 292-93.

83   "Cheboygan Man Relates Fall of Strang's Empire," *Detroit Free Press*, 11 January 1914 (internal quotation marks omitted).

84   "Born on Lakes Sailed 50 Years," *Escanaba Morning Press*, 21 May 1915.

85   Powers, *History of Northern Michigan and Its People*, 1005-06, GB. Note: Powers gives the names of the *Isaac Toucey* as the "Issi Tousey."

86   "Records of the United States Revenue Cutter Service, NARA, last reviewed 11 January 2023, https://www.archives.gov/research/military/coast-guard/revenue-cutter-service.

87   "Erie, 1833," United States Coast Guard, last modified 30 December 2020, https://www.history.uscg.mil/Browse-by-Topic/Assets/Water/All/Article/2459729/erie-1833/.

88   "Ingham, 1849," United States Coast Guard, last modified 30 March 2022, https://www.history.uscg.mil/Browse-by-Topic/Assets/Water/All/Article/2983145/ingham-1849/.

89   "Toucey (Isaac Toucey), 1857," United States Coast Guard, last modified 11 September 2020, https://www.history.uscg.mil/Browse-by-Topic/Assets/Water/All/Article/2344206/toucey-isaac-toucey-1857/.

90   1860 U.S. Census, Holmes Township, Michilimackinac County, Michigan, population schedule, p. 87, dwelling 939, family 546, lines 1-7, Eli Bouchard, AC.

91   1860 U.S. Census, Holmes Township, Michilimackinac County, Michigan, population schedule, p. 88, dwelling 948, family 555, lines 11-13, Remi Bouchard, AC.

92   1860 U.S. Census, Holmes Township, Michilimackinac County, Michigan, population schedule, p. 75, dwelling 827, family 462, lines 1-2, Edward Buchard, AC.

93   1860 U.S. Census, Delta Township, Delta County, Michigan, population schedule, p. 134, dwelling 1282, family 867, lines 37-39, Simon and Harriet Bouchard, AC; 1860 U.S. Census, Delta Township, Delta County, Michigan, population schedule, p. 139, dwelling 1318, family 903, lines 20-21, Mary Olive and Joseph Bouchard, AC.

94   1870 U.S. Census, St. Martin Island, Delta County, Michigan, population schedule, p. 2 (handwritten), dwelling 10, family 10, line 26, Abner Cady, FS.

95   Willis F. Dunbar and George S. May, *Michigan: A History of the Wolverine State*, 3rd Ed. (Grand Rapids: Wm. B. Eerdmans Publishing Co., 1995), 323.

96   Hyde, *Born of Lakes and Plains*, 260.

97   Dunbar and May, *Michigan*, 324; Letter from Brian Russell to Marion Jean Bouchard Perry, undated, FS, shared by Hilary Hinckley; George H. Turner, comp., *Record of Service of Michigan Volunteers in the Civil War, 1861 - 1865* (Kalamazoo: Ihling Bros. & Everard, 1909), 37:5, 22, HT.

98   Mackinac County, Michigan, Deed Book L:149-50 (Eli Bouchard to Joseph Wilmette, Recorded 23 August 1864), FS.

99   Aaron Greeley, *Plan of the Town and Harbor of Michilimacinac, Mackinac Island*, 15 July 1848, Records of the Bureau of Land Management, NAID: 301095564, NARA.

100   1870 U.S. census, Mackinac County, Michigan, population schedule, Holmes Township, p. 8 (handwritten), dwelling 52, family 53, Eli Bouchard, AC.

101   Mackinac County, Michigan, Deed Book M:218-219 (Charles Wachter to Edward Bouchard, Recorded 25 October 1870), FS.

102   Mackinac County, Michigan, Deed Book M:489-90 (Edward A. and Mary E. Bouchard to John McNeal, Recorded 19 February 1873), FS.

103   "Application for Admittance to the Sailors' Snug Harbor – Eli Bouchard," 9 October 1877, Sub-Series A: Files, 1869-2005, Sailors' Snug Harbor Records, 1757-2008, SC-0016, SBLL.

104   "Sailors' Snug Harbor Register and Record of Inmates for Eli Bouchard," Page 941, Sub-Series A: Files, 1869-2005, Sailors' Snug Harbor Records, 1757-2008, SC-0016, SBLL.

105   Karamanski, *Schooner Passage*, 164.

106   Dan Austin, "Marine Hospital," *HistoricDetroit.org*, , accessed 13 October 2022, https://historicdetroit.org/buildings/marine-hospital.

107   Application for Admittance to the Sailors' Snug Harbor – Eli Bouchard," 9 October 1877, Sub-Series A: Files, 1869-2005, Sailors' Snug Harbor Records, 1757-2008, SC-0016, SBLL.

108   Barnett Shepherd, *Sailors' Snug Harbor, 1801-1976* (New York City: Snug Harbor Cultural Center, 1979), 14-15, 18; Louis Bagger, "The Sailors' Snug Harbor," *Harper's New Monthly Magazine* Vol. XLVI, December 1872 to May 1873, 192, Archive.org; Gerald J. Barry, *The Sailors' Snug Harbor: A History* (New York City: Fordham University Press, 2000), xii.

109   Barry, *Sailors' Snug Harbor*, xii.

110   Shepherd, *Sailors' Snug Harbor, 1801-1976*, 16.

111   Bagger, "Sailors' Snug Harbor," 190.

112   Barry, *Sailors' Snug Harbor*, xiii.

113 "Brief History," The Trustees of the Sailors' Snug Harbor in the City of New York, accessed 10 July 2024, https://thesailorssnugharbor.org/brief-history/.

114 "Application for Admittance to the Sailors' Snug Harbor – Eli Bouchard," 9 October 1877, Sub-Series A: Files, 1869-2005, Sailors' Snug Harbor Records, 1757-2008, SC-0016, SBLL.

115 J. W. Weeks & Co., *Annual City Directory of the Inhabitants, Business Firms, Incorporated Companies, etc., of Detroit for 1873-4* (Detroit: J. W. Weeks & Co., 1873), 50, 56, 325, HT.

116 "Names of Persons Admitted and Died in the Sailors Snug Harbor from Sept 24th to Dec 14th 1877," Page 364, *Reports to the Trustees, 1867 - 1878*, SC-0016-III-A-2, Sailors' Snug Harbor Records, 1757-2008, SC-0016, SBLL.

117 Shepherd, *Sailors' Snug Harbor, 1801-1976*, 50.

118 "Application for Admittance to the Sailors' Snug Harbor – Eli Bouchard," 9 October 1877, Sub-Series A: Files, 1869-2005, Sailors' Snug Harbor Records, 1757-2008, SC-0016, SBLL.

119 "Application for Admittance to the Sailors' Snug Harbor – Eli Bouchard," 9 October 1877, Sub-Series A: Files, 1869-2005, Sailors' Snug Harbor Records, 1757-2008, SC-0016, SBLL.

120 Shepherd, *Sailors' Snug Harbor, 1801-1976*, 19-20.

121 Shepherd, *Sailors' Snug Harbor, 1801-1976*, 23, 25.

122 Shepherd, *Sailors' Snug Harbor, 1801-1976*, 23-25.

123 Barry, *Sailors' Snug Harbor*, 83.

124 "Daily Allowance for Each Inmate in Sailors Snug Harbor," *Reports to the Trustees, 1867 - 1878*, SC-0016-III-A-2, Page 242, Sailors' Snug Harbor Records, 1757-2008, SC-0016, SBLL.

125 Shepherd, *Sailors' Snug Harbor, 1801-1976*, 50.

126 Shepherd, *Sailors' Snug Harbor, 1801-1976*, 19.

127 Shepherd, *Sailors' Snug Harbor, 1801-1976*, 25.

128 "Sailors' Snug Harbor Death Report for Eli Bouchard," 25 October 1879, Sub-Series A: Files, 1869-2005, Sailors' Snug Harbor Records, 1757-2008, SC-0016, SBLL; "Town Talk," *Northern Tribune* (Cheboygan, MI), 15 November 1879, CA.

129 "Sailors' Snug Harbor Register and Record of Inmates for Eli Bouchard," Page 941, Sub-Series A: Files, 1869-2005, Sailors' Snug Harbor Records, 1757-2008, SC-0016, SBLL.

130 Barry, *Sailors' Snug Harbor*, 84.

131 "Inquisition into the Death of Eli Bouchard, Sailor," Sub-Series A: Files, 1869-2005, Sailors' Snug Harbor Records, 1757-2008, SC-0016, SBLL.

132 "Facts About the History of St. Peter's R.C. Church on Staten Island," *St. George Civic Association*, accessed 4 July 2022, https://preserve.org/stgeorge/stgeorge.htm.

133 "Sailors' Snug Harbor Death Report for Eli Bouchard," 25 October 1879, Sub-Series A: Files, 1869-2005, Sailors' Snug Harbor Records, 1757-2008, SC-0016, SBLL; *Find A Grave*, indexed database (http://www.findagrave.com : accessed February 9, 2018), Eli Bouchard (1794-1879), Sailors Snug Harbor Cemetery, Staten Island, NY, Memorial No. 178357030.

134 E.A. Bouchard to Thomas Melville, 5 January 1879 [sic], Sailors' Snug Harbor Records, 1757-2008, SC-0016-III-A-1-0143, SBLL. Note: Edward Bouchard's letter appears to be mistakenly dated January 5, 1879, and was likely written in January 1880 as Elie passed away on 25 October 1879.

135 Bouchard to Melville, 5 January 1879.

136 Tom Wrobleski, "Historic Cemetery, Scene of Boozy St. Patrick's Parade Teen Bacchanal, Donated to NYC Parks," *Staten Island Advance*, 7 June 2024, https://www.silive.com/news/2024/06/historic-cemetery-scene-of-boozy-st-patricks-parade-teen-bacchanal-donated-to-nyc-parks.html.

Grandparents of Simon Bouschor

4.   Abel François Alexis Bouchard

Born: 23 August 1767 in Petite-Rivière, Province of Quebec (Petite-Rivière-Saint-François, Capitale-Nationale, Quebec)

Died: 6 February 1833 in Saint-Roch, Lower Canada (Saint-Roch-de-l'Achigan, Lanaudière, Quebec)

5.   Agathe Blanche LeBlanc

Born: Approximately 1768–1770 in Tracadigash, Province of Quebec (Carleton-sur-Mer, Gaspésie–Îles-de-la-Madeleine, Quebec)

Died: 19 December 1854 in Saint-Roch, Province of Canada (Saint-Roch-de-l'Achigan, Lanaudière, Quebec)

Abel François Alexis Bouchard (known as Alexis), the fourth child and fourth son of Louis Bouchard and Marie Françoise Dufour, was born on 23 August 1767 in Petite-Rivière, Province of Quebec (present-day Petite-Rivière-St-François in Quebec's Charlevoix region).[1] Petite-Rivière was the birthplace of Alexis' father, Louis Bouchard, and the childhood home of his grandfather, Antoine Bouchard. Alexis' great-grandparents, Claude Bouchard and Louise Gagne, were two of Petite-Rivière's first French settlers in 1675. A deeper discussion of Petite-Rivière's founding is contained in the section detailing their lives.

Agathe Blanche LeBlanc,[*] the fifth child and third daughter of Pierre Benjamin LeBlanc and Marie Dugas, was born around 1768 to 1770 in Tracadigash, Province of Quebec (present-day Carleton-sur-Mer, Quebec, on the Gaspé Peninsula's Chaleur Bay). A group of Acadians that included Agathe's parents who had been expelled from Acadia and were temporarily living in nearby Bonaventure came to Tracadigash in approximately 1766. Tracadigash, also known as Tracadièche, comes from a Mi'kmaq Indian name meaning "place where there are herons." Around twenty-five families, led by Charles Dugas and Benjamin LeBlanc, settled the traditionally-Mi'kmaq territory on the Baie des Chaleurs.[2] Tracadigash's name was later changed to Carleton in 1787 after American Loyalists settled in the area. Finally, on 4 October 2000, Carleton and the neighboring community of Saint-Omer merged into the united community of Carleton–Saint-Omer, which morphed into the present-day name of Carleton-sur-Mer five years later.[3]

Alexis and Agathe were married on 17 May 1790 in Carleton, Province of Quebec, at Sainte Anne de Restigouche Catholic Church by the Acadian-born parish priest Father Joseph Mathurin Bourg. Agathe's father, Benjamin LeBlanc, and her siblings, Luc LeBlanc and Désiré LeBlanc, all witnessed the marriage ceremony.[4] Alexis and Agathe's first three children were born in Carleton in the early 1790s and baptized by Father Bourg. Alexis also acted as a witness at his older brother Joseph Bouchard's 24 September 1793 marriage to Emerentienne Tremblay in Petite-Rivière. It's not known what brought Alexis Bouchard from Petite-Rivière to Carleton.

Alexis and Agathe had twelve children:

   i.   **Alexandre Bouchard**, b. Carleton, Province of Quebec, 17 November 1791; d. Unknown[5]
   ii.   **Marie Olivette Bouchard**, b. Carleton, Lower Canada, 30 December 1792; m. Louis Du-

---

*   The LeBlanc surname is sometimes written as "Leblanc" or "Le Blanc." This volume uses the LeBlanc variant for consistency except in direct quotes utilizing an alternative version.

rant, Carleton, Lower Canada, 28 October 1811; d. Saint-Jean-sur-Richelieu, Montérégie, Quebec, Canada, 26 February 1848[6]

iii.   **Elie A. Bouchard**, b. Carleton, Lower Canada, 13 September 1794; m. Josette Champagne, Michilimackinac Island, Michilimackinac County, Michigan Territory, 2 December 1828; d. Staten Island, Richmond County, New York, 25 October 1879[7]

iv.   **Pascal Bouchard**, b. Carleton, Lower Canada, 26 March 1796; d. Carleton, Lower Canada, 10 June 1797[8]

v.   **Marie Constance Bouchard**, b. Carleton, Lower Canada, 15 June 1798; m. Charles Courteau, Carleton, Lower Canada, 30 October 1819; d. Carleton, Lower Canada, 8 Septem 1872[9]

vi.   **Joseph Bouchard**, b. Carleton, Lower Canada, 4 November 1799; d. Carleton, Lower Canada, 8 May 1807[10]

vii.   **Théotiste Bouchard**, b. Carleton, Lower Canada, 12 June 1801; d. Carleton, Lower Canada, 13 May 1802[11]

viii.   **François Xavier Bouchard**, b. Carleton, Lower Canada, 14 March 1803; d. Carleton, Lower Canada, 21 August 1809[12]

ix.   **Édouard Benjamin Bouchard**, b. Carleton, Lower Canada, 12 October 1804; m. Sarah Ann Holmes, Mineral Point, Iowa County, Wisconsin, 10 March 1852; d. Mineral Point, Iowa County, Wisconsin, 22 March 1881[13]

x.   **Théotiste Bouchard**, b. Carleton, Lower Canada, 3 January 1807; m. Louis Archambault, Carleton, Lower Canada, 26 November 1832; d. Unknown[14]

xi.   **Leon Bouchard**, b. Carleton, Lower Canada, 5 April 1811; m. Armeline d'Odet d'Orsonnens, Carleton, Lower Canada, 23 November 1840; d. Unknown[15]

xii.   **Zaïde Bouchard**, b. Carleton, Lower Canada, 2 April 1813; d. Carleton, Lower Canada, 11 May 1814[16]

Sometime between 1794 and 1796, the family relocated from Carleton on the Gaspé Peninsula to Saint-Roch (Saint-Roch-de-l'Achigan), as Elie's younger brother Pascal Bouchard was born in Saint-Roch in approximately May 1796. Saint-Roch is a small community located in Quebec's Lanaudière administrative region northeast of Montreal on the Achigan River. Saint-Roch was settled in the 1770s, and the parish of Saint-Roch-de-l'Achigan was formed in 1787, a few years prior to the Bouchard family's arrival. While the community was originally known simply as Saint-Roch, the municipality renamed itself Saint-Roch-de-l'Achigan in 1957 to distinguish the community from other towns and regions also bearing the name Saint-Roch.[17]

Alexis held several occupations while the family lived in Saint-Roch. The 10 June 1797 burial record for their son Pascal, 15 June 1798 baptismal record for their daughter Marie Constance, and 12 June 1801 baptismal record for their daughter Théotiste all list Alexis' occupation as *menusier*, or carpenter. However, by the 14 May 1802 burial record for Théotiste, Alexis' occupation is listed as *aubergiste de cette paroisse* (innkeeper of this parish), and the following year as *marchand de cette paroisse* (merchant of this parish) in their son François Xavier's baptismal record. However, by the time of their daughter Théotiste's birth (the second Théotiste) on 3 January 1807, his occupation is listed as *cultivateur* or farmer. In 1809, upon the death of his son François, Alexis' occupation is listed as *chantre et bédeau* (cantor and beadle), and again in the 1811 baptismal record for his child Theo. The same is listed for the baptismal and burial records of their youngest child, Zaïde, dated 2 April 1813 and 12 May 1814, respectively.[18] In his capacity with the church, Alexis signed many of the burial records for the Saint-Roch parish indicating his presence at the interment. Many of these records are likewise signed by his friend Jean Noel Labreque. The beadle, or bedeau, assisted the priest in maintaining, cleaning, and operating the church,

A view of the Saint-Roch presbytery and Catholic church where Alexis served as the church's cantor and beadle — Built in 1803, the church burned down in 1958 and was replaced by the present-day structure, but the presbytery remains in place

A 1922 view of Saint-Roch's main street with the church in the background

and often worked as the churchyard gravedigger.[19]

The 1825 Census of Lower Canada lists Alexis as living in Saint-Roch (Leinster District, St. Henri de Maskouche Subdistrict) in a family consisting of one married male between forty and sixty years of age, one married female over forty-five, and one unmarried female between fourteen and forty-five.[20] In addition to Alexis and Agathe, the third member of the family was likely their youngest surviving daughter, Théotiste, as she was approximately eighteen at the time of the census.

Six years later, the 1831 Census of Lower Canada reflects that Alexis continued to live in Saint-Roch in a family consisting of one married male over the age of sixty, one married female over the age of forty-five, one unmarried female between the ages of fourteen and forty-five, and one child under the age of five. As Théotiste did not marry until the following year, she is again likely the unmarried female mention. The 1831 census record lists Alexis's occupation as *tonnelier*, which translates to cooper in English.[21]

In 1832, Saint-Roch was part of the L'Assomption seigniory of Lachenaie County. It numbered 1,036 inhabitants with a church and two schools—along with six taverns. In the same year, Joseph Bouchette observed of Saint-Roch that it "occupies the centre of the fief, its handsome church and a few well-built houses round it are seated on a beautiful and well-chosen pot in a bend of the R. Achigan."[22]

Three months prior to Alexis' death, their youngest daughter, Théotiste, married Louis Archambault in Saint-Roch. The marriage record reflects that Alexis was still the *chantre de la paroisse* (cantor of the parish). Alexis died on 6 February 1833 at the age of sixty-five in Saint-Roch and was buried two days later in the Saint-Roch-de-l'Achigan parish churchyard cemetery.[23]

Agathe outlived Alexis by over twenty-one years before passing away in Saint-Roch on 19 December 1854 at the age of eighty-four. She was buried the following day in the Saint-Roch-de-l'Achigan churchyard cemetery.[24]

6.   Simon Champagne

Born: 21 March 1765 in Montreal, Province of Quebec (Montreal, Montreal, Quebec)
Died: 10 May 1852 on Mackinac Island, Mackinac County, Michigan

7.   Te Pi Ma Guain (Marguerite Champagne)

Born: Approximately 1780, likely on Michilimackinac Island, Province of Quebec (Mackinac Island, Mackinac County, Michigan)
Died: Approximately 1850 in Wisconsin

Simon Champagne was born Simon Marmotte to parents Nicolas Noël Marmotte dit Champagne[†] and Marie Geneviève Bissonnette the morning of 21 March 1765 in Montreal, Province of Quebec, shortly after the Treaty of Paris awarded France's Canadian colonies to Great Britain. He was baptized the same day in the Montreal parish, likely in the old Notre Dame Church, with Simon Audin Rochefort and Therese Bissonet serving as godparents.[25] Simon likely grew up in Montreal, and he served as a witness at the 31 March 1788 wedding of his younger sister Marie Josephe Marmotte to her husband, Jacques Rouillard, at Montreal.[26] He eventually made his way to the Great Lakes region

---

[†]   A "dit name" is an alternative family name frequently used to denote a place of origin, profession, or other distinguishing characteristic in French families. Dit names were frequently used to distinguish between different families sharing the same surname. In this case, Nicolas Noël's surname was Marmotte, but his dit name was Champagne, almost certainly in honor of his home region in France. His son Simon's baptismal record likewise lists his surname as "Marmotte."

and Mackinac Island, where he would spend the rest of his life.

A Simon Champagne of "La Cote des Anges" is referenced as working as an *engagé* for merchant Toussaint Pothier in 1803. Pothier was originally from Montreal and worked as an agent of the Michilimackinac Company and later the South West Fur Company out of Mackinac Island in the first decades of the 1800s.[27]

Simon came to Michilimackinac Island sometime before July 1799. Edwin Orin Wood's *Historic Mackinac* gives a picture of Michilimackinac Island around the time of Simon's arrival via the description of Major Caleb Swan, who arrived in August 1796 as part of the island's transition from British to American control:

> On the south side of the Island, there is a small bason [sic], of a segment of a circle, serving as an excellent harbour for vessels of any burden, and for canoes. Around this bason the village is built, having two streets of nearly a mile in length, a Roman chapel, and containing eighty-nine houses and stores; some of them spacious and handsome, with white lime plastering in front, which shews to great advantage the sea. At one end and in the rear of the town, is an elegant government house, of immense size, and finished with great taste. . . . The fort, the village, the neighbouring islands and channels seem prostrated at your feet; while, to the south-west, you look in the immensity of Lake Michigan, which loses itself in the southern hemisphere; and, to the north-west, the great Lake Huron lies expanded to the bounds of the horizon. It was a beautiful morning when I had this view.[28]

The "Roman chapel" referenced in Major Swan's recollections is almost certainly Ste. Anne Catholic Church, which remains an island landmark to this day. The Mackinac Island parish records reflect that on 20 July 1799, Simon made his mark on a baptismal register as godfather to Henry McGulpin, son of Patrice McGulpin and Madeline Crequé. The baptismal record reflects Simon could not sign his name. Simon also witnessed the marriage of Jacques Jauvan and Angelique Roy, and that of Charles Marly and Josephe Vaillancourt, both held on 16 July 1804 on Mackinac Island before Father J. Dilhet.[29]

Michilimackinac Land Claim

Simon came to own over 150 acres of land on Mackinac Island. An 1828 survey of private claims for the island, reproduced on the following page, depicts a substantial section of land totaling 157 acres on the western edge of the island, surrounded by U.S. government-owned land.[30] On maps, including those created long after the acreage passed out of Simon's hands, the parcel is known as Private Claim No. 2 or Sunset Forest.

It took Simon over two decades to establish full title to this acreage. Although the British had purchased Mackinac Island from the Ojibwa in 1781 (thereby extinguishing Native American title to formerly Indian lands), considerable doubt over title to individual parcels vexed American officials, owing in part to "extremely loose" transaction records and poor descriptions.[31] President Jefferson appointed a commission in 1804 to adjudicate land claims in Michigan Territory, including those on Mackinac Island. These land boards allowed residents to register claims. One such board was established at Detroit, and efforts to clarify ownership resulted in several maps of Mackinac Island and the village.[32] A survey created in 1810 by Michigan Deputy Surveyor Aaron Greeley showing island claims outside the village depicts the land largely corresponding with that of Simon Champagne as being claimed by David Mitchell (a former British army surgeon and trader). Mitchell likewise claimed a similar parcel of 122.73 acres on the south side of the island (site of the present-day Grand Hotel Golf Course), while Michael Dousman claimed 200 acres on the island's north end.[33] Mitchell's putative claim for Simon's parcel noted that he maintained a small house on the land along with planted acres of turnips and

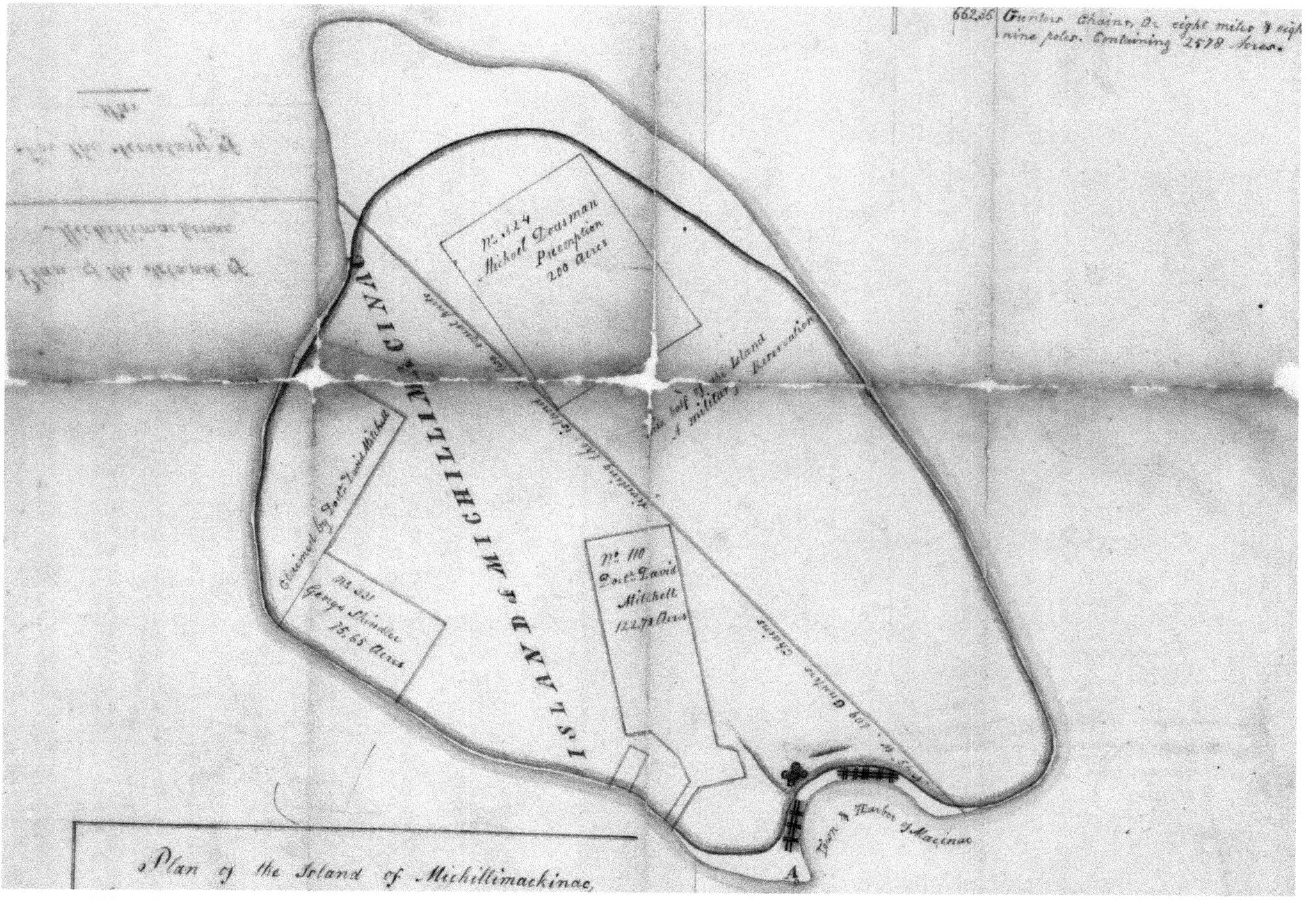

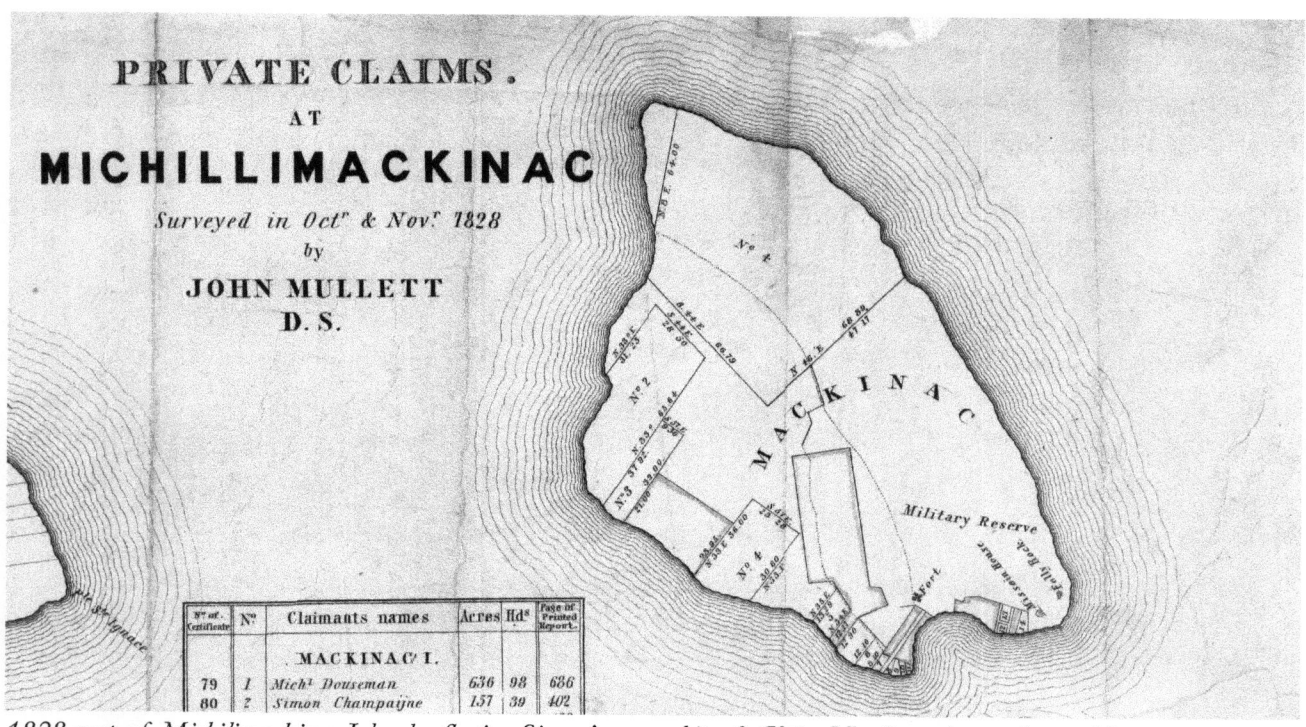

1810 Aaron Greeley plan of Michilimackinac Island showing Simon Champagne's future parcel on the island's southwest side and listed as claimed by David Mitchell

1828 map of Michilimackinac Island reflecting Simon's ownership of Claim No. 2 on the southwest side

potatoes, but the land board ultimately rejected Mitchell's claim.[34] Mitchell later rejoined the British army and assisted with the British capture of Fort Michilimackinac on 17 July 1812. Following conclusion of hostilities in 1815, Mitchell permanently left Mackinac Island for nearby Drummond Island while his wife, Elizabeth, remained behind to manage their extensive estate.[35]

On 11 December 1805, Simon filed a land claim with the Commissioners of the Detroit Land Office. In 1810, he appeared before the Commissioners of the Land Office in Detroit regarding to claimed land. Joseph Numainville testified on Simon's behalf that "on the 1st July, 1796, Jean Baptiste Gatien was in possession and occupancy of the premises, and continued so until he sold to the claimant, who has constantly occupied the same to this day: a dwelling house is erected thereon." The commissioners approved Simon's claim and ordered that he conduct a survey of the land and file a plot with the Register of the Land Office at Detroit.[36] Simon also testified as a witness regarding numerous other land claims on Michilimackinac Island. The Detroit Land Office ultimately issued Simon Certificate No. 703 on 3 July 1812, granting him title to 3,563 square feet of land on Mackinac Island, described as follows:

> Beginning on a line between this lot and a lot confirmed to Dominick Rousseau; thence North twenty seven degree thirty five minutes east fifty five feet, to the South line of a lot confirmed to Pierre Lacroix; thence South sixty four degrees East, fifty two feet, one tenth of a foot to a lane; thence South fourteen degrees west, fifty six feet, two tenths of a foot to a lane; thence North sixty four degrees West, sixty five feet, five tenths of a foot to the place of beginning: There is granted by the United States unto the said Simon Champagne, the tract, or parcel of land above described; to have and to hold, the said tract or parcel of land, with the appurtenances, unto the said Simon Champagne, his heirs and assigns.[37]

Simon's land claims continued into the next decade. On 21 February 1823, congress enacted another law striving to address the conundrum of land ownership on Mackinac Island. The act provided for another commission to adjust land claims in Michigan Territory and established a 1 October 1823 deadline for claimants to file a petition. To obtain confirmation of title, the commission required a claimant to establish two things: "that he should have occupied the land claimed on July 1, 1812; the other, that he should have continued to submit to the authority of the United States." The 1 July 1812 date was notable, as the 1807 land act required a showing of occupancy beginning in 1796.[38]

Accordingly, in 1823, Simon entered a claim "to a tract of land on the island of Mackinac, commencing on the border of the lake, running southerly or westerly 65 chains 64 links to a post, and fronting on the lake nine acres; running northerly thereabouts, containing about two hundred acres; on the north line running easterly; on the east line running southerly by public lands." On 31 July 1823, Morrice Montaigne, Ambrose R. Davenport, and Jeane Bt. Tesserron appeared before Judge J. D. Doty sitting at Mackinac and testified that Simon occupied and cultivated the described tract "mentioned in the annexed notice of claims during the years 1811, 1812, and 1813," and that Simon "had a very considerable field enclosed and under cultivation" and was occupying the lot on 1 July 1812. The commissioners issued an order on 28 October 1823 determining Simon "be confirmed in a tract not to contain more than the quantity claimed, (two hundred acres,) nor to extend more than eighty arpents from the shore of the lake, nor so far from said lake as to interfere with other claims, comprehending, however, the ground occupied and cultivated by the claimant on the 1st of July, 1812."[39] John Mullett's survey of Mackinac Island begun on 13 October 1828 and completed on 15 November 1828 depicts parcels claimed as private property on Mackinac Island and likewise confirmed the boundaries of Simon Champagne's Private Claim No. 2. Copies of Mullett's survey were sent to the General Land Office in Washington, D.C.[40]

Simon's Private Claim No. 2 remained in his and Margaret's possession until 1830. On 26 February 1830 at Holmes Township, they executed a deed conveying the parcel of land to Michael Dousman, a pioneer fur trader and merchant. The parcel was described as: "Lot Number Two, beginning at the Border of Lake Huron bounded on the west line of Lot Number Three confirmed to François Louisgnon, thence north thirty three Degrees east sixty five chains and sixty four links to a post, thence north forty four degrees west twenty eight chains and fifty links to a post, thence south thirty three degrees west thirty one chains and twenty five links to a fur tree on the border of the Lake, thence along the border of said Lake to the place of beginning." The deed conveying the land to Dousman was recorded on 1 November 1830 at five o'clock.[41]

Michael Dousman was one of the largest private landowners on Mackinac Island, and the Champagne land only added to a parcel comprising nearly the island's entire northwest quarter. Historian Edwin Orin Wood later observed, "No plat of ground in America has more romantic, picturesque or historic associations. Over its fields the Indians, French, English, and Americans have trod. Here the British crossed in 1812, when they captured Fort Mackinac. Here the memorable Battle of Mackinac Island took place, and the life blood of brave soldiers was spilled. On this farm are some of the most interesting natural curiosities in the entire country. The farms are now owned by the Early brothers, worthy members of a fine family connected with some of the leading citizens of Michigan."[42]

Mackinac Island Private Claim No. 2 later came into the possession of Jacob A.T. Wendell. There apparently remained some question regarding title to the property, for in 1879 two of Simon Champagne's heirs executed quitclaim deeds conveying their interest in the property to Wendell. Raphael Oliver Bouchard and his wife Josephine conveyed their interest in Private Claim No. 2 to Wendell for $15 via a quitclaim deed executed on 4 March 1879.[43]

Similarly, on 2 April 1879, Raphael's older brother Edward A. Bouchard—listed as "one of the heirs of the late Simon Champaigne [sic]"—executed a quitclaim deed conveying all his interest in Private Claim No. 2 to Wendell, also in exchange for $15.[44]

Simon's 150-acre Mackinac Island land eventually passed into ownership of Cudahy Packing Company founder Michael Cudahy, who built a mansion named Stonecliffe on the grounds. The mansion and surrounding grounds are today operated as the Inn at Stonecliffe.[45] This land comprises the community governed by the Sunset Forest Association, an organization dedicated to "protecting the unique character of Sunset Forest as a private Mackinac Island community."[46] The remaining portion of Simon's former land is dominated by the Grand Hotel's Woods back nine golf course, designed by Jerry Matthews and opened to the public in 1994.

Te Pi Ma Guain and the Odawa People

By the early 1800s, Simon started a family with an Odawa Indian woman, Te Pi Ma Guain.[‡] Scant verifiable information is available regarding Te Pi Ma Guain, who later adopted the name Marguerite. As she went by Marguerite Champagne or Shampine later in life, this work will refer to her as Marguerite, except where otherwise indicated. It's believed she was born in approximately 1780, likely on Michilimackinac Island or in the vicinity of present-day Sault Sainte Marie in what was then the British-controlled Province of Quebec. Marguerite belonged to the Odawa people of Mackinac Island.

The Odawa, also known as the Ottawa, belong to the Algonquian language family and lived in the Mackinac Straits area of northern Michigan and the nearby islands, including Mackinac Island. They called themselves the O-dah-wah or Adawa, rendered as Outaoucas by the French, which later morphed into the current "Ottawa" or "Odawa" in use today. The most widely accepted meaning of their name, as put forth by William Warren, is

---

‡   Historian Virgil J. Vogel noted that most Indians were not accorded a given name at birth, but later received a suitable name based on his or her accomplishments or personal characteristics. Dr. Vogel further observed that a name could change later in one's life. *See* Virgil J. Vogel, *Indian Names in Michigan* (Ann Arbor: The University of Michigan Press, 1986), 27.

"trading people." This stems from their long-time role as a go-between for white traders and other Indian groups living in the area.[47] While Indians are estimated to have lived in the northern Great Lakes region for approximately 12,000 years, the Odawa and the Ojibwe originally lived in eastern Canada near the Saint Lawrence River. Around the sixteenth century they migrated west towards the Great Lakes region following raids by Iroquois tribes.[48] The predecessors to the Ojibwa, Odawa, and Pottawatomi lived during the Late Woodland Period (800 CE to 1600 CE) and are believed to be the first peoples to have established lakeside fishing villages around the Upper Peninsula and western Ontario during the summer months.[49]

Upon the arrival of the first French explorers to the Great Lakes region in the 1600s, the Odawa numbered approximately 3,000 individuals. Jesuit priests encountered large communities in the mid-1600s when they arrived in the region seeking converts.[50] At the time Samuel Champlain, and later Jean Nicolet, first encountered the Odawa people in the summer of 1615, they initially called them the Cheveaux Releves (owing to their roached hair) or the Courtes Oreilles (short ears).[51] The Odawa were allied with the Huron people and comprised four groups or bands: Outaouosinigouek (black squirrel people), Kichkagoueiak (cut-tail or bear people), Negaouichiriniouek (people of the sandy beach), and Nassaauaketon (people of the fork).[52] While the French tended to identify them as a single group—the Odawa—the people themselves recognized the importance of the four distinct groups united by a common language and shared interests.[53] For residences, the Odawa built dwellings comprised of saplings that were then covered with bark and skins to form dome-like structures.[54]

The combined impact of disease introduced by European settlers and war with the Five Nations Iroquois in the 1640s disrupted the Huron Confederacy and displaced both the Huron and Odawa tribes from their homelands on the eastern shore of Lake Huron and present-day Ontario, initially pushing them west to the Straits of Mackinac by 1651. However, continued conflict with the Iroquois fur-

Habit of an Ottawa an Indian . Nation of N. America

Indien de la Nation Ottawa dans l'Amerique septentrional.

297

Depiction of an Odawa Indian in the mid-1700s

ther displaced them, first to the present-day Green Bay area, then northward to Chequamagon Bay on Lake Superior by 1660. After a ten-year period on the bay, some Odawa returned to the Straits of Mackinac in 1671 when Jesuit missionaries established the mission at St. Ignace while others went to Manitoulin Island. Their motivation for relocating was in part due to the proximity of Dakota Indians and harsh weather on Lake Superior, whereas the straits provided better access.[55] Although some Odawa and other tribes followed the French when they abandoned Fort de Buade for the newly established Fort Pontchartrain du Detroit around 1697, others remained in Michilimackinac.[56] Even though both Huron and Odawa lived at Michilimackinac near the Jesuit mission and Fort de Buade, they maintained separate and distinct villages, with both tribes engaging in fishing and hunting, as well as growing limited crops during the growing season.[57]

The Odawa people formed a close relationship with the French, and their alliance and trading history remains storied. The Odawa and other Anishinaabe peoples welcomed several technological advances, such as guns and household items made from iron and tailored cloth. Other European introductions, such as Christianity and the concept of private property, remained foreign and never completely took hold.[58] Regarding the religious beliefs of the Odawa, Jesuit Priest Claude-Jean Allouez observed in the paternalistic tone of his time and station:

> There is here a false and abominable religion, resembling in many respects the belies of some of the ancient Pagans. The savages of these regions recognize no sovereign master of Heaven and Earth, but believe there are many spirits—some of whom are beneficent, as the Sun, the Moon, the Lake, the Rivers, and Woods; others malevolent, as the adder, the dragon, cold, and storms. And, in general, whatever seems to them either helpful or hurtful they call a Manitou, and pay it the worship and veneration which we render only to the true God.[59]

Father Allouez goes on to detail the practices of animal sacrifice to appease the Manitous and other ceremonies to ensure a hearty fishing catch.[60]

While the Odawa initially acknowledged the transfer of sovereignty over the Great Lakes area to the British in 1763 following the French and Indian War, a change in practices from those formerly observed under the French resulted in dissatisfaction with the British. Under the guise of a friendly game of lacrosse, Ojibwa and Odawa living in the vicinity of Fort Michilimackinac launched a wide-scale assault on the fort on 4 July 1763, resulting in seventy British deaths and numerous prisoners taken. An alliance spearheaded by Odawa chief Pontiac rebelled against the British, resulting in a favorable treaty in 1765.[61]

Michilimackinac was an important location to the Odawa and other tribes in the region. The Natives established seasonal villages around the straits and island.[62] These summer villages typically comprised between 50 and 75 people and featured houses made from birchbark sheets that covered bent saplings.

The inhabitants frequently planted small gardens and devoted considerable energy to processing and smoking the fish caught through with gill nets. The village would last until the weather turned cold in fall and families dispersed inland where game was easier to obtain.[63]

A visitor to Mackinac Island, Ann Jameson, recorded her observations of a visit to an Odawa village in 1837:

> Though all these lodges seem nearly alike to a casual observer, I was soon aware of differences and gradations in the particular arrangements, which are amusingly characteristic of the various inhabitants. There is one lodge, a little to the east of us, which I call the Chateau. It is rather larger and loftier than the others: the mats which cover it are whiter and of a neater texture than usual. The blanket which hangs before the opening is new and clean. The inmates, ten in number, are well and handsomely dressed; even the women and children have abundance of ornaments; and as for the gay cradle of the baby, I quite covet it—it is so gorgeously elegant. I supposed at first that this must be the lodge of a chief; but I have since understood that the chief is seldom either so well lodged or so well dressed as the others, it being a part of his policy to avoid everything like ostentation, or rather to be ostentatiously poor and plain in his apparel and possessions. This wigwam belongs to an Ottawa, remarkable for his skill in hunting, and for his habitual abstinence from the "fire-water." He is a baptized Roman Catholic, belonging to the mission at Arbre Croche, and is reputed a rich man.
>
> Not far from this, and almost immediately in front of our house, stands another wigwam, a most wretched concern. The owners have not mats enough to screen them from the weather; and the bare poles are exposed through the "looped and windowed raggedness" on every side. The woman, with her

long neglected hair, is always seen cowering despondingly over the embers of her fire, as if lost in sad reveries. Two naked children are scrambling among the pebbles on the shore. The man wrapt in a dirty ragged blanket, without a single ornament, looks the image of savage inebriety and ferocity. Observe that these are the two extremes, and that between them are many gradations of comfort, order, and respectability. An Indian is respectable in his own community, in proportion as his wife and children look fat and well fed; this being a proof of his prowess and success as a hunter, and his consequent riches.[64]

Despite living under the succession of French, British, and American rule throughout most of the seventeenth and eighteenth centuries, the Odawa did not formally relinquish their claim on the Michilimackinac region, including Mackinac Island, until ceding the territory to the United States via the Treaty of Greenville on 3 August 1795 following negotiations over the course of that summer held in Greenville, Ohio.[65] It was the first treaty between the United States and tribes of the Upper Great Lakes region. The treaty itself between the Odawa, eleven other tribes, and the United States framed the cession as follows:

The post of Michilimackinac, and all the land on the island on which that post stands, and the main land adjacent, of which the Indian title has been extinguished by gifts or grants to the French or English governments; and a piece of land on the main to the north of the island, to measure six miles, on lake Huron, or the strait between

An Ottawa indian village on the shore of Mackinac Island in approximately 1842

115

lakes Huron and Michigan, and to extend three miles back from the water of the lake or strait; and also, the Island De Bois Blanc, being an extra and voluntary gift of the Chippewa nation.[66]

Although treaties tended to be negotiated amongst various tribes, it was the local band comprising multiple families of Indians that was key to decision-making within the Indian community itself. As a result, when it came time to execute a treaty, multiple individuals representing each distinct band of Indians needed to sign in order to bind a given band.[67]

While many Indians had converted to Catholicism, Father Gabriel Richard observed "a profound indifference to religion" during a 1799 visit and noted the deleterious effects of alcohol on the Odawa people.[68] The American government likewise recognized the negative influence of alcohol on the Native inhabitants and attempted to control and curtail the problem by implementing what was called the Factory System in 1802. The Factory System created an exclusive system of government-operated trading posts in the upper Great Lakes. Due to an inability to achieve complete control of trade—and with liquor and other goods still flowing courtesy of the Northwest, Mackinac, and American fur companies—the U.S. government abandoned the Factory System in 1822.[69]

Around the time Simon met Marguerite at the turn of the century, the Odawa population around the Great Lakes numbered around 4,000 according to an estimate by North West Company officials.[70] Mackinac Island remained central to the lives of many Odawa even after the Treaty of Greenville. In 1808, the United States established an Indian factory—one of the exclusive trading houses operated by the government for trade with Indians—on Mackinac Island.[71] Natives, including the Odawa, established summer camps on the island. The presence of the Indian agency and proximity of the island to other locales made it attractive.[72]

During the early years of the nineteenth century,

Michigan's Indians—including the Odawa—played a vital role in trade and the relationship between the British and American forces vying for control of the region. However, the 1815 Treaty of Ghent formally resolving the War of 1812 resulted in undisputed American control over Michigan. The decline of the fur trade and amelioration of the critical role Indians played in facilitating trade significantly lessened Indian influence over the region.[73]

While many Michigan Indians experienced deportation west to places like Kansas and Oklahoma, many of the Odawa and Chippewa of Lake Superior avoided this fate. The strategic value of the Michilimackinac region gave the Odawa and Ojibwe people of the region considerable leverage in negotiations with Europeans. Cession negotiations in Sault Ste. Marie between representatives of the United States represented by Lewis Cass and Henry Rowe Schoolcraft and Ojibwa tribal leaders in 1820 demonstrated that the balance of the region's territory belonged to the Ojibwa people and that negotiation between the tribes and the United States government would be necessary for any transfer of sovereignty from one to the other.[74]

However, between the execution of the 1820 Sault Ste. Marie Treaty and 1836, the non-Native population in Michigan Territory swelled dramatically from 8,765 to 174,543.[75] This increase put considerable pressure on territory retained by the Native inhabitants from settlers entering northern Michigan and the Upper Peninsula from lower Michigan. As a result, the Odawa and Ojibwa bands entered into negotiations with the United States government in Washington, D.C. The resulting Treaty of Washington was signed on 28 March 1836 and ratified by the United States Senate on 27 May 1836—with considerable unilateral changes that hadn't been agreed to in negotiations. The Odawa and Ojibwa only agreed to the subsequent changes under threat from Henry Schoolcraft that the money and goods due under the treaty would be withheld absent Indian acquiescence.[76]

The 1836 Treaty of Washington awarded payment to Josette Bouchard and several of her children and likewise reserved 142,000 acres in Northern Michigan and the Upper Peninsula. While the Treaty of Washington purported to be between the United States and the "Ottawa and Chippewa Nation," in execution it included multiple bands of Odawa and Ojibwa Indians from across the region.[77] While they would later lose much of this land following changes in government policy, including recission of the extensive reservations promised by the treaty as negotiated, the effects of the treaty allowed many Indians to remain in the area, where their descendants live to this day.[78] The 1836 Treaty also provided for mixed-descent families, in recognition of their influence resulting from fur trade connections.[79]

A subsequent treaty entered into in 1854 between the U.S. government and the Sault Ste. Marie, L'Anse, and La Pointe bands of Ojibwe Indians prevented removal of their tribal members and avoided the fate suffered by so many other tribes forced to move long distances south and west from their ancestral homelands.[80] As a result, many Odawa still call Michigan home, though Odawa reservations were created in Kansas and northeastern Oklahoma owing to removal policies.

Simon's child, Simon Junior, appears in the 1908 Durant Roll of Chippewa and Ottawa Indians, which stated the following about his mother:

> The mother of Simon Champaign [sic] was an Indian of the Ottawa and Chippewa tribe of the Mackinaw Band; Simon says she died before 1870, that he used to draw with his mother; that his father was a Frenchman; Simon's mother was a cousin of wife of Chief Kesis, of the Nahma sub-band; his mother also had an allotment of land near Mackinaw Island.[81]

At the time of Marguerite's birth and through the first half of the nineteenth century, Native Americans comprised the majority of Mackinac Island's residents. Another Mackinac Island resident and contemporary of Marguerite Champagne, Agatha Biddle, is illustrative. Ms. Biddle was of mixed French, Odawa, and Ojibwe heritage, and while she identified as Odawa, her ancestry gave her an immense familial network through the region.[82] The kinship between a European and an Odawa woman further bonded the European to the Odawa's allies, the Ojibwe and the Huron in the region.[83] As a result, the Metis of Mackinac Island formed a large and powerful community of multi-racial individuals—both male and female—with its members exerting considerable control over the island's affairs.[84] Agatha Biddle and Magdelaine La Framboise are examples of powerful Metis woman who left a profound and indelible influence on the island.

Central to the Anishinaabe way of life was the concept of kinship, whether through blood relationship or adoption into the family.[85] Relationships between Ojibwe women, other Indian tribes, fur traders, and European settlers in the Great Lakes region were crucial in building alliances with allies in the region. The children born to mixed-blood marriages cemented alliances between maternal clans, and annual feast ceremonies served as opportunities to renew these alliances and pay homage to the ancestors.[86]

Relationships between French fur traders and Indian women in the Great Lakes had long occurred following the arrival of Europeans to the region, but a French minister issued an edict in the late 1600s officially encouraging intermarriage with local tribes, as nearly a quarter of all French colonists had moved into the fur trade seeking riches.[87] Many of the voyageurs not only lived amongst the Ojibwa, Huron, and Odawa, but adopted Indian dress, customs, and lifestyle. Both Indian and French inhabitants attained a high degree of fluency in Ojibwa and/or Odawa as well as French.[88] Indeed, religious leader James J. Strang, in his *Ancient and Modern Michilimackinac*, noted that the region's French settlers were "a mixed race, partaking more of the Indian than the European."[89]

The Jay Treaty of 1807 resulted in residents of the Great Lakes region gaining U.S. citizenship.[90] It's possible Marguerite and her children would have been considered citizens at the time of the state of Michigan's founding, as the definition of "White" then included people of mixed-descent and some Indian residents.[91] However, only a few years later, in 1824, leaders were already looking at whether an individual lived more like an Indian or like a European in making citizenship determinations.[92] The Michigan Constitution of 1850 included language allowing a pathway to citizenship for "civilized Indians" who renounced their tribal membership. Despite the pressures to conform to European ways of life, the Odawa and other Great Lakes Natives nonetheless attempted to maintain their culture while adopting some imported practices and customs.[93]

While many Odawa Indian bands obtained federal recognition through the process established by the federal government in the 1934 Indian Reorganization Act, other bands of Odawa continue to seek recognition. This includes the Mackinac Band of Chippewa and Ottawa Indians (bands 11 through 17 of the former Northern Michigan Ottawa Association), whose representatives signed the 1820, 1836, and 1855 treaties with the United States. Among these are the descendants of the Odawa people who lived in the Mackinac Island and Michilimackinac area during the early years of European settlement. The Mackinac Band are headquartered in St. Ignace and are engaged in the laborious process of obtaining federal recognition as a tribe.[94]

In all likelihood, Simon and Marguerite were initially married *à la façon du pays*, as was common in that era for relationships between French-Canadian men and Native women. The 1883 *History of the Upper Peninsula of Michigan* described intermarriage between French immigrants and the Native population as follows:

> The one trait in which the French immigrants differed widely from the English and Spanish settlers in America, was their friendliness toward the aboriginal inhabitants. This kindly disposition was appreciated by the Indians; so that the two races,

whenever they fairly understood each other, lived in peace together. Intermarriage was not very frequent, nor was this relationship often entered into by the peasantry of this part of the continent. It was common enough at the remoter posts, down even to our own time. The Indian trader, whether Frenchman, Scotchman, or Yankee, prompted partly by interest, usually took to himself an Indian wife. At such places as Mackinac and Sault de Ste. Marie, half-breeds were quite numerous, as they had been at Detroit at an earlier day. The classes known as voyageurs—the *coureurs des bois* of the older times—have become, to a very considerable extent, of mixed blood.[95]

These marriages *à la façon du pays* were outright recognized by other Native people, the Canadian government, and various fur trade companies. The Catholic Church tolerated these unions, though it encouraged local priests to see that people who had married *à la façon du pays* formalized their relationship even years into it.[96]

Indeed, Simon and Marguerite later solemnized their union through a formal Catholic marriage on 14 December 1822—over twenty years after the birth of their first child—in a ceremony on Michilimackinac Island.[97] Simon and Marguerite (listed only as "a woman Savage of the Sehiouse nation") first appear in the Mackinac Island parish baptismal records on 11 October 1801 for the baptism of their son, Charles Michael Champagne, born the previous day. He was baptized by Adhemar St. Martin, a United States justice of the peace. The Mackinac Island baptismal records also record a second baptism for Charles Michael on 17 June 1804 with Charles Marley and Josephe Vaillancour serving as his godparents, as well as the baptism of their first daughter, Marguerite Louise, whose godparents were Pierre LaCroix and Louise Vasseur.[98]

Simon and Marguerite had the following children:§

---

§   Several family trees in online databases like Ancestry.com and FamilySearch.org reference other possible children born to Simon Champagne and Marguerite, such as Jean Baptiste Champagne (also known as John Shampine) (1806–1892) and Julie Champagne (1825–unknown). The author was unable to locate any sources corroborating the existence of these children.

    i.   **Charles Michael Champagne**, b. Michilimackinac Island, Wayne County, Indiana Territory, 10 October 1801; d. Unknown[99]

    ii.   **Marguerite Louise Champagne**, b. Michilimackinac Island, Wayne County, Indiana Territory, 6 October 1803; m. Augustin Rousseau, date and location unknown; d. After 1880[100]

    iii.   **Mary Genevieve Champagne**, b. Michilimackinac Island, Wayne County, Michigan Territory, approximately 1808–09; m. David McGulpin, Michilimackinac Island, Michilimackinac County, Michigan Territory, 21 May 1827; d. After 1880[101]

    iv.   **Josette Champagne**, b. Michilimackinac Island, Wayne County, Michigan Territory, approximately 1812; m. Elie Bouchard, Michilimackinac Island, Michilimackinac County, Michigan Territory, 2 December 1828; d. Green Bay, Brown County, Wisconsin, approximately 1845–46[102]

On 27 January 1817, Simon and Marguerite (under the name Te Pi Ma Guain) entered into an agreement with George Johnston, also of Mackinac Island, providing for their eight-year-old daughter Mary Genevieve Champagne to be indentured to Mr. Johnston as a housekeeper until she reached the age of seventeen or married. The indenture agreement required that Mr. Johnston instruct Mary in the "craft, mystery, and occupation of housekeeping" and provide for her needs in addition to teaching Mary her prayers and duty to God.[103]

The 1830 U.S. Census lists Simon as living in Pokagon Township on Mackinac Island and as being the sole inhabitant of his home.[104] Given his remarriage a few years later to Françoise Bevien, it's possible Simon and Marguerite had separated by this point. However, they both appeared before public notary Samuel Abbott on 26 February 1830 and made their marks on the deed conveying the 150-acre Private Claim No. 2 to Michael Dousman.[105]¶

Even after marriage to European men, many Ojibwe and Odawa women continued to live indigenous lives. They planted corn, harvested maple syrup, gathered berries including gooseberries and blueberries, and participated in the gathering of wild rice during fall.[106]

Marriage, however, was not necessarily an obstacle to relationships with others outside the marital bond. It wasn't uncommon for marriages to end even if solemnized, and Native women who exited a partnership or marriage could rely on their extended kin networks for support. Some men who had married and started families with Indian women who felt the need to advance in Canadian society would move on with another partner but continue to support their Native wives and mixed-descent children.[107] For reasons unknown to us, Marguerite and Simon eventually separated and went their separate ways sometime in the early 1830s.

Marriage to Françoise Bevien and Later Life

Simon later married a woman named Françoise Bevien or Bouvier in approximately 1834. Simon and Françoise are believed to have had at least six children together:

Readers with additional records or information regarding the children of Simon and Marguerite Champagne are encouraged to contact the author.

¶   It's also worth considering whether the Simon Champagne who married Marguerite (Te Pi Ma Guain) and was father to Josette Champagne Bouchard was a different person than the Simon Champagne who married Françoise Bevien and had at least five children with her before dying on 10 May 1852. As noted above, the 1830 U.S. Census lists Simon as being between the ages of sixty and seventy and living alone. However, the 1840 U.S. Census lists Simon as being between fifty and sixty and having five children. The 1850 U.S. Census likewise gives his age as sixty-seven, and his 1852 burial record lists his age as seventy. If Simon Champagne was born 21 March 1765, he would have been eighty-seven at the time of his death. Given the lack of clarity, this volume shall treat Simon Champagne as a single person until further information becomes available.

i. **Louis Champagne**, b. Michigan Territory, approximately 1828; d. Unknown [108]

ii. **August Champagne (a.k.a. August Shampine)**, b. Michigan Territory, approximately 1831; m. Susan Martin, approximately 1854; d. Manistique, Schoolcraft County, Michigan, 14 November 1901 [109]

iii. **Susan Champagne**, b. Michigan Territory, approximately 1833; m. William Henry Andress, Bois Blanc Island, Mackinac County, Michigan, 9 June 1894; d. Mackinaw Township, Cheboygan County, Michigan, 23 January 1913 [110]

iv. **Moses Champagne (a.k.a. Moses Shampine)**, b. Michigan Territory, approximately 1836; m. Sarah Plante, unknown date and location; d. Moran Township, Mackinac County, Michigan, 29 March 1895 [111]

v. **John Baptiste Champagne (a.k.a. John B. Champine)**, b. Michigan, 13 March 1838; m. Mary Anne Vallier, St. Ignace, Mackinac County, Michigan, 5 May 1867; d. Thompson, Schoolcraft County, Michigan, 21 April 1912 [112]

vi. **Simon Champagne (a.k.a. Simon Shampine)**, b. Michigan, approximately 1843–44; m. (1) Adelene Derusha, St. Ignace, Mackinac County, Michigan, 13 May 1867; m. (2) Madeline Leveille, approximately 1869–70; d. Pentland Township, Luce County, Michigan, 5 October 1929 [113]

The 1840 U.S. Census lists Simon Champagne as living on Mackinac Island. Also living in the household were a woman between twenty and twenty-nine, a boy between ten and fourteen, another boy between five and nine, and two boys and two girls under the age of five. [114] This would roughly correspond with children Louis, August, Susan, Moses, John Baptiste, and an unknown girl under the age of five.

In 1850, Simon and Françoise lived in Mackinac Island with their six children and a forty-eight-year-old fisherman named Joseph Tremblay. Françoise's age is given as forty while Simon is listed as only being sixty-five—considerably younger than his 1765 birthday would indicate. The six named children are twenty-two-year-old Louis, nineteen-year-old August, seventeen-year-old Susan, fourteen-year-old Moses, thirteen-year-old John B., and seven-year-old Simon. The 1850 U.S. Census reflects that sixty-five-year-old Simon still worked as a fisherman and that he could neither read nor write. [115]

Simon died on 10 May 1852 on Mackinac Island. [116] Information on his burial is unavailable. Françoise lived for several years after Simon's death. The 1870 U.S. Census references a seventy-six-year-old woman named Francis Champain as living in the household of Austin Champain in Warner Township, Chippewa County, Michigan. [117] Austin Champain is believed to be the same person as August Champagne or Shampine, who was born in 1831 to Simon and Françoise and died in Manistique on 14 November 1901. According to the Mackinac County death records, a Françoise Champaigne died on 8 December 1877 on Mackinac Island at the age of ninety. The entry notes she was a widow and the daughter of a man named Bevien or Bovien. [118]

Marguerite's Life in Wisconsin

Following Marguerite and Simon's separation, Marguerite evidently moved to the Green Bay, Wisconsin Territory area and lived with the family of her daughter and son-in-law, Margaret and Augustin Rousseau. Margaret Rousseau was born Marguerite Louise Champagne to Simon and Te Pi Ma Guain on 6 October 1803, and later married Augustin Rousseau (1799–1857). [119] Augustin Rousseau worked as a fur trader for the American Fur Company, and the family settled in the Bay Settlement area north of present-day Green Bay in 1835 where they worked the land as farmers. [120] The 1840 U.S. Census lists one female between the ages of sixty and seventy living in the Rousseau household. [121] As Marguerite Champagne was approximately sixty in 1840, it is reasonably possible she resided in her daughter and son-in-law's Bay Settlement household as early as 1840. She served as godmother at the 3 February 1844 baptism of her grandson, Raphael Oliver Bouchard, youngest child of Elie and Josette Bouchard.[122] The 1850 U.S. Census expressly lists a seventy-year-old "Margaret Shampan" as living in the household of Augustin and Margaret Rousseau. Oddly, the record lists her birthplace as "Mississippi," although this may be a misprint for Michilimackinac.[123]

Marguerite Champagne died in approximately 1850 in the newly admitted State of Wisconsin, likely in Bay Settlement. She is believed to be buried in Bay Settlement's Old Holy Cross Cemetery near the grave of her daughter, Josette Champagne Bouchard.

Notes

ABBREVIATIONS

AC. Ancestry.com, https://www.ancestry.com/

BLM GLO. Bureau of Land Management, General Land Records Office, https://glorecords.blm.gov/default.aspx

CA. Chronicling America, Library of Congress, https://chroniclingamerica.loc.gov/

DI-GQ. Drouin Institute – Genealogy Quebec, https://www.genealogiequebec.com/en/

FS. FamilySearch https://www.familysearch.org/en/united-states/

GB. Google Books, https://books.google.com/

HT. HathiTrust Digital Library, https://www.hathitrust.org/

MO. Michiganology, https://michiganology.org/

PRDH-IGD. Le Programme de Recherche en Démographie Historique, https://www.prdh-igd.com

SBLL. Stephen B. Luce Library, SUNY Maritime College, https://www.sunymaritime.edu/library

UPDN. Upper Peninsula Digital Network, https://uplink.nmu.edu/

1   Abel François Alexis Bouchard Baptismal Record, 23 August 1767, Record No. 740255, DI-GQ.

2   "Carleton-sur-Mer—The Herons of Tracadièche Are Still There," Acadie: On the Roads of the Acadian People, accessed 16 May 2021, https://acadie.cheminsdelafrancophonie.org/en/carleton-sur-mer-the-herons-of-tracadieche-are-still-there/.

3   "Carleton-sur-Mer, Province of Quebec - Commission de toponymie accessed 19 July 2024, https://toponymie.gouv.qc.ca/ct/ToposWeb/fiche.aspx?no_seq=385498.

4   Marriage Record for Abel-François-Alexis Bouchard and Agathe-Blanche LeBlanc, 17 May 1790, Record No. 774553, DI-GQ.

5   Baptismal Record for Alexandre Bouchard, 18 November 1791, Record No. 604622, DI-GQ.

6   Baptismal Record for Marie Olivette Bouchard, 30 December 1792, Record No. 605300, DI-GQ; Marriage Record of Louis Durant and Marie Olive Bouchard, 28 October 1811, Record No. 2212376, DI-GQ; Family Record for Alexis Bouchard & Agathe Blanche LeBlanc, Couple No. 90687, PRDH-IGD.

7   Elie Bouchard Baptismal Record, 13 September 1794, Record No. 605393, DI-GQ; Marriage Record of Elvi [sic] Bouchard to Josette Champagne, 2 December 1828, Mackinac County, Michigan, County Marriages, 1822-1940, AC; "Sailors' Snug Harbor Death Report for Eli Bouchard," 25 October 1879, Sub-Series A: Files, 1869-2005, Sailors' Snug Harbor Records, 1757-2008, SC-0016, SBLL.

8   Baptismal Record for Pascal Bouchard, 26 March 1796, Record No. 683872, DI-GQ; Burial Record for Pascal Bouchard, 10 June 1797, Record No. 527112, DI-GQ.

9   Baptismal Record for Marie Constance Bouchard, 15 June 1798, Record No. 684124, DI-GQ; Marriage Record of Charles Courteau and Constance Bouchard, 30 October 1819, DI-GQ, https://www.genealogiequebec.com/Membership/LAFRANCE/img/tag/d1p_01120763.jpg; *Marie Constance Bouchard Headstone*, photograph, June 2010, AC.

10   Baptismal Record for Joseph Bouchard, 4 November 1799, Record No. 684313, DI-GQ; Individual Record for Joseph Bouchard, Individual No. 2195732, PRDH-IGD.

11   Baptismal Record for Théotiste Bouchard, 12 June 1801, Record No. 2921757, DI-GQ; Burial Record for Théotiste Bouchard, 14 May 1802, Record No. 2925579, DI-GQ; Family Record for Alexis Bouchard & Agathe Blanche LeBlanc, Couple No. 90687, PRDH-IGD.

12   Baptismal Record for François Xavier Bouchard, 15 March 1803, Record No. 2921992, DI-GQ; Burial Record for François Xavier Bouchard, 22 August 1809, Record No. 2926165, DI-GQ.

13   Baptismal Record for Édouard Benjamin Bouchard, 13 October 1804, Record No. 2922223, DI-GQ; Record of Marriage for Edward D. Beouchard and Sarah Ann Holmes, 10 March 1852, Record No. 02125, Vol. 1, Page 194,

Wisconsin Pre-1907 Marriage Records, Wisconsin Historical Society; "Obituary – Edward D. Beouchard," *Iowa County Democrat* (Mineral Point, WI), 25 March 1881, CA.

14   Baptismal Record for Théotiste Bouchard, 3 January 1807, Record No. 2922586, DI-GQ; Marriage Record of Louis Archambault and Théotiste Bouchard, 26 November 1832, Record No. 3451999, PRDH-IGD.

15   Baptismal Record for Leon Bouchard, 5 April 1811, Record No. 2923141, DI-GQ; Marriage Record of Leon Bouchard to Armeline d'Odet d'Orsonnens, 23 November 1840, Record No. 3453996, DI-GQ; Family Record for Alexis Bouchard & Agathe Blanche LeBlanc, Couple No. 90687, PRDH-IGD.

16   Baptismal Record for Zaïde Bouchard, 2 April 1813, Record No. 2923412, DI-GQ; Burial Record for Zaïde Bouchard, 12 May 1814, Record No. 2926537, DI-GQ.

17   "Saint-Roch-de-l'Achigan," Province of Quebec - Commission de toponymie, accessed 15 June 2024, https://toponymie.gouv.qc.ca/ct/toposweb/fiche.aspx?no_seq=395767.

18   Burial Record for Pascal Bouchard, 10 June 1797, Record No. 527112, DI-GQ; Baptismal Record for Marie Constance Bouchard, 15 June 1798, Record No. 684124, DI-GQ; Baptismal Record for Théotiste Bouchard, 12 June 1801, Record No. 2921757, DI-GQ; Burial Record for Théotiste Bouchard, 14 May 1802, Record No. 2925579, DI-GQ; Baptismal Record for François Xavier Bouchard, 15 March 1803, Record No. 2921992, DI-GQ; Baptismal Record for Théotiste Bouchard, 3 January 1807, Record No. 2922586, DI-GQ; Burial Record for François Xavier Bouchard, 22 August 1809, Record No. 2926165, DI-GQ; Baptismal Record for Zaïde Bouchard, 2 April 1813, Record No. 2923412, DI-GQ; Burial Record for Zaïde Bouchard, 12 May 1814, Record No. 2926537, DI-GQ.

19   "Le Bedeau – The Beadle," The French Canadian Genealogist, accessed 19 July 2024, https://www.tfcg.ca/beadle-old-occupation.

20   1825 Census of Lower Canada, St. Roch Parish, Leinster, Lower Canada, Record for Alexis Bouchard, FS.

21   1831 Census of Lower Canada, St. Roch Parish, Lachenaie, Lower Canada, Line 24, record for Alex Bouchard, FS.

22   Joseph Bouchette, *A Topographical Dictionary of the Province of Lower Canada* (London: Longman, Rees, Orme, Brown, Green, and Longman, 1832), n.p., GB.

23   Marriage Record of Louis Archambault and Théotiste Bouchard, 26 November 1832, Record No. 3451999, PRDH-IGD; Burial Record for Alexis Bouchard, 8 February 1833, Record No. 3397309, DI-GQ.

24   Burial Record for Agathe Leblanc, 20 December 1854, Record No. 5605435, DI-GQ.

25   Baptismal Record for Simon Marmotte, 21 March 1765, Record No. 298050, DI-GQ.

26   Marriage Record of Jacques Rouillard to Marie Josephe Marmotte, 31 March 1788, Record No. 341937, DI-GQ.

27   Les and Jeanne Rentmeester, *The Wisconsin Fur-Trade People* (Green Bay: Howard-Suamico Historical Society, Inc., 2009), 168, http://wi-research.info/wisconsin-history/The%20Wisconsin%20Fur%20Trade%20People.pdf; "Toussaint Pothier (1771–1845)," Assemblée Nationale du Québec, updated April 2021, http://www.assnat.qc.ca/fr/patrimoine/anciens-parlementaires/pothier-toussaint-333.html.

28   Edwin Orr Wood, *Historic Mackinac* (New York: Macmillan Company, 1918), 1:280, GB.

29   Reuben Gold Thwaites, Ed., *Collections of the State Historical Society of Wisconsin* (Madison: Wisconsin Historical Society, 1910), 19:114, HT; Reuben Gold Thwaites, Ed., *Collections of the State Historical Society of Wisconsin* (Madison: Wisconsin Historical Society, 1908), 18:508-09, 511, HT.

30   *Private Claims at Michillimackinac*, 1828, cadastral map, 43 x 59 cm., Stephen S. Clark Library, University of Michigan Library Digital Collections.

31   Brian Leigh Dunnigan, *A Picturesque Situation: Mackinac before Photography, 1615-1860* (Detroit: Wayne State University Press, 2008), 76, 179.

32   Western Historical Company, *History of the Upper Peninsula of Michigan* (Chicago: Western Historical Company, 1883), 90, HT; Dunnigan, *A Picturesque Situation*, 90.

33   Dunnigan, *A Picturesque Situation*, 97; Keith R. Widder, "Magdelaine LaFramboise: The First Lady of Mackinac Island," *Mackinac History* IV, No. 1 (Mackinac Island: Mackinac Island State Park Commission, 2007), 5.

34   Dunnigan, *A Picturesque Situation*, 99.

35   David A. Armour, "MITCHELL, DAVID," in Dictionary of Canadian Biography, vol. 6, University of Toronto/Université Laval, 2003–, accessed April 17, 2023, http://www.biographi.ca/en/bio/mitchell_david_6E.html

36   Walter Lowrie and Matthew St. Clair Clarke, Eds., *Documents, Legislative and Executive, of the Congress of the United States* (Washington, D.C.: Gales and Seaton, 1832), 8:1:545, HT.

37   Simon Champagne Land Patent, Certificate No. 703, 3 July 1812, BLM GLO.

38   Dunnigan, *A Picturesque Situation*, 187.

39   Asbury Dickins and John W. Forney, Eds., *American State Papers: Documents, Legislative and Executive, of the Congress of the United States* (Washington, D.C.: Gales & Seaton, 1860), 5:48, 228-29.

40   "Claim No. 2 Simon Champaigne," *Survey of Mackinac Islands and Private Claims, also Private Claims at Point St. Ignace*, Michigan Department of Natural Resources, Real estate Division Survey Notes, MO; Dunnigan, *A Picturesque Situation*, 185-86.

41   Mackinac County, Michigan, Deed Book B:46 (Simon Champagne to Michael Dousman, Recorded 1 November 1830), FS.

42   Edwin Orin Wood, *Historic Mackinac* (New York: Macmillan Company, 1918), 1:530-31, GB.

43   Mackinac County, Michigan, Deed Book N:285-86 (Raphael Oliver and Josephine Bouchard to Jacob A.F. Wendell, Recorded 12 June 1879), FS.

44   Mackinac County, Michigan, Deed Book O:62 (Edward A. Bouchard to Jacob A.F. Wendell, Recorded 4 April 1879), FS. Note: Six years earlier, Edward A. and Mary E. Bouchard had conveyed another lot located on Water Street in the village of Mackinac by warranty deed to John McNeal for $170. This was likely around the time Edward and Mary relocated across the Straits of Mackinac to Cheboygan. *See* Mackinac County, Michigan, Deed Book M:489 (Edward A. and Mary E. Bouchard to John McNeal, Recorded 19 February 1873), FS.

45   "The Inn at Stonecliffe: Our Story," The Inn at Stonecliffe, accessed 21 June 2020, https://www.theinnatstonecliffe.com/our-history.

46   "Sunset Forest Association Mission Statement," Sunset Forest Association, accessed 20 March 2024, https://www.sunsetforest.org/.

47   Virgil J. Vogel, *Indian Names in Michigan* (Ann Arbor: The University of Michigan Press, 1986), 9; Charles E. Cleland, *Rites of Conquest: The History and Culture of Michigan's Native Americans* (Ann Arbor: The University of Michigan Press, 1992), 86.

48   Cleland, *Rites of Conquest*, 11; Anne F. Hyde, *Born of Lakes and Plains: Mixed-Descent Peoples and the Making of the American West* (New York: W.W. Norton & Co., 2022), 5.

49   Cleland, *Rites of Conquest*, 23, 25.

50   Willis F. Dunbar and George S. May, *Michigan: A History of the Wolverine State*, 3rd Ed. (Grand Rapids: Wm. B. Eerdmans Publishing Co., 1995), 13; Hyde, *Born of Lakes and Plains*, 16.

51   Cleland, *Rites of Conquest*, 80, 86.

52   Cleland, *Rites of Conquest*, 86.

53   Cleland, *Rites of Conquest*, 102-103.

54   Dunbar and May, *Michigan*, 15.

55   Dunnigan, *A Picturesque Situation*, 2, 15; Cleland, *Rites of Conquest*, 88, 90, 93-94.

56   Dunnigan, *A Picturesque Situation*, 23.

57   Cleland, *Rites of Conquest*, 98-99.

58   Cleland, *Rites of Conquest*, 78.

59   Reuben Gold Thwaites, ed., *The Jesuit Relations and Allied Documents: Travels and Explorations of the Jesuit Missionaries in New France 1610–1791* (Cleveland: Burrows Brothers Company, 1899), 50:285.

60   Thwaites, *Jesuit Relations and Allied Documents*, 50:286-289.

61   Vogel, *Indian Names in Michigan*, 46-47; Cleland, *Rites of Conquest*, 138.

62   Dunnigan, *A Picturesque Situation*, 1-2.

63   Cleland, *Rites of Conquest*, 45-46.

64   Anna Jameson, *Winter Studies and Summer Rambles in Canada* (New York: Wiley and Putnam, 1839), 2:136-137, GB.

65   Dunbar and May, *Michigan*, 100-01; Cleland, *Rites of Conquest*, 156.

66   Charles J. Kappler, ed., *Indian Affairs: Laws and Treaties* (Washington, D.C.: Government Printing Office, 1904), 2:40, GB.

67   Cleland, *Rites of Conquest*, 192-93.

68   Dunbar and May, *Michigan*, 88, 111.

69   Cleland, *Rites of Conquest*, 176-77.

70   Hyde, *Born of Lakes and Plains*, 69.

71   Dunnigan, *A Picturesque Situation*, 78.

72   Dunnigan, *A Picturesque Situation*, 145.

73   Dunbar and May, *Michigan*, 138.

74   Hyde, *Born of Lakes and Plains*, 122.

75   Cleland, *Rites of Conquest*, 209.

76   Cleland, *Rites of Conquest*, 227-28.

77   Cleland, *Rites of Conquest*, 204-05.

78   Dunbar and May, *Michigan*, 152; Cleland, *Rites of Conquest*, 228.

79   Hyde, *Born of Lakes and Plains*, 144.

80   Hyde, *Born of Lakes and Plains*, 229.

81   National Archive Microfilm Publications, *Correspondence, Field Notes, and the Census Roll of All Members or Descendants of Members Who Were on the Roll of the Ottawa and the Chippewa Tribes of Michigan in 1870, and Living on March 4, 1907 (Durant Roll)*, Microfilm Publication M2039, Roll 1, Census Page 57, FS; *Ibid.* at Roll 2, Field Notes to Page 16, Line 50 of the

1870 Census. Note that Simon Champaign is thought to be the child of Simon Champagne and Françoise Bevien—Simon Senior's second spouse. It's unclear if Françoise was of Indian heritage as well.

82   Lynn Armitage, "Mackinac Island Finally Telling Native Side of History," *Indian Country Today*, 30 March 2017, https://newsmaven.io/indiancountrytoday/archive/mackinac-island-finally-telling-native-side-of-history-5UI0AK-2BCEm4JEcvJu8ppA/.

83   Hyde, *Born of Lakes and Plains*, 10.

84   Cleland, *Rites of Conquest*, 179-80.

85   Cleland, *Rites of Conquest*, 41-42.

86   Hyde, *Born of Lakes and Plains*, 8.

87   Hyde, *Born of Lakes and Plains*, 17.

88   Cleland, *Rites of Conquest*, 107, 146.

89   James J. Strang, *Ancient and Modern Michilimackinac*, 1854, 10.

90   Hyde, *Born of Lakes and Plains*, 94.

91   Hyde, *Born of Lakes and Plains*, 118.

92   Hyde, *Born of Lakes and Plains*, 128.

93   Cleland, *Rites of Conquest*, 243.

94   "About Us," Mackinac Band of Chippewa and Ottawa Indians, accessed 26 July 2023, https://www.mackinacband.com/about-us.

95   Western Historical Company, *History of the Upper Peninsula of Michigan*, 89.

96   Hyde, *Born of Lakes and Plains*, 33.

97   Record of Marriage of Simon Champagne and Margaret (Indian Woman), 14 December 1822, Mackinac County (Michigan) Marriages 1820-1832, Michigan State Library, FS.

98   Reuben Gold Thwaites, Ed., *Collections of the State Historical Society of Wisconsin* (Madison: Wisconsin Historical Society, 1910), 19:119, 122, HT.

99   State Historical Society of Wisconsin, *Mackinac Register of Baptisms and Internments, 1695-1821* (Madison, WI: State Historical Society of Wisconsin, 1910), 119, 122, Library of Congress.

100   State Historical Society of Wisconsin, *Mackinac Register of Baptisms and Internments, 1695-1821*, 122; 1880 U.S. Census, Scott, Brown, Wisconsin, population schedule, enumeration district 23, p. 13, dwelling 83, family 83, line 42, Margaret Rouseau, AC.

101   Indenture Papers of Mary Genieve [sic] Champagne, 27 January 1817, AC; Record of Marriage of David McGulpin and Mary Champagne, 21 May 1827, Record No. 47, Mackinac County (Michigan) Marriages 1820-1832, Michigan State Library, FS; 1880 U.S. Census, Cross Village, Emmet, Michigan, population schedule, enumeration district 60, p. 12, dwelling 94, family 94, line 16, Mary J. McGulpin, FS.

102   Record of Marriage of Elvi Bouchard and Josette Champagne, 2 December 1828, Record No. 56, Mackinac County (Michigan) Marriages 1820-1832, Michigan State Library, FS; Powers, Perry F, *A History of Northern Michigan and Its People* (Chicago, Lewis Publishing Company, 1912), 3:1005-06, GB.

103   Indenture Papers of Mary Genieve [sic] Champagne, 27 January 1817, AC.

104   1830 U.S. Census, Mackinac Island, Michilimackinac County, Michigan Territory, p. 200, Simon Champagne.

105   Mackinac County, Michigan, Deed Book B:46 (Simon Champagne to Michael Dousman, 26 February 1830), FS.

106   Hyde, *Born of Lakes and Plains*, 57.

107   Hyde, *Born of Lakes and Plains*, 34, 69.

108   1850 U.S. Census, Michilimackinac County, Michigan, population schedule, p. 223, dwelling 283, family 290, line 27, Louis Champagne, AC.

109   1860 U.S. Census, Moran Township, Mackinac County, Michigan, population schedule, p. 108, dwelling 1098, family 688, line 17, Augustus Champigne, AC; Certificate and Record of Death for August Shampine, Filed 15 November 1901, Reg. No. 72, State of Michigan, Department of State - Vital Statistics Division, MO; "August Champine Dead," *Manistique Pioneer-Tribune*, 15 November 1901, UPDN.

110   1850 U.S. Census, Michilimackinac County, Michigan, population schedule, p. 223, dwelling 283, family 290, line 30, Susan Champagne, AC; Record of Marriage for William Henry Andress and Susan Cadotte, 9 June 1894, "Michigan Marriages, 1822-1995," FS; Certificate of Death for Susan Andress, Filed 21 February 1913, Reg. No. 3, State of Michigan, Department of State - Division of Vital Statistics, MO.

111   1870 U.S. Census, Moran Township, Mackinac County, Michigan, population schedule, p. 2, dwelling 13, family 13, line 38, Moses Champagne; Record of Death for Moses Shampine, Recorded 1 June 1896, Record No. 3, Return of Deaths in the County of Mackinac for the Year Ending December 31, A.D. 1895, Michigan Department of Vital Records, FS.

112   Record of Marriage for Jean B. Champain and Mary Vallier, 5 May 1867, Record No. 18, Return of Marriages in the County of Mackinac for the Year Ending December 31st, 1867, Michigan Department of Vital Records, FS; Certif-

icate of Death for John B. Champine, Filed 25 April 1912, Reg. No. 5, Michigan Department of State – Division of Vital Statistics, AC; "Died at Thompson," *Manistique Pioneer-Tribune*, 26 April 1912, UPDN.

113   Record of Marriage for Simon Champagne and Adelene Derocha, 13 May 1867, Record No. 15, Return of Marriages in the County of Mackinac for the Years 1866 and 1867, Michigan Department of Vital Records, FS; 1900 U.S. Census, Manistique, Schoolcraft County, Michigan, population schedule, enumeration district 165, p. 8A, dwelling 121, family 141, line 9, Simon Champine, FS; Certificate of Death for Simon Shampine, Filed 7 October 1929, Reg. No. 95, State of Michigan, Department of Health - Division of Vital Statistics, MO.

114   1840 U.S. Census, Michilimackinac County, Michigan, p. 220, line 6, Semo Champan, AC.

115   1850 U.S. Census, Michilimackinac County, Michigan, population schedule, p. 223, dwelling 283, family 290, line 25, Simon Champagne, AC.

116   Burial Record for Simon Champagne, 10 May 1852, Mackinac Island Burial Records, Garden Peninsula Historical Society.

117   1870 U.S. Census, Warner Township, Chippewa County, Michigan, population schedule, p. 2, dwelling 9, family 10, line 6, Francis Champain, AC.

118   Record of Death for Françoise Champagine, Recorded 3 October 1878, Record No. 102, State of Michigan, Michigan Secretary of State, FS.

119   State Historical Society of Wisconsin, *Mackinac Register of Baptisms and Internments, 1695-1821*, 122.

120   Pauline LaFrombois, *A Glimpse into the Past: A History of the Town of Scott* (New Franken, WI: John Grall Publishing, 2007), Archive.org.

121   1840 U.S. Census, Brown County, Wisconsin Territory, p. 2, Augustus Rousseau, AC.

122   Baptismal Record for Raphael Oliver Bouchard, 3 February 1844, File 1842-1844, Page 124, Diocese of Green Bay Archives, Courtesy of Georgia Tillotson.

123   1850 U.S. Census, Green Bay, Brown County, Michigan, population schedule, p. 51, family 417, Margaret Shampan [sic], AC.

Great-Grandparents of Simon Bouschor

8.   Louis Bouchard

Born: 17 May 1729 in Petite-Rivière, Canada (Petite-Rivière-St-François, Capitale-Nationale, Quebec)
Died: 16 November 1780 in Petite-Rivière, Province of Quebec (Petite-Rivière-St-François, Capitale-Nationale, Quebec)

9.   Marie Françoise Dufour

Born: 27 December 1739 in Baie-Saint-Paul, Canada (Baie-Saint-Paul, Capitale-Nationale, Quebec)
Died: 12 June 1815 in Petite-Rivière, Lower Canada (Petite-Rivière-St-François, Capitale-Nationale, Quebec)

Louis Bouchard, the youngest child of Antoine Bouchard and Marie Madeleine Simard, was born on 17 May 1729 in Petite-Rivière, Canada (present-day Petite-Rivière-St-François), and baptized the following day in the Petite-Rivière Parish Church by the Baie-Saint-Paul parish priest Pierre Joseph Resche. His godparents were Louis Tremblay and Catherine Biville.[1] Petite-Rivière was settled by immigrants from France in the late 1600s, including Louis' grandparents, Claude Bouchard and Louise Gagne. The section detailing their lives features more information on Petite-Rivière's founding.

Marie Françoise Dufour, the daughter of Bonaventure Dufour and Elisabeth Tremblay, was born just downriver from Louis in Baie-Saint-Paul, Canada, on 27 December 1739. She was baptized over four months later in Baie-Saint-Paul in a *cérémonies supple* (supplemental ceremony), likely due to a winter-related delay in baptism.[2] Baie-Saint-Paul is a small city just upriver from Petite-Rivière. Its history will be covered in greater detail in the section focusing on Antoine Bouchard and Marie Madeleine Simard.

Marie Françoise and Louis Bouchard married on 14 November 1757 in Petite-Rivière.[3] They had twelve children:

i.   **Louise Côme Bouchard**, b. Petite-Rivière, Canada, 16 October 1758; d. Petite-Rivière, Canada, 20 February 1759[4]

ii.   **Louis Bouchard**, b. Petite-Rivière, Canada, approximately 1759; m. Dorothée Ursule Gagne, Petite-Rivière, Lower Canada, 23 May 1791; d. Baie-Saint-Paul, Lower Canada, 15 January 1819[5]

iii.   **Jean Baptiste Bouchard**, b. Petite-Rivière, Canada, 24 October 1760; m. (1) Ursule Tremblay (1768–1809), Petite-Rivière, Province of Quebec, 18 November 1788; m. (2) Marie Felicite Gagne, Baie-Saint-Paul, Lower Canada, 21 January 1812; d. Baie-Saint-Paul, Lower Canada, 11 August 1828[6]

iv.   **Joseph Marie Bouchard**, b. Petite-Rivière, Canada, 4 April 1762; m. Emerentienne Tremblay, 24 September 1793; d. Baie-Saint-Paul, Lower Canada, 5 November 1838[7]

v.   **Antoine Abraham Bouchard**, b. Petite-Rivière, Province of Quebec, 9 June 1764; m. Veronique Marie Bouchard, Petite-Rivière, Lower Canada, 26 May 1800; d. Petite-Rivière, Lower Canada, 23 September 1838[8]

vi.   **Abel François Alexis Bouchard**, b. Petite-Rivière, Province of Quebec, 23 August 1767, m. Agathe Blanche LeBlanc, Carleton, Province of Canada, 17 May 1790; d. Saint-Roch, Province of Quebec, 6 February 1833[9]

vii.   **André Bouchard**, b. Approximately 1769; d. Petite-Rivière, Lower Canada, 9 December

Ancestors of
Abel François Alexis Bouchard

Claude Bouchard
Born: Approximately 1626
Saint-Cosme-en-Vairais, Maine, France
Died: 25 November 1699
Petite-Rivière, Canada

Louise Gagne
Born: 21 January 1642
Igé, Perche, France
Died: 27 April 1721
Petite-Rivière, Canada

Noel Simard dit Lombrette
Born: Approximately 1637
Angoulême, Angoumois, France
Died: 24 July 1715
Baie-Saint-Paul, Canada

Marie Madeleine Racine
Born: 25 July 1646
Quebec, Canada
Died: 3 December 1746
Baie-Saint-Paul, Canada

Gabriel Robert Dufour
Born: Approximately 1669
Lisieux, Normandy, France
Died: 26 June 1720
Saint-Joachim, Canada

Louise Gagne
Born: 20 September 1683
Petite-Rivière, Canada
Died: 24 September 1747
Baie-Saint-Paul, Canada

Louis Tremblay
Born: 29 September 1667
Château-Richer, Canada
Died: Unknown

Françoise Morel
Born: 16 October 1680
Sainte-Anne-de-Beaupré, Canada
Died: 3 May 1715

Grandparents

Antoine Bouchard
Born: 15 October 1682
Sainte-Anne-de-Beaupré, Canada
Died: 24 June 1759
Petite-Rivière, Province of Quebec

Marie Madeleine Simard
Born: 19 January 1689
Baie-Saint-Paul, Canada
Died: 20 February 1769
Petite-Rivière, Province of Quebec

Bonaventure Dufour
Born: Approximately 1706
Sainte-Anne-de-Beaupré, Canada
Died: 14 April 1783
Petite-Rivière, Province of Quebec

Marie Elisabeth Tremblay
Born: 4 March 1715
Baie-Saint-Paul, Canada
Died: 15 May 1799
Petite-Rivière, Province of Quebec

Parents

Louis Bouchard
Born: 17 May 1729
Petite-Rivière, Canada
Died: 16 November 1780
Petite-Rivière, Province of Quebec

Marie Françoise Dufour
Born: 27 December 1739
Baie-Saint-Paul, Canada
Died: 12 June 1815
Petite-Rivière, Lower Canada

Abel François Alexis Bouchard
Born: 23 August 1767
Petite-Rivière, Province of Quebec
Died: 6 February 1833
Saint-Roch, Lower Canada

1795[10]

viii. **Marie Madeleine Bouchard**, Petite-Rivière, Province of Quebec, 30 April 1772; m. François Tremblay, Petite-Rivière, Lower Canada, 26 May 1800; d. Petite-Rivière, Province of Canada, 26 May 1852[11]

ix. **Élie Bouchard**, b. Petite-Rivière, Province of Quebec, 13 July 1774; m. Théophile Girard, Baie-Saint-Paul, Lower Canada, 23 April 1805; d. Saint-Joachim, Province of Canada, 3 June 1860[12]

x. **François Bouchard**, b. Petite-Rivière, Province of Quebec, 30 May 1776; m. Helene Tremblay, Baie-Saint-Paul, Lower Canada, 18 July 1808; d. Petite-Rivière, Lower Canada, 16 February 1837[13]

xi. **Denis Bouchard**, b. Petite-Rivière, Province of Quebec, 23 May 1778; m. Marie Pilote, Baie-Saint-Paul, Lower Canada, 10 September 1811; d. Unknown[14]

xii. **Marie Judith Bouchard**, b. Petite-Rivière, Province of Quebec, 25 July 1781; m. Jean Baptiste Dupere, Petite-Rivière, Lower Canada, 4 February 1805; d. Baie-Saint-Paul, Province of Canada, 30 December 1853[15]

Louis died on 16 November 1780 in Petite-Rivière, Province of Quebec, at the age of fifty-one and was buried two days later in the Petite-Rivière-St-François parish church cemetery.[16] Eight months later, his and Françoise's last child, Marie Judith Bouchard, was born on 25 July 1781.

Françoise outlived Louis for nearly thirty-five years before passing away on 12 June 1815 in Petite-Rivière, Lower Canada. She was likewise buried in the Petite-Rivière-St-François parish church cemetery two days later on 14 June.[17]

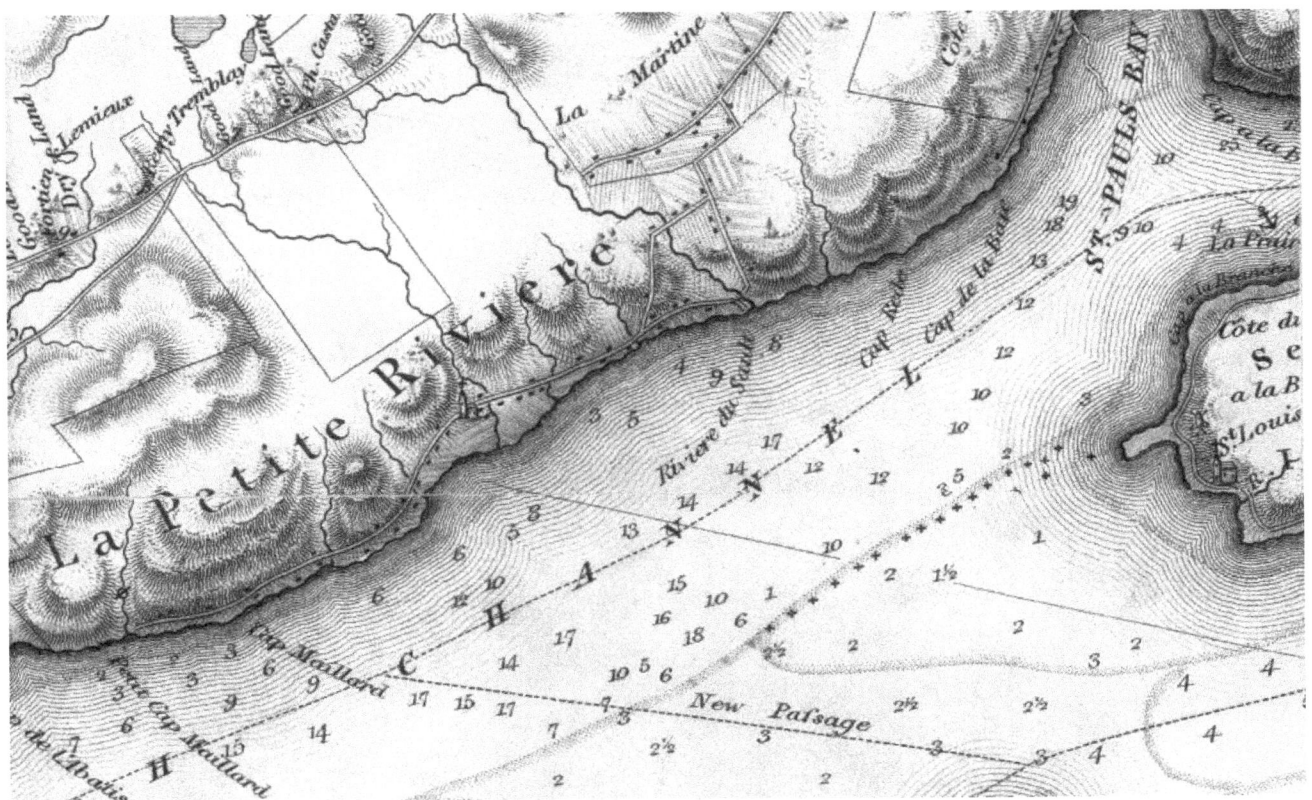

1831 Map of Quebec depicting the Petite-Rivière region settled by Claude Bouchard and Louise Gagne in 1675 and long-time home to the family of Louis Bouchard and Marie Françoise Dufour

Ancestors of Agathe Blanche LeBlanc

René LeBlanc Pere
Born: Approximately 1657
Port-Royal, Acadia
Died: 3 January 1734
Grand-Pré, Acadia

Anne Bourgeois
Born: Approximately 1661
Port-Royal, Acadia
Died: 28 December 1747
Grand-Pré, Acadia

Pierre Thibault
Born: Approximately 1675
Saint-Malo, Brittany, France
Died: Unknown

Jeanne Comeau
Born: Approximately 1682
Port-Royal, Acadia
Died: 12 July 1737
Grand-Pré, Acadia

Joseph Dugas
Born: Approximately 1689
Port-Royal, Acadia
Died: 4 September 1733
Louisbourg, Acadia

Marguerite Richard
Born: Approximately 1690
Port-Royal, Acadia
Died: 15 September 1746
Grand-Pré, Acadia

Pierre LeBlanc
Born: Approximately 1685
Rivière-Aux-Canards, Acadia
Died: 22 October 1769
Montreal, Province of Quebec

Françoise Landry
Born: Approximately 1693
Grand-Pré, Acadia
Died: 3 October 1767

René LeBlanc Fils
Born: Approximately 1684
Port-Royal, Acadia
Died: 6 February 1758
Philadelphia, Philadelphia County,
Province of Pennsylvania

Marguerite Thibault
Born: 19 October 1704
Port-Royal, Acadia
Died: Approximately 1750

Charles Dugas
Born: 10 December 1711
Grand-Pré, Acadia
Died: 25 January 1801
Carleton, Lower Canada

Anne Suzanne LeBlanc
Born: 16 March 1718
Grand-Pré, Acadia
Died: 15 April 1776
Tracadigash, Province of Canada

Pierre Benjamin LeBlanc
Born: January–February 1740
Grand-Pré, Acadia
Died: 25 February 1805
Carleton, Lower Canada

Marie Dugas
Born: Approximately 1740
Grand-Pré, Acadia
Died: 2 July 1839
Carleton, Lower Canada

Agathe Blanche LeBlanc
Born: Approximately
1768–1770
Tracadigash, Province of
Quebec
Died: 19 December 1854
Saint-Roch, Province of
Canada

10. Pierre Benjamin LeBlanc

Born: January–February 1740 in Grand-Pré, Acadia (Grand-Pré, Kings County, Nova Scotia)
Died: 25 February 1805 in Carleton, Lower Canada (Carleton-sur-Mer, Gaspésie–Îles-de-la-Madeleine, Quebec)

11. Marie Dugas

Born: Approximately 1740 in Grand-Pré, Acadia (Grand-Pré, Kings County, Nova Scotia)
Died: 2 July 1839 in Carleton, Lower Canada (Carleton-sur-Mer, Gaspésie–Îles-de-la-Madeleine)

Pierre Benjamin LeBlanc, the son of René LeBlanc Fils and Marguerite Thibault, was born in January or February 1740, in Grand-Pré, Acadia (present-day Kings County, Nova Scotia). He was the twin brother of Esther LeBlanc, and he was baptized along with Esther in the Saint-Charles-Des-Mines parish church in early 1740 by the parish priest with Pierre Doucet acting as his godfather and Marguerite LeBlanc as his godmother.[18]

The region commonly known as Acadia, or *L'Acadie* in French, comprised the modern-day Canadian provinces of Nova Scotia, New Brunswick, Prince Edward Island, and part of Maine.[19] The French first settled Acadia in 1606 by establishing a fort and colony at Port-Royal on the northwestern shore of Acadia. Over the next 150 years, control of Acadia vacillated between England and France, with the latter ceding Acadia to England via the 1713 Treaty of Utrecht.[20]

Acadians also founded the hamlet of Grand-Pré in approximately 1682.[21] Located on the Gaspereau River and translated as the "great meadow," Grand-Pré stretched along the southern shore of the Minas Basin and became the province's breadbasket, according to historian John Mack Faragher.[22] A complex series of dikes on the basin's rivers allowed agriculture to flourish in Grand-Pré and generated enough grain to sustain eight gristmills by the 1690s.[23]

Life in Grand-Pré and other communities in Acadia could appropriately be described as idyllic. Low mortality and healthy lifestyles encouraged rapid population expansion, and the Acadians enjoyed exceptionally long lifespans for the era.[24] They primarily subsisted by working the land at farming and raising livestock, while they consumed the healthy bounty produced by their efforts.[25] One French official commented, "These French Acadians are hard-working by nature . . . they are born smiths, joiners, coopers, carpenters, and builders. They themselves make the cloth and the fabrics in which they are dressed."[26]

Marie Dugas, the daughter of Charles Dugas and Anne-Suzanne LeBlanc, was born in approximately 1740, also in Grand-Pré. Both Pierre and Marie came of age during the expulsion of the Acadians from Grand-Pré, and both were likely expelled during *le grand dérangement* of 1755, along with their parents. Following the English occupation of Acadia, pressure steadily increased until the English resolved to remove the Acadian settlers from their homelands. Anti-Acadian activity reached fever pitch in summer 1755 beginning with a raid and seizure of firearms from Grand-Pré and other hamlets in the Minas Basin settlement on 2 June 1755.[27]

The English pressure culminated in a roundup of all Acadians in August through October 1755, followed by their dispersal to various seaports along the East Coast colonies in fractured numbers to prevent the Acadians from regrouping. Acadians from Annapolis Royal and Minas were sent to Pennsylvania, New York, Connecticut, Massachusetts, Virginia, and Maryland.[28] On 16 August 1755, English militia commander John Winslow led 300 British soldiers into Minas and held the Acadian men hostage.[29] The men were first rounded up in September and made to board troopships anchored

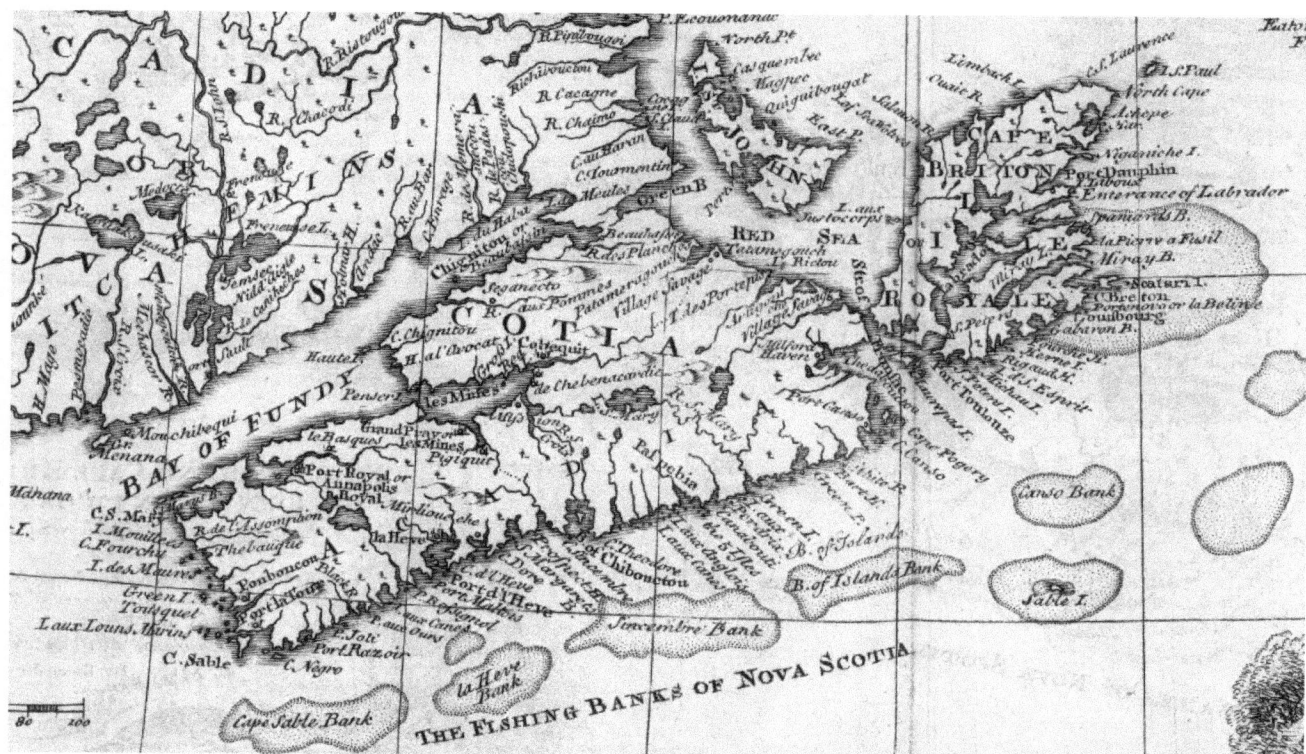

Detail from an 1747 map of eastern Canada depicting Acadia prior to the 1755 expulsion of the Acadians

offshore in the basin, while the women followed the next month. Soon, no Acadians were left in the Minas Basin region that they had called home for well over one hundred years.

Not all Acadians met the fate of being herded aboard troopships and exiled to the eastern seaboard. Some avoided deportation and fled to other corners of the French empire, such as French Canada and the territory now known as New Brunswick. These refuges became home to thousands of displaced Acadian refugees.[30]

Nonetheless, the next decade presented great difficulties for the Acadians who remained in Canada owing to the on-going war between the English and French. It wasn't until the war ended in 1763 that many Acadians could permanently settle, albeit far from their Acadian homelands. After the expulsion,

Benjamin found his way to the Baie des Chaleurs region of French Canada on the Gaspé Peninsula. The bay and the Restigouche River, which drains into it, form the boundary between Quebec and New Brunswick. The region, known as the North Shore, became home to around 2,000 Acadians by 1770 following conclusion of hostilities.[31]

Benjamin and Marie likely initially settled in Bonaventure, a small village on the North Shore of the Baie des Chaleurs. Bonaventure was one of the "Little Cadies" in present-day Quebec that became landing spots for exiled Acadians following the expulsion.[32]

Benjamin and Marie married in approximately 1760, likely in Bonaventure or another of the nascent Acadian communities on the Baie des Chaleurs.[33] They had thirteen children:

i. **Benjamin LeBlanc**, b. Approximately 1760–1761; m. Judith Comeau, Carleton, Province of Quebec, 16 November 1789; d. Carleton, Province of Canada, 21 February 1853[34]

ii. **Scholastique LeBlanc**, b. Approximately 1763; m. Joseph Audet, Tracadigash, Province of Quebec, 20 November 1786; d. Carleton, Lower Canada, 24 December 1813[35]

iii. **Luc LeBlanc**, b. Approximately 1766; m. Elisabeth Jeanson, Carleton, Province of Quebec, 19 October 1790; d. Carleton, Province of Canada, 21 October 1855[36]

iv. **Marie Charlotte LeBlanc**, b. Approximately 1766; m. Gabriel Audet, Tracadigash, Province of Quebec, 16 April 1787; d. Carleton, Lower Canada, 15 June 1818[37]

v. **Agathe Blanche LeBlanc**, b. Tracadigash, Province of Quebec, approximately 1768–1770; m. Abel François Alexis Bouchard, Carleton, Province of Quebec, 17 May 1790; d. Saint-Roch, Lower Canada, 19 December 1854[38]

vi. **Monique LeBlanc**, b. Tracadigash, Province of Quebec, 7 November 1773; m. Louis Etiambre, Restigouche, Province of Quebec, 20 May 1794; d. Carleton, Lower Canada, 19 December 1832[39]

vii. **Désiré LeBlanc**, b. Tracadigash, Province of Quebec, 17 September 1775; m. Marie Victoire Comeau, Carleton, Lower Canada, 3 January 1798; d. Quebec, Lower Canada, 22 July 1834[40]

viii. **Théotiste LeBlanc**, b. Tracadigash, Province of Quebec, 21 April 1777; m. Urbain Boudreau, Carleton, Lower Canada, 22 January 1799; d. Carleton, Province of Canada, 23 October 1853[41]

ix. **Joseph Hilaire LeBlanc**, b. Tracadigash, Province of Quebec, 4 April 1779; m. Marie Bernard, Carleton, Lower Canada, 28 May 1804; d. Unknown[42]

x. **Colette Marie LeBlanc**, b. Tracadigash, Province of Quebec, 23 July 1781; m. (1) Basile Mius Dentremont, Carleton, Lower Canada, 14 June 1808; m. (2) Jean Baptiste Barriault, Carleton, Lower Canada, 28 April 1823; d. Unknown[43]

xi. **Marie Luce LeBlanc**, b. Tracadigash, Province of Quebec, 14 October 1783; m. Luc Johnson, Carleton, Lower Canada, 6 November 1810; d. Unknown[44]

xii. **Elisabeth LeBlanc**, b. Tracadigash, Province of Quebec, 27 May 1785; m. Charles Boudreau, Carleton, Lower Canada, 7 January 1806; d. Carleton, Province of Canada, 24 May 1855[45]

xiii. **Marie Rufine LeBlanc**, b. Carleton, Province of Canada, 25 September 1787; m. Antoine Cyr, Carleton, Lower Canada, 17 January 1809; d. Unknown[46]

A 1765 census of the Baie des Chaleurs region lists Benjamin and Marie as living in Bonaventure, along with a child under the age of fifteen—likely their oldest daughter, Scholastique Leblanc.[47] Their time in Bonaventure appears to have been short-lived, for following the conclusion of hostilities in 1763, the Treaty of Paris awarded French Canada to the English and many lands once belonging to exiled Acadians were once again distributed to English settlers.[48]

Benjamin helped found the exile community of Saint-Joseph de Tracadièche, Canada—also known as Tracadigash—in the 1760s along with Charles Dugas following the expulsion.[49] Tracadigash was renamed Carleton following its occupation by American Loyalists in 1787. Carleton now comprises part of the present-day community of Carleton-sur-Mer on the Gaspé Peninsula in Quebec.

The 1777 census of Tracadigash lists thirty-seven-year-old Benjamin and thirty-two-year-old Marie as living in Tracadigash along with three sons and five daughters.[50] The census likewise lists Benjamin as being an *officier de malice* with the rank of lieutenant under the command of Captain Joseph Gravois.

Benjamin died on 25 February 1805 in Carleton, Lower Canada (present-day Carleton-sur-Mer, Quebec) at the age of sixty-five or sixty-six, and he was buried on 27 February in the Carleton parish cemetery.[51]

Marie outlived him by over thirty years before passing away around the age of ninety-nine on 2 July 1839 in Carleton as well. She was buried two days later in the Carleton parish cemetery.[52]

Ancestors of Simon Champagne

Gerard Marmotte
Born: Approximately 1670
Contreuve, Champagne, France
Died: Unknown

Poncette Gueri
Born: Approximately 1675
France
Died: Unknown

Nicolas Garaudel
Born: Approximately 1675
France
Died: Unknown

Marguerite Guillot
Born: Approximately 1680
France
Died: Unknown

Jean Bissonnette
Born: 24 July 1669
Quebec, Canada
Died: 15 May 1715
Quebec, Canada

Marie Charlotte Davenne
Born: 13 April 1676
L'Ancienne-Lorette, Canada
Died: 20 October 1707
Quebec, Canada

Nicolas Binet
Born: 11 February 1671
Quebec, Canada
Died: 29 July 1753
Beauport, Canada

Geneviève Brisson dit DuTilly
Born: 27 February 1678
Quebec, Canada
Died: 3 March 1758

Claude Marmotte dit Champagne
Born: Approximately 1700
Monthois, Champagne, France
Died: Unknown

Nicole Garaudel
Born: Approximately 1705
Monthois, Champagne, France
Died: Unknown

Louis Bissonnette
Born: 28 May 1706
Saint-Michel-de-Bellechasse, Canada
Died: 15 May 1760
Lachine, Canada

Marie Geneviève Binet
Born: 12 January 1707
Beauport, Canada
Died: 12 May 1745
Lachine, Canada

Nicolas Noël Marmotte dit Champagne
Born: 25 December 1727
Monthois, Champagne, France
Died: 18 June 1774
Montreal, Province of Quebec

Marie Geneviève Bissonnette
Born: 26 February 1732
Beauport, Canada
Died: 16 February 1790
Montreal, Province of Quebec

Simon Champagne
Born: 21 March 1765
Montreal, Province of Quebec
Died: 10 May 1852
Mackinac Island, Mackinac
County, Michigan

12. Nicolas Noël Marmotte dit Champagne

Born: 25 December 1727 in Monthois, Champagne, France (Monthois, Ardennes, Grand Est, France)
Died: 18 June 1774 in Montreal, Province of Quebec (Montreal, Montreal, Quebec)

13. Marie Geneviève Bissonnette

Born: 26 February 1732 in Beauport, Canada (Borough of Beauport, Quebec City, Quebec)
Died: 16 February 1790 in Montreal, Province of Canada (Montreal, Montreal, Quebec)

Nicolas Noël Marmotte dit Champagne, the son of Claude Marmotte dit Champagne and Nicole Garaudel, was born on 25 December 1727 and baptized in the Catholic Church on the same day in Monthois, located in the historic Champagne province of France.[53] The present-day commune of Monthois has fewer than 400 residents as of 2021 and forms part of the Ardennes department, Grand Est region, France.[54]

His future wife, Marie Geneviève Bissonnette, was born on 26 February 1732 in Beauport, Canada, to parents Louis Bissonnette and Marie Geneviève Bi-net, and was baptized that same day at Beauport Parish's Church of the Nativité-de-Notre-Dame.[55] Beauport is a present-day borough of Quebec City.

Nicolas came to Canada in approximately 1755 as one of General Montcalm's troops enlisted in the Béarn Regiment, Montredon Company.[56] Nicolas and Marie Geneviève married on 9 January 1758 in Montreal's Notre-Dame-de-Montréal parish when Nicolas was thirty and Marie Geneviève twenty-five.[57]

Nicolas and Marie Geneviève had eight children:[58]

i. **Geneviève Marmotte**, b. Lachine, Canada, 29 September 1758; d. Montreal, Lower Canada, 22 November 1819[59]

ii. **François Nicolas Marmotte**, b. Montreal, Canada, 29 July 1761; m. Marie Josephe Cazelais, Montreal, Province of Quebec, 16 April 1787; d. Montreal, Lower Canada, 21 May 1832[60]

iii. **Marie Josephe Marmotte**, b. Montreal, Province of Quebec, 25 July 1763; d. Montreal, Province of Quebec, 26 July 1763[61]

iv. **Françoise Veronique Marmotte**, b. Montreal, Province of Quebec, 25 July 1763; d. Montreal, Province of Quebec, 26 July 1763[62]

v. **Simon Marmotte Champagne**, b. Montreal, Province of Quebec, 21 March 1765; m. (1) Te Pi Ma Guain, Michilimackinac Island, Michilimackinac County, Michigan Territory, 14 December 1822; m. (2) Françoise Bevien, 6 June 1834; d. Mackinac Island, Mackinac County, Michigan, 14 December 1852[63]

vi. **Marie Therese Marmotte**, b. Montreal, Province of Quebec, 13 August 1767; d. Montreal, Province of Quebec, 13 June 1769[64]

vii. **Marie Josephe Marmotte**, b. Montreal, Province of Quebec, 17 March 1770; m. Jacques Rouillard, Montreal, Province of Quebec, 31 March 1788; d. Unknown[65]

viii. **Jean Baptiste Marmotte**, b. Montreal, Province of Quebec, 14 October 1773; d. Montreal, Province of Quebec, 17 December 1776[66]

The growing family of Nicolas and Marie Geneviève appears to have been impoverished. After the death of their twenty-two-month-old daughter Marie Therese Marmotte on 13 June 1769, she was buried *dans le cimetière des pauvres* (in the poor cemetery) located a short distance from Montreal's first

Notre-Dame Church at the corner of Rue Saint-Jacques and Rue Saint-Jean.[67] Only four of their eight children lived to adulthood.

Shortly after the birth of their eighth child in 1773, Nicolas Marmotte dit Champagne died on 18 June 1774 in Montreal, Province of Quebec, at the age of forty-seven and was buried the following day in Montreal's Proche de la Poudriere Cemetery, located in the Notre-Dame churchyard.[68]

Marie Geneviève Bissonnette died on 16 February 1790 in Montreal, Province of Canada, just short of her fifty-eighth birthday and was buried the following day, presumably in the Proche de la Poudriere Cemetery as well.[69]

14.   Unknown (Maternal Great-Grandparent of Simon Bouschor)

15.   Unknown (Maternal Great-Grandparent of Simon Bouschor)

We do not know the identities of the parents or other ancestors of Simon's maternal grandmother, Marguerite Champagne (Te Pi Ma Guain). Information regarding the Odawa Indian people is discussed at greater length in the section detailing Marguerite's life beginning on page 112.

Notes

ABBREVIATIONS

DI-GQ. Drouin Institute – Genealogy Quebec, https://www.genealogiequebec.com/en/

FS. Familysearch.org, https://www.familysearch.org/en/united-states/

PRDH-IGD. Le Programme de Recherche en Démographie Historique, https://www.prdh-igd.com

1   Baptismal Record for Louis Bouchard, 18 May 1729, Record No. 9878, DI-GQ.

2   Baptismal Record for Marie Françoise Dufour, 4 April 1740, Record No. 110612, DI-GQ.

3   Marriage Record of Louis Bouchard and Marie Françoise Dufour, 14 November 1757, Record No. 195504, DI-GQ.

4   Baptismal Record of Louise Côme Bouchard, 16 October 1758, Record No. 195451, DI-GQ; Burial Record of Louise Côme Bouchard, 20 February 1759, Record No. 195547, DI-GQ.

5   Marriage Record for Louis Bouchard and Ursule Gagné, 23 May 1791, Record No. 346814, DI-GQ; Burial Record for Louis Bouchard, 15 January 1819, Record No. 2429569, DI-GQ; Family Record for Louis Bouchard & Marie Françoise Dufour, Family No. 34214, PRDH-IGD.

6   Baptismal Record for Jean Baptiste Bouchard, 24 October 1760, Record No. 195460, DI-GQ; Marriage Record for Jean Baptiste Bouchard and Ursule Tremblay, 18 November 1788, Record No. 346811, DI-GQ; Marriage Record for Jean Bouchard and Felicite Gagne, 21 January 1812, Record No. 2200223, DI-GQ; Burial Record for Jean Baptiste Bouchard, 13 August 1828, Record No. 6048379, DI-GQ; Family Record for Louis Bouchard & Marie Françoise Dufour, Family No. 34214, PRDH-IGD.

7   Baptismal Record for Joseph Marie Bouchard, 4 April 1762, Record No. 195467, DI-GQ; Marriage Record for Joseph Bouchard and Emerentienne Tremblay, 24 September 1793, Record No. 346818, DI-GQ; Burial Record for Joseph Bouchard, 7 November 1838, DI-GQ.

8   Baptismal Record for Antoine Abraham Bouchard, 9 June 1764, Record No. 195480, DI-GQ; Marriage Record for Abraham Bouchard and Veronique Bouchard, 26 May 1800, Record No. 2201081, DI-GQ; Burial Record for Abraham Bouchard, 13 January 1839, Record No. 4135165, DI-GQ.

9   Baptismal Record for Abel François Alexis Bouchard, August 23, 1767, Record No. 740255, DI-GQ; Marriage Record for Abel François Alexis Bouchard and Agathe Blanche LeBlanc, May 17, 1790, Record No. 774553, DI-GQ; Burial Record for Alexis Bouchard, 8 February 1833, Record No. 3397309, DI-GQ.

10   Burial Record for André Bouchard, 27 December 1795, Record No. 513596, DI-GQ.

11   Baptismal Record for Marie Madeleine Bouchard, 30 April 1772, Record No. 740269, DI-GQ; Marriage Record for François Tremblay and Madeleine Bouchard 26 April 1800, Record No. 2201082, DI-GQ; Burial Record for Madeleine Bouchard, 26 May 1852, Record No. 5758288, DI-GQ.

12   Baptismal Record for Elie Bouchard, 13 April 1774, Record No. 461651, DI-GQ; Marriage Record of Elie Bouchard and Theophile Girard, 23 April 1805, Record No. 2200089, DI-GQ; Burial Record for Elie Bouchard, 5 June 1860, Record No. 5603042, DI-GQ.

13   Baptismal Record for François Bouchard, 13 June 1776, Record No. 461664, DI-GQ; Marriage Record for François Bouchard and Helene Tremblay, 18 July 1808, Record No. 2200151, DI-GQ; Burial Record for François Bouchard, 18 February 1837, Record No. 4135157, DI-GQ.

14   Baptismal Record for Denis Bouchard, 23 May 1778, Record No. 461678, DI-GQ; Marriage Record for Denis Bouchard and Marie Pilotte, 10 September 1811, Record No. 2200214, DI-GQ.

15   Baptismal Record for Judith Bouchard, 25 July 1781, Record No. 461702, DI-GQ; Marriage Record for Jean Baptiste Dupere and Marie Judith Bouchard, 4 February 1805, Record No. 2201089, DI-GQ; Burial Record for Judith Bouchard, 1 January 1854, Record No. 5908953, DI-GQ.

16   Burial Record for Louis Bouchard, 18 November 1780, Record No. 367372, DI-GQ.

17   Burial Record for Françoise Dufour, 14 June 1815, Record No. 2381998, DI-GQ.

18   Baptismal Record for Pierre Benjamin LeBlanc, 1740, Record No. 6147173, DI-GQ (Note: The Baptismal Record is undated but is recorded between an earlier record dated 2 January 1740 and a later record dated 17 February 1740).

19   John Mack Faragher, *A Great and Noble Scheme: The Tragic Story of the Expulsion of the French Acadians from their American Homeland* (New York: W.W. Norton & Company, Inc., 2005), 6.

20   Faragher, *Great and Noble Scheme*, 8-9, 59; Christopher Hodson, "Exile on Spruce Street: An Acadian History," *The William and Mary Quarterly* 67, no. 2 (2010): 259, https://doi.org/10.5309/willmaryquar.67.2.249.

21   Faragher, *Great and Noble Scheme*, 76.

22   Faragher, *Great and Noble Scheme*, 76-77.

23   Hodson. "Exile on Spruce Street," 258.

24   Faragher, *Great and Noble Scheme*, 181.

25   Faragher, *Great and Noble Scheme*, 181-82.

26   Faragher, *Great and Noble Scheme*, 183.

27   Faragher, *Great and Noble Scheme*, 314.

28   Faragher, *Great and Noble Scheme*, 335-36.

29   Faragher, *Great and Noble Scheme*, 340.

30   Faragher, *Great and Noble Scheme*, 393.

31   Faragher, *Great and Noble Scheme*, 437.

32   "The Acadian Refugees in Quebec," Acadie: On the Roads of the Acadian People, accessed 22 July 2024, https://acadie.cheminsdelafrancophonie.org/en/geographical-areas/quebec-2/.

33   "Généalogie Marie Dugas," Généalogie du Québec et d'Amérique française, accessed 8 December 2019, https://www.nosorigines.qc.ca/GenealogieQuebec.aspx?genealogie=Dugas_Marie&pid=993212.

34   Marriage Record for Benjamin LeBlanc and Judith Commeau, 16 November 1789, Record No. 774548, DI-GQ; Burial Record for Benjamin LeBlanc, 23 February 1853, Record No. 5935402, DI-GQ.

35   Marriage Record for Joseph Audet and Scholastique Leblanc, 20 November 1786, Record No. 774506, DI-GQ; Burial Record for Scholastique LeBlanc, 28 December 1813, Record No. 2867610, DI-GQ.

36   Marriage Record for Luc LeBlanc and Elisabeth Jeanson, 19 October 1790, Record No. 774558, DI-GQ; Burial Record for Luc LeBlanc, 23 October 1855, Record No. 5935491, DI-GQ.

37   Marriage Record for Gabriel Audet and Charlotte LeBlanc, 16 April 1787, Record No. 774509, DI-GQ; Burial Record for Charlotte LeBlanc, 17 June 1818, Record No. 2867716, DI-GQ.

38   Marriage Record for Alexis Bouchard and Agathe Blanche LeBlanc, 17 May 1790, Record No. 774553, DI-GQ; Burial Record for Agathe Leblanc, 20 December 1854, Record No. 5605435, DI-GQ.

39   Baptismal Record for Monique LeBlanc, 7 November 1773, Record No. 774656, DI-GQ; Marriage Record for Louis Etiambre and Monique LeBlanc, 20 May 1794, Record No. 345169, DI-GQ; Burial Record for Monique LeBlanc, 21 December 1832, Record No. 4075271, DI-GQ.

40   Baptismal Record for Désiré LeBlanc, 17 September 1775, Record No. 774687, DI-GQ; Marriage Record for Désiré LeBlanc and Marie Victorie Comeau, 3 January 1798, Record No. 774599, DI-GQ; Burial Record for Désiré LeBlanc, 22 July 1834, Record No. 4102580, DI-GQ.

41   Baptismal Record for Theotiste LeBlanc, 21 April 1777, Record No. 774751, DI-GQ; Marriage Record for Urbain Boudreau and Theotiste LeBlanc, 22 January 1799, Record No. 774608, DI-GQ; Burial Record for Theotiste LeBlanc, 25 October 1853, Record No. 5935422, DI-GQ.

42   Baptismal Record for Joseph Hilaire LeBlanc, 4 April 1779, Record No. 774815, DI-GQ; Marriage Record for Hilaire LeBlanc and Marie Bernard, 28 May 1804, Record No. 2294523, DI-GQ.

43   Baptismal Record for Colette LeBlanc, 23 July 1781, Record No. 774945, DI-GQ; Marriage Record for Basile Miousse, 14 June 1808, DI-GQ; Marriage Record for Jean-Baptiste Barriault and Marie-Colette LeBlanc, 28 April 1823, Record No. 2295078, DI-GQ; Individual Record for Colette Marie LeBlanc, Individual No. 599764, PRDH-IGD.

44   Baptismal Record for Marie Luce LeBlanc, 14 October 1783, Record No. 774993, DI-GQ; Marriage Record for Luc Johnson and Marie Luce LeBlanc, 6 November 1810, Record No. 2294699, DI-GQ.

45   Baptismal Record for Elisabeth LeBlanc, 27 April 1785, Record No. 775067, DI-GQ; Marriage Record for Charles Boudreau and Elisabeth LeBlanc, 7 January 1806, Record No. 2294556, DI-GQ; Burial Record for Elisabeth LeBlanc, 24 May 1855, Record No. 5935474, DI-GQ.

46   Baptismal Record for Marie LeBlanc, 29 September 1787, Record No. 775135, DI-GQ; Marriage Record for Antoine Cyr and Marie Rufine LeBlanc, 17 January 1809, Record No. 2294616, DI-GQ; Family Record for Benjamin LeBlanc & Marie Dugas, Couple No. 90686, PRDH-IGH.

47   "Recensement de la Baye des Chaleurs, Bonaventure (1765)," Acadian Home, accessed 10 August 2019, http://www.acadian-home.org/1765-Census-BaieChaleur-Binder1.pdf.

48   "Bonaventure, Quebec," Wikipedia, The Free Encyclopedia, accessed 10 August 2019, https://en.wikipedia.org/wiki/Bonaventure,_Quebec.

49   "Carleton-sur-Mer—The Herons of Tracadièche Are Still There," Acadie: On the Roads of the Acadian People, accessed 16 May 2021, https://acadie.cheminsdelafrancophonie.org/en/carleton-sur-mer-the-herons-of-tracadieche-are-still-there/.

50   "Recensement de Carleton pour l'année 1777," Acadian Home, accessed 10 August 2019, http://www.acadian-home.org/1777-Census-Carleton-Binder1.pdf.

51   Burial Record for Benjamin LeBlanc, 27 February 1805, DI-GQ, https://www.genealogiequebec.com/Membership/LAFRANCE/img/acte/2867451.

52   Burial Record for Marie Dugas, 4 July 1839, DI-GQ, https://www.genealogiequebec.com/Membership/LA-FRANCE/img/acte/4075470.

53   Baptismal Record for Nicolas Noël Marmotte, 25 December 1727, Registres paroissiaux et d'état civil, Archives départementales des Ardennes, https://archives.cd08.fr/ark:/75583/s00532d3d74ca4c8/532d3d74cd156.

54   "Population légales 2021 – Commune de Monthois (08303)," L'Institut national de la statistique et des études économiques, last updated 28 December 2023, https://www.insee.fr/fr/statistiques/7725600?geo=COM-08303.

55   Individual Record for Marie Geneviève Bissonnette, Individual Record No. 155423, PRDH-IGD.

56   "Marmotte / Champagne, Nicolas (b. Nicolas-Noël)," Fichier Origine, last modified 5 March 2022, https://fichierorigine.com/recherche?numero=021147.

57   Marriage Record of Nicolas Marmotte Champagne and Marie Geneviève Bissonnette, 26 February 1732, Record No. 298764, DI-GQ; Family Record for Nicolas Marmotte Champagne & Marie Genevieve Bissonnet, Couple No. 34405, PRDH-IGD.

58   Généalogie Nicolas Marmotte, Généalogie du Québec et d'Amérique française, accessed 19 September 2019, https://www.nosorigines.qc.ca/GenealogieQuebec.aspx?genealogie=Marmotte_Nicolas&pid=54440.

59   Baptismal Record for Geneviève Marmotte, 29 September 1758, Record No. 274898, DI-GQ.

60   Baptismal Record for François Nicolas Marmotte, 30 July 1761, Record No. 296760, DI-GQ; Marriage Record for Nicolas Marmotte and Marie Josephe Cazelet, 16 April 1787, Record No. 341893, DI-GQ; Burial Record for Nicolas Marmotte dit Champagne, 23 May 1832, Record No. 4213481, DI-GQ.

61   Baptismal Record for Marie Josephe Marmotte, 25 July 1763, Record No. 297469, DI-GQ; Burial Record for Marie Joseph Marmotte, 26 July 1763, Record No. 302808, DI-GQ.

62   Baptismal Record for Françoise Veronique Marmotte, 25 July 1763, Record No. 297470, DI-GQ; Burial Record for Françoise Veronique Marmotte, 27 July 1763, Record No. 302809, DI-GQ.

63   Baptismal Record for Simon Marmotte, 21 March 1765, Record No. 298050, DI-GQ; Record of Marriage of Simon Champagne and Margaret (Indian Woman), 14 December 1822, Mackinac County (Michigan) Marriages 1820-1832, Michigan State Library, FS; Burial Record for Simon Champagne, 10 May 1852, Mackinac Island Burial Records, Garden Peninsula Historical Society.

64   Baptismal Record for Marie Therese Marmotte, 14 August 1767, Record No. 611392, DI-GQ; Burial Record for Marie Therese Marmotte, 13 June 1769, Record No. 487703, DI-GQ.

65   Baptismal Record for Marie Josephe Marmotte, 18 March 1770, Record No. 612348, DI-GQ; Marriage Record for Jacques Rouillard and Marie Joseph Marmotte, 31 March 1788, Record No. 341937, DI-GQ.

66   Baptismal Record for Jean Baptiste Marmotte, 14 October 1773, Record No. 615583, DI-GQ; Burial Record for Jean Baptiste Marmotte, 18 December 1776, Record No. 588237, DI-GQ.

67   Burial Record for Marie Therese Marmotte, 13 June 1767, Record No. 487703, DI-GQ.

68   Nicolas Marmotte Champagne Burial Record, 19 September 1774, Record No. 395485, DI-GQ.

69   Marie Geneviève Bissonnet Burial Record, 17 February 1790, Record No. 380597, DI-GQ.

Great-Great-Grandparents of Simon Bouschor

16.   Antoine Bouchard

Born: 15 October 1682 in Sainte-Anne-de-Beaupré, Canada (Sainte-Anne-de-Beaupré, Capitale-Nationale, Quebec)

Died: 24 June 1759 in Petite-Rivière, Province of Quebec (Petite-Rivière-Saint-François, Capitale-Nationale, Quebec)

17.   Marie Madeleine Simard dit Lombrette

Born: 19 January 1689 in Baie-Saint-Paul, Canada (Baie-Saint-Paul, Capitale-Nationale, Quebec)

Died: 20 February 1769 in Petite-Rivière, Province of Quebec (Petite-Rivière-Saint-François, Capitale-Nationale, Quebec)

Antoine Bouchard, the youngest child of Claude Bouchard and Louise Gagne, was born on 15 October 1682 in Sainte-Anne-de-Beaupré, Canada (present-day Sainte-Anne-de-Beaupré, Capitale-Nationale, Quebec, Canada). He was baptized on 25 October 1682 in Baie-Saint-Paul with Antoine Baillon and Marguerite Bouchard acting as his godparents.[1]

Marie Madeleine Simard dit Lombrette was born on 19 January 1689 in Baie-Saint-Paul to parents Noel Simard and Marie Madeleine Racine. Father Gagnon of the Baie-Saint-Paul parish baptized Marie that same day with Pierre Paré and Anne Dodier serving as her godparents.[2]

Antoine and Marie Madeleine married on 20 November 1704 in Baie-Saint-Paul when Antoine was twenty-two and Marie fifteen.[3] They had eleven children:

i.   **Félicité Bouchard**, b. Baie-Saint-Paul, Canada, 29 November 1705; m. Pierre Perron, Baie-Saint-Paul, Canada, 10 January 1729; d. Baie-Saint-Paul, Canada, 16 December 1757[4]

ii.   **Jean Baptiste Noël Bouchard**, b. Baie-Saint-Paul, Canada, 13 June 1707; m. Marie Catherine Tremblay, Les Éboulements, Canada, 28 July 1734; d. Baie-Saint-Paul, Canada, 10 January 1778[5]

iii. **Marie Catherine Bouchard**, b. Baie-Saint-Paul, Canada, 19 June 1709; d. Baie-Saint-Paul, Canada, 2 May 1710[6]

iv.   **Antoine Bouchard**, b. Baie-Saint-Paul, Canada, 22 February 1711; m. Jeanne Gagnon, Les Éboulements, Canada, 20 November 1738; d. Les Éboulements, Province of Canada, 1 July 1776[7]

v.   **Jacques Bouchard**, b. Baie-Saint-Paul, Canada, 3 January 1713; m. Louise Françoise Rousset, L'Isle-aux-Coudres, Canada, 13 November 1741; d. L'Isle-aux-Coudres, Province of Canada, 16 May 1772[8]

vi.   **Marie Madeleine Bouchard**, b. Baie-Saint-Paul, Canada, 14 November 1714; m. Pierre Jacques Alard, Petite-Rivière, Canada, 8 January 1737; d. Petite-Rivière, Lower Canada, 30 October 1793[9]

vii. **Joseph Bouchard**, b. Baie-Saint-Paul, Canada, 7 January 1718; m. Marie Françoise Fortin, Baie-Saint-Paul, Canada, 14 November 1746; d. Petite-Rivière, Lower Canada, 2 September 1803[10]

viii. **Marguerite Bouchard**, b. Baie-Saint-Paul, Canada, 11 March 1720; m. (1) Joseph Tremblay, Petite-Rivière, Canada, 6 November 1742; m. (2) François LeClerc, L'Isle-aux-Coudres, Province of Quebec, 8 October 1764; d. L'Isle-aux-Coudres, Lower Canada, 9 August 1799[11]

ix. **Emerentienne Bouchard**, b. Baie-Saint-Paul, Canada, 1 April 1722; m. François Perron, Petite-Rivière, Canada, 5 February 1743; d. Petite-Rivière, Canada, 29 May 1744[12]

x. **Michel Bouchard**, b. Baie-Saint-Paul, Canada, 11 August 1725; m. Marie Louise Tremblay, Petite-Rivière, Canada, 15 November 1750; d. L'Acadie, Province of Quebec, 19 November 1789[13]

xi. **Louis Bouchard**, b. Petite-Rivière, Canada, 17 May 1729; m. Marie Françoise Dufour, Petite-Rivière, Canada, 14 November 1757; d. Baie-Saint-Paul, Province of Quebec, 16 November 1780[14]

All but one of Antoine and Marie's eleven children were born in Baie-Saint-Paul. Baie-Saint-Paul is a small city on the Saint Lawrence River, and it today numbers over 7,000 people and serves as the seat of the Charlevoix Regional County Municipality. However, by 1729, the family had moved to the community of Petite-Rivière, located just upriver from Baie-Saint-Paul. Their youngest child, Louis, was born there in 1729. Antoine and Marie Madeleine would remain in Petite-Rivière the rest of their lives.

Antoine died on or about 24 June 1759 in the vicinity of Petite-Rivière while hiding in the woods from

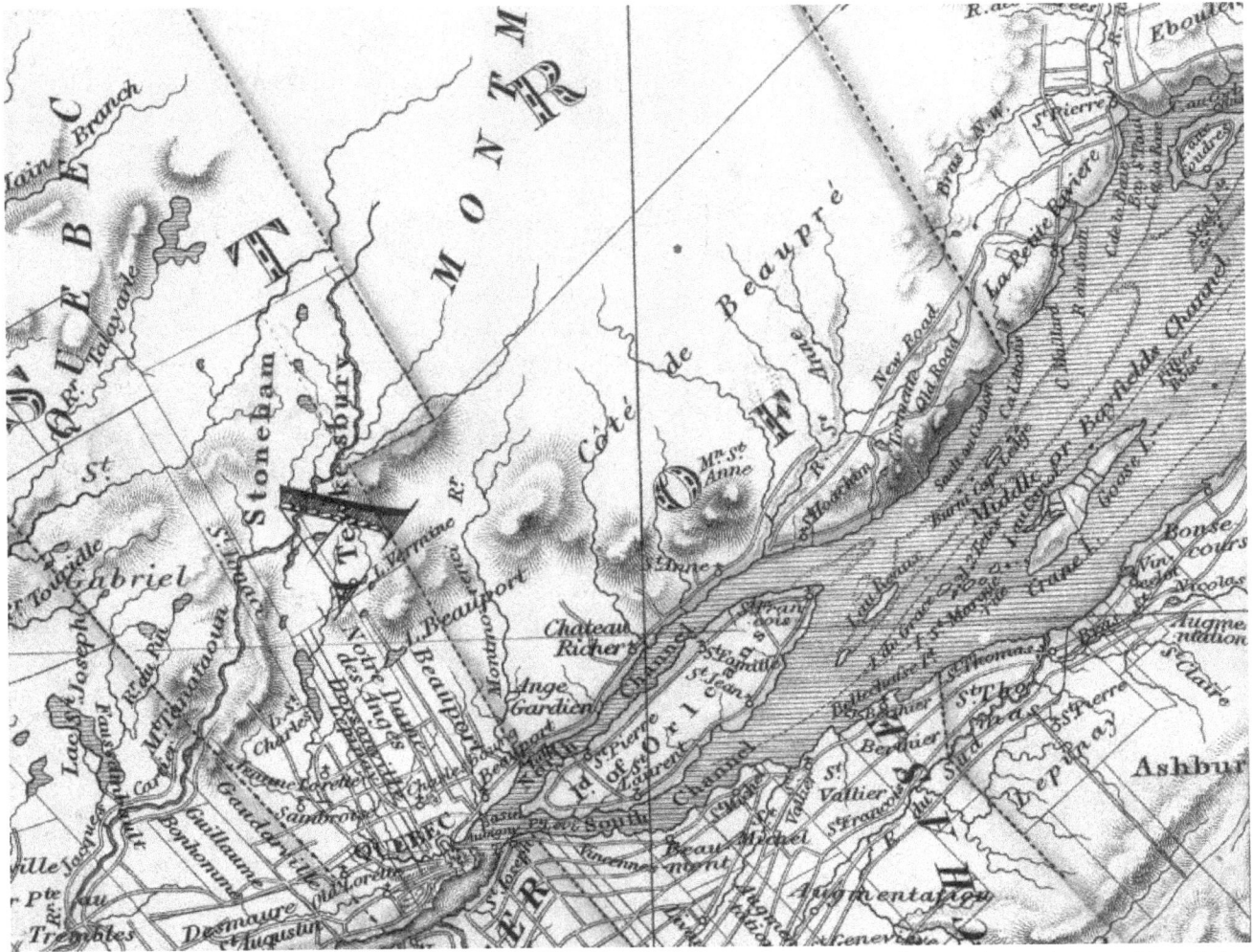

1831 map of Quebec depicting the stretch of the Saint Lawrence River from Quebec City in the southwest to Baie-Saint-Paul in the northeast and including la Côte-de-Beaupré region home to many Bouchard ancestors

General James Wolfe's English troops. He was buried at the Petite-Rivière-Saint-François parish cemetery on 24 June.[15] As part of the Seven Years' War between the French and English, General Wolfe's English forces fought their way up the Saint Lawrence River during the summer of 1759 before successfully laying siege to the city of Quebec. Despite perishing in battle, General Wolfe led his troops to a pivotal victory in the Battle of the Plains of Abraham on 13 September 1759, which resulted in France's loss of Quebec and other territory to the English following the 1763 Treaty of Paris.[16]

Marie Madeleine survived the skirmishes of the Seven Years' War and outlived Antoine by nearly ten years before passing away on 20 February 1769 in Petite-Rivière at the age of eighty. She was likewise buried at the Petite-Rivière-Saint-François parish cemetery.[17]

18.   Bonaventure Dufour

Born: Approximately 1706 in Sainte-Anne-de-Beaupré, Canada (Sainte-Anne-de-Beaupré, Capitale-Nationale, Quebec)
Died: 14 May 1783 in Petite-Rivière, Province of Canada (Petite-Rivière-Saint-François, Capitale-Nationale, Quebec)

19.   Marie Elisabeth Tremblay

Born: 4 March 1715 in Baie-Saint-Paul, Canada (Baie-Saint-Paul, Capitale-Nationale, Quebec)
Died: 15 May 1799 in Petite-Rivière, Province of Quebec (Petite-Rivière-Saint-François, Capitale-Nationale, Quebec)

Bonaventure Dufour, the great-grandfather of Elie Bouchard, was born in approximately 1706 in Sainte-Anne-de-Beaupré, Canada (present-day Sainte-Anne-de-Beaupré, Capitale-Nationale, Quebec, Canada), to parents Gabriel Robert Dufour and Louise Gagne.

Marie Elisabeth Tremblay, the daughter of Louis Tremblay and Françoise Morel, was born on 4 March 1715 in Baie-Saint-Paul, Canada (present-day Baie-Saint-Paul, Capitale-Nationale, Quebec, Canada). She was baptized the following day in the Baie-Saint-Paul parish by Father Jacques LeBlond, with Etienne Debien and Marie Lavoye acting as her godparents.[18]

Bonaventure and Elisabeth married on 8 November 1734 in Petite-Rivière, Canada.[19] They had eight children:

i.   **Marie Reine Dufour**, b. Approximately 1735; m. Pierre LaVoie, Petite-Rivière, Canada, 17 November 1756; d. Cap-Saint-Ignace, Lower Canada, 23 October 1812[20]

ii.   **Augustin Roch Dufour**, b. Petite-Rivière, Canada, 11 November 1737; m. Therese Tremblay, Petite-Rivière, Canada, 9 November 1772; d. Baie-Saint-Paul, Lower Canada, 13 June 1821[21]

iii.   **Marie Françoise Dufour**, b. Baie-Saint-Paul, Canada, 27 December 1739; m. Louis Bouchard, Petite-Rivière, Canada, 14 November 1757; d. Petite-Rivière, Lower Canada, 12 June 1815[22]

iv.   **Jean Baptiste Dufour**, b. Petite-Rivière, Canada, 12 November 1742; m. Marie Genevieve Bouchard, Baie-Saint-Paul, Province of Canada, 17 November 1768; d. Petite-Rivière, Lower Canada, 1 June 1810[23]

v.   **Joseph Michel Dufour**, b. Petite-Rivière, Canada, 7 October 1744; m. Charlotte Tremblay, L'Isle-aux-Coudres, Province of Quebec, 2 September 1771; d. L'Isle-aux-Coudres, Lower Canada, 15 December 1829[24]

vi.   **Constance Colombe Dufour**, b. Petite-Rivière, Canada, 30 December 1746; m. Jean Baptiste Tremblay, Baie-Saint-Paul, Province of Canada, 17 November 1768; d. Petite-Rivière, Province of Canada, 18 December 1776[25]

vii. **Unnamed Dufour**, b. Petite-Rivière, Canada, 17 March 1749; d. Petite-Rivière, Canada, 17 March 1749[26]

viii. **Zacharie Dufour**, b. Petite-Rivière, Canada, 23 March 1750; m. (1) Marie Anne Theriault, Baie-Saint-Paul, Province of Canada, 8 January 1781; m. (2) Théotiste Dube, Saint-Roch-des-Aulnaies, Lower Canada, 11 January 1820; d. Saint-Roch-des-Aulnaies, Lower Canada, 17 March 1833[27]

ix.   **Unnamed Dufour**, b. Petite-Rivière, Canada, 30 October 1755; d. Petite-Rivière, Canada, 30 October 1755[28]

x.   **Marie Josephe Dufour**, b. Petite-Rivière, Canada, 28 May 1757; m. Elie Mailloux, Petite-Rivière, Province of Canada, 9 November 1777; d. L'Isle-aux-Coudres, Lower Canada, 24 November 1833[29]

Bonaventure died on 14 April 1783 in Petite-Rivière. He wasn't buried until over a month later, when he was interred in the Petite-Rivière parish cemetery on 23 May 1783.[30]

Elisabeth outlived Bonaventure by over fifteen years before passing away on 15 May 1799 in Petite-Rivière at the age of eighty-four. She was buried the following day in the Petite-Rivière parish cemetery.[31]

20.   René LeBlanc Fils

Born: Approximately 1684 in Port-Royal, Acadia (Annapolis Royal, Annapolis County, Nova Scotia)
Died: 6 February 1758 in Philadelphia, Philadelphia County, Province of Pennsylvania (Philadelphia, Philadelphia County, Pennsylvania)

21.   Marguerite Thibault

Born: 19 October 1704 in Port-Royal, Acadia (Annapolis Royal, Annapolis County, Nova Scotia)
Died: Approximately 1750 in Unknown

René LeBlanc Fils[*] was born in approximately 1684 to parents René LeBlanc Père and Anne Bourgeois in the Acadian community of Port-Royal (present day Annapolis Royal, Nova Scotia).[†] The 1686 Acadian census reflects that at the age of two, René lived in Port-Royal with his parents and two older brothers.[32] Seven years later, René lived in Grand-Pré in the Minas Basin with his parents and siblings.[33] Many Acadians from the Port-Royal area had relocated to the Minas Basin in the 1680s to take advantage of the fertile soil.[34]

René first married Elisabeth Melançon (1673–1714), the widow of Pierre Alain Bugeaud, on 30 July 1709 in Grand-Pré's Saint-Charles-les-Mines parish church.[35] Elisabeth was born in Port-Royal

---

*   The French word *Fils* translates to "son" but is often used to designate a younger member of a generation bearing the same name, similar to the use of "junior" in English.
†   The Acadian settlement of Port-Royal was renamed Annapolis Royal following its capture in 1710 by the British. Events occurring there prior to 1710 shall be referred to as occurring in Port-Royal, while events occurring in 1710 or later will be referenced as occurring in Annapolis Royal.

in approximately 1673 and died only five years after her marriage to René in 1714. Elisabeth brought five children from her marriage to Pierre Alain into the family. Elisabeth and René had four additional children:[36]

i. **Benjamin LeBlanc**, b. 6 April 1711, Grand-Pré, Acadia; d. Unknown[37]

ii. **Marie Josephe LeBlanc**, b. Approximately 1714; m. Joseph Meunier, Saint-Charles-des-Mines, Grand-Pré, Acadia, 27 April 1734; d. Unknown[38]

iii. **Desire LeBlanc**, b. approximately 1717; m. Madeleine Landry, approximately 1740; d. L'Ascension, Province of Quebec, 5 March 1777[39]

iv. **Elisabeth LeBlanc**, b. 6 December 1718, Grand-Pré, Acadia; d. Unknown[40]

Elisabeth died on 12 December 1718 in Grand-Pré.[41] René subsequently married Marguerite Thibault on 26 November 1720 in Port-Royal.[42] Marguerite Thibault (also known as Thébeau or Thebaut), the daughter of Pierre Thibault and Jeanne Comeau, was born on 19 October 1704 in Port-Royal, Acadia.[43] René and Marguerite had fourteen children:[44]

i. **Marguerite LeBlanc**, b. Grand-Pré, Acadia, 25 July 1721; m. Joseph Babin, Grand-Pré, Acadia, 22 November 1745; d. Unknown[45]

ii. **Marie LeBlanc**, b. Grand-Pré, Acadia, 25 July 1721; d. Unknown[46]

iii. **Anne LeBlanc**, b. Grand-Pré, Acadia, 25 July 1721; d. Unknown[47]

iv. **Anne LeBlanc**,‡ b. Grand-Pré, Acadia, 29 September 1724; m. René Theriault, Grand-Pré, Acadia, 23 November 1744; d. Unknown[48]

v. **Marie LeBlanc**, b. Grand-Pré, Acadia, 19 March 1726; m. (1) Cyprien Leprince, approximately 1754; m. (2) Eustache Alain Trahan, 10 February 1766; d. Unknown[49]

vi. **Blanche LeBlanc**, b. Grand-Pré, Acadia, 19 March 1726; m. Michel Bonhomme, L'Ancienne-Lorette, Quebec, 5 October 1762; d. L'Ancienne-Lorette, Canada, 30 June 1763[50]

vii. **Madeleine LeBlanc**, b. Grand-Pré, Acadia, 19 November 1727; m. Charles Broussard, Grand-Pré, Acadia, 7 Jun 1746; d. Unknown[51]

viii. **Simon LeBlanc**, b. Grand-Pré, Acadia, 10 November 1731; d. Unknown[52]

ix. **René LeBlanc**, b. Grand-Pré, Acadia, 10 November 1731; m. Anne Blanchard, approximately 1752; d. Unknown[53]

x. **Françoise LeBlanc**, b. Grand-Pré, Acadia, 1 May 1734; m. Charles Grajon, approximately 1752; d. Chambly, Province of Quebec, 18 February 1791[54]

xi. **Ursule LeBlanc**, b. Grand-Pré, Acadia, 27 December 1735; m. Jacques Christophe Babuty, Quebec, Canada, 6 February 1758; d. Chambly, Lower Canada, 31 October 1794[55]

xii. **Pierre Benjamin LeBlanc**, b. Grand-Pré, Acadia, 2 January 1740; m. Marie Dugas, Carleton, Province of Quebec, approximately 1764; d. Carleton, Lower Canada, 25 February 1805[56]

xiii. **Marie Esther LeBlanc**, b. Grand-Pré, Acadia, 2 January 1740; m. Raymond Bourdage, Rivière-Saint-Jean, Acadia, 17 November 1760; d. Bonaventure, Lower Canada, 17 May 1805[57]

xiv. **Jean Baptiste Marie LeBlanc**, b. Grand-Pré, Acadia, 25 June 1744; m. Marguerite Boudreau, approximately 1770; d. Carleton, Lower Canada, 1 November 1824[58]

---

‡   René and Margeurite appear to have had two daughters named Anne (one born as a set of triplets in 1721 and one born in 1724) and two daughters named Marie (one born in the 1721 set of triplets and a second born in 1726). It's possible that the Anne and Marie born in 1721 died shortly after birth or as young children.

René and Marguerite lived in Acadia during its heyday in the first half of the eighteenth century before the 1755 expulsion. Acadia developed a unique culture owing to its French ancestry, but distinct from anywhere else in the world. While most Acadians were illiterate, they spoke an old-fashioned French dialect that retained characteristics of early-modern French due to Acadia's relative isolation from other French-speaking areas. Further compounding this isolation was the limitations on immigration from French-speaking areas imposed by British colonial rule from 1713. In lieu of linguistic influence from France and other parts of French Canada, Acadian French borrowed from the English and Algonquin languages.[59]

Like most Acadians, René cooperated with the English during the occupation leading up to the expulsion, and he became the community's leading go-between with the provincial British government. In 1732, the English awarded René the contract for construction of an English blockhouse at Minas.[60] Although the English told René the blockhouse was for storage, they intended it for use in lodging English troops. After work commenced in July 1732, three Mi'kmaq Indians confronted and threatened René regarding the construction of the fort, and he ultimately abandoned efforts to complete it.[61]

René was appointed as royal notary at Les Mines, Acadia on 17 December 1744. During a skirmish in late 1749 between the English and local Mi'kmaq, Abenaki, and Maliseet Indians supported by the French, the native fighters took René prisoner, along with nineteen English soldiers. René would spend at least two years in captivity in the early 1750s.[62] Marguerite purportedly died of grief due to the stress of the separation.[63] After René's release from captivity, he returned to Grand-Pré and resumed his duties as notary.

Henry Wadsworth Longfellow immortalized René as a character in *Evangeline*, his epic 1847 poem about the expulsion of the Acadians. While of questionable historical accuracy, Longfellow offers the following description of the aged René and memorializes his time spent in captivity:

Bent like a laboring oar, that toils in the surf
of the ocean,
Bent, but not broken, by age was the form
of the notary public;
Shocks of yellow hair, like the silken floss
of the maize, hung
Over his shoulders; his forehead was high;
and glasses with horn bows
Sat astride on his nose, with a look of wisdom supernal.
Father of twenty children was he, and more
than a hundred
Children's children rode on his knee, and
heard his great watch tick.
Four long years in the times of the war had
he languished a captive,
Suffering much in an old French fort as the
friend of the English.
Now, though warier grown, without all guile
or suspicion,
Ripe in wisdom was he, but patient, and
simple, and childlike.
He was beloved by all, and most of all by
the children;
For he told them tales of the Loup-garou
in the forest,
And of the goblin that came in the night to
water the horses,
And of the white Létiche, the ghost of a
child who unchristened
Died, and was doomed to haunt unseen the
chambers of children;
And how on Christmas eve the oxen talked
in the stable,
And how the fever was cured by a spider
shut up in a nutshell,
And of the marvellous powers of four-
leaved clover and horseshoes,
With whatsoever else was writ in the lore of
the village.[64]

Marguerite died in approximately 1750, likely in Grand-Pré, and was spared the horrors of the expulsion. In August 1755, British troops at the command of John Winslow occupied Grand-Pré and the Minas Basin and initiated the removal of the Acadians. The British established their headquar-

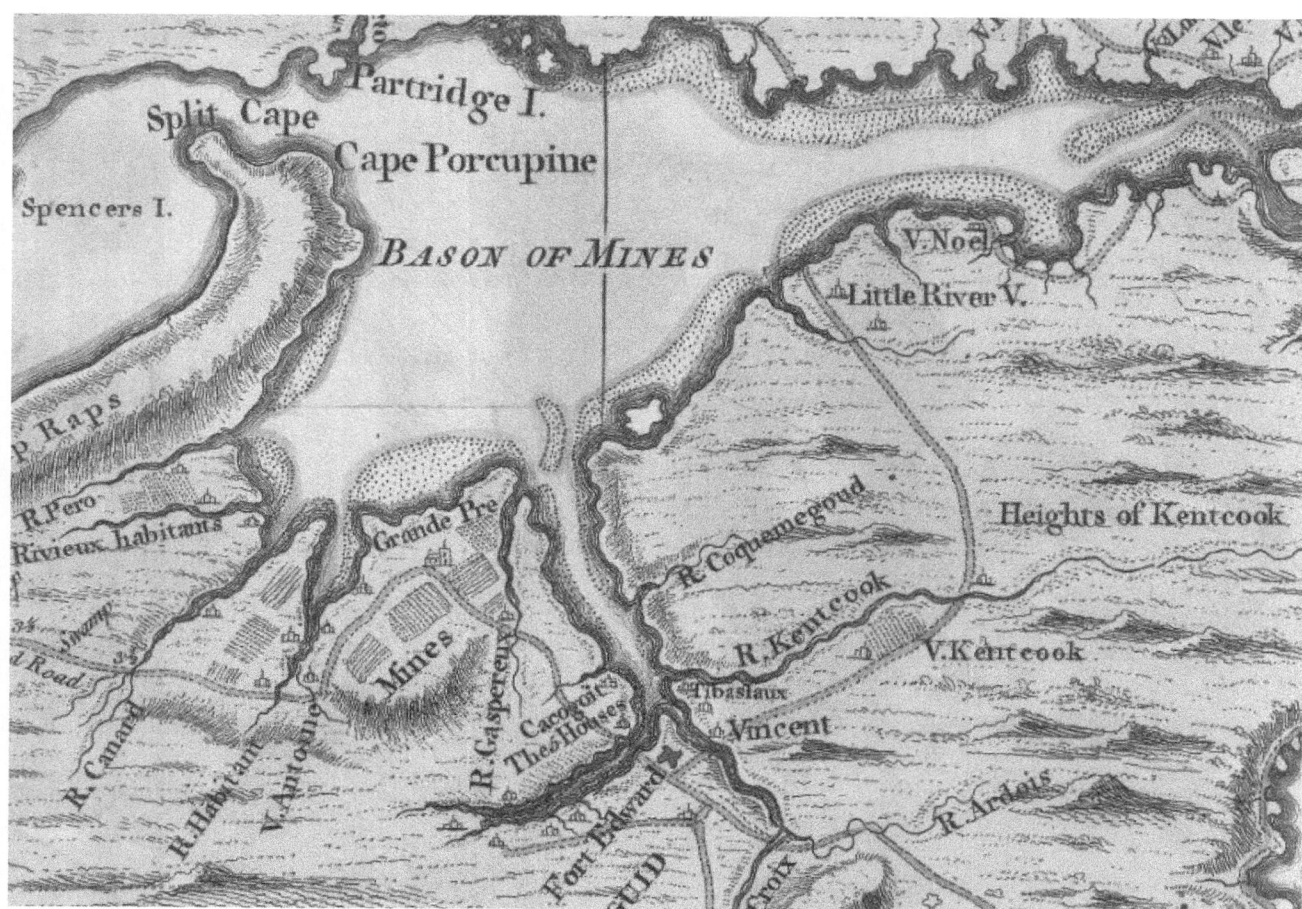

Map of the Minas Basin with the Acadian village of Grand-Pré located on the basin's southern shore

ters at the Saint-Charles-des-Mines church, and it was there that René and several other elders went in August 1755 to meet with Commander Winslow and plead for his people.[65] Shortly thereafter, several British transport ships arrived in Minas. As the threat of removal grew palpable, the Acadians became ever more fearful. Groups of Acadians gathered at the Grand-Pré homes of René and François Landry to discuss the impending expulsion. The elders advised cooperation with the British. According to historian John Mack Faragher, some 418 men and boys representing four generations of some seventy families entered the Saint-Charles-des-Mines church later that afternoon and sat in the church pews to await their fate.[66] Commander Winslow then informed the assembled Acadians that their property and livestock were forfeited to the Crown, save for household goods and money, and that they were to be removed from Acadia. René and other elders again attempted to appeal to Commander Winslow, but without success.[67]

On 11 September 1755, the British forcibly ordered the Acadian men of Grand-Pré out of their homeland of over one hundred years and onto several troopships at anchor offshore a mile and a half away.[68] René made one additional attempt to intercede on the Acadians' behalf by presenting Commander Winslow with a memorial noting his people's fidelity and submission, and attaching an affidavit of fidelity from 1730, along with other documents from René's notarial files.[69] A month later, on 8 October 1755, the women and children of Grand-Pré were likewise driven out of their homes and made to board other troopships waiting offshore.[70] In the overwhelming confusion, many families were separated, including the LeBlancs. René's family was separated amongst three transport ships that dispersed their passengers at different locations along the eastern seaboard from Massachusetts to Virginia.[71]

By 13 October 1755 all the Acadians of Grand-Pré

were being held captive aboard five troopships anchored offshore.[72] Conditions aboard were abysmal, with poor ventilation and little food and water, and two people were made to share a space measuring four by four feet and only six feet deep.[73] Countless people died of exhaustion, starvation, and disease before the ships even reached their intended destinations. Three ships—the *Hannah*, the *Three Friends*, and the *Swan*—with 454 Acadians aboard made their way south along the eastern seaboard over the next month, bound for Pennsylvania colony.[74]

By the third week of November, the three ships arrived in Pennsylvania colony. Colonial officials were far from happy to see them, and due to an outbreak of smallpox aboard one ship, the colonial governor of Pennsylvania ordered them to land at Province Island. Located south of the city of Philadelphia, Province Island then served as the city's "pest house," but today is the site of the Philadelphia International Airport. It wasn't until February of the following year that colonial officials relented and allowed the Acadians into Philadelphia and other parts of Pennsylvania.[75]

René died in exile in Philadelphia, Pennsylvania Colony, on 6 February 1758. He was initially buried in a potter's field then known as Southeast Square and later renamed Washington Square in 1825. Longfellow recounted René's exile in Pennsylvania and passing in part two, section 5 of *Evangeline*:

In that delightful land which is washed by the Delaware waters,
Guarding in sylvan shades the name of Penn the apostle,
Stands on the banks of its beautiful stream the city he founded.
There all the air is balm, and the peach is the emblem of beauty,
And the streets still re-echo the names of the trees of the forest,
As if they fain would appease the Dryads whose haunts they molested.
There from the troubled sea had Evangeline landed, an exile,
Finding among the children of Penn a home and a country.
There old René Leblanc had died; and when he departed,
Saw at his side only one of all his hundred descendants.[76]

1893 George Craig painting illustrating the expulsion of the Grand-Pré Acadians

René's remains presumably lie interned in an unmarked grave beneath Philadelphia's Washington Square, far from his Acadian homeland.

22.   **Charles Dugas**

Born: 10 December 1711 in Grand-Pré, Acadia (Grand-Pré, Kings County, Nova Scotia)
Died: 25 January 1801 in Carleton, Lower Canada (Carleton-sur-Mer, Gaspésie–Îles-de-la-Madeleine, Quebec)

23.   **Anne Suzanne LeBlanc**

Born: 16 March 1718 in Grand-Pré, Acadia (Grand-Pré, Kings County, Nova Scotia)
Died: 15 April 1776 in Tracadigash, Province of Canada (Carleton-sur-Mer, Gaspésie–Îles-de-la-Madeleine, Quebec)

Charles Dugas, son of Joseph Dugas and Marguerite Richard, was born on 10 December 1711 in Grand-Pré, Acadia (present-day Grand-Pré, Kings County, Nova Scotia, Canada).[77]

His future wife, Anne Suzanne LeBlanc, was born on 16 March 1718 in Grand-Pré as well, to parents Pierre LeBlanc and Françoise Landry.[78] Charles and Anne married on 7 January 1739 in Grand-Pré in the Saint-Charles-les-Mines parish church.[79] They had the following children:

i.   **Charles Dugas**, b. Grand-Pré, Acadia, 23 September 1739; m. Felicite Bujold, approximately 1772; d. Carleton, Lower Canada, 9 March 1806[80]

ii.   **Marie Dugas**, b. Grand-Pré, Acadia, approximately 1740; m. Pierre Benjamin LeBlanc, approximately 1760; d. Carleton, Lower Canada, 2 July 1839[81]

iii.   **Anne Dugas**, b. Grand-Pré, Acadia, 16 December 1740; d. Unknown[82]

iv.   **Abraham Dugas**, b. approximately 1741; m. (1) Marguerite Pelagie Bujold, Bonaventure, Province of Quebec, 22 April 1776; m. (2) Marie Amable Joli, Saint-Roch, Lower Canada, 11 February 1800; d. Saint-Esprit, Lower Canada, 9 April 1826[83]

v.   **Pierre Dugas**, b. Grand-Pré, Acadia, 14 September 1742; m. Françoise Robichaud, Bonaventure, Province of Quebec, 15 April 1776; d. Carleton, Lower Canada, 27 April 1832[84]

vi.   **Joseph Dugas**, b. Grand-Pré, Acadia, 14 September 1742; m. Agathe Landry, Caraquet, New Brunswick, approximately 1770–1771; d. Caraquet, New Brunswick, 4 June 1820[85]

vii.   **Amand Herculin Dugas**, b. Grand-Pré, Acadia, 7 November 1743; d. Unknown[86]

viii.   **Hélène Dugas**, b. Approximately 1746; m. Claude Landry, Quebec, Canada, 16 October 1770; d. Carleton, Lower Canada, 23 April 1830[87]

ix.   **Françoise Dugas**, b. Approximately 1747; m. Joseph LeBlanc, approximately 1773; d. Carleton, Lower Canada, 5 April 1834[88]

x.   **Angelique Dugas**, b. Approximately 1750; m. Hilaire Poirier, Carleton, Province of Quebec, 8 November 1773; d. Saint-Jacques-de-l'Achigan, Lower Canada, 30 November 1825[89]

xi.   **Marthe Dugas**, b. Approximately 1756; m. Jean Landry, Carleton, Province of Canada, 6 May 1776; d. Carleton, Lower Canada, 5 February 1840[90]

Following the expulsion of the Acadians, Charles and Anne relocated to the Gaspé Peninsula in New France, initially settling in the Acadian exile community of Bonaventure on the north shore of the

Baie des Chaleurs. The 1765 census of the inhabitants of the Baie des Chaleurs reflects Charles as living in a household in Bonaventure with three women, one child over the age of fifteen, and three children under the age of fifteen.[91]

In the following decade, Charles helped found the town of Saint-Joseph de Tracadièche, also known in English as Tracadigash, along with his future son-in-law, Pierre Benjamin LeBlanc.[92] Tracadigash's name was changed in 1787 to Carleton by American Loyalists.

Anne died in Tracadigash around 15 April 1776.[93] Charles passed away a quarter century later at the age of ninety in the Acadian exile community rechristened Carleton on 25 January 1801. He was buried the following day in the Carleton parish cemetery.[94]

24.   Claude Marmotte dit Champagne

Born: Approximately 1700 in Monthois, Champagne, France (Monthois, Ardennes, Champagne, France)
Died: Unknown

25.   Nicole Garaudel

Born: Approximately 1705 in Monthois, Champagne, France (Monthois, Ardennes, Champagne, France)
Died: Unknown

Claude Marmotte dit Champagne, son of Gerard Marmotte and Poncette Gueri, was born in approximately 1700 in Monthois in France's historic province of Champagne. Monthois is located east of Rheims, approximately twenty miles from the French border with Belgium. Claude was likely called Champagne owing to his birthplace.

Nicole Garaudel, also known as Nicole Garaudelle, was born in approximately 1705 in Monthois as well, to parents Nicolas Garaudel and Marguerite Guillot.

Claude and Nicole married on 7 January 1727 in Contreuve, a community near Monthois in Champagne province.[95] They had at least one child:

> i.   **Nicolas Noël Marmotte dit Champagne**, b. Monthois, Champagne, France, 25 December 1727; m. Genevieve Bissonnette, Montreal, Canada, 9 January 1758; d. Montreal, Province of Quebec, 18 June 1774[96]

It is unknown if or when Claude and Nicole immigrated to New France, and the author was unable to locate any additional information on their lives following their marriage in 1727 and subsequent birth of their child, Nicolas.

26.   Louis Bissonnette

Born: 28 May 1706 in Saint-Michel-de-Bellechasse, Canada (Saint-Michel-de-Bellechasse, Chaudière-Appalaches, Quebec)
Died: 15 May 1760 in Lachine, Canada (Borough of Lachine, Montreal, Quebec)

27.   Marie Geneviève Binet

Born: 12 January 1707 in Beauport, Canada (Borough of Beauport, Quebec City, Quebec)

Died: 12 May 1745 in Lachine, Canada (Borough of Lachine, Montreal, Quebec)

Louis Bissonnette (also known as Louis Bissonnet) was born on 28 May 1706 to parents Jean Bissonnette and Marie Charlotte Davenne in Saint-Michel-de-Bellechasse, Canada, a small village on the southern bank of the Saint Lawrence River located in the former seigniory of La Durantaye. He was baptized on 3 June 1706 in the Saint-Michel-de-Bellechasse parish.[97]

Marie Geneviève Binet, the daughter of Nicolas Binet and Geneviève Brisson dit DuTilly, was born on 12 January 1707 in Beauport, Canada, a parish slightly upriver from Saint-Michel-de-Bellechasse and a present-day suburb of Quebec City.[98]

Louis and Geneviève married on 9 August 1729 in Beauport when Louis was twenty-three and Geneviève twenty-two.[99] They had at least eight children:

i.   **Louis Bissonnette**, b. Beauport, Canada, 17 June 1730; d. Unknown[100]
ii. **Marie Geneviève Bissonnette**, b. Beauport, Canada, 26 February 1732; m. Nicolas Marmotte Champagne, Montreal, Canada, 9 January 1758; d. Montreal, Province of Quebec, 16 February 1790[101]
iii. **François Bissonnette**, b. Montreal, Canada, 27 April 1735; d. Unknown[102]
iv. **Elisabeth Bissonnette**, b. Montreal, Canada, 21 March 1737; d. Montreal, Canada, 18 April 1762[103]
v.   **Marie Angelique Bissonnette**, b. Montreal, Canada, 28 January 1739; d. Montreal, Lower Canada, 9 April 1825[104]
vi. **Marie Catherine Bissonnette**, b. Montreal, Canada, 12 May 1740; m. Jean Baptiste Demers, Montreal, Province of Quebec, 21 November 1763; d. Montreal, Province of Quebec, 23 September 1767[105]
vii. **Pierre Bissonnette**, b. Montreal, Canada, 3 March 1742; d. Unknown[106]
viii. **Andre Amable Bissonnette**, b. Lachine, Canada, 30 November 1744; d. Unknown[107]

Sometime between 1732 and 1735, the family moved from Beauport to Montreal, as five of their children born between 1735 and 1742 were born in Montreal. Sometime before 1742 they moved to the nearby community of Lachine,§ as their last child, Andre Amable, was born there in 1744, and Geneviève died on 12 May 1745 in Lachine at the age of thirty-eight. She was buried the following day in the Saints-Anges-de-Lachine parish cemetery.[108]

Louis remarried on 16 August 1746 in Montreal to twenty-four-year-old Marie Anne Langevin dit Lacroix of Montreal.[109] Louis and Marie Anne had at least five children:

i.   **Jean Baptiste Bissonnette**, b. Lachine, Canada, 26 November 1747; d. Unknown[110]
ii. **Marie Ann Bissonnette**, b. Lachine, Canada, 23 December 1748; d. Unknown[111]
iii. **Therese Bissonnette**, b. Lachine, Canada, 26 January 1750; m. Joseph Renaud, Montreal, Province of Quebec, 29 July 1771; d. Pointe-Claire, Lower Canada, 2 March 1817[112]
iv. **Marie Josephe Bissonette**, b. Lachine, Canada, 21 September 1751; d. Montreal, Province of Quebec, 21 October 1780[113]
v.   **Unnamed Bissonnette**, b. Lachine, Canada, 1 July 1755; d. Lachine, Canada, 1 July 1755[114]

Louis lived into his early fifties before passing away on 15 May 1760 in Lachine, Canada, and was also

---

§   Lachine is the present-day Borough of Lachine, a suburb of Montreal.

buried in the Saints-Anges-de-Lachine parish cemetery the same day.[115] Marie Anne passed away twelve years later at the age of fifty-three on 10 May 1772 at Montreal's Hôpital General run by the Sisters of Charity of Montreal, also known as the Gray Nuns.[116]

28.   Unknown (Maternal Great-Great-Grandparent of Simon Bouschor)

29.   Unknown (Maternal Great-Great-Grandparent of Simon Bouschor)

30.   Unknown (Maternal Great-Great-Grandparent of Simon Bouschor)

31.   Unknown (Maternal Great-Great-Grandparent of Simon Bouschor)

No information is available about the maternal great-great-grandparents of Simon Bouschor—the grandparents of Marguerite Champagne (Te Pi Ma Guain). See the discussion above beginning on page 112 for more information on the history of the Odawa people.

Notes

ABBREVIATIONS

DI-GQ. Drouin Institute – Genealogy Quebec, https://www.genealogiequebec.com/en/

PRDH-IGD. Le Programme de Recherche en Démographie Historique, https://www.prdh-igd.com

1   Baptismal Record for Antoine Bouchard, 25 October 1682, Record No. 27726, DI-GQ.

2   Baptismal Record for Marie Madeleine Simard, 19 January 1689, Record No. 9478, DI-GQ.

3   Marriage Record for Antoine Bouchard and Marie Madeleine Simard, 20 November 1704, Record No. 9898, DI-GQ.

4   Baptismal Record for Félicité Bouchard, 29 November 1705, Record No. 9561, DI-GQ; Marriage Record for Pierre Perron and Félicité Bouchard, 10 January 1729, Record No. 9938, DI-GQ; Burial Record for Félicité Bouchard, 17 December 1757, Record No. 201869, DI-GQ.

5   Baptismal Record for Noël Bouchard, 13 June 1707, Record No. 9569, DI-GQ; Marriage Record for Jean Baptiste Noël Bouchard and Marie Catherine Tremblay, 28 July 1734, Record No. 111042, DI-GQ; Individual Record for Jean Baptiste Noel Bouchard, Individual No. 88165, PRDH-IGD.

6   Baptismal Record for Catherine Bouchard, 19 June 1709, Record No. 9583, DI-GQ; Burial Record for Catherine Bouchard, May 1710, Record No. 9957, DI-GQ.

7   Baptismal Record for Antoine Bouchard, 22 February 1711, Record No. 9595, DI-GQ; Marriage Record for Antoine Bouchard and Marie Jeanne Gagnon, 20 November 1738, Record No. 111047, DI-GQ; Burial Record for Antoine Bouchard, 3 July 1776, Record No. 367329, DI-GQ.

8   Baptismal Record for Jacques Bouchard, 8 January 1713, Record No. 9609, DI-GQ; Marriage Record for Jacques Bouchard and Marie Madeleine Bouchard, 13 November 1714, Record No. 111308, DI-GQ; Burial Record for Jacques Bouchard, 18 May 1772, Record No. 367395, DI-GQ.

9   Baptismal Record for Marie Madeleine Bouchard, 16 November 1714, Record No. 9620, DI-GQ; Marriage Record for Pierre Jacques Alard and Marie Madeleine Bouchard, 8 January 1737, Record No. 111207, DI-GQ; Burial Record for Marie Madeleine Bouchard, 1 November 1793, Record No. 384694, DI-GQ.

10   Baptismal Record for Joseph Bouchard, 2 February 1718, Record No. 9661, DI-GQ; Marriage Record for Joseph Bouchard and Françoise Fortin, 14 November 1746, Record No. 110845, DI-GQ; Burial Record for Joseph Bouchard, 26 September 1803, Record No. 2381952, DI-GQ.

11   Baptismal Record for Marguerite Bouchard, 11 March 1720, Record No. 9704, DI-GQ; Marriage Record for Marguerite Bouchard and Joseph Tremblay, 6 November 1742, Record No. 111214, DI-GQ; Marriage Record for Marguerite Bouchard and François LeClerc, 8 October 1764, Record No. 202299, DI-GQ; Burial Record for Marguerite Bouchard, 10 August 1799, Record No. 384841, DI-GQ.

12   Baptismal Record for Emerentienne Bouchard, 1 April 1722, Record No. 9736, DI-GQ; Marriage Record for Emerentienne Bouchard and François Perron, 5 February 1743, Record No. 111215, DI-GQ; Burial Record for Emerentienne Bouchard, 29 May 1744, Record No. 111244, DI-GQ.

13   Baptismal Record for Michel Bouchard, 12 August 1725, Record No. 9793, DI-GQ; Marriage Record for Michel Bouchard and Marie Louise Tremblay, 15 November 1750, Record No. 195485, DI-GQ; Burial Record for Michel Bouchard, 20 November 1789, Record No. 394862, DI-GQ.

14   Baptismal Record for Louis Bouchard, 18 May 1729, Record No. 9878, DI-GQ; Marriage Record of Louis Bouchard and Marie Françoise Dufour, 14 November 1757, Record No. 195504, DI-GQ; Burial Record for Louis Bouchard, 18 November 1780, Record No. 367372, DI-GQ.

15   Burial Record for Antoine Bouchard, 24 June 1759, Record No. 195549, DI-GQ.

16   Francis Parkman, *France and England in North America Vol. 2: Count Frontenac and New France under Louis XIV, A Half-Century of Conflict, Montcalm and Wolfe* (New York: Library of America, 1983), 1399-1400, 1472.

17   Généalogie Marie-Madeleine Simard, Généalogie du Québec et d'Amérique française, accessed 26 October 2019, https://www.nosorigines.qc.ca/GenealogieQuebec.aspx?genealogie=Simard_Marie-Madeleine&pid=1400.

18   Baptismal Record for Elisabeth Tremblay, 5 March 1715, DI-GQ.

19   Marriage Record for Bonaventure Dufour and Elisabeth Tremblay, 8 November 1734, DI-GQ.

20   Marriage Record for Pierre LaVoie and Marie Reine Dufour, 17 November 1756, Record No. 195501, DI-GQ; Burial Record for Marie Reine Dufour, 25 October 1812, Record No. 2878610, DI-GQ.

21   Baptismal Record for Augustin Roch Dufour, 13 November 1737, Record No. 111117, DI-GQ; Marriage Record for Augustin Roch Dufour and Therese Tremblay, 9 November 1772, Record No. 361376, DI-GQ; Burial Record for Augustin Roch Dufour, 15 June 1821, Record No. 2429675, DI-GQ.

22   Baptismal Record for Marie Françoise Dufour, 4 April 1740, Record No. 110612, DI-GQ; Marriage Record of Louis Bouchard and Marie Françoise Dufour, 14 November 1757, Record No. 195504, DI-GQ; Burial Record for Françoise Dufour, 14 June 1815, Record No. 2381998, DI-GQ.

23   Baptismal Record for Jean Baptiste Dufour, 15 November 1742, Record No. 111153, DI-GQ; Marriage Record for Jean Baptiste Dufour and Marie Genevieve Bouchard, 17 November 1768, Record No. 216800; Burial Record for Jean Baptiste Dufour, 13 June 1810, Record No. 2381971, DI-GQ.

24   Baptismal Record for Joseph Michel Dufour, 14 October 1744, Record No. 111168, DI-GQ; Marriage Record for Joseph Michel Dufour and Charlotte Tremblay, 2 September 1771, Record No. 216999, DI-GQ; Burial Record for Joseph Michel Dufour, 16 December 1829, Record No. 3311954, DI-GQ.

25   Baptismal Record for Constance Colombe Dufour, 13 January 1747, Record No. 111180, DI-GQ; Marriage Record for Constance Colombe Dufour and Jean Baptiste Tremblay, 17 November 1768, Record No. 216801, DI-GQ; Burial Record for Constance Colombe Dufour, 19 December 1776, Record No. 367364, DI-GQ.

26   Individual Record for Anonyme Dufour, Individual No. 138821, PRDH-IGD.

27   Baptismal Record for Zacharie Dufour, 23 Mar 1750, Record No. 195401, DI-GQ; Marriage Record for Zacharie Dufour and Marie Anne Theriault, 8 January 1781, Record No. 222243, DI-GQ; Burial Record for Zacharie Dufour, 18 March 1833, Record No. 3385762, DI-GQ.

28   Individual Record for Anonyme Dufour, Individual No. 65593, PRDH-IGD.

29   Baptismal Record for Marie Joseph Dufour, 28 May 1757, Record No. 195444, DI-GQ; Marriage Record for Elie Mailloux and Marie Josephe Dufour, 9 November 1777, Record No. 2198900, DI-GQ; Burial Record for Marie Josephe Dufour, 26 November 1833, Record No. 3311993, DI-GQ; Family Record for Bonaventure & Marie Elisabeth Tremblay, Couple No. 19169, PRDH-IGD.

30   Burial Record for Bonaventure Dufour, 23 May 1783, Record No. 367378, DI-GQ.

31   Burial Record for Elisabeth Tremblay, 16 May 1799, Record No. 384810, DI-GQ.

32   Lucie LeBlanc Consentino, "1686 Acadian Census," Acadian Census Records, accessed 29 November 2019, http://www.acadian-home.org/census1686.html.

33   Lucie LeBlanc Consentino, "1693 Acadian Census," Acadian Census Records, accessed 29 November 2019, http://www.acadian-home.org/census1693.html.

34   Christopher Hodson, "Exile on Spruce Street: An Acadian History," *The William and Mary Quarterly* 67, no. 2 (2010): 258, https://doi.org/10.5309/willmaryquar.67.2.249.

35   Marriage Record for René LeBlanc and Elizabeth Melançon, 30 July 1709, DI-GQ; Individual Record for Elisabeth Melancon Lavendure, Individual No. 3765891, PRDH-IGD.

36   "Généalogie Rene Leblanc," Généalogie du Québec et d'Amérique française, accessed 4 May 2019, https://www.nosorigines.qc.ca/GenealogieQuebec.aspx?pid=660313&partID=21566.

37   Baptismal Record for Benjamin LeBlanc, 8 December 1711, Record No. 6146118, DI-GQ.

38   Marriage Record for Joseph Meunier and Marie Josephe LeBlanc, 27 April 1734, DI-GQ.

39   "Généalogie Desire Leblanc," Généalogie du Québec et d'Amérique française, accessed 7 December 2019, https://www.nosorigines.qc.ca/GenealogieQuebec.aspx?genealogie=Leblanc_Desire&pid=660316.

40   Baptismal Record for Elisabeth LeBlanc, 8 December 1718, Record No. 6146187, DI-GQ.

41   "Généalogie Rene Leblanc," Généalogie du Québec et d'Amérique française, accessed 29 November 2019, https://www.nosorigines.qc.ca/GenealogieQuebec.aspx?pid=660313&partID=21566.

42   Marriage Record for René Leblanc and Marguerite Thibault, 26 November 1720, DI-GQ.

43   Baptismal Record for Marguerite Thibault, 20 October 1704, Record No. 6143177, DI-GQ.

44   "Généalogie Rene Leblanc," Généalogie du Québec et d'Amérique française, accessed 4 May 2019, https://www.nosorigines.qc.ca/GenealogieQuebec.aspx?pid=660313&partID=21566.

45   Baptismal Record for Marguerite LeBlanc, 25 July 1721, DI-GQ; Marriage Record for Joseph Babin and Marguerite LeBlanc, 22 November 1745, DI-GQ.

46   Baptismal Record for Marie LeBlanc, 25 July 1721, DI-GQ.

47   Baptismal Record for Anne LeBlanc, 25 July 1721, DI-GQ.

48   Baptismal Record for Anne LeBlanc, 28 October 1724, Record No. 6146304, DI-GQ; Marriage Record for Rene Theriault and Anne LeBlanc, 23 November 1744, DI-GQ.

49   Baptismal Record for Marie LeBlanc, 19 March 1726, Record No. 6146909, DI-GQ; "Généalogie Marie Leblanc," Généalogie du Québec et d'Amérique française, accessed 7 December 2019, https://www.nosorigines.qc.ca/GenealogieQuebec.aspx?pid=660341&partID=660342.

50   Baptismal Record for Blanche LeBlanc, 19 March 1726, Record No. 6146908, DI-GQ; Marriage Record for Michel Bonhomme and Blanche LeBlanc, 5 October 1762, Record No. 259235, DI-GQ; Burial Record for Blanche LeBlanc, 1 July 1763, Record No. 259744, DI-GQ.

51   Baptismal Record for Marie Madeleine LeBlanc, 21 November 1727, Record No. 6146354, DI-GQ; "Généalogie

Madeleine Leblanc," Généalogie du Québec et d'Amérique française, accessed 7 December 2019, https://www.nos-origines.qc.ca/GenealogieQuebec.aspx?genealogie=Leblanc_Madeleine&pid=660350.

52 Baptismal Record for Simon LeBlanc, 17 November 1731, Record No. 6146450, DI-GQ.

53 Baptismal Record for Rene LeBlanc, 17 November 1731, Record No. 6146450, DI-GQ; "Généalogie Rene Leblanc," Généalogie du Québec et d'Amérique française, accessed 7 December 2019, https://www.nosorigines.qc.ca/GenealogieQuebec.aspx?genealogie=Leblanc_Rene&pid=660371.

54 Baptismal Record for Françoise LeBlanc, 4 May 1734, Record No. 6146492, DI-GQ; "Généalogie Françoise Leblanc," Généalogie du Québec et d'Amérique française, accessed 7 December 2019, https://www.nosorigines.qc.ca/GenealogieQuebec.aspx?genealogie=Leblanc_Francoise&pid=660362; Family Record for Rene LeBlanc & Marguerite Thibault, Couple No. 13587, PRDH-IGD.

55 Baptismal Record for Ursule LeBlanc, 27 December 1735, Record No. 6147085, DI-GQ; Marriage Record for Jacques Christophe Babuty and Ursule LeBlanc, 6 February 1758, Record No. 250021, DI-GQ; Burial Record for Ursule LeBlanc, 2 November 1794, Record No. 384257, DI-GQ.

56 Baptismal Record for Pierre Benjamin LeBlanc, 1740, Record No. 6147173, DI-GQ (Note: The Baptismal Record is undated but is recorded between an earlier record dated 2 January 1740 and a later record dated 17 February 1740); Burial Record for Benjamin LeBlanc, 27 February 1805, Record No. 2867451, DI-GQ.

57 Baptismal Record for Esther LeBlanc, 1740, Record No. 6147173, DI-GQ (Note: The Baptismal Record is undated but is between an earlier record dated 2 January 1740, and a later record dated 17 February 1740.); "Généalogie Esther Leblanc," Généalogie du Québec et d'Amérique française, accessed 7 December 2019, https://www.nosorigines.qc.ca/GenealogieQuebec.aspx?genealogie=Leblanc_Esther&pid=103981; Burial Record for Esther LeBlanc, 18 May 1805, Record No. 2880353, DI-GQ.

58 Baptismal Record for Jean Baptiste LeBlanc, 25 June 1744, Record No. 6147303, DI-GQ; "Généalogie Jean-Baptiste Leblanc," Généalogie du Québec et d'Amérique française, accessed 7 December 2019, https://www.nosorigines.qc.ca/GenealogieQuebec.aspx?genealogie=Leblanc_Jean-Baptiste&pid=660369; Burial Record for Jean Baptiste LeBlanc, 5 November 1824, Record No. 2867838, DI-GQ.

59 John Mack Faragher, *A Great and Noble Scheme: The Tragic Story of the Expulsion of the French Acadians from their American Homeland* (New York: W.W. Norton & Company, Inc., 2005), 78-79.

60 Faragher, *Great and Noble Scheme*, 201-202.

61 Faragher, *Great and Noble Scheme*, 202.

62 Faragher, *Great and Noble Scheme*, 262, 341; Hodson, "Exile on Spruce Street," 262.

63 WikiTree Contributors, "Marguerite Thébeau (1704 - abt. 1750)," WikiTree: The Free Family Tree, last modified 21 July 2024, https://www.wikitree.com/wiki/Th%C3%A9beau-21.

64 Henry Wadsworth Longfellow, "Evangeline," in *English Poetry III: From Tennyson to Whitman*, Vol. XLII The Harvard Classics (New York: P.F. Collier & Son, 1910), GB.

65 Faragher, *Great and Noble Scheme*, 340-41.

66 Faragher, *Great and Noble Scheme*, 343-44.

67 Faragher, *Great and Noble Scheme*, 344-45.

68 Faragher, *Great and Noble Scheme*, 353-54.

69 Faragher, *Great and Noble Scheme*, 353-55.

70 Faragher, *Great and Noble Scheme*, 358-59.

71 Faragher, *Great and Noble Scheme*, 359-60.

72 Faragher, *Great and Noble Scheme*, 361.

73 Faragher, *Great and Noble Scheme*, 361.

74 "Exile Destination: Pennsylvania," Acadian-Cajun Genealogy & History, accessed 10 August 2019, https://freepages.rootsweb.com/~acadiancajun/genealogy/expa.htm.

75 Faragher, *Great and Noble Scheme*, 376-77; Hodson, "Exile on Spruce Street," 263-64.

76 Henry Wadsworth Longfellow, "Evangeline," in *English Poetry III: From Tennyson to Whitman*, Vol. XLII The Harvard Classics (New York: P.F. Collier & Son, 1910), GB.

77 Baptismal Record for Charles Dugas, 17 December 1711, Record No. 6146119, DI-GQ.

78 Baptismal Record for Anne Suzanne LeBlanc, 16 March 1718, Record No. 6146763, DI-GQ.

79 Marriage Record for Charles Dugas and Anne Suzanne LeBlanc, 7 January 1739, DI-GQ.

80 Baptismal Record for Charles Dugas, 23 September 1739, Record No. 6147162, DI-GQ; "Généalogie Charles Dugas," Généalogie du Québec et d'Amérique française, accessed 8 December 2019, https://www.nosorigines.qc.ca/GenealogieQuebec.aspx?genealogie=Dugas_Charles&pid=165583; Burial Record for Charles Dugas, 16 March 1806, Record No. 2867480, DI-GQ.

81 "Généalogie Marie Dugas," Généalogie du Québec et d'Amérique française, accessed 8 December 2019, https://www.nosorigines.qc.ca/GenealogieQuebec.aspx?genealogie=Dugas_Marie&pid=993212; Burial Record for Marie

Dugas, 4 July 1839, Record No. 4075470, DI-GQ.

82   Baptismal Record for Anne Dugas, 16 December 1740, Record No. 6147190, DI-GQ.

83   Marriage Record for Abraham Dugas and Marguerite Pelagie Bujold, 22 April 1776, Record No. 774449, DI-GQ; Marriage Record for Abraham Dugas and Marie Amable Joli, 11 February 1800, Record No. 2210435, DI-GQ; Burial Record for Abraham Dugas, 10 April 1826, Record No. 4159309, DI-GQ.

84   Baptismal Record for Pierre Dugas, 14 September 1742, Record No. 6147247, DI-GQ; Marriage Record for Pierre Dugas and Françoise Robichaud, 15 April 1776, Record No. 774447, DI-GQ; Individual Record for Pierre Dugas, Individual No. 364276, PRDH-IGD.

85   Baptismal Record for Joseph Dugas, 14 September 1742, Record No. 6147247, DI-GQ; "Généalogie Joseph Dugas," Généalogie du Québec et d'Amérique française, accessed 8 December 2019, https://www.nosorigines.qc.ca/GenealogieQuebec.aspx?genealogie=Dugas_Joseph&pid=1417322.

86   Baptismal Record for Amand Herculin Dugas, 7 November 1743, Record No. 6147287, DI-GQ.

87   Marriage Record for Claude Landry and Helene Dugas, 16 October 1770, Record No. 212255, DI-GQ; Burial Record for Helene Dugas, 25 April 1830, Record No. 4075198, DI-GQ.

88   "Généalogie Françoise Dugas," Généalogie du Québec et d'Amérique française, accessed 8 December 2019, https://www.nosorigines.qc.ca/GenealogieQuebec.aspx?genealogie=Dugas_Francoise&pid=861614; Burial Record for Françoise Dugas, 7 April 1834, Record No. 4075297, DI-GQ.

89   Marriage Record for Hilaire Poirier and Angelique Dugas, 8 November 1773, Record No. 774442, DI-GQ; Burial Record for Angelique Dugas, 1 December 1825, Record No. 3379308, DI-GQ.

90   Marriage Record for Jean Landry and Marthe Dugas, 6 May 1776, Record No. 774451, DI-GQ; Burial Record for Marthe Dugas, 7 February 1840, Record No. 4075491, DI-GQ.

91   "Recensement de la Baye des Chaleurs, Bonaventure (1765)," Acadian Home, accessed 10 August 2019, http://www.acadian-home.org/1765-Census-BaieChaleur-Binder1.pdf.

92   "Carleton-sur-Mer—The Herons of Tracadièche Are Still There," Acadie: On the Roads of the Acadian People, accessed 16 May 2021, https://acadie.cheminsdelafrancophonie.org/en/carleton-sur-mer-the-herons-of-tracadieche-are-still-there/.

93   WikiTree Contributors, "Anne (Leblanc) LeBlanc (1718-abt.1776)," WikiTree: The Free Family Tree, last modified 13 September 2022, https://www.wikitree.com/wiki/Leblanc-459.

94   Burial Record for Charles Dugas, 26 January 1801, Record No. 2867422, DI-GQ.

95   Marriage Record for Claude Marmotte and Nicole Garaudel, 7 January 1727, Registres paroissiaux et d'état civil, Archives départementales des Ardennes, https://archives.cd08.fr/ark:/75583/s00532d83791654f/532d83791fd05.

96   Marriage Record of Nicolas Marmotte Champagne and Marie Geneviève Bissonnet, 26 February 1732, Record No. 298764, DI-GQ; Nicolas Marmotte Champagne Burial Record, 19 September 1774, Record No. 395485, DI-GQ.

97   Baptismal Record for Louis Bissonnette, 3 June 1706, Record No. 1196, DI-GQ.

98   Baptismal Record for Marie Geneviève Binet, 12 January 1707, Record No. 76511, DI-GQ.

99   Marriage Record for Louis Bissonnette and Marie Geneviève Binet, 9 August 1729, Record No. 77536, DI-GQ.

100   Individual Record for Louis Bissonnet, Individual No. 71226, PRDH-IGD.

101   Baptismal Record for Marie Geneviève Bissonnette, 26 February 1732, Record No. 170015, DI-GQ; Marriage Record of Nicolas Marmotte Champagne and Marie Geneviève Bissonnette, 9 January 1758, Record No. 298764, DI-GQ; Marie Geneviève Bissonnette Burial Record, 17 February 1790, Record No. 380597, DI-GQ.

102   Baptismal Record for François Bissonnette, 27 April 1735, Record No. 146237, DI-GQ.

103   Baptismal Record for Elisabeth Bissonnette, 22 March 1737, Record No. 146644, DI-GQ; Burial Record for Elisabeth Bissonnette, 19 April 1762, Record No. 302518, DI-GQ.

104   Baptismal Record for Marie Angelique Bissonnette, 29 January 1739, Record No. 147056, DI-GQ; Individual Record for Marie Angelique Bissonnet, Individual No. 88636, PRDH-IGD.

105   Baptismal Record for Marie Catherine Bissonnette, 13 May 1740, Record No. 147353, DI-GQ; Marriage Record for Jean Baptiste Demers and Catherine Bissonnette, 21 November 1763, Record No. 299187, DI-GQ; Burial Record for Marie Catherine Bissonnette, 24 September 1767, Record No. 363172, DI-GQ.

106   Baptismal Record for Pierre Bissonnette, 4 March 1742, Record No. 147734, DI-GQ.

107   Baptismal Record for Andre Amable Bissonnette, 30 November 1744, Record No. 115790, DI-GQ.

108   Burial Record for Marie Geneviève Binet, 13 May 1745, Record No. 116152, DI-GQ.

109   Marriage Record for Louis Bissonnette and Marie Anne Langevin, 16 August 1746, Record No. 150294, DI-GQ.

110   Baptismal Record for Jean Baptiste Bissonnette, 27 November 1747, Record No. 115861, DI-GQ.

111   Individual Record for Marie Anne Bissonnet, Individual No. 2653508, PRDH-IGD; Baptismal Record for Marie Anne Bissonnette, 24 December 1748, Record No. 115892, DI-GQ.

112   Baptismal Record for Therese Bissonnette, 27 January 1750, Record No. 274676, DI-GQ; Marriage Record for Joseph Renaud and Therese Bissonnette, 29 July 1771, Record No. 213237, DI-GQ; Burial Record for Therese Bissonnette,

4 March 1817, Record No. 2802971, DI-GQ.

113   Baptismal Record for Marie Josephe Bissonnette, 22 September 1751, Record No. 274715, DI-GQ; Burial Record for Marie Joseph Bissonnette, 22 October 1780, Record No. 364009, DI-GQ.

114   Burial Record for Unnamed Bissonnette, 1 July 1755, Record No. 275306, DI-GQ.

115   Burial Record for Louis Bissonnette, 15 May 1760, Record No. 275397, DI-GQ.

116   "Généalogie Marie-Anne Langevin," Généalogie du Québec et d'Amérique française, accessed 17 November 2019, https://www.nosorigines.qc.ca/GenealogieQuebec.aspx?genealogie=Langevin_Marie-Anne&pid=54435.

Great-Great-Great Grandparents of Simon Bouschor

32.   Claude Bouchard

Born: Approximately 1626 in Saint-Cosme-en-Vairais, Maine, France (Saint-Cosme-en-Vairais, Sarthe, Pays-de-la-Loire, France)

Died: 25 November 1699 in Petite-Rivière, Canada (Petite-Rivière-Saint-François, Capitale-Nationale, Quebec)

33.   Louise Gagne

Born: 21 January 1642 in Igé, Perche, France (Igé, Orne, Normandy, France)

Died: 27 April 1721 in Petite-Rivière, Canada (Petite-Rivière-Saint-François, Capitale-Nationale, Quebec)

Claude Bouchard and Louise Gagne are the founding Bouchard family ancestors who came to New France from Europe in the 1600s. Claude Bouchard was born to parents Jacques Bouchard and Noelle Touschard in approximately 1626 in the small French village of Saint-Cosme-en-Vairais in the historic province of Maine near the border of the Perche province. Little is known about Claude's parents, Jacques and Noelle, except that Jacques was a tailor like his son would become.[1]

Located in France's Sarthe department in the present-day Pays-de-la-Loire region, Saint-Cosme is approximately twenty-three miles northeast of Le Mans, France. At the time of Claude's birth and until reorganization during the French Revolution, Saint-Cosme belonged to France's historic Maine region. Just under 2,000 people call Saint-Cosme home today.[2] A plaque in honor of Claude Bouchard graces Saint-Cosme's main street at 100 Rue Nationale, noting the 100,000 Canadian Bouchards descended from him.[3] In addition, a primary school in Saint-Cosme, the *Ecole Claude Bouchard*, bears his name.

Known as "the Petite Claude," he was one of several Bouchards who left France and settled in New France (present-day Quebec). Legend has it that in 1650, one of the early colonizers and promoters of New France, seigneur Robert Giffard, came to the White Horse Inn in Saint-Cosme and gave a lecture on the opportunities in New France. Evidently, Claude was taken with Giffard's presentation, for he and his friends Julien Fortin and Gervais Bisson resolved to move to New France. Flush with dreams of new opportunity, Claude left Saint-Cosme in 1650 from the French port of Dieppe, arriving in New France approximately three months later.[4] He initially settled on the Beaupré coast northeast of Saint-Anne-de-Beaupré after obtaining a land grant on 26 October 1650 from Olivier Letardif, the attorney for the Compagnie de Beaupré.[5] The Compagnie de Beaupré managed the settlement of the Seigneurie de Beaupré with responsibility over territory spanning from just northeast of present-day Quebec City downriver to near Baie-Saint-Paul.[6] The seigneurial system in New France resulted in the distribution of land granted to favored colonists who in turn allocated land to tenants known as *habitants* like Claude and other settlers.[7] Claude later sold the thirty arpent parcel of land* to Louis Guimond on 1 October 1657 for 600 livres after receiving permission from the colonial authorities organized as the Company of One Hundred Associates.[8]

Claude married Louise Gagne, also known as Louise Gasnier, on 25 May 1654 in Quebec's Notre-

---

*   An arpent of land equals approximately 0.85 acres. *See Merriam-Webster Collegiate Dictionary*, 11th ed. (2020), s.v. "arpent."

Dame-de-Québec parish church in the presence of the missionary Paul Ragueneau.[9]

Louise was born on 21 January 1642 to parents Louis Gagne (also known as Gasnier) and Marie Michel in the commune of Igé, in France's historic region of Perche. Igé—a neighbor of Saint-Cosme less than ten miles northeast—is currently located in the Orne department of France's Normandy region. Louise came to New France as a small child in approximately 1644. On 30 October 1653, she entered into a marriage contract with Claude Bouchard at the home of her parents before notary Aubert.[10] Louise was only twelve at the time of the marriage, which occurred the following May, but their first child, Marie, was not born until 27 October 1659 when she was seventeen. Louise was confirmed in the Catholic church at Château-Richer on 2 February 1660 at the age of eighteen, accompanied by Claude, her parents, and several siblings.[11]

Claude and Louise had twelve children:

i. **Marie Bouchard**, b. Quebec, Canada, 27 October 1659; d. Montreal, Canada, 29 April 1739[12]

ii. **Jacques Bouchard**, b. Approximately 1662; d. Château-Richer, Canada, 12 December 1690[13]

iii. **Gilles Bouchard**, b. Château-Richer, Canada, 8 March 1664; d. Château-Richer, Canada, 22 March 1664[14]

iv. **Marguerite Bouchard**, b. Château-Richer, Canada, 15 October 1665; m. René Levoie, Sainte-Anne-de-Beaupré, Canada, 4 November 1683; d. Baie-Saint-Paul, Canada, 6 April 1731[15]

v. **Louise Bouchard**, b. Approximately 1668; d. Petite-Rivière, Canada, 8 December 1696[16]

vi. **Anne Bouchard**, b. Sainte-Anne-de-Beaupré, Canada, 20 February 1670; m. Louis Jobidon, L'Ange-Gardien, Canada, 20 November 1690; d. Château-Richer, Canada, 8 April 1731[17]

vii. **Genevieve Bouchard**, b. Sainte-Anne-de-Beaupré, Canada, 25 April 1672; m. Michel Tremblay, Baie-Saint-Paul, Canada, 20 June 1686; d. Petite-Rivière, Canada, 23 March 1754[18]

viii. **François Bouchard**, b. Sainte-Anne-de-Beaupré, Canada, 8 April 1674; m. Marguerite Simard dit Lombrette, Baie-Saint-Paul, Canada, 15 June 1699; d. Petite-Rivière, Canada, 12 October 1756[19]

ix. **Rosalie Bouchard**, b. Sainte-Anne-de-Beaupré, Canada, 6 April 1676; m. Etienne Simard dit Lombrette, Baie-Saint-Paul, Canada, 22 November 1695; d. Baie-Saint-Paul, Canada, 22 June 1733[20]

x. **Claude Bouchard**, b. Sainte-Anne-de-Beaupré, Canada, 14 October 1678; d. Sainte-Anne-de-Beaupré, Canada, 28 October 1678[21]

xi. **Louis Bouchard**, b. Sainte-Anne-de-Beaupré, Canada, 12 February 1680; m. (1) Suzanne Lefebvre, La Prairie, Canada, 25 February 1715; m. (2) Françoise Dania, La Prairie, Canada, 2 December 1724; d. Montreal, Canada, 17 November 1727[22]

xii. **Antoine Bouchard**, b. Sainte-Anne-de-Beaupré, Canada, 15 October 1682; m. Marie Madeleine Simard dit Lombrette, Baie-Saint-Paul, Canada, 20 November 1704 d. Petite-Rivière, Province of Quebec, 24 June 1759[23]

On 30 July 1657, Claude obtained a six-year lease on the Saint-Charles smallholding near Cap Tourmente on the Beaupré coast (located approximately thirty miles northeast of Quebec City near the present-day community of Saint-Joachim).[24] Cap Tourmente owed its name to stormy conditions generated by wind along the river and is today home to the Cap Tourmente National Wildlife Area.[25]

1615 map of New France depicting the region shortly before the arrival of Claude Bouchard and other Bouschor-family ancestors

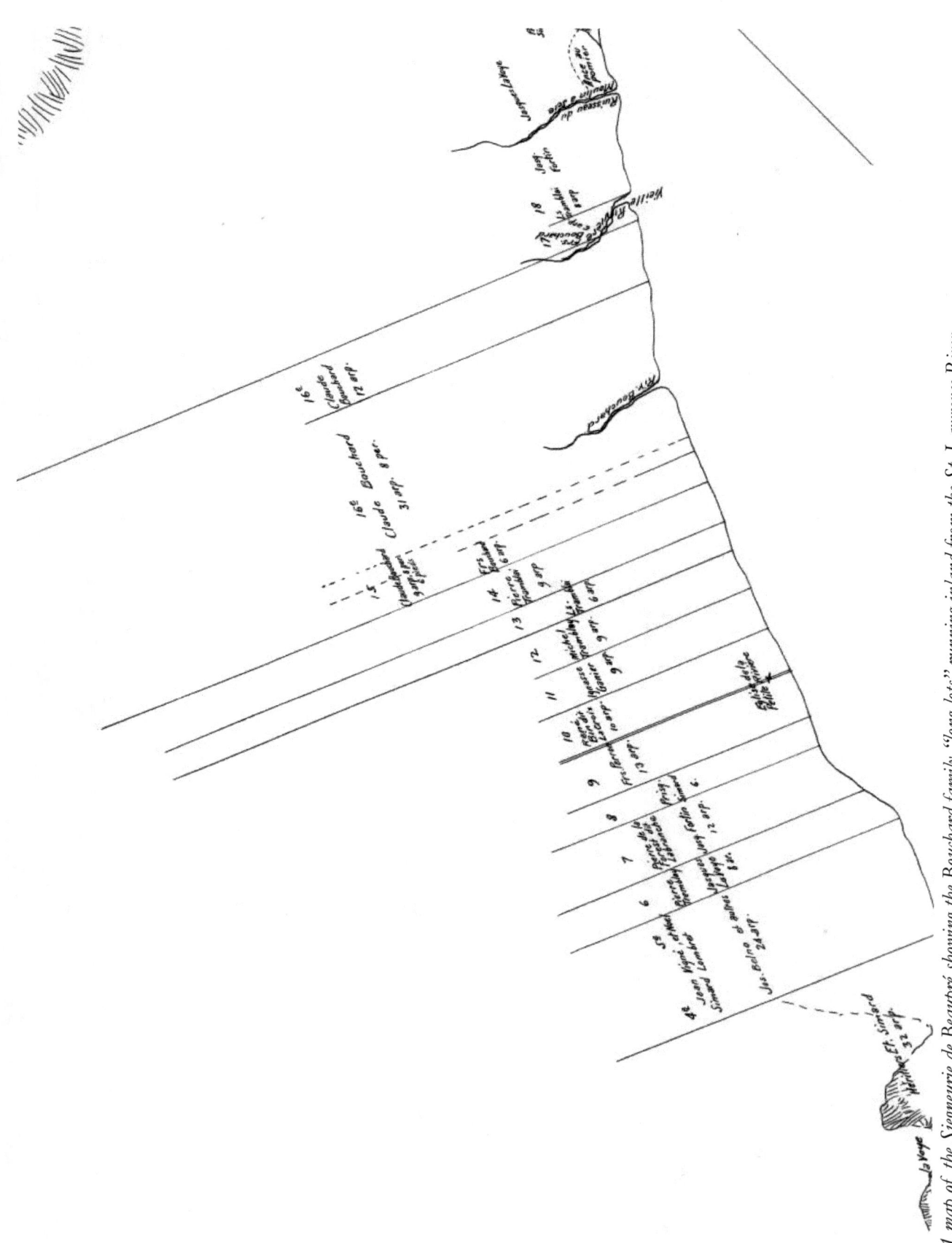

1751 map of the Siegneurie de Beaupré showing the Bouchard family "long lots" running inland from the St. Lawrence River

Although Claude bought another four arpents of land in the area on 4 December 1657, the region's governor ordered Claude and family to abandon the land in 1661 due to increased ransacking by the Mohawks.[26] The family initially took refuge in Château-Richer, but the following year they returned to the Cap Tourmente region. Claude obtained three arpents of land half a league deep near Petit-Cap de Saint-Joachim just downriver from Sainte-Anne-de-Beaupré on 11 April 1662 from Charles Aubert de la Chesnaye, the agent of the Lords of Beaupré. Claude built his family a house on the land and, on the following 8 September 1663, bought additional land from his neighbor Nicolas Maniere for 255 pounds.[27†] These narrow parcels ("seigneuries") running inland from the water were known as "long lots" or "ribbon farms," with the intent being to provide both water and transportation access to the landowners.[28]

The first census of New France taken in 1666 lists forty-year-old Claude, twenty-four-year-old Louise, and their three eldest surviving children—Marie, Jacques, and Marguerite—as living in the Beaupré region, with Claude working as a *tailleur d'habits*.[29] Based on this census, he continued to practice his craft as a tailor while working his land. Another census taken the following year finds the family still living in Beaupré and having eight arpents of land and seven animals.[30] Through a rental contract executed on 7 November 1668, Claude obtained additional land for a period of seven years at the rate of 500 pounds and 6 capons per year. These debts ultimately grew to be too much, and Claude was forced to sell his land on 28 May 1675 for 1,500 livres to pay his debts.[31]

Despite these setbacks, Claude and Louise were not deterred in their determination to succeed in the New World. The Bouchard family next moved to the nearby parish of Saint-François-Xavier-de-la-Petite-Rivière (present-day Petite-Rivière-Saint-François), more commonly known as Petite-Riv-

ière, and became the first settlers in the area.[32] He obtained a concession to work twelve arpents of land fronting the Saint Lawrence River from Monseigneur de Laval, the Bishop of Quebec and Lord of Beaupré, on 28 May 1675—the same day he had disposed of his farm at Cap Tourmente.[33] Petite-Rivière was at the northern end of the Beaupré Seignory (Seigneurie de Beaupré), several miles downriver from their former home at Cap Tourmente. A plaque at Petite-Rivière dedicated by its citizens in 1975 commemorates Claude's arrival 300 years earlier on 28 May 1675. Today, Petite-Rivière remains a small hamlet in Charlevoix, with a population of 953 inhabitants as of 2021.[34]

Claude would spend the remaining twenty-plus years of his life in Petite-Rivière. Monseigneur de Laval granted Claude an additional twelve arpents of land on 20 October 1676. He performed work on behalf of the church and is recorded as supervising a group of carpenters in 1678 and providing them with butter.[35] A Quebec census taken in 1681 shows Claude and Louise, together with their children Marie, Jacques, Marguerite, François, Louise, Angelique, Jean, and Roslie, living on six arpents of land in the Seigneurie de Beaupré and owning two flintlock muskets and ten *bêtes à cornes* (horned beasts).[36] Claude lost six of the arpents granted to him in 1675 on 26 July 1694 due to inability to make his rent payments, but the Bishop of Quebec nonetheless regranted the six arpents to Claude and Louise's eldest surviving son, François Bouchard, on the following 2 August 1695.[37] On 19 October 1698, a year prior to Claude's death, he and Louise granted each of their three surviving sons—François, Louis, and Antoine—ten arpents of land fronting the Saint Lawrence River.[38] The 1751 map on the opposite page depicts the Bouchard family landholdings in Petite-Rivière.

Claude died at the age of seventy on 25 November 1699 in Petite-Rivière and was buried the following day in the cemetery of St-François Xavier Church

---

†   While the Bouchard family is believed to have moved to the Petit Cap region in 1662, at least two of their children born during their time in Petit-Cap, Gilles Bouchard and Marguerite Bouchard, were baptized in the Visitation-de-Notre-Dame parish located upriver in their former home of Château-Richer. It's possible the family returned to Château-Richer for the baptisms or that the Visitation-de-Notre-Dame parish priest traveled to Petit-Cap to perform religious services.

in Petite-Rivière.[39]

Louise outlived Claude by over twenty years before

passing away around 27 April 1721 at the age of seventy-nine in Petite-Rivière and was buried the same day at St-François Xavier Church.[40]

34.   Noel Simard dit Lombrette

Born: Approximately 1637 in Angoulême, Angoumois, France (Angoulême, Charente, Nouvelle-Aquitaine, France)
Died: 24 July 1715 in Baie-Saint-Paul, Canada (Baie-Saint-Paul, Capitale-Nationale, Quebec)

35.   Marie Madeleine Racine

Born: 25 July 1646 in Quebec, Canada (Quebec City, Capitale-Nationale, Quebec)
Died: 3 December 1746 in Baie-Saint-Paul, Canada (Baie-Saint-Paul, Capitale-Nationale, Quebec)

Noel Simard dit Lombrette, the son of Pierre Simard and Suzanne Durand, was born in 1637 in Angoulême in the historic Angoumois province of France (present-day Angoulême, Charente department, Nouvelle-Aquitaine region). Noel and his father, Pierre, left France in approximately May 1657, possibly aboard the ship *Le Taureau* from La Rochelle and arrived in Canada on approximately 21 June 1657.[41] They settled on the Beaupré coast and set about cultivating land.

Noel's future spouse, Marie Madeleine Racine, was born on 25 July 1646 in Quebec, Canada, to parents Etienne Racine and Marguerite Martin dit l'Ecossais and was baptized the same day in Quebec's Notre-Dame-de-Québec parish.[42] Noel and Marie Madeleine married on 22 November 1661 in the parish church of Château-Richer, Canada, in a ceremony officiated by Father Thomas Morel.[43] They had fourteen children:

i.   **Pierre Simard**, b. Château-Richer, Canada, 30 April 1663; m. Claire Dodier, Baie-Saint-Paul, Canada, 6 December 1690; d. Sainte-Anne-de-Beaupré, Canada, 7 November 1724[44]

ii. **Noel Simard**, b. Château-Richer, Canada, 7 October 1664; m. Anne Dodier, Baie-Saint-Paul, Canada, 26 April 1689; d. Baie-Saint-Paul, Canada, 9 April 1726[45]

iii. **Marie Madeleine Simard**, b. Château-Richer, Canada, 4 January 1667; m. Pierre Tremblay, Sainte-Anne-de-Beaupré, Canada, 3 November 1683; d. Sainte-Anne-de-Beaupré, Canada, 24 August 1684[46]

iv. **Etienne Simard**, b. Château-Richer, Canada, 4 March 1669; m. Rosalie Bouchard, Baie-Saint-Paul, Canada, 22 November 1695; d. Baie-Saint-Paul, Canada, 14 November 1750[47]

v.   **Françoise Simard**, b. Sainte-Anne-de-Beaupré, Canada, 11 September 1671; m. (1) Jean Allaire, Baie-Saint-Paul, Canada, 28 April 1688; m. (2) Noel Boucher, Canada, approximately 1706; d. Unknown, 16 August 1714[48]

vi. **Joseph Simard**, b. Sainte-Anne-de-Beaupré, Canada, 11 February 1674; m. (1) Gertrude Caron, Sainte-Anne-de-Beaupré, Canada, 20 April 1700; m. (2) Marie Boivin, Sainte-Anne-de-Beaupré, Canada, 30 October 1702; d. Sainte-Anne-de-Beaupré, Canada, 25 September 1738[49]

vii. **Augustin Simard**, b. Sainte-Anne-de-Beaupré, Canada, 2 April 1676; m. Marguerite Pare, unknown location, 24 June 1710; d. Sainte-Anne-de-Beaupré, Canada, 20 August 1735[50]

viii. **François Simard**, b. Sainte-Anne-de-Beaupré, Canada, 22 September 1678; m. Ursule Pare, unknown location, 23 June 1712; d. Baie-Saint-Paul, Canada, 7 December 1732[51]

ix. **Rosalie Simard**, b. Baie-Saint-Paul, Canada, 14 November 1680; m. Jean Caron, Baie-

Saint-Paul, Canada, 29 October 1696; d. Sainte-Anne-de-Beaupré, Canada, 19 July 1714[52]

x.   **Paul Simard**, b. Baie-Saint-Paul, Canada, 25 November 1681; m. Genevieve Gagnon, unknown location, 10 June 1716; d. Baie-Saint-Paul, Canada, 15 August 1733[53]

xi.   **Marguerite Simard**, b. Sainte-Anne-de-Beaupré, Canada, 14 January 1684; m. François Bouchard, Baie-Saint-Paul, Canada, 15 June 1699; d. Unknown[54]

xii.   **Jean Simard**, b. Baie-Saint-Paul, Canada, 27 May 1686; m. Genevieve Gravel, unknown location, 12 November 1714; d. Baie-Saint-Paul, Canada, 4 August 1715[55]

xiii.   **Marie Madeleine Simard**, b. Baie-Saint-Paul, Canada, 19 January 1689; m. Antoine Bouchard, Baie-Saint-Paul, Canada, 20 November 1704; d. Baie-Saint-Paul, Canada, 20 February 1769[56]

xiv.   **Catherine Simard**, b. Baie-Saint-Paul, Canada, 4 May 1692; m. Noel Castonguay, Baie-Saint-Paul, Canada, 4 June 1716; d. Baie-Saint-Paul, Canada, 16 December 1748[57]

The Simard and Bouchard families were neighbors on the Beaupré coast, as shown in the 1751 map on page 160. Three of Noel and Marie Madeleine's children married three children of Claude Bouchard and Louise Gagne: Etienne, Marguerite, and Marie Madeleine Simard to Rosalie, François, and Antoine Bouchard, respectively. Based on baptismal records, the family lived in several places along the Saint Lawrence River, beginning with Château-Richer, where their first three children were born, and then Sainte-Anne-de-Beaupré from approximately 1669 to 1678 or 1679. The Simard family later moved to the Petite-Rivière region sometime before November 1680, as their remaining six children were all born and baptized in the nearby Baie-Saint-Paul parish.

A 1666 census of the Habitants of Beaupré lists "Pierre Simar dit Lombrette, 64," a "maçon" or builder, living next to the Claude and Louise Bouchard family along with "Marie Racine, 20, sa femme" and two young children, Pierre and Noel.[58] This listing is somewhat confusing, as Pierre Simard was the father of Noel Simard, but the young children Pierre and Noel were the two eldest children of Noel and Marie Madeleine (Racine). It's possible Noel Simard was away from home at the time this census was taken. It's believed they were living in or around Château-Richer or Cap Tour-

mente at this time, just upriver from Sainte-Anne-de-Beaupré, which makes sense, as at least two of Claude and Louise Bouchard's children were baptized in the Château-Richer area and the Bouchard family farmed near Cap Tourmente during this time. The author was unable to locate a listing for the Simard family in the 1667 Quebec census taken the following year.

In 1681, the Quebec census lists forty-six-year-old Noel and thirty-two-year-old Marie Madeleine as living with Noel's father, sixty-year-old Pierre Simard, in the Seigneurie de Beaupré. Baie-Saint-Paul was part of the Seigneurie de Beaupré at the time. Also living there were Noel and Marie Madeleine's children Noel, Etienne, Marie, Pierre, Françoise, Joseph, Augustin, François, and Rosalie. The family owned three flintlock muskets and counted twenty *bêtes à cornes* (horned beasts) on their thirty arpents of land.[59]

Noel died on 24 July 1715 in Baie-Saint-Paul at the age of approximately seventy-eight and was buried by the people of the town in the parish church cemetery, as the priest was absent.[60] Marie Madeleine passed away eleven years later, on 3 December 1726, in Baie-Saint-Paul and was also buried in the Baie-Saint-Paul parish church cemetery.[61]

36.   Gabriel Robert Dufour

Born: Approximately 1669 in Lisieux, Normandy, France (Lisieux, Calvados, Normandy, France)

Died: 26 June 1720 in Saint-Joachim, Canada (Saint-Joachim, Saint-Joachim, Canada, Quebec)

37.   Louise Gagne

Born: 20 September 1683 in Petite-Rivière, Canada (Petite-Rivière-Saint-François, Capitale-Nationale, Quebec)

Died: 24 September 1747 in Baie-Saint-Paul, Canada (Baie-Saint-Paul, Capitale-Nationale, Quebec)

Gabriel Robert Dufour (known as Robert) was born in approximately 1669 in Lisieux, a town in France's historic Normandy region, to parents François Dufour and Françoise Morin.

Robert was married twice. He first married Anne Migneron, daughter of Laurent Migneron and Anne St-Denis, on 1 May 1694 at an unknown location in Canada.[62] They had three children:

i.   **Angelique Dufour**, b. Château-Richer, Canada, 23 May 1695; m. Ignace Gagne, approximately 1719; d. Baie-Saint-Paul, Province of Quebec, 19 August 1768[63]

ii.   **Marie Josephe Dufour**, b. Château-Richer, Canada, 19 September 1697; m. Pierre Gagne, Parish of Saint-François-de-Sales, Canada, 14 May 1725; d. Unknown[64]

iii.   **Agnes Dufour**, b. Approximately 1702; m. Louis Bolduc; Saint-Joachim, Canada, 8 October 1725; d. Unknown[65]

After Anne Migneron's death during an epidemic in approximately 1703, Robert married Louise Gagne (1683–1747) in Baie-Saint-Paul on 23 August 1707.[66]

Louise Gagne, the daughter of Ignace Gagne and Barbe Dodier, was born on 20 September 1683 in Petite-Rivière and baptized in the Baie-Saint-Paul parish church on 24 September.[67] Her aunt Louise Gagne and uncle Claude Bouchard acted as her godparents. Shortly before Louise's birth, the 1681 Quebec census reflects that twenty-five-year-old Ignace and eighteen-year-old Barbe lived on two arpents of land in the Seigneurie de Beaupré and possessed one flintlock musket and three cows.[68] Robert and Louise had seven children:

i.   **Marie Reine Dufour**, b. Approximately 1707; m. François Xavier Tremblay, Baie-Saint-Paul, Canada, 6 November 1726; d. Petite-Rivière, Province of Quebec, 14 April 1790[69]

ii.   **Joseph Dufour**, b. Approximately 1709; m. (1) Marie Anne Tremblay, Baie-Saint-Paul, Canada, 29 October 1732; m. (2) Felicite Simard, Baie-Saint-Paul, Canada, 23 June 1750; d. La Malbaie, Province of Quebec, 14 August 1774[70]

iii.   **Ignace Dufour**, b. Approximately 1711; m. Marie Reine Tremblay, Petite-Rivière, Canada, 28 November 1736; d. Baie-Saint-Paul, Canada, 7 October 1762[71]

iv.   **Bonaventure Dufour**, b. Approximately 1713; m. Elisabeth Tremblay, Petite-Rivière, Canada, 8 November 1734; d. Petite-Rivière, Province of Quebec, 14 April 1783[72]

v.   **Louise Dufour**, b. Approximately 1713; d. Baie-Saint-Paul, Canada, 8 September 1759[73]

vi.   **Barbe Dufour**, b. Approximately 1715; m. Etienne Simard, Baie-Saint-Paul, Canada, 23 November 1733; d. Baie-Saint-Paul, Lower Canada, 19 October 1799[74]

vii.   **Gabriel Dufour**, b. Approximately 1717; m. (1) Genevieve Tremblay, L'Isle-aux-Coudres, Canada, 21 May 1742; m. (2) Madeleine Boissonneau, Saint-Jean, Canada, 9 June 1756; d. L'Isle-aux-Coudres, Province of Quebec, approximately 1783[75]

Baptismal records do not exist for Robert and Louise's seven children, but they were likely all born in the Baie-Saint-Paul or Petite-Rivière area.

Robert Dufour died on 26 June 1720 in Saint-Joachim, Quebec, purportedly due to drowning in the Saint Lawrence River.[76] On 30 October 1726, Louise married Guillaume Boily (1682–1764) in Baie-

Saint-Paul.[77] Louise and Guillaume had one child:

    i.   **Jean Baptiste Boily**, b. Baie-Saint-Paul, Canada, 6 June 1728; m. (1) Ursule Duchesne, Baie-Saint-Paul, Canada, 22 January 1748; m. (2) Amable Cote, Baie-Saint-Paul, Province of Quebec, 14 September 1779; d. L'Isle-aux-Coudres, Lower Canada, 30 November 1805[78]

Louise died in Baie-Saint-Paul on 24 September 1747 at the age of sixty-four and was buried in the Baie-Saint-Paul parish church cemetery the same day.[79]

Louise's second husband, Guillaume Boily, outlived her by seventeen years before passing away on 17 February 1764 in Baie-Saint-Paul. He was buried the following day in the Baie-Saint-Paul parish cemetery.[80]

38.   Louis Tremblay

Born: 29 September 1667 in Château-Richer, Canada (Château-Richer, Capitale-Nationale, Quebec)
Died: Unknown

39.   Françoise Morel

Born: 16 October 1680 in Sainte-Anne-de-Beaupré, Canada (Sainte-Anne-de-Beaupré, Capitale-Nationale, Quebec)
Died: 3 May 1715 in Baie-Saint-Paul, Canada (Baie-Saint-Paul, Capitale-Nationale, Canada, Quebec)

Louis Tremblay, the son of Pierre Tremblay and Ozanne Jeanne Achon, was born on 29 September 1667 in Château-Richer, Canada. He was baptized the following day in the Château-Richer parish by Father Thomas Morel, with Louis Levasseur and Genevieve Marsolet acting as his godparents.[81] The 1667 Quebec census lists Louis as living with his parents in the Cote de Beaupré region on nine arpents of land with two *beastiaux*.[82] A census taken fourteen years later reflects that Pierre and Ozanne continued to live in the Beaupré region with ten children on ten arpents of land next to the Noel Simard family, but for whatever reason, Louis was omitted amongst the children.[83]

Louis was married four times in total. He first married Marie Perron (1667–1706), daughter of François Daniel Perron and Louise Gargottin, on 27 November 1691 in L'Ange-Gardien, Canada.[84] Louis and Marie had six children:

    i.   **Marie Dorothee Tremblay**, b. L'Ange-Gardien, Canada, 28 September 1692; m. Etienne Desbiens, Baie-Saint-Paul, Canada, 21 January 1715; d. Les Éboulements, Canada, 9 March 1734[85]

    ii.   **François Xavier Tremblay**, b. Petite-Rivière, Canada, 11 April 1695; m. Marie Madeleine Bouchard, Baie-Saint-Paul, Canada, 24 November 1718; d. L'Isle-aux-Coudres, Canada, November 1755[86]

    iii.   **Louise Tremblay**, b. Petite-Rivière, Canada, 22 June 1697; m. François Roussel, Baie-Saint-Paul, Canada, 17 November 1720; d. Les Éboulements, Canada, 11 December 1733[87]

    iv.   **Marie Rosalie Tremblay**, b. Petite-Rivière, Canada, 29 September 1699; m. Sebastien Hervé, Baie-Saint-Paul, Canada, 17 November 1722; d. Baie-Saint-Paul, Canada, 22 August 1740[88]

    v.   **Marie Madeleine Tremblay**, b. Petite-Rivière, Canada, 15 October 1701; m. François

Xavier Fortin, Baie-Saint-Paul, Canada, 5 November 1726; d. Baie-Saint-Paul, Province of Quebec, 22 February 1778[89]

vi. **Louis Tremblay**, b. Petite-Rivière, Canada, 14 August 1703; m. Marie Brigitte Fortin, Petite-Rivière, Canada, 11 November 1726; d. Petite-Rivière, Canada, 7 April 1757[90]

Louis and Marie settled in the Petite-Rivière area upriver from Baie-Saint-Paul, where five of their six children were born. Marie died on or around 7 April 1706 during childbirth (*morte en couches*) in Petite-Rivière and was buried in the Baie-Saint-Paul parish cemetery.[91]

Louis next married Françoise Morel (1680–1715) seven months later, on 19 November 1706 in Sainte-Anne-de-Beaupré.[92] The marriage record reflects Louis lived in Petite-Rivière at the time of the marriage.

Françoise was born on 16 October 1680 in Sainte-Anne-de-Beaupré to parents Guillaume Morel and Catherine Pelletier. Parish priest Guillaume Gaultier baptized Françoise in October in the Sainte-Anne-de-Beaupré parish church. Françoise's grandfather, Georges Pelletier, served as her godfather while Françoise LeHoux acted as her godmother.[93] The 1681 Quebec census reveals that Françoise, who was a year old at the time, lived with her parents in the Seigneurie de Beaupré.[94] Louis and Françoise had five children:

i. **Guillaume Tremblay**, b. Petite-Rivière, Canada, 20 June 1707; m. Marie Jeanne Dinelle, Baie-Saint-Paul, Canada, 23 November 1729; d. L'Isle-aux-Coudres, Canada, November

View of Quebec's Baie-Saint-Paul — home to numerous Bouchard ancestors

1755[95]

ii. **Marie Françoise Tremblay**, b. Petite-Rivière, Canada, 28 December 1708; m. Michel Poitevin, Petite-Rivière, Canada, 14 November 1735; d. Baie-Saint-Paul, Province of Quebec, 29 May 1778[96]

iii. **Etienne Tremblay**, b. Baie-Saint-Paul, Canada, 13 November 1710; m. Marie Louise Bonneau, Petite-Rivière, Canada, 11 November 1734; d. L'Isle-aux-Coudres, Canada, November 1755[97]

iv. **Marie Reine Tremblay**, b. Baie-Saint-Paul, Canada, 6 December 1712; m. Ignace Dufour, Petite-Rivière, Canada, 28 November 1736; d. Baie-Saint-Paul, Canada, 17 October 1758[98]

v. **Elisabeth Tremblay**, b. Baie-Saint-Paul, Canada, 4 March 1715; m. Bonaventure Dufour, Petite-Rivière, Canada, 8 November 1734; d. Baie-Saint-Paul, Lower Canada, 15 May 1799[99]

Françoise died on 3 May 1715 in Baie-Saint-Paul at the age of thirty-five shortly after the birth of her fifth child. She was buried in the Saint-François-Xavier parish church cemetery in Petite-Rivière.[100] Louis' third marriage took place the following year, to Marie Letartre (1681–1726), widow of Charles Brisson, in L'Ange-Gardien, Canada, on 26 August 1716.[101] Marie had six children with Charles Brisson prior to his death in 1712.[102] Louis and Marie had three children:

i. **Marie Josephe Tremblay**, b. Petite-Rivière, Canada, 2 June 1717; m. François Simard, Petite-Rivière, Canada, 10 January 1735; d. Baie-Saint-Paul, Canada, 24 November 1735[103]

ii. **Andre Tremblay**, b. Petite-Rivière, Canada, 23 April 1719; m. Catherine Bouchard, Baie-Saint-Paul, Canada, 28 April 1739; d. L'Isle-aux-Coudres, Lower Canada, 8 June 1804[104]

iii. **Joseph Tremblay**, b. Petite-Rivière, Canada, 13 August 1720; m. Marguerite Bouchard, Petite-Rivière, Canada, 6 November 1742; d. L'Isle-aux-Coudres, Canada, 17 November 1758[105]

Marie entered Quebec's Hôpital Hôtel-Dieu du Précieux-Sang de Québec—the first hospital in New France—on 21 June 1726, and passed away a month later on 20 July 1726 at the age of forty-five. She was buried the following day in the hospital's cemetery for the poor.[106] Louis was married for the final time the following year, to Madeleine Marquis (1675–1747), widow of Henri François Chateauneuf, on 29 July 1727 at Quebec's Notre-Dame-de-Québec parish church.[107]

Madeleine died on 5 March 1747 in Petite-Rivière and was buried two days later in the Petite-Rivière parish cemetery.[108] Louis' date of death cannot be determined with any degree of accuracy due to incomplete parish records from Petite-Rivière. Three of Louis' children—François Xavier, Guillaume, and Etienne—along with the spouses of François Xavier and Etienne, died in a smallpox epidemic that swept through Quebec in late 1755 and were buried in a communal grave on L'Isle-aux-Coudres in November 1755.[109]

40.   René LeBlanc Père

Born: Approximately 1657 in Port-Royal, Acadia (Annapolis Royal, Annapolis County, Nova Scotia)
Died: 3 January 1734 in Grand-Pré, Acadia (Grand-Pré, Kings County, Nova Scotia)

41.   Anne Bourgeois

Born: Approximately 1661 in Port-Royal, Acadia (Annapolis Royal, Annapolis County, Nova Scotia)

Died: 28 December 1747 in Grand-Pré, Acadia (Grand-Pré, Kings County, Nova Scotia)

René LeBlanc Père was born in approximately 1657 in Port-Royal, Acadia (present-day Annapolis Royal, Nova Scotia) to parents Daniel LeBlanc and Françoise Gaudet.[110] Daniel LeBlanc was born in approximately 1626 in France and was one of the early settlers in Acadia. He met and married Françoise Gaudet in 1650 in Port-Royal. Daniel and Françoise established a ten-arpent farm in the vicinity of Port-Royal and built a highly effective series of dikes constructed of Acadian shoreline sod to create a prosperous estate by French and Acadian standards.[111] As reflected in the 1671 Acadian census, fourteen-year-old René lived with his parents and six siblings in Port-Royal.[112] Both Daniel and Françoise continued to live in Port-Royal before passing away in 1695 and 1699, respectively.

René married Anne Bourgeois (1661–1747) in Port-Royal, Acadia, in approximately 1678.[113] The 1678 Acadian census lists them as being in the same household without any children.[114]

Anne Bourgeois was born in approximately 1661, likely in Acadia, to parents Jacques Bourgeois and Jeanne Trahan. Jacques Bourgeois was a French-born surgeon who came to Acadia aboard the *St. François* in 1641. Jeanne came over with her parents, Guillaume Trahan and Françoise Charbonneau, and a younger sister in 1636 aboard the *St. Jehan*, which set sail from LaRochelle, France, on 1 April 1636. Jacques and Jeanne married in 1643 in Port-Royal.[115] Developed by Governor of Acadia Charles de Menou d'Aulnay in the 1630s, Port-Royal grew during the seventeenth century into an important village and fort on Acadia's northwest coast. Jacques prospered in Port-Royal and, after learning English, traded with Boston merchants and eventually served as president of the inhabitants' council prior to the English occupation.[116] At ten years old, Anne lived with her parents and siblings in Port-Royal, per the 1671 Acadian census.[117]

Sometime later in 1671, Jacques Bourgeois moved his family from Port-Royal to a region known as

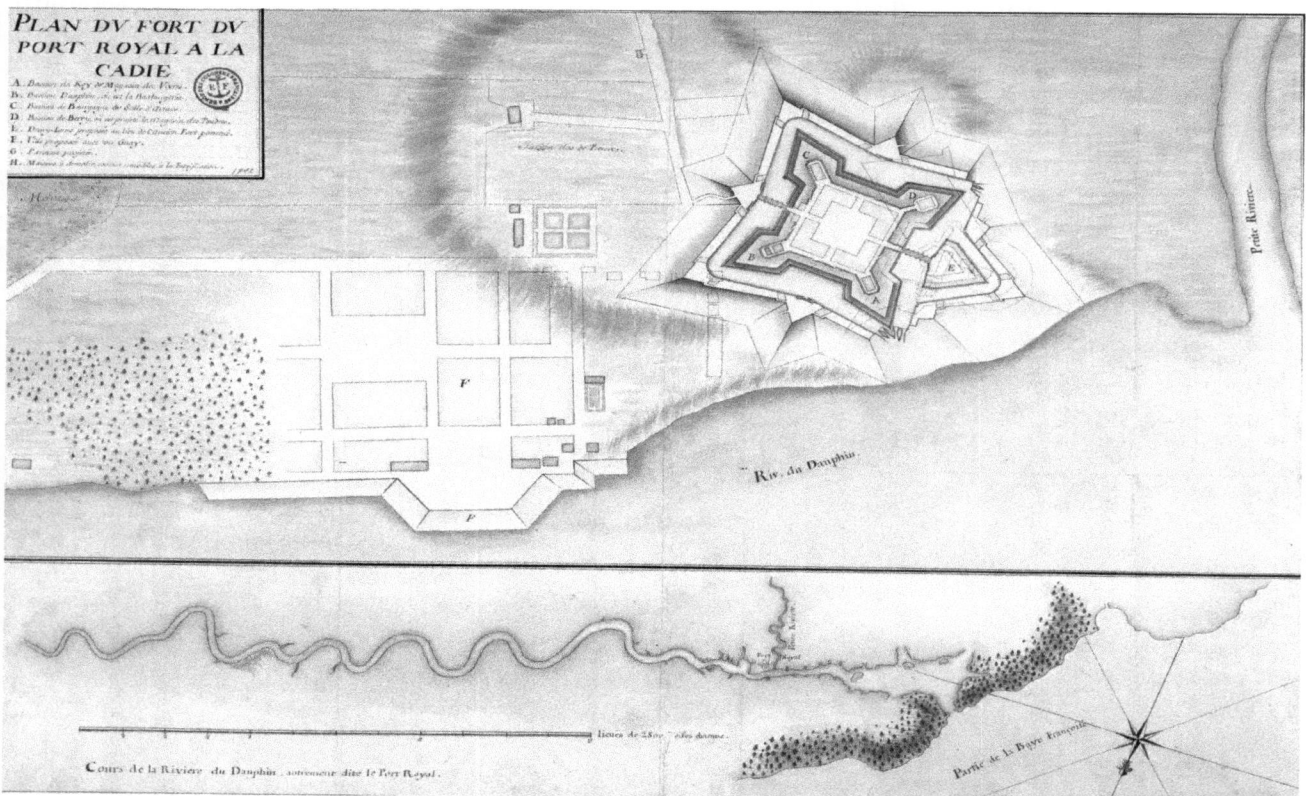

1702 map of the French fort and townsite at Port-Royal and the Dauphin River (present-day Annapolis River)

Chignecto, which sat on a ten-mile-long isthmus connecting mainland Canada to the Acadian peninsula.[118] Specifically, the Bourgeois family settled in the Beaubassin area and proceeded to make the area home. They cleared the land for the homestead, constructed dikes, and brought in livestock. Installation of a sawmill and gristmill enabled them to engage in lucrative trade, including with merchants along the New England coast.[119] Many other families followed, making Beaubassin a center of Acadian life. Ten-year-old Anne undoubtedly spent her formulative years in Beaubassin.

René and Anne had at least ten children:[‡]

i. **Jacques LeBlanc**, b. Port-Royal, Acadia, approximately 1678; m. Catherine Landry, Grand-Pré, Acadia, 8 October 1702; d. Grand-Pré, Acadia, October 1755[120]

ii. **François LeBlanc**, Acadia, approximately 1680; m. Jeanne Hebert, Acadia, approximately 1703; d. St-Ours-sur-Richelieu, Province of Quebec, 5 March 1770[121]

iii. **René LeBlanc Fils**, b. Port-Royal, Acadia, approximately 1682; m. (1) Elisabeth Melanson, Grand-Pré, Acadia, 30 July 1709; m. (2) Marguerite Thibault, Port-Royal, Acadia, 26 November 1720; d. Philadelphia, Pennsylvania Colony, 6 February 1758[122]

iv. **Pierre LeBlanc**, b. Port-Royal, Acadia, approximately 1684; m. Jeanne Theriault, Grand-Pré, Acadia, 26 October 1711; d. Unknown[123]

v. **Joseph LeBlanc**, b. Approximately 1688; d. Unknown[124]

vi. **Etienne LeBlanc**, b. Approximately 1688; m. Ann Mailoux, Quebec, Canada, 23 November 1716; d. Unknown[125]

vii. **Claude LeBlanc**, b. Grand-Pré, Acadia, approximately 1691; m. Jeanne Dugas, Grand-Pré, Acadia, 4 May 1718; d. Approximately 1763[126]

viii. **Marie LeBlanc**, b. Approximately 1694; m. Jacques Theriault, Grand-Pré, Acadia, 2 October 1713; d. Grand-Pré, Acadia, 19 November 1725[127]

ix. **Jean Baptiste LeBlanc**, b. Grand-Pré, Acadia, approximately 1697; d. Quebec, Canada, 20 January 1718[128]

x. **Claire LeBlanc**, b. Approximately 1700; m. Jean Landry, Grand-Pré, Acadia, approximately 1717; d. Unknown[129]

In 1686, René, Anne, and their three eldest children all lived in Port-Royal. However, by 1693, the LeBlancs and their seven children lived in the Grand-Pré area. The 1693 Acadian census also records that they had a dozen cattle, sheep, and hogs a piece, as well as sixteen arpents of land, and one gun. By 1701, the LeBlanc family still lived in Grand-Pré on ten acres of land with eighteen cattle, eighteen sheep, twelve hogs, and one gun. Two years later, the 1703 Acadian census reflects that the family comprised three boys and three girls in addition to René and Anne, with one being an arms bearer.[130]

In 1707, the Acadian census lists the LeBlanc family as living in Minas on six arpents of land with three boys over fourteen, one younger boy, and one girl less than twelve years old, in addition to four cattle, twelve sheep, and twelve hogs. In 1714, per the Acadian census from that year, René and Anne were still living in Minas with two sons and one daughter. The following year, the 1715 census of heads of household in Grand-Pré records both René and his father's households.[131] Unfortunately, no other Acadian census records were taken until 1751, and we have no further details on René and Anne's life after 1714 until their deaths.

René died on 3 January 1734 in Grand-Pré, Acadia, and was buried the following day in the Saint-Charles-des-Mines parish cemetery.[132] Anne passed

---

‡ Records from Acadia during this era are incomplete at best. Documented events are cited, but the remain dates are based on the conjecture of previous researchers.

away nearly fourteen years later on 28 December 1747, in Grand-Pré, and the following day she was also buried in Grand-Pré's Saint-Charles-des-Mines parish cemetery.[133]

42. Pierre Thibault

Born: Approximately 1675 in Saint-Malo, Brittany, France (Saint-Malo, Ille-et-Vilaine, Brittany, France)
Died: Unknown

43. Jeanne Comeau

Born: Approximately 1682 in Port-Royal, Acadia (Annapolis Royal, Annapolis County, Nova Scotia)
Died: 12 July 1737 in Grand-Pré, Acadia (Grand-Pré, Kings County, Nova Scotia)

Pierre Thibault (also known as Thébeau or Tibeau), the son of Mathurin Thibault and Perrine Moran, was born in approximately 1675 in Saint-Malo, France.[134] Nothing is known about Pierre until his 26 November 1703 marriage to Jeanne Comeau in Port-Royal, Acadia.[135]

Jeanne Comeau was born in approximately 1682 in Port-Royal, Acadia, the daughter of Pierre Comeau and Jeanne Bourg.[136] At the age of four in 1686, Jeanne lived with her parents and five siblings in Port-Royal, along with ten cattle, ten sheep, eight hogs, and one gun, per the 1686 census. The 1693 Acadian census reflects that the Comeau–Bourg family lived in Port-Royal on twenty arpents of land with fifteen cattle, twenty sheep, a dozen hogs, and one gun. By 1698, the Comeau–Bourg family, including fifteen-year-old Jeanne and her twelve siblings, still lived in Port-Royal. They now had twenty-six arpents of land and owned eleven cattle, fifteen sheep, eight hogs, thirty fruit trees, and one gun. Three years later, the family numbered ten children, and they lived on twelve arpents of land with fifteen cattle, twenty sheep, fourteen hogs, and one gun. In 1703, the family comprised one boy and four girls in addition to Pierre Comeau and Jeanne Bourg.[137] This was likely the last time Jeanne Comeau was included in her parents' household as she married Pierre Thibault later that year.

Pierre and Jeanne had at least two children:

    i.   **Marguerite Thibault**, b. Port-Royal, Acadia, 19 October 1704; m. René Leblanc Fils, Port-Royal, Acadia, 26 November 1720; d. approximately 1750[138]

    ii.   **Jacques François Thibault**, b. Port-Royal, Acadia, 2 May 1706; m. Anne Melanson, Grand-Pré, Acadia, 4 August 1733; d. Unknown[139]

Pierre apparently died sometime before 1714, as the 1714 Acadian census lists a woman named "La Tibodeau (widow)" along with one daughter in Port-Royal.[140]

Jeanne outlived him by over thirty years before passing away in Grand-Pré as well on 12 July 1737.[141] The author was unable to locate any other information on Pierre or Jeanne.

44. Joseph Dugas

Born: Approximately 1689 in Port-Royal, Acadia (Annapolis Royal, Annapolis County, Nova Scotia)
Died: 4 September 1733 in Louisbourg, Acadia (Louisbourg, Cape Breton County, Nova Scotia)

45. Marguerite Richard

Born: Approximately 1690 in Port-Royal, Acadia (Annapolis Royal, Annapolis County, Nova Scotia)
Died: 15 September 1746 in Grand-Pré, Acadia (Grand-Pré, Kings County, Nova Scotia)

Joseph Dugas was born in approximately 1689 in Port-Royal, Acadia, to parents Abraham Dugas Fils and Jeanne Guilbeau.[142] Abraham was the son of Acadian settlers Abraham Dugas Pere and Marguerite Doucet and was born in approximately 1662 in Port-Royal. Marguerite Doucet was the daughter of the commander of Port-Royal's garrison, Germain Doucet.[143] Joseph's mother, Jeanne Guilbeau, was also born in Port-Royal, in approximately 1670, to Pierre Guilbault and Catherine Thériot (or Theriault).[144]

The 1693 Acadian census reflects that Joseph, his parents, and one sibling lived south of Port-Royal, on Cap-de-Sable Island along with sixteen cattle, thirteen hogs, and one gun. By 1703, however, the family is listed as living in the Minas region. Four years later, the family—comprising Abraham and Jeanne, one boy over fourteen, and three girls over twelve—lived on only one arpent of land but with eight cattle, sixteen sheep, and ten hogs.[145]

Joseph and Marguerite Richard married on 12 January 1711 in Grand-Pré, Acadia.[146] Marguerite was likewise born in approximately 1690 in Port-Royal to parents Pierre Jean Richard and Marguerite Marie Landry.[147] The Richard family, including five boys and four girls, are reflected in the 1703 Acadian census as living in the Minas basin, like in Grand-Pré. The Richard family still lived in Minas in 1707 on six arpents of land with fifteen cattle, eleven sheep, and sixteen hogs.[148]

Joseph and Marguerite had at least nine children:

i. **Charles Dugas**, b. Grand-Pré, Acadia, 10 December 1711; m. Anne Suzanne LeBlanc, Grand-Pré, Acadia, 7 January 1739; d. Carleton, Lower Canada, 25 January 1801[149]

ii. **Joseph Dugas**, b. Grand-Pré, Acadia, 1714; m. (1) Catherine Louise Milly, Acadia, approximately 1739; m. (2) Marguerite LeBlanc, Grand-Pré, Acadia, approximately 1740; m. (3) Louise-Isabelle Arsenault, Miquelon, Canada, 2 October 1762; d. Saint-Servan, France, 10 January 1779[150]

iii. **Marguerite Dugas**, b. Grand-Pré, Acadia, approximately 1717; d. Louisbourg, Acadia, 7 December 1732[151]

iv. **Anne Dugas**, b. Grand-Pré, Acadia, approximately 1720; d. Louisbourg, Acadia, 28 June 1733[152]

v. **Angélique Dugas**, b. Unknown, approximately 1725; d. Grand-Pré, 4 November 1743[153]

vi. **Abraham Dugas**, b. Grand-Pré, Acadia, approximately 1726; m. Marguerite LeBlanc, Grand-Pré, Acadia, 16 July 1748; d. Unknown[154]

vii. **Etienne Dugas**, b. Louisbourg, Acadia, 25 February 1729; d. Louisbourg, Acadia, 20 November 1730[155]

viii. **Jeanne Dugas**, b. Louisbourg, Acadia, 16 October 1731; m. Pierre Bois, Port-Toulouse, Acadia, approximately 1750; d. Chéticamp, Nova Scotia, 16 October 1817[156]

ix. **Marie Madeleine Dugas**, b. Unknown; d. Louisbourg, Acadia, 10 December 1732[157]

Joseph, Marguerite, and their two eldest sons lived in the Minas basin, likely in Grand-Pré, per the 1714 Acadian census.[158] Joseph Dugas is also listed in the 1715 head of household census of Minas Basin inhabitants.[159] Between 1726 and 1729, the family moved to Louisbourg, on the far eastern coast of Acadia in present-day Cape Breton Island.

Joseph died on 4 September 1733 in Louisbourg, Acadia, in a smallpox epidemic that also took the lives of his daughters Marie Madeleine, Marguerite, and Anne. He was buried the following day in Louisbourg.[160] After Joseph's death, Marguerite remarried to Charles de Saint-Étienne de la Tour on 13 January 1736 in Louisbourg.[161] Marguerite and

Charles had twin daughters:

i.   **Anne de Saint-Étienne de la Tour**, b. Louisbourg, Acadia, 23 December 1737; d. Unknown[162]

ii. **Jeanne Angelique de Saint-Étienne de la Tour**, b. Louisbourg, Acadia, 23 December 1737; d. Unknown[163]

Marguerite and her second husband moved back to Grand-Pré in approximately 1738, where she died on 15 September 1746.[164]

46.   Pierre LeBlanc

Born: Approximately 1685 in Rivière-Aux-Canards, Grand-Pré, Acadia (Grand-Pré, Kings County, Nova Scotia)
Died: 22 October 1769 in Montreal, Province of Quebec (Montreal, Montreal, Quebec)

47.   Françoise Landry

Born: Approximately 1693 in Grand-Pré, Acadia (Grand-Pré, Kings County, Nova Scotia)
Died: 3 October 1767 in Lavaltrie, Province of Quebec (Lavaltrie, Lanaudière, Quebec)

Pierre LeBlanc, son of Antoine LeBlanc and Marie Bourgeois, was born around 1685 in Riviere-Aux-Canards, Acadia, a small village in the Minas Basin near Grand-Pré.[165] Antoine was the son of Daniel LeBlanc and Françoise Gaudet, the founders of the LeBlanc family in North America, and was the younger brother of René LeBlanc Pere discussed above. At the age of eight in 1693, Pierre lived in the Minas basin with his parents and four siblings on sixteen arpents of land. The family had twelve cattle, six sheep, and twelve hogs. The 1701 Acadian census lists the LeBlanc family as continuing to live on sixteen arpents of land in Grand-Pré, now with twenty cattle, fifteen sheep, ten hogs, and one gun. While the 1703 Acadian census lists Antoine LeBlanc and his wife, no children are recorded as living in the household; by this time Pierre may have struck out on his own, possibly outside Acadia. However, the 1707 Acadian census lists Antoine LeBlanc and his wife as living in Minas with two boys fourteen or older, four younger boys, and three girls under twelve on eight arpents of land with twelve cattle, ten sheep, and fourteen hogs.[166]

Françoise Landry was born around 1693 in Grand-Pré to parents Antoine Landry and Anne Marie Thibodeau. Around the time of her birth, the family lived on twelve arpents of land and had fifteen cattle, eight sheep, six hogs, and one gun to their name. The Landry–Thibodeau family still lived in the Minas basin in 1703 with two boys and two girls, one of whom was likely Françoise. Although Antoine Landry and his wife show up in the 1707 Acadian census, the household doesn't list any girls, so it's unknown where Françoise lived during this time.[167]

Pierre LeBlanc married Françoise Landry on 16 February 1711 in Grand-Pré.[168] They had fourteen children:

i.   **Agnes LeBlanc**, b. Grand-Pré, Acadia, 15 March 1712; m. Pierre Gaudreau, Grand-Pré, Acadia, 15 October 1731; d. Cobequid, Acadia, 28 September 1749[169]

ii. **Ursule LeBlanc**, b. Grand-Pré, Acadia, approximately 1713; m. Joseph Broussard, Grand-Pré, Acadia, 29 February 1740; d. Cherbourg, France, 4 December 1758[170]

iii. **Anne Suzanne LeBlanc**, b. Grand-Pré, Acadia, 16 March 1718; m. Charles Dugas, Grand-Pré, Acadia, 7 January 1739; d. Carleton, Province of Quebec, 15 April 1776[171]

iv. **Theodore LeBlanc**, b. Grand-Pré, Acadia, 23 December 1719; m. Marie Cormier, Beaubassin, Acadia, 4 June 1740; d. Unknown[172]

v. **Marie Angelique LeBlanc**, b. Grand-Pré, Acadia, 27 May 1722; m. Germain Dupuis, approximately 1747; d. Unknown[173]

vi. **Marie Madeleine LeBlanc**, b. Grand-Pré, Acadia, 10 September 1723; d. Unknown[174]

vii. **Augustin LeBlanc**, b. Grand-Pré, Acadia, 25 November 1724; m. Françoise Hebert, Grand-Pré, Acadia, December 1753; d. Yamachiche, Province of Quebec, 14 July 1786[175]

viii. **Joseph LeBlanc**, b. Grand-Pré, Acadia, 11 February 1726; d. Unknown[176]

ix. **Françoise LeBlanc**, b. Grand-Pré, Acadia, 27 July 1727; m. (1) Louis Syvain Dupuis, Grand-Pré, Acadia, approximately 1745; m. (2) Antoine Boudreau, L'Acadie, Lower Canada, 28 September 1801; d. L'Acadie, Lower Canada, 24 November 1802[177]

x. **Marie LeBlanc**, b. Grand-Pré, Acadia, 7 April 1729; m. François Gaudreau, Grand-Pré, Acadia, 10 July 1748; d. Approximately 1755[178]

xi. **Pierre Raymond LeBlanc**, b. Grand-Pré, Acadia, 7 January 1731; d. Grand-Pré, Acadia, 13 January 1731[179]

xii. **Marie Rose LeBlanc**, b. Grand-Pré, Acadia, 25 March 1732; m. Jean Baptiste Hebert, Boston, Province of Massachusetts Bay, 24 August 1762; d. Bécancour, Province of Quebec, 21 May 1771[180]

xiii. **Marguerite Monique LeBlanc**, b. Grand-Pré, Acadia, 27 April 1734; m. Charles Hebert, Acadia, approximately 1754; d. Saint-Malo, France, 25 January 1759[181]

xiv. **Pierre Hilaire LeBlanc**, b. Grand-Pré, Acadia, 12 January 1736; m. (1) Isabelle Hebert, Guilford, Connecticut Colony, 13 October 1762; m. (2) Marie Catherine Granger, L'Acadie, Province of Quebec, 25 October 1784; d. L'Acadie, Lower Canada, 28 July 1800[182]

Pierre LeBlanc and Françoise Landry first appear together in the 1714 Acadian census and are listed as living in Minas with two daughters, likely Agnes and Ursule.[183] The following year, Pierre appears in a census of the heads of household living in Grand-Pré.[184]

Both Pierre and Françoise died in exile. Françoise passed away first, on 3 October 1767 in Lavaltrie, a small community halfway between Montreal and Quebec City in Quebec's Lanaudière administrative region. She was buried the following day in the Lavaltrie parish cemetery.[185]

Pierre died two years later on 22 October 1769 in the Hôtel-Dieu de Montréal located in Old Montreal and was buried the following day in the hospital's cemetery.[186]

48. Gerard Marmotte

Born: Approximately 1670 in Contreuve, Champagne, France (Contreuve, Ardennes, Grand Est, France)
Died: Unknown

49. Poncette Gueri

Born: Approximately 1675 in France
Died: Unknown

Gerard Marmotte was born in approximately 1670 in Contreuve, France. His future wife, Poncette

Gueri, was born in approximately 1675 in France as well.[187] Gerard and Poncette had at least one child:

    i.   **Claude Marmotte dit Champagne**, b. Monthois, Champagne, France, approximately 1700; m. Nicole Garaudel, Contreuve, Champagne, France, 7 January 1727; d. Unknown[188]

The author was unable to locate any further information on Gerard or Poncette. It's likely they remained in France while their son and daughter-in-law, Claude Marmotte and Nicole Garaudel, immigrated to New France.

50.   Nicolas Garaudel

Born: Approximately 1675 in France
Died: Unknown

51.   Marguerite Guillot

Born: Approximately 1680 in France
Died: Unknown

Nicolas Garaudel was born in approximately 1675 in France. Marguerite Guillot was likewise born in France in approximately 1680.[189] Nicolas and Marguerite had at least one child:

    i.   **Nicole Garaudel**, b. Monthois, Champagne, France, 1705; m. Claude Marmotte dit Champagne, Monthois, Champagne, France, 7 January 1727; d. Unknown[190]

The author was unable to locate any further information on Nicolas or Marguerite. It's likely they also remained in France while their daughter and son-in-law, Nicole Garaudel and Claude Marmotte, immigrated to New France.

52.   Jean Bissonnette

Born: 24 July 1669 in Quebec, Canada (Quebec City, Capitale-Nationale, Quebec)
Died: 15 May 1715 in Quebec, Canada (Quebec City, Capitale-Nationale, Quebec)

53.   Marie Charlotte Davenne

Born: 13 April 1676 in L'Ancienne-Lorette, Canada (L'Ancienne-Lorette, Capitale-Nationale, Quebec)
Died: 20 October 1707 in Quebec, Canada (Quebec City, Capitale-Nationale, Quebec)

Jean Bissonette (or Bissonnet), son of Pierre Bissonnette and Marie D'Allon, was born on 24 July 1669 in Quebec (present-day Quebec City). Father Hugues Pommier baptized Jean that same day in the Notre-Dame-de-Québec parish church.[191] At the age of twelve, Jean is listed in the 1681 Quebec census as living with his parents, Pierre and Marie, and five siblings on seven arpents of land in the Comté de Saint-Laurent region, located on the Île d'Orléans, an island located midway across the Saint Lawrence River. The family owned one flintlock musket and two horned beasts.[192]

Marie Charlotte Davenne (or Daveine), daughter of Charles Davenne and Marie DeNoyon, was born on 13 April 1676 in L'Ancienne-Lorette, Canada (the present-day municipality of L'Ancienne-Lorette, Quebec is surrounded entirely by Quebec City), and baptized the following day in the parish church.[193] At the age of approximately five, Marie Charlotte lived with her parents and siblings Gabriel, Madeleine, and Françoise in the Seigneurie de la Durantaye on three arpents of land.[194]

Jean and Charlotte married in approximately 1692 in La Durantaye, Canada.[195] They lived in Saint-Michel-de-Bellechasse and La Durantaye on the southern shore of the Saint Lawrence River for several years, and most of their children were born there. Jean and Charlotte had the following children:

i. **Marie Charlotte Bissonnette**, b. Saint-Michel-de-Bellechasse, Canada, 16 January 1693; m. Charles Flibotte, Saint-Michel-de-Bellechasse, Canada, 29 July 1708; d. Montreal, Canada, 19 May 1733[196]

ii. **Suzanne Bissonnette**, b. Approximately 1695; m. Gabriel Brias, Beaumont, Canada, 29 January 1714; d. Montreal, Canada, 19 December 1741[197]

iii. **Jean Bissonnette**, b. Saint-Michel-de-Bellechasse, Canada, 25 August 1698; m. Marie Lavoie, Baie-Saint-Paul, Canada, 19 July 1720; d. Saint-Michel-de-Bellechasse, Canada, 1 May 1756[198]

iv. **François Bissonnette**, b. Saint-Michel-de-Bellechasse, Canada, 4 February 1700; m. Marguerite Guay, Quebec, Canada, 14 February 1722; d. Les Cèdres, Canada, 29 June 1756[199]

v. **Françoise Hilaire Bissonnette**, b. Saint-Michel-de-Bellechasse, Canada, 30 May 1702; d. Unknown[200]

vi. **Charles Alexandre Bissonnette**, b. Saint-Michel-de-Bellechasse, Canada, 2 December 1703; m. Marie Quemeneur dit LaFlamme, Saint-François, Canada, 29 October 1727; d. Unknown[201]

vii. **Louis Bissonnette**, b. Saint-Michel-de-Bellechasse, Canada, Canada, 28 May 1706; m. (1) Marie Geneviève Binet, Beauport, Canada, 9 August 1729; m. (2) Marie Anne Langevin, Montreal, Canada, 16 August 1746; d. Lachine, Canada, 15 May 1760[202]

Charlotte died on 20 October 1707 at the Hotel-Dieu de Québec in Quebec at the age of thirty-one.[203] Jean remarried a year and a half later on 11 January 1709 in Quebec, to twenty-six-year-old Marie Jeanne LeBlanc (1683–1750).[204] Jean and Marie Jeanne had three children:

i. **Marie Jeanne Bissonnette**, b. Saint-Michel-de-Bellechasse, Canada, 6 May 1710; d. Saint-Michel-de-Bellechasse, Canada, 25 May 1710[205]

ii. **Joseph Bissonnette**, b. Beaumont, Canada, 22 November 1711; d. Beaumont, Canada, 8 December 1711[206]

iii. **Pierre Bissonnette**, b. Beaumont, Canada, 17 January 1713; d. Baie-Saint-Paul, Canada, 17 April 1731[207]

iv. **Suzanne Bissonnette**, b. Beaumont, Canada, 11 February 1714; m. Gabriel Bilodeau, Berthier-sur-Mer, Canada 13 August 1731; d. Berthier-sur-Mer, Lower Canada, 9 June 1799[208]

Jean passed away at the Hotel-Dieu de Québec in Quebec City on 15 May 1715 at the age of forty-five.[209] His second wife, Marie Jeanne LeBlanc, later married a man named Jean Baptiste Coulombe and lived for another thirty-five years before passing away on 18 March 1750 in Berthier-sur-Mer, Canada, slightly downriver from Beaumont and La Durantaye.[210]

54. Nicolas Binet

Born: 11 February 1671 in Quebec, Canada (Quebec City, Capitale-Nationale Quebec)
Died: 29 July 1753 in Beauport, Canada (Beauport Borough, Quebec City, Capitale-Nationale Quebec)

55. Geneviève Brisson dit DuTilly

Born: 27 February 1678 in Quebec, Canada (Quebec City, Capitale-Nationale Quebec)
Died: 3 March 1758 in Beauport, Canada (Beauport Borough, Quebec City, Capitale-Nationale Quebec)

Nicolas Binet, son of René Binet and Catherine Bourgeois, was born on 11 February 1671 in Quebec, Canada. His parents both immigrated to New France in the 1660s and married in Quebec on 19 October 1667.[211] Father Henri de Bernières baptized Nicolas on 11 February 1671 in Notre-Dame-de-Québec Church with Nicolas DuPont and Anne Madeleine Gaultier acting as his godparents.[212] The Parish of Quebec was the first Catholic parish established in New France, presided over by Bishop François de Laval at the time of Nicolas' birth. When Nicolas was ten years old, he and his parents, along with his siblings Anne, François, Marie, and René, relocated to the Seigneurie de Beauport where there lived on a full forty arpents of land with one flintlock musket and ten horned beasts.[213]

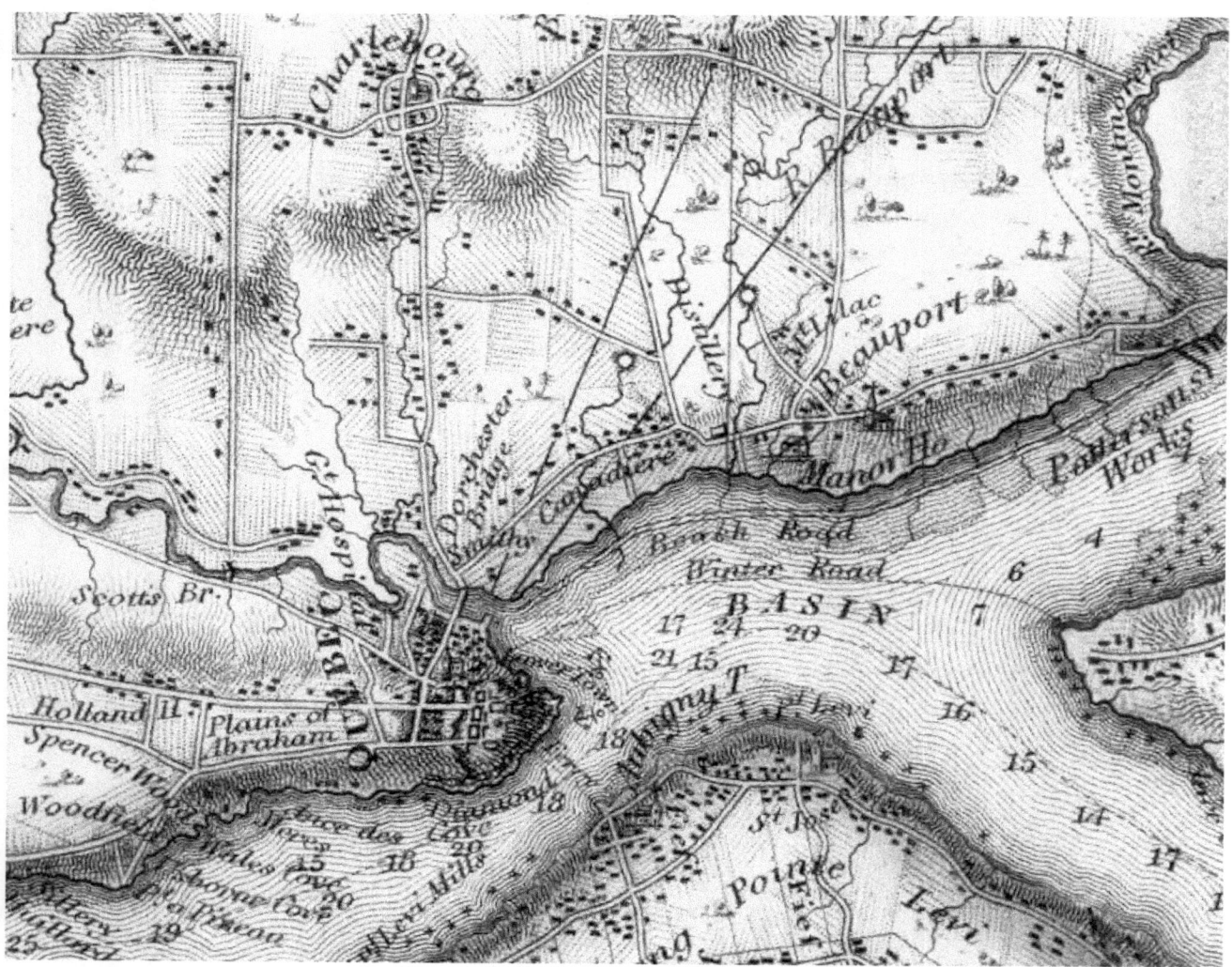

1831 map of the Quebec City region including the community of Beauport to the northeast

Geneviève Brisson dit DuTilly was born on 27 February 1678 in Quebec, Canada (present day Quebec City), to parents René Brisson and Anne Vezina. At the time of her birth, the family lived in the Basee-Ville (Lower Town) neighborhood of Quebec. She was baptized the following day in Notre-Dame-de-Québec Church also by Father de Bernières.[214] As of 1681, Geneviève continued to live with her parents in Quebec's Lower Town along with her siblings René, Charles, Anne, Marie, and Catherine, where her father worked as a *boucher* ("butcher"),

and they owned one cow.[215]

Nicolas married Geneviève on 12 November 1697 in L'Ange-Gardien, Canada, a parish located upriver from Quebec.[216] They settled further upriver in Beauport, a community on the north bank of the Saint Lawrence River that is now a borough of present-day Quebec City resulting from the 2002 municipal merger. All of Nicolas and Geneviève's children were born in Beauport. Nicolas and Geneviève had the following children:

i.   **Marguerite Binet**, b. Beauport, Canada, 3 September 1698; m. (1) Jean Girou, Beauport, Canada, 14 November 1718; m. (2) Alexandre Boissel, Beauport, Canada, 27 September 1723; m. (3) Jacques Paradis, Beauport, Canada, 7 August 1747; d. Beauport, Canada, 13 February 1759[217]

ii.   **Charles Binet**, b. Beauport, Canada, 10 March 1700; d. Beauport, Canada, 7 February 1721[218]

iii. **Nicolas Binet**, b. Beauport, Canada, 17 April 1702; d. Montreal, Canada, 28 August 1749[219]

iv.   **Raphael Binet**, b. Beauport, Canada, 20 February 1704; m. Marie Josephe Turgeon, Beauport, Canada, 22 November 1728; d. Unknown[220]

v.   **Marie Geneviève Binet**, b. Beauport, Canada, 20 December 1705; d. Beauport, Canada, 25 January 1706[221]

vi.   **Marie Geneviève Binet**, b. Beauport, Canada, 12 January 1707; m. Louis Bissonnette, Beauport, Canada, 9 August 1729; d. Lachine, Canada, 12 May 1745[222]

vii. **Louis Binet**, b. Beauport, Canada, 23 August 1709; m. (1) Marie Angelique Landry, Beauport, Canada, 1 October 1731; m. (2) Madeleine Giroux, Beauport, Canada, 16 February 1756; d. Beauport, Canada, 29 August 1757[223]

viii. **Ange Binet**, b. Beauport, Canada, 30 October 1711; m. Marie Ursule Tardif, Beauport, Canada, 1 October 1742; d. Beauport, Province of Quebec, 20 December 1763[224]

ix.   **Marie Françoise Binet**, b. Beauport, Canada, 10 September 1714; m. Louis Rodrigue, Beauport, Canada, 3 February 1738; d. Beauport, Province of Quebec, 4 April 1774[225]

x.   **François Binet**, b. Approximately 1717; m. Charlotte Parant, Montreal, Canada, 21 May 1742; d. Pointe-Claire, Montreal, Province of Quebec, 13 August 1792[226]

xi.   **Genevieve Binet**, b. Beauport, Canada, 3 January 1720; m. Ignace Crevier, Pointe-Claire, Canada, 19 October 1761; d. Saint-Eustache, Province of Quebec, 14 April 1779[227]

Nicolas and Geneviève spent the remainder of their lives in Beauport. Nicholas died on 29 July 1753 in Beauport, Quebec, and was buried the following day in the Beauport parish cemetery.[228] Geneviève outlived Nicolas by nearly five years before passing away on 3 March 1758 in Beauport as well. She was likewise buried the following day in the Beauport parish cemetery.[229]

Individuals 56 through 63 are unknown (Great-Great-Great-Grandparents of Simon Bouschor)

Notes

ABBREVIATIONS

CH. Canadiana Héritage – Canadian Research Knowledge Network, https://heritage.canadiana.ca/

DI-GQ. Drouin Institute – Genealogy Quebec, https://www.genealogiequebec.com/en/

HT. HathiTrust, https://www.hathitrust.org/

PRDH-IGD. Le Programme de Recherche en Démographie Historique, https://www.prdh-igd.com

1   Patrimoine du Vairais, "Bouchard Claude dit Le Petit Claude (vers 1626-1699)," *Les Carnets du Vairais*, 7 September 2016, 19, https://www.patrimoineduvairais.fr/app/download/22512070/Revue+n%C2%B07.pdf.

2   "Commune de Saint-Cosme-en-Vairais (72276)," Populations légales 2021, L'Institut national de la statistique et des études économiques, last updated 28 December 2023, https://www.insee.fr/fr/statistiques/7725600?-geo=COM-72276.

3   "Claude Bouchard," Perche-Québec, accessed March 30, 2020, http://www.perche-quebec.com/files/perche/individus/bouchard-claude.htm#1.

4   "Bouchard Claude dit Le Petit Claude (vers 1626-1699)," *Les Carnets du Vairais*, 19.

5   "Bouchard Claude dit Le Petit Claude (vers 1626-1699)," *Les Carnets du Vairais*, 19; Thomas J. Laforest, *Our French-Canadian Ancestors* vol. 3 (Palm Harbor, FL: LISI Press, 1985), 38, https://obsessedwithmypast.wordpress.com/wp-content/uploads/2021/12/claude-bouchard-1.jpeg?w=1024.

6   "Seigneurie de Beaupré," Séminaire De Québec, accessed 4 August 2024, https://www.seminairedequebec.org/qui-nous-sommes/seigneurie-de-beaupre/.

7   Jacques Mathieu, "Seigneurial System," *Canadian Encyclopedia*, last modified 4 March 2015, https://www.thecanadianencyclopedia.ca/en/article/seigneurial-system.

8   Thomas J. Laforest, *Our French-Canadian Ancestors* vol. 3, 38.

9   Marriage Record for Claude Bouchard and Louise Gasnier, 25 May 1654, Record No. 66447, DI-GQ; Thomas J. Laforest, *Our French-Canadian Ancestors* vol. 12 (Madison, WI: LISI Press, 1983), 131.

10   Janet Manseau, "My Pioneer Ancestor Jacques Bouchard," last modified 8 February 2010, https://www.genealogy.com/forum/surnames/topics/bouchard/1170/.

11   Laforest, *Our French-Canadian Ancestors* vol. 3, 43.

12   Baptismal Record for Marie Bouchard, 11 November 1659, Record No. 57761, DI-GQ; Burial Record for Marie Bouchard, 1 May 1739, Record No. 152021, DI-GQ.

13   Burial Record for Jacques Bouchard, 14 December 1690, Record No. 30586, DI-GQ.

14   Baptismal Record for Gilles Bouchard, 8 March 1664, Record No. 28875, DI-GQ; Burial Record for Gilles Bouchard, 22 March 1664, Record No. 30453, DI-GQ.

15   Baptismal Record for Marguerite Bouchard, 21 October 1665, Record No. 28976, DI-GQ; Marriage Record for René Levoie and Marguerite Bouchard, 4 November 1683, Record No. 28371, DI-GQ; Burial Record for Marguerite Bouchard, 6 April 1731, Record No. 110862, DI-GQ.

16   Burial Record for Louise Bouchard, 10 December 1696, Record No. 9947, DI-GQ.

17   Baptismal Record for Anne Bouchard, 20 February 1670, Record No. 27605, DI-GQ; Marriage Record for Louis Jobidon and Anne Bouchard, 20 November 1690, Record No. 34320, DI-GQ; Burial Record for Anne Bouchard, 8 April 1731, Record No. 140205, DI-GQ.

18   Baptismal Record for Genevieve Bouchard, 29 April 1672, Record No. 27628, DI-GQ; Marriage Record for Michel Tremblay and Genevieve Bouchard, 20 June 1686, Record No. 9891, DI-GQ; Burial Record for Genevieve Bouchard, 23 March 1754, Record No. 195533, DI-GQ.

19   Baptismal Record for François Bouchard, 9 April 1674, Record No. 27649, DI-GQ; Marriage Record for François Bouchard and Marguerite Simard, 15 June 1699, Record No. 9897, DI-GQ; Burial Record for François Bouchard, 12 October 1756, Record No. 195541, DI-GQ.

20   Baptismal Record for Rosalie Bouchard, 7 April 1676, Record No. 27671, DI-GQ; Marriage Record for Etienne Simard and Rosalie Bouchard, 22 November 1695, Record No. 9895, DI-GQ; Burial Record for Rosalie Bouchard, 23 June 1733, Record No. 210485, DI-GQ.

21   Baptismal Record for Claude Bouchard, 14 October 1678, Record No. 27692, DI-GQ; Burial Record for Claude Bouchard, 30 October 1678, Record No. 28519, DI-GQ.

22   Baptismal Record for Louis Bouchard, 20 April 1680, Record No. 27706, DI-GQ; Marriage Record for Louis Bouchard and Suzanne Lefebvre, 25 February 1715, Record No. 18938, DI-GQ; Marriage Record for Louis Bouchard and Françoise Dania, 2 December 1724, Record No. 19001, DI-GQ; Burial Record for Louis Bouchard, 18 November 1727, Record No. 52520, DI-GQ.

23   Baptismal Record for Antoine Bouchard, 25 October 1682, Record No. 27726, DI-GQ; Marriage Record for Antoine Bouchard and Marie Madeleine Simard, 20 November 1704, Record No. 9898, DI-GQ; Burial Record for Antoine Bouchard, 24 June 1759, Record No. 195549, DI-GQ.

24   Lease Agreement between Olivier Letardif and Claude Bouchard, 30 July 1657, https://www.communitystories.ca/v2/portraits-de-nos-ancetres_portraits-of-our-ancestors/wp-content/uploads/sites/106/2019/11/bail-2.jpg.

25   Canada Wildlife Service, *Cap Tourmente National Wildlife Area: Between Two Worlds* (Environment Canada, 1987), 6, https://publications.gc.ca/collections/collection_2023/eccc/cw66/CW66-88-1987-eng.pdf.

26   "Bouchard Claude dit Le Petit Claude (vers 1626-1699)," *Les Carnets du Vairais*, 19; Laforest, *Our French-Canadian Ancestors* vol. 3, 39.

27   "Bouchard Claude dit Le Petit Claude (vers 1626-1699)," *Les Carnets du Vairais*, 19; Laforest, *Our French-Canadian Ancestors* vol. 3, 39-40.

28   Brian Leigh Dunnigan, *A Picturesque Situation: Mackinac before Photography, 1615-1860* (Detroit: Wayne State University Press, 2008), 182.

29   "Habittans de Beaupré," The First Census of New France (Quebec) – 1666, accessed 29 November 2019, http://www.cangenealogy.com/armstrong/qc1666bpre.htm.

30   Benjamin Sulte, *Histoire des Canadiens-Français 1608-1880* Vol. 4 (Montréal: Wilson & Cie, 1882), 75, HT.

31   "Bouchard Claude dit Le Petit Claude (vers 1626-1699)," *Les Carnets du Vairais*, 19; Laforest, *Our French-Canadian Ancestors* vol. 3, 40.

32   "Claude Bouchard," Perche-Québec, accessed 30 March 2020, http://www.perche-quebec.com/files/perche/individus/bouchard-claude.htm#1.

33   "Bouchard Claude dit Le Petit Claude (vers 1626-1699)," *Les Carnets du Vairais*, 19; Laforest, *Our French-Canadian Ancestors* vol. 3, 40.

34   "Petite-Rivière-Saint-François, Municipalité (MÉ) Quebec," Census Profile 2021 Census of Population, Statistics, Canada, released 15 November 2023, https://www12.statcan.gc.ca/census-recensement/2021/dp-pd/prof/index.cfm?Lang=E.

35   Laforest, *Our French-Canadian Ancestors* vol. 3, 40-41.

36   Sulte, *Histoire des Canadiens-Français*, 78.

37   Laforest, *Our French-Canadian Ancestors* vol. 3, 41.

38   Laforest, *Our French-Canadian Ancestors* vol. 3, 43.

39   Burial Record for Claude Bouchard, 26 November 1699, Record No. 9952, DI-GQ.

40   Burial Record for Louise Gagne, 27 April 1721, Record No. 9986, DI-GQ.

41   "Passengers du Tareau 1657," Geni, accessed 4 August 2024, https://www.geni.com/projects/Passagers-du-Taureau-1657/24670.

42   Baptismal Record for Marie Madeleine Racine, 25 July 1646, Record No. 57242, DI-GQ.

43   Marriage Record for Noel Simard and Marie Madeleine Racine, 22 November 1661, DI-GQ.

44   Baptismal Record for Pierre Simard, 1 May 1663, Record No. 28835, DI-GQ; Marriage Record for Pierre Simard and Claire Dodier, 6 December 1690, Record No. 9894, DI-GQ; Burial Record for Pierre Simard, 8 November 1724, Record No. 28727, DI-GQ.

45   Baptismal Record for Noel Simard, 8 October 1664, Record No. 28917, DI-GQ; Marriage Record for Noel Simard and Anne Dodier, 26 April 1689, Record No. 9893, DI-GQ; Burial Record for Noel Simard, 9 April 1726, Record No. 9996, DI-GQ.

46   Baptismal Record for Marie Madeleine Simard, 5 January 1667, Record No. 29034, DI-GQ; Marriage Record for Pierre Tremblay and Marie Madeleine Simard, 3 November 1683, Record No. 28370, DI-GQ; Burial Record for Marie Madeleine Simard, 27 August 1684, Record No. 28529, DI-GQ.

47   Baptismal Record for Etienne Simard, 4 March 1669, Record No. 29108, DI-GQ; Marriage Record for Etienne Simard and Rosalie Bouchard, 22 November 1695, Record No. 9895, DI-GQ; Burial Record for Etienne Simard, 15 November 1750, Record No. 201828, DI-GQ.

48   Baptismal Record for Françoise Simard, 11 September 1671, Record No. 27618, DI-GQ; Marriage Record for Jean Allaire and Françoise Simard, 28 April 1688, Record No. 9892, DI-GQ; "Généalogie Françoise Simard," Généalogie du Québec et d'Amérique française, accessed 22 November 2019, https://www.nosorigines.qc.ca/GenealogieQuebec.aspx?genealogie=Simard_Francoise&pid=1840.

49   Baptismal Record for Joseph Simard, 11 February 1674, Record No. 27643, DI-GQ; Marriage Record for Joseph Simard and Gertrude Caron, 20 April 1700, Record No. 28405, DI-GQ; Marriage Record for Joseph Simard and Marie

Boivin, 30 October 1702, Record No. 28417, DI-GQ; Burial Record for Joseph Simard, 26 September 1738, Record No. 139532, DI-GQ.

50 Baptismal Record for Augustin Simard, 3 April 1676, Record No. 27670, DI-GQ; "Généalogie Augustin Simard," Généalogie du Québec et d'Amérique française, accessed 22 November 2019, https://www.nosorigines.qc.ca/GenealogieQuebec.aspx?genealogie=Simard_Augustin&pid=1845; Burial Record for Augustin Simard, 20 August 1735, Record No. 139514, DI-GQ.

51 Baptismal Record for François Simard, 22 September 1678, Record No. 27690, DI-GQ; "Généalogie François Simard," Généalogie du Québec et d'Amérique française, accessed 22 November 2019, https://www.nosorigines.qc.ca/GenealogieQuebec.aspx?genealogie=Simard_Francois&pid=1847; Burial Record for François Bouchard, 8 December 1732, Record No. 110885, DI-GQ.

52 Baptismal Record for Rosalie Simard, 2 May 1681, Record No. 99700, DI-GQ; Marriage Record for Jean Caron and Rosalie Simard, 29 October 1696, Record No. 9896, DI-GQ; Burial Record for Rosalie Simard, 20 July 1714, Record No. 28658, DI-GQ.

53 Baptismal Record for Paul Simard, 7 May 1682, Record No. 99569, DI-GQ; "Généalogie Paul Simard," Généalogie du Québec et d'Amérique française, accessed 22 November 2019, https://www.nosorigines.qc.ca/GenealogieQuebec.aspx?genealogie=Simard_Paul&pid=1851; Burial Record for Paul Simard, 17 August 1733, Record No. 210487, DI-GQ.

54 Baptismal Record for Marguerite Simard, 22 February 1684, Record No. 9467, DI-GQ; Marriage Record for François Bouchard and Marguerite Bouchard, 15 June 1699, Record No. 9897, DI-GQ.

55 Baptismal Record for Jean Simard, 27 May 1686, Record No. 9473, DI-GQ; Marriage Record for Jean Simard & Genevieve Gravelle, Couple No. 194184, PRDH-IGD; Burial Record for Jean Simard, 4 August 1715, Record No. 9972, DI-GQ.

56 Baptismal Record for Marie Madeleine Simard, 19 January 1689, Record No 9478, DI-GQ; Marriage Record for Antoine Bouchard and Marie Madeleine Simard, 20 November 1704, Record No. 9898, DI-GQ.

57 Baptismal Record for Catherine Simard, 4 May 1692, Record No. 9478, DI-GQ; Marriage Record for Noel Castonguay and Catherine Simard, 4 June 1716, Record No. 9914, DI-GQ; Burial Record for Catherine Simard, 17 December 1748, Record No. 110959, DI-GQ.

58 Sulte, *Histoire des Canadiens-Français*, 55.

59 Sulte, *Histoire des Canadiens-Français*, 78.

60 Burial Record for Noel Simard, 24 July 1715, Record No. 9970, DI-GQ.

61 Burial Record for Marie Madeleine Simard, 3 December 1726, Record No. 9997, DI-GQ.

62 "Généalogie Gabriel-Robert Dufour," Généalogie du Québec et d'Amérique française, accessed 24 November 2019, https://www.nosorigines.qc.ca/GenealogieQuebec.aspx?genealogie=Dufour_Gabriel-Robert&pid=1920.

63 Baptismal Record for Angelique Dufour, 23 May 1695, Record No. 29463, DI-GQ; "Généalogie Angelique Dufour," Généalogie du Québec et d'Amérique française, accessed 24 November 2019, https://www.nosorigines.qc.ca/GenealogieQuebec.aspx?genealogie=Dufour_Angelique&pid=25916; Burial Record for Angelique Dufour, 20 August 1768, Record No. 367251, DI-GQ.

64 Baptismal Record for Marie Josephe Dufour, 19 September 1697, Record No. 29513, DI-GQ; Marriage Record for Pierre Gagne and Marie Joseph Dufour, 14 May 1725, Record No. 37793, DI-GQ.

65 "Généalogie Agnes Dufour," Généalogie du Québec et d'Amérique française, accessed 24 November 2019, https://www.nosorigines.qc.ca/GenealogieQuebec.aspx?genealogie=Dufour_Agnes&pid=30763.

66 "Généalogie Gabriel-Robert Dufour," Généalogie du Québec et d'Amérique française, accessed 24 November 2019, https://www.nosorigines.qc.ca/GenealogieQuebec.aspx?genealogie=Dufour_Gabriel-Robert&pid=1920.

67 Baptismal Record for Louise Gagne, 24 September 1683, Record No. 99701, DI-GQ.

68 Sulte, *Histoire des Canadiens-Français*, 78.

69 Marriage Record for François Tremblay and Marie Reine Dofour, 6 November 1726, Record No. 9935, DI-GQ; Burial Record for Marie Reine Dufour, 16 April 1790, Record No. 384799, DI-GQ.

70 Marriage Record for Joseph Dufour and Marie Anne Tremblay, 29 October 1732, Record No. 195585, DI-GQ; Marriage Record for Joseph Dufour and Felicite Simard, 23 June 1750, Record No. 201755, DI-GQ; Burial Record for Joseph Dufour, 2 September 1774, Record No. 367426, DI-GQ.

71 Marriage Record for Ignace Dufour and Marie Reine Tremblay, 28 November 1736, Record No. 111205, DI-GQ; Burial Record for Ignace Dufour, 8 October 1762, Record No. 201931, DI-GQ.

72 Marriage Record for Bonaventure Dufour and Elisabeth Tremblay, 8 November 1734, Record No. 111198, DI-GQ; Burial Record for Bonaventure Dufour, 23 May 1783, Record No. 367378, DI-GQ.

73 Burial Record for Louise Dufour, 9 September 1759, Record No. 201897, DI-GQ.

74 Marriage Record for Etienne Simard and Barbe Dufour, 23 November 1733, Record No. 110824, DI-GQ; Burial Record for Barbe Dufour, 21 October 1799, Record No. 384751, DI-GQ.

75   Marriage Record for Gabriel Robert Dufour and Genevieve Tremblay, 21 May 1742, Record No. 111309, DI-GQ; Marriage Record for Gabriel Robert Dufour and Madeleine Boissonneau, 9 June 1756, Record No. 239309, DI-GQ.

76   "Généalogie Gabriel-Robert Dufour," Généalogie du Québec et d'Amérique française, accessed 24 November 2019, https://www.nosorigines.qc.ca/GenealogieQuebec.aspx?genealogie=Dufour_Gabriel-Robert&pid=1920.

77   Marriage Record for Guillaume Boily and Louise Gagne, 30 October 1726, Record No. 9933, DI-GQ.

78   Baptismal Record for Jean Baptiste Boily, 9 June 1728, Record No. 9849, DI-GQ; Marriage Record for Jean Baptiste Boily and Ursule Duchesne, 22 January 1748, Record No. 110852, DI-GQ; Marriage Record for Jean Baptiste Boily and Amable Cote, 14 September 1779, Record No. 216889, DI-GQ; Burial Record for Jean Baptiste Boily, 2 December 1805, Record No. 2380734, DI-GQ.

79   Burial Record for Louise Gagne, 24 September 1747, Record No. 110943, DI-GQ.

80   Burial Record for Guillaume Boily, 18 February 1764, Record No. 201935, DI-GQ.

81   Baptismal Record for Louis Tremblay, 30 September 1667, Record No. 29060, DI-GQ.

82   Sulte, *Histoire des Canadiens-Français*, 74.

83   Sulte, *Histoire des Canadiens-Français*, 78.

84   Marriage Record for Louis Tremblay and Marie Perron, 27 November 1691, Record No. 34327, DI-GQ.

85   Baptismal Record for Marie Dorothee Tremblay, 28 September 1692, Record No. 33644, DI-GQ; Marriage Record for Etienne Desbiens and Marie Dorothee Tremblay, 21 January 1715, Record No. 9909, DI-GQ; Burial Record for Marie Dorothee Tremblay, 9 March 1734, Record No. 111065, DI-GQ.

86   Baptismal Record for François Xavier Tremblay, 12 April 1695, Record No. 9498, DI-GQ; Marriage Record for François Xavier Tremblay and Marie Madeleine Bouchard, 24 November 1718, Record No. 9921, DI-GQ; Burial Record for François Xavier Bouchard, November 1755, Record No. 202313, DI-GQ.

87   Baptismal Record for Louise Tremblay, 24 June 1697, Record No. 9507, DI-GQ; Marriage Record for François Rousset and Louise Tremblay, 17 November 1720, Record No. 9924, DI-GQ; Burial Record for Louise Tremblay, 12 December 1733, Record No. 111064, DI-GQ.

88   Baptismal Record for Rosalie Tremblay, 29 September 1699, Record No. 9522, DI-GQ; Marriage Record for Sebastian Hervé and Rosalie Tremblay, 17 November 1722, Record No. 9926, DI-GQ; Burial Record for Rosalie Tremblay, 23 August 1740, Record No. 110909, DI-GQ.

89   Baptismal Record for Marie Madeleine Tremblay, 30 October 1701, Record No. 9535, DI-GQ; Marriage Record for François Xavier Fortin and Marie Madeleine Tremblay, 5 November 1726, Record No. 9934, DI-GQ; Burial Record for Marie Madeleine Tremblay, 23 February 1778, Record No. 367280, DI-GQ.

90   Baptismal Record for Louis Tremblay, 14 August 1703, Record No. 9550, DI-GQ; Marriage Record for Louis Tremblay and Brigitte Fortin, 11 November 1726, Record No. 9936, DI-GQ; Burial Record for Louis Tremblay, 7 April 1757, Record No. 195542, DI-GQ.

91   Burial Record for Marie Perron, 7 April 1706, Record No. 9955, DI-GQ.

92   Marriage Record for Louis Tremblay and Françoise Morel, 19 November 1706, Record No. 28424, DI-GQ.

93   Baptismal Record for Françoise Morel, 18 October 1680, Record No. 27710, DI-GQ.

94   Sulte, *Histoire des Canadiens-Français*, 79.

95   Baptismal Record for Guillaume Tremblay, 22 June 1707, Record No. 9570, DI-GQ; Marriage Record for Guillaume Tremblay and Marie Jeanne Dinelle, 23 November 1729, Record No. 9941, DI-GQ; Burial Record for Guillaume Tremblay, November 1755, Record No. 202311, DI-GQ.

96   Baptismal Record for Françoise Tremblay, 29 December 1708, Record No. 9579, DI-GQ; Marriage Record for Michel Poitevin and Françoise Tremblay, 14 November 1735, Record No. 111201, DI-GQ; Burial Record for Françoise Tremblay, 30 May 1778, Record No. 367282, DI-GQ.

97   Baptismal Record for Etienne Tremblay, 13 November 1710, Record No. 9592, DI-GQ; Marriage Record for Etienne Tremblay and Marie Louise Bonneau, 11 November 1734, Record No. 111199, DI-GQ; Burial Record for Etienne Tremblay, November 1755, Record No. 202316, DI-GQ.

98   Baptismal Record for Marie Reine Tremblay, 11 December 1712, Record No. 9608, DI-GQ; Marriage Record for Marie Reine Tremblay and Ignace Dufour, 28 November 1736, Record No. 111205, DI-GQ; Burial Record for Marie Reine Tremblay, 18 October 1758, Record No. 201884, DI-GQ.

99   Baptismal Record for Elisabeth Tremblay, 5 March 1715, Record No. 9628, DI-GQ; Marriage Record for Bonaventure Dufour and Elisabeth Tremblay, 8 November 1734, Record No. 111198, DI-GQ; Burial Record for Elisabeth Tremblay, 16 May 1799, Record No. 384810, DI-GQ.

100   Burial Record for Françoise Morel, 3 May 1715, Record No. 9966, DI-GQ.

101   Marriage Record for Louis Tremblay and Marie Letarte, 26 August 1716, Record No. 34425, DI-GQ.

102   "Généalogie Marie Letartre," Généalogie du Québec et d'Amérique française, accessed 28 November 2019, https://www.nosorigines.qc.ca/GenealogieQuebec.aspx?pid=1348&partID=1349.

103   Baptismal Record for Marie Josephe Tremblay, 4 June 1717, Record No. 9652, DI-GQ; Marriage Record for François

Simard and Marie Josephe Tremblay, 10 January 1735, Record No. 111200, DI-GQ; Burial Record for Marie Josephe Tremblay, 24 November 1735, Record No. 110899, DI-GQ.

104   Baptismal Record for Andre Tremblay, 23 April 1719, Record No. 9687, DI-GQ; Marriage Record for Andre Tremblay and Catherine Bouchard, 28 April 1739, Record No. 111208, DI-GQ; Burial Record for Andre Tremblay, 2 July 1804, Record No. 2380729, DI-GQ.

105   Baptismal Record for Joseph Tremblay, 17 August 1720, Record No. 9712, DI-GQ; Marriage Record for Joseph Tremblay and Marguerite Bouchard, 6 November 1742, Record No. 111214, DI-GQ; Burial Record for Joseph Tremblay, 17 November 1758, Record No. 202324, DI-GQ.

106   Burial Record for Marie Letartre, 21 July 1726, Record No. 73798, DI-GQ.

107   Marriage Record for Louis Tremblay and Madeleine Marquis, 29 July 1727, Record No. 68552, DI-GQ.

108   Burial Record for Marie Madeleine Marquis, 7 March 1747, Record No. 111246, DI-GQ.

109   "Généalogie François-Xavier Tremblay," *Généalogie du Québec et d'Amérique française*, accessed 19 June 2024, https://www.nosorigines.qc.ca/GenealogieQuebec.aspx?genealogie=Tremblay_Francois-Xavier&pid=1381; "Généalogie Guillaume Tremblay," *Généalogie du Québec et d'Amérique française*, accessed 19 June 2024, https://www.nosorigines.qc.ca/GenealogieQuebec.aspx?genealogie=Tremblay_Guillaume&pid=1391; "Généalogie Etienne Tremblay," *Généalogie du Québec et d'Amérique française*, accessed 19 June 2024, https://www.nosorigines.qc.ca/GenealogieQuebec.aspx?genealogie=Tremblay_Etienne&pid=32280.

110   Stephen A. White, *Dictionnaire Généalogique Des Familles Acadiennes* (Moncton, N.B.: Centre D'études Acadiennes, Université De Moncton, 1999), 987-988.

111   Christopher Hodson, "Exile on Spruce Street: An Acadian History," *The William and Mary Quarterly* 67, no. 2 (2010): 258, https://doi.org/10.5309/willmaryquar.67.2.249.

112   Lucie LeBlanc Consentino, "1671 Acadian Census," Acadian Census Records, accessed 29 November 2019, http://www.acadian-home.org/census1671.html.

113   White, *Dictionnaire Généalogique Des Familles Acadiennes*, 987-988.

114   Lucie LeBlanc Consentino, "1678 Acadian Census," Acadian Census Records, accessed 29 November 2019, http://www.acadian-home.org/census1678.html.

115   "Bourgeois Family Arrived in 1632," *Daily Advertiser* (Lafayette, LA), 2 June 1996, https://www.acadian.org/genealogy/families/bourgeois/; "Bourgeois Update," *Assumption Pioneer* (Napoleonville, LA), 3 October 1996, Newspapers.com.

116   "History – Fort Anne National Historic Site," Parks Canada, Government of Canada, last modified 18 April 2024, https://parks.canada.ca/lhn-nhs/ns/fortanne/culture/histoire-history; John Mack Faragher, *A Great and Noble Scheme: The Tragic Story of the Expulsion of the French Acadians from their American Homeland* (New York: W.W. Norton & Company, Inc., 2005), 71, 73.

117   Consentino, "1671 Acadian Census."

118   Faragher, *Great and Noble Scheme*, 71.

119   Faragher, *Great and Noble Scheme*, 71-72.

120   "Généalogie Jacques LeBlanc," *Généalogie du Québec et d'Amérique française*, accessed 10 December 2019, https://www.nosorigines.qc.ca/GenealogieQuebec.aspx?genealogie=Leblanc_Jacques&pid=94236.

121   "Généalogie François LeBlanc," *Généalogie du Québec et d'Amérique française*, accessed 10 December 2019, https://www.nosorigines.qc.ca/GenealogieQuebec.aspx?genealogie=Leblanc_Francois&pid=18754; Burial Record for François LeBlanc, 5 March 1770, DI-GQ.

122   "Généalogie René LeBlanc," *Généalogie du Québec et d'Amérique française*, accessed 10 December 2019, https://www.nosorigines.qc.ca/GenealogieQuebec.aspx?genealogie=Leblanc_René&pid=660313.

123   "Généalogie Pierre LeBlanc," *Généalogie du Québec et d'Amérique française*, accessed 10 December 2019, https://www.nosorigines.qc.ca/GenealogieQuebec.aspx?genealogie=Leblanc_Pierre&pid=96778.

124   White, *Dictionnaire Généalogique Des Familles Acadiennes*, 987.

125   White, *Dictionnaire Généalogique Des Familles Acadiennes*, 987; Marriage Record for Etienne LeBlanc and Ann Mailoux, 23 November 1716, DI-GQ.

126   White, *Dictionnaire Généalogique Des Familles Acadiennes*, 1492.

127   Marriage Record for Jacques Theriault and Marie LeBlanc, 2 October 1713, DI-GQ; "Généalogie Marie LeBlanc," *Généalogie du Québec et d'Amérique française*, accessed 10 December 2019, https://www.nosorigines.qc.ca/GenealogieQuebec.aspx?genealogie=Leblanc_Marie&pid=96773.

128   White, *Dictionnaire Généalogique Des Familles Acadiennes*, 988; Burial Record for Jean Baptiste LeBlanc, 20 January 1718, Record No. 71600, DI-GQ.

129   White, *Dictionnaire Généalogique Des Familles Acadiennes*, 925, 988.

130   Consentino, "1686 Acadian Census;" Lucie LeBlanc Consentino, "1693 Acadian Census," Acadian Census Records, accessed 29 November 2019, http://www.acadian-home.org/census1693.html; Lucie LeBlanc Consentino, "1701

Acadian Census," Acadian Census Records, accessed 29 November 2019, http://www.acadian-home.org/census1701.html; Lucie LeBlanc Consentino, "1703 Acadian Census," Acadian Census Records, accessed 29 November 2019, http://www.acadian-home.org/census1703.html.

131   Lucie LeBlanc Consentino, "1707 Acadian Census," Acadian Census Records, accessed 29 November 2019, http://www.acadian-home.org/census1707.html; Lucie LeBlanc Consentino, "1714 Acadian Census," Acadian Census Records, accessed 29 November 2019, http://www.acadian-home.org/census1714.html; "1715 Grand Pré Les Mines Census," Nova Scotia and Cape Breton, Original Correspondence (CO217): C-9120, of the National Archives of Canada "Acadie Recensements 1671 – 1752," Images 610-613, CH.

132   Burial Record for René LeBlanc, 4 January 1734, Record No. 6147512, DI-GQ.

133   Burial Record for Anne Bourgeois, 29 December 1747, Record No. 6147597, DI-GQ.

134   WikiTree Contributors, "Pierre Thébeau (abt. 1675 - bef. 1714)," WikiTree: The Free Family Tree, last modified 21 July 2024, https://www.wikitree.com/wiki/Th%C3%A9beau-155.

135   Marriage Record for Pierre Thibault and Jeanne Comeau, 26 November 1703, DI-GQ.

136   WikiTree Contributors, "Marie-Jeanne Comeau (abt. 1683 - 1737)," WikiTree: The Free Family Tree, last modified 5 August 2024, https://www.wikitree.com/wiki/Comeau-62; Consentino, "1686 Acadian Census."

137   Consentino, "1686 Acadian Census."; Consentino, "1693 Acadian Census;" Lucie LeBlanc Consentino, "1698 Acadian Census," Acadian Census Records, accessed 30 November 2019, http://www.acadian-home.org/census1698.html; Consentino, "1701 Acadian Census;" Consentino, "1703 Acadian Census."

138   Baptismal Record for Marguerite Thibault, 20 October 1704, Record No. 6143177, DI-GQ; Marriage Record for René Leblanc and Marguerite Thibault, 26 November 1720, DI-GQ.

139   Baptismal Record for Jacques François Thibault, 2 May 1706, DI-GQ; Marriage Record for Jacques François Thibault and Anne Melanson, 4 August 1733, DI-GQ.

140   Consentino, "1714 Acadian Census."

141   WikiTree Contributors, "Jeanne Comeau (abt. 1683 – 1737)," WikiTree: The Free Family Tree, last modified 19 October 2019, https://www.wikitree.com/wiki/Comeau-62.

142   WikiTree Contributors, "Joseph Dugas (1689 - 1733)," WikiTree: The Free Family Tree, last modified 18 August 2023, https://www.wikitree.com/wiki/Dugas-246.

143   Faragher, Great and Noble Scheme, 45-46.

144   WikiTree Contributors, "Jeanne Guilbeau (1670 - abt. 1728)," WikiTree: The Free Family Tree, last modified 18 April 2024, https://www.wikitree.com/wiki/Guilbeau-460 citing Stephen A. White, Dictionnaire Généalogique des Familles Acadiennes (2 vols., Moncton, New Brunswick: Centre d'Études Acadiennes, 1999) p. 780.

145   Consentino, "1693 Acadian Census;" Consentino, "1703 Acadian Census;" Consentino, "1707 Acadian Census."

146   Marriage Record for Joseph Dugas and Marguerite Richard, 12 January 1711, DI-GQ.

147   WikiTree Contributors, "Marguerite Richard (aft. 1693 - 1746)," WikiTree: The Free Family Tree, last modified 28 August 2022, https://www.wikitree.com/wiki/Richard-632 citing Stephen A. White, Dictionnaire Généalogique des Familles Acadiennes (2 vols., Moncton, New Brunswick: Centre d'Études Acadiennes, 1999) p. 1376.

148   Consentino, "1703 Acadian Census;" Consentino, "1707 Acadian Census."

149   Baptismal Record for Charles Dugas, 17 December 1711, Record No. 6146119, DI-GQ; Marriage Record for Charles Dugas and Anne Suzanne LeBlanc, 7 January 1739, DI-GQ; Burial Record for Charles Dugas, 26 January 1801, Record No. 2867422, DI-GQ.

150   WikiTree Contributors, "Joseph Dugas (1714 – 1779)," WikiTree: The Free Family Tree, last modified 4 June 2024, https://www.wikitree.com/wiki/Dugas-620.

151   Burial Record for Marguerite Dugas, 7 December 1732, Record No. 6139101, DI-GQ.

152   Burial Record for Anne Dugas, 28 June 1733, Record No. 6139174, DI-GQ.

153   Burial Record for Angélique Dugas, 5 November 1743, Record No. 6147555, DI-GQ.

154   Marriage Record for Abraham Dugas and Marguerite LeBlanc, 16 July 1748, DI-GQ.

155   Baptismal Record for Etienne Dugas, 26 February 1729, Record No. 6137920, DI-GQ; Burial Record for Etienne Dugas, 21 November 1730, Record No. 6139014, DI-GQ.

156   Baptismal Record for Jeanne Dugas, 16 October 1731, Record No. 6137982, DI-GQ; Denis Savard, "Racines acadiennes – Jeanne Dugas élevée au rang de personnage historique," Acadie Nouvelle, 13 March 2016, https://www.acadienouvelle.com/chroniques/2016/02/28/jeanne-dugas-elevee-au-rang-de-personnage-historique/.

157   Burial Record for Marie Madeleine Dugas, 11 December 1732, Record No. 6139103, DI-GQ.

158   Consentino, "1714 Acadian Census."

159   "1715 Grand Pré Les Mines Census," Nova Scotia and Cape Breton, Original Correspondence (CO217): C-9120, of the National Archives of Canada "Acadie Recensements 1671 – 1752," Images 610-613, CH.

160   Burial Record for Joseph Dugas, 5 September 1733, Record No. 6139180, DI-GQ.

161   Marriage Record for Charles de Saint-Étienne de la Tour and Marguerite Richard, 16 January 1736, Record No.

6136235, DI-GQ.

162   Baptismal Record for Anne de Saint-Étienne de la Tour, 23 December 1737, Record No. 6138142, DI-GQ.

163   Baptismal Record for Jeanne Angelique de Saint-Étienne de la Tour, 23 December 1737, Record No. 6138142, DI-GQ.

164   Denis Savard, "Racines acadiennes – Jeanne Dugas élevée au rang de personnage historique," Acadie Nouvelle, 13 March 2016, https://www.acadienouvelle.com/chroniques/2016/02/28/jeanne-dugas-elevee-au-rang-de-personnage-historique/.

165   Individual Record for Pierre LeBlanc, Individual No. 219004, PRDH-IGD.

166   Consentino, "1693 Acadian Census;" Consentino, "1701 Acadian Census;" Consentino, "1703 Acadian Census;" Consentino, "1707 Acadian Census."

167   Consentino, "1693 Acadian Census;" Consentino, "1703 Acadian Census;" Consentino, "1707 Acadian Census."

168   Marriage Record for Pierre LeBlanc and Françoise Landry, 16 February 1711, DI-GQ.

169   Baptismal Record for Agnes LeBlanc, 15 March 1712, Record No. 6146738, DI-GQ; "Généalogie Agnes Leblanc," Généalogie du Québec et d'Amérique française, accessed 16 December 2019, https://www.nosorigines.qc.ca/GenealogieQuebec.aspx?genealogie=Leblanc_Agnes&pid=84328.

170   Marriage Record for Joseph Broussard and Ursule LeBlanc, 29 February 1740, DI-GQ; "Généalogie Ursule Leblanc," Généalogie du Québec et d'Amérique française, accessed 16 December 2019, https://www.nosorigines.qc.ca/GenealogieQuebec.aspx?genealogie=Leblanc_Ursule&pid=1129114.

171   Baptismal Record for Anne Suzanne LeBlanc, 16 March 1718, Record No. 6146763, DI-GQ; Marriage Record for Charles Dugas and Anne Suzanne LeBlanc, 7 January 1739, DI-GQ; WikiTree Contributors, "Anne (Leblanc) LeBlanc (1718-abt.1776)," WikiTree: The Free Family Tree, last modified 13 September 2022, https://www.wikitree.com/wiki/Leblanc-459.

172   Baptismal Record for Theodore LeBlanc, 23 December 1719, Library and Archives Canada, Fonds de la paroisse catholique Saint-Charles-des-Mines (Grand-Pré, N.-É.) - 1869, Parish registers: Nova Scotia : C-1869 (Image 124), CH; Marriage Record for Theodore LeBlanc and Marie Cormier, 4 June 1740, Library and Archives Canada Fonds des Archives départementales de la Charente-Maritime [La Rochelle, France] : C-1207 Registres de Beaubassin - reel_c1207 MG 6 A 2 (Image 69), CH.

173   Baptismal Record for Angelique LeBlanc, 27 May 1722, Library and Archives Canada, Fonds de la paroisse catholique Saint-Charles-des-Mines (Grand-Pré, N.-É.) - 1869, Parish registers: Nova Scotia : C-1869 (Image 161), CH.

174   Baptismal Record for Marie-Madeleine LeBlanc, 10 September 1723, Library and Archives Canada, Fonds de la paroisse catholique Saint-Charles-des-Mines (Grand-Pré, N.-É.) - 1869, Parish registers: Nova Scotia : C-1869 (Image 179), CH.

175   Baptismal Record for Augustin LeBlanc, 25 November 1724, Library and Archives Canada, Fonds de la paroisse catholique Saint-Charles-des-Mines (Grand-Pré, N.-É.) - 1869, Parish registers: Nova Scotia : C-1869 (Image 205), CH; Burial Record for Augustin LeBlanc, 14 July 1786, Record No. 394032, DI-GQ.

176   Baptismal Record for Joseph LeBlanc, 18 February 1726, Library and Archives Canada, Fonds de la paroisse catholique Saint-Charles-des-Mines (Grand-Pré, N.-É.) - 1869, Parish registers: Nova Scotia : C-1869 (Image 224), CH.

177   Baptismal Record for Françoise LeBlanc, 9 September 1727, Library and Archives Canada, Fonds de la paroisse catholique Saint-Charles-des-Mines (Grand-Pré, N.-É.) - 1869, Parish registers: Nova Scotia : C-1869 (Image 246), CH; "Généalogie Françoise Leblanc," Généalogie du Québec et d'Amérique française, accessed 18 December 2019, https://www.nosorigines.qc.ca/GenealogieQuebec.aspx?pid=563559&partID=563552; Marriage Record for Antoine Boudreau and Françoise LeBlanc, 28 September 1801, Record No, 2255362, DI-GQ; Burial Record for Françoise LeBlanc, 25 November 1802, Record No. 2822908, DI-GQ.

178   Baptismal Record for Marie LeBlanc, 7 April 1729, Library and Archives Canada, Fonds de la paroisse catholique Saint-Charles-des-Mines (Grand-Pré, N.-É.) - 1869, Parish registers: Nova Scotia : C-1869 (Image 265), CH; Marriage Record for Françoise Gaudreau and Marie LeBlanc, 10 July 1748, Library and Archives Canada, Fonds de la paroisse catholique Saint-Charles-des-Mines (Grand-Pré, N.-É.) - 1869, Parish registers: Nova Scotia : C-1869 (Image 804), CH.

179   Baptismal Record for Pierre Raymond LeBlanc, 10 January 1731, Library and Archives Canada, Fonds de la paroisse catholique Saint-Charles-des-Mines (Grand-Pré, N.-É.) - 1869, Parish registers: Nova Scotia : C-1869 (Image 292-293), CH; Burial Record for Pierre-Raymond LeBlanc, 13 January 1731, Library and Archives Canada, Fonds de la paroisse catholique Saint-Charles-des-Mines (Grand-Pré, N.-É.) - 1869, Parish registers: Nova Scotia : C-1869 (Image 837), CH.

180   Baptismal Record for Marie LeBlanc, 5 April 1732, Library and Archives Canada, Fonds de la paroisse catholique Saint-Charles-des-Mines (Grand-Pré, N.-É.) - 1869, Parish registers: Nova Scotia : C-1869 (Image 313), CH; Burial Record for Marie Rose LeBlanc, 22 May 1771, Record No. 375315, DI-GQ.

181   Baptismal Record for Marguerite Monique LeBlanc, 4 May 1734, Library and Archives Canada, Fonds de la paroisse

catholique Saint-Charles-des-Mines (Grand-Pré, N.-É.) - 1869, Parish registers: Nova Scotia : C-1869 (Image 345), CH; WikiTree Contributors, "Marguerite Monique Leblanc (1734)," WikiTree: The Free Family Tree, last modified 9 October 2023, https://www.wikitree.com/wiki/Leblanc-7604; Burial Record for Marguerite LeBlanc, 26 January 1759, Archives en ligne Ille-et-Vilaine, Registres paroissiaux et état civil, 10 NUM 35288 732 > SAINT-MALO > 1759 > Sépultures > COMMUNE > p. 5 of 41, https://archives-en-ligne.ille-et-vilaine.fr/thot_internet/gestionARK.asp?a=49933%2Ftht80gb5p56b%2F140177%2F5.

182   Baptismal Record for Pierre Hilaire LeBlanc, 12 January 1736, Library and Archives Canada, Fonds de la paroisse catholique Saint-Charles-des-Mines (Grand-Pré, N.-É.) - 1869, Parish registers: Nova Scotia : C-1869 (Image 373), CH; Marriage Record for Pierre-Hiliare LeBlanc and Marie Granger, 25 October 1784, Record No. 225499, DI-GQ; Burial Record for Pierre Hilaire LeBlanc, 29 July 1800, Record No. 2822688, DI-GQ.

183   Consentino, "1714 Acadian Census."

184   "1715 Grand Pré Les Mines Census," Nova Scotia and Cape Breton, Original Correspondence (CO217): C-9120, of the National Archives of Canada, "Acadie Recensements 1671 – 1752", Images 610-613, CH.

185   Burial Record for Marie Françoise Landry, 4 October 1767, Record No. 365686, DI-GQ.

186   Burial Record for Pierre LeBlanc, 23 October 1769, Record No. 375810, DI-GQ.

187   "Marmotte / Champagne, Nicolas (b. Nicolas-Noël)," Fichier Origine, last modified 5 March 2022, https://fichierorigine.com/recherche?numero=021147.

188   Marriage Record for Claude Marmotte and Nicole Garaudel, 7 January 1727, Registres paroissiaux et d'état civil, Archives départementales des Ardennes, https://archives.cd08.fr/ark:/75583/s00532d83791654f/532d83791fd05.

189   "Marmotte / Champagne, Nicolas (b. Nicolas-Noël)," Fichier Origine, last modified 5 March 2022, https://fichierorigine.com/recherche?numero=021147.

190   Marriage Record for Claude Marmotte and Nicole Garaudel, 7 January 1727, Registres paroissiaux et d'état civil, Archives départementales des Ardennes, https://archives.cd08.fr/ark:/75583/s00532d83791654f/532d83791fd05.

191   Baptismal Record for Jean Bissonette, 24 July 1669, Record No. 58324, DI-GQ.

192   Sulte, *Histoire des Canadiens-Français*, 86.

193   Baptismal Record for Charlotte Davenne, 14 April 1676, Record No. 78116, DI-GQ.

194   Sulte, *Histoire des Canadiens-Français*, 77.

195   "Généalogie Jean Bissonette," Généalogie du Québec et d'Amérique française, accessed 17 November 2019, https://www.nosorigines.qc.ca/GenealogieQuebec.aspx?genealogie=Bissonnette_Jean&pid=4253.

196   Baptismal Record for Marie Charlotte Bissonette, 23 January 1693, Record No. 1000, DI-GQ; Marriage Record for Charles Flibot and Charlotte Bissonnette, 29 July 1708, Record No. 1315, DI-GQ; Burial Record for Marie-Charlotte Bissonette, 20 May 1733, Record No. 151244, DI-GQ.

197   Marriage Record for Gabriel Brias and Suzanne Bissonnette, 29 January 1714, Record No. 717, DI-GQ; Burial Record for Suzanne Bissonnette, 20 December 1741, Record No. 152389, DI-GQ.

198   Baptismal Record for Jean Bissonnette, 26 August 1698, Record No. 1035, DI-GQ; Marriage Record for Jean Bissonette and Marie Lavoie, 19 July 1720, Record No. 9923, DI-GQ; Burial Record for Jean Bissonette, 2 May 1756, Record No. 198581, DI-GQ.

199   Baptismal Record for François Bissonnette, 5 February 1700, Record No. 1063, DI-GQ; Marriage Record for François Bissonnette and Marguerite Guay, 14 February 1722, Record No. 68326, DI-GQ; Burial Record for François Bissonnette, 30 June 1756, Record No. 307276, DI-GQ.

200   Baptismal Record for Françoise Hilaire Bissonnette, 31 May 1702, Record No. 1108, DI-GQ.

201   Baptismal Record for Charles Alexandre Bissonnette, 5 December 1703, Record No. 1134, DI-GQ; Marriage Record for Charles Alexandre Bissonnette and Marie LaFlamme, 29 October 1727, Record No. 37804, DI-GQ.

202   Baptismal Record for Louis Bissonnette, 3 June 1706, Record No. 1196, DI-GQ; Marriage Record for Louis Bissonnette and Marie Geneviève Binet, 9 August 1729, Record No. 77536, DI-GQ; Marriage Record for Louis Bissonnette and Marie Anne Langevin, 16 August 1746, Record No. 150294, DI-GQ; Burial Record for Louis Bissonnette, 15 May 1760, Record No. 275397, DI-GQ.

203   Burial Record for Marie Charlotte Davenne, 20 October 1707, Record No. 73230, DI-GQ.

204   "Généalogie Jean Bissonnette," Généalogie du Québec et d'Amérique française, accessed 17 November 2019, https://www.nosorigines.qc.ca/GenealogieQuebec.aspx?genealogie=Bissonnette_Jean&pid=4253.

205   Baptismal Record for Marie Jeanne Bissonnette, 7 May 1710, Record No. 1261, DI-GQ; "Généalogie Marie-Jeanne Bissonnette," Généalogie du Québec et d'Amérique française, accessed 17 November 2019, https://www.nosorigines.qc.ca/Genealogie_Canada_Children.aspx?genealogie=Marie-Jeanne&pid=46105.

206   Baptismal Record for Joseph Bissonnette, 24 November 1711, Record No. 219, DI-GQ; Burial Record for Joseph Bissonnette, 8 December 1711, Record No. 837, DI-GQ.

207   Baptismal Record for Pierre Bissonnette, 18 January 1713, Record No. 248, DI-GQ; Individual Record for Pierre Bissonnet, Individual No. 12586, PRDH-IGD.

208   Baptismal Record for Suzanne Bissonnette, 11 February 1714, Record No. 279, DI-GQ; Marriage Record for Suzanne Bissonnette and Gabriel Bilodeau, 13 August 1731, Record No. 138130, DI-GQ; Burial Record for Suzanne Bissonnette, 11 June 1799, Record No. 391092, DI-GQ.

209   Burial Record for Jean Bissonnette, 15 May 1715, Record No. 73493, DI-GQ.

210   Burial Record for Marie LeBlanc, 18 March 1750, Record No. 232598, DI-GQ.

211   WikiTree contributors, "René Binet (1638-1699)," WikiTree: The Free Family Tree, last modified 3 April 2023, https://www.wikitree.com/wiki/Binet-38.

212   Baptismal Record for Nicolas Binet, 11 February 1671, Record No. 58535, DI-GQ.

213   Sulte, *Histoire des Canadiens-Français*, 81.

214   Baptismal Record for Geneviève Brisson, 28 February 1678, Record No. 59640, DI-GQ.

215   Sulte, *Histoire des Canadiens-Français*, 55.

216   Marriage Record for Nicolas Binet and Geneviève Brisson, 12 November 1697, Record No. 34352, DI-GQ.

217   Baptismal Record for Marguerite Binet, 3 September 1698, Record No. 76279, DI-GQ; Marriage Record for Jean Girou and Marguerite Binet, 14 November 1718, Record No. 77451, DI-GQ; Marriage Record for Alexandre Boissel and Marguerite Binet, 27 September 1723, Record No. 77484, DI-GQ; Marriage Record for Marguerite Binet and Jacques Paradis, 7 August 1747, Record No. 170936, DI-GQ; Burial Record for Marguerite Binet, 13 February 1759, Record No. 257950, DI-GQ.

218   Baptismal Record for Charles Binet, 10 March 1700, Record No. 76330, DI-GQ; Burial Record for Charles Binet, 7 February 1721, Record No. 77994, DI-GQ.

219   Baptismal Record for Nicolas Binet, 17 April 1702, Record No. 76392, DI-GQ; Burial Record for Nicolas Binet, 29 August 1749, Record No. 153919, DI-GQ.

220   Baptismal Record for Raphael Binet, 21 February 1704, Record No. 76440, DI-GQ; Marriage Record for Raphael Binet and Marie Joseph Turgeon, 22 November 1728, Record No. 77531, DI-GQ.

221   Baptismal Record for Marie Geneviève Binet, 20 December 1705, Record No. 76483, DI-GQ; Burial Record for Marie Geneviève Binet, 26 January 1706, Record No. 77763, DI-GQ.

222   Baptismal Record for Marie Geneviève Binet, 12 January 1707, Record No. 76511, DI-GQ; Marriage Record for Louis Bissonnette and Marie Geneviève Binet, 9 August 1729, Record No. 77536, DI-GQ; Burial Record for Marie Geneviève Binet, 13 May 1745, Record No. 116152, DI-GQ.

223   Baptismal Record for Louis Binet, 23 August 1709, Record No. 76584, DI-GQ; Marriage Record for Louis Binet and Marie Angelique Landry, 1 October 1731, Record No. 170821, DI-GQ; Marriage Record for Louis Binet and Madeleine Giroux, 16 February 1756, Record No. 257547, DI-GQ; Burial Record for Louis Binet, 30 August 1757, Record No. 257879, DI-GQ.

224   Baptismal Record for Ange Binet, 30 October 1711, Record No. 76649, DI-GQ; Marriage Record for Ange Binet and Marie Ursule Tardif, 1 October 1742, Record No. 170896, DI-GQ; Burial Record for Ange Binet, 21 December 1763, Record No. 258122, DI-GQ.

225   Baptismal Record for Marie Françoise Binet, 11 September 1714, Record No. 76740, DI-GQ; Marriage Record for Louis Rodrigue and Françoise Binet, 3 February 1738, Record No. 170859, DI-GQ; Burial Record for Marie Françoise Binet, 4 April 1774, Record No. 376246, DI-GQ.

226   Marriage Record for François Binet and Charlotte Parant, 21 May 1742, Record No. 150116, DI-GQ; Burial Record for François Binet, 15 August 1792, Record No. 385725, DI-GQ.

227   Baptismal Record for Geneviève Binet, 5 January 1720, Record No. 76908, DI-GQ; Marriage Record for Ignace Crevie and Geneviève Binet, 19 October 1761, Record No. 277985, DI-GQ; Burial Record for Geneviève Binet, 15 April 1779, Record No. 368014, DI-GQ.

228   Burial Record for Nicolas Binet, 30 July 1753, Record No. 257752, DI-GQ.

229   Burial Record for Marie Geneviève Brisson, 3 March 1758, Record No. 257905, DI-GQ.

Part Four

Ancestors of Harriette Isabella Gray Bouschor

Generation 1 – Harriette Isabella Gray

1. **Harriette Isabella GRAY**, daughter of David GRAY and Isabella KINREAD, b. Hartford, Hartford County, Connecticut, 9 December 1839; m. Simon Bouschor, Washington Island, Door County, Wisconsin, 6 July 1854; d. Manistique, Schoolcraft County, Michigan, 18 December 1906

Generation 2 – Parents of Harriette Isabella Gray

2. **David GRAY**, son of unknown GRAY and Esther GRAY, b. Nova Scotia Colony, approximately 1796; m. Isabella Kinread, possibly Nova Scotia Colony, before 1827; d. Fairbanks, Delta County, Michigan, 15 May 1880

3. **Isabella KINREAD**, daughter of George Henry KINREAD and Ann FORD, b. England, approximately 1806; m. David Gray, possibly Nova Scotia Colony, before 1827; d. Garden, Delta County, Michigan, 2 August 1884

Generation 3 – Grandparents of Harriette Isabella Gray

4. **Unknown GRAY** (Paternal grandfather of Harriette Isabella Gray)

5. **Esther GRAY**, daughter of unknown GRAYs, b. Nova Scotia Colony, approximately 1778; m. Unknown; d. Unknown

6. **George Henry KINREAD**, son of John KINREAD and Isabel GAWN, b. Malew Parish, Rushen Sheading, Isle of Man, approximately 5 May 1782; m. Ann Ford, United Kingdom, approximately 1806; d. Rexton, Kent County, New Brunswick Colony, approximately 1865

7. **Ann FORD**, daughter of unknown FORDs, b. England, approximately 1782; m. George Henry Kinread, United Kingdom, approximately 1806; d. approximately 1830, Rexton, Kent County, New Brunswick Colony

---

Generation 4 – Great-Grandparents of Harriette Isabella Gray

8 – 11. **UNKNOWN** (paternal great-grandparents of Harriette Isabella Gray)

12. **John KINREAD**, son of John KINREAD and Anne COWIN, b. Braddan Parish, Middle Sheading, Isle of Man, approximately 30 November 1760; m. Isabel Gawn, Malew Parish, Rushen Sheading, Isle of Man, 1 July 1781; d. Braddan Parish, Middle Sheading, Isle of Man, 23 November 1837

13. Isabel GAWN, daughter of Thomas GAWN and Mary NELSON, b. Rushen Parish, Rushen Sheading, Isle of Man, approximately 16 January 1756; m. John Kinread, Malew Parish, Rushen Sheading, Isle of Man, 1 July 1781; d. Unknown

14 – 15. UNKNOWN (maternal great-grandparents of Harriette Isabella Gray)

Ancestors of
Harriette Isabella Gray

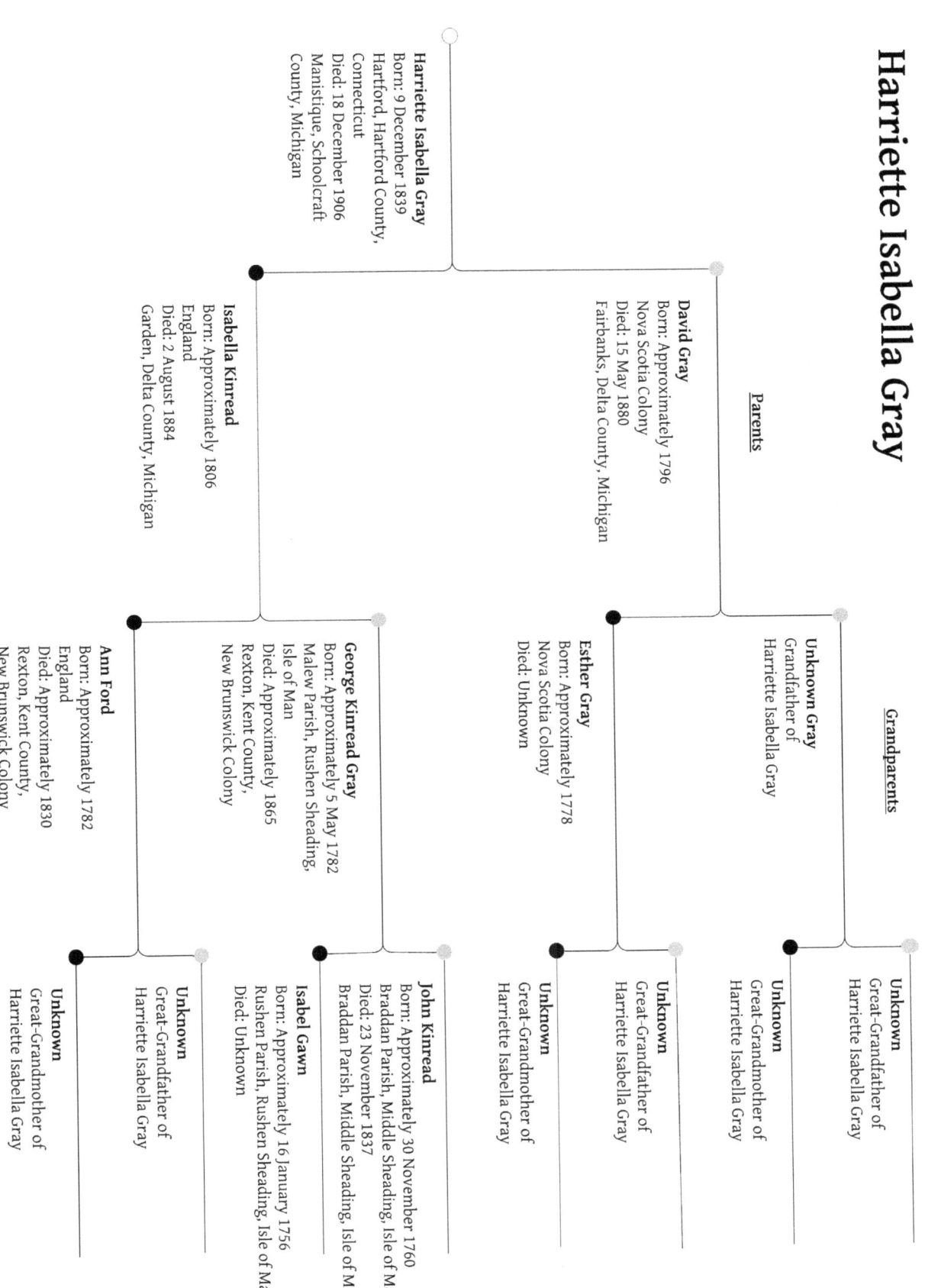

Parents

Grandparents

Great-Grandparents

Harriette Isabella Gray
Born: 9 December 1839
Hartford, Hartford County,
Connecticut
Died: 18 December 1906
Manistique, Schoolcraft
County, Michigan

David Gray
Born: Approximately 1796
Nova Scotia Colony
Died: 15 May 1880
Fairbanks, Delta County, Michigan

Isabella Kinread
Born: Approximately 1806
England
Died: 2 August 1884
Garden, Delta County, Michigan

Unknown Gray
Grandfather of
Harriette Isabella Gray

Esther Gray
Born: Approximately 1778
Nova Scotia Colony
Died: Unknown

George Kinread Gray
Born: Approximately 5 May 1782
Malew Parish, Rushen Sheading,
Isle of Man
Died: Approximately 1865
Rexton, Kent County,
New Brunswick Colony

Ann Ford
Born: Approximately 1782
England
Died: Approximately 1830
Rexton, Kent County,
New Brunswick Colony

Unknown
Great-Grandfather of
Harriette Isabella Gray

Unknown
Great-Grandmother of
Harriette Isabella Gray

Unknown
Great-Grandfather of
Harriette Isabella Gray

Unknown
Great-Grandmother of
Harriette Isabella Gray

John Kinread
Born: Approximately 30 November 1760
Braddan Parish, Middle Sheading, Isle of Man
Died: 23 November 1837
Braddan Parish, Middle Sheading, Isle of Man

Isabel Gawn
Born: Approximately 16 January 1756
Rushen Parish, Rushen Sheading, Isle of Man
Died: Unknown

Unknown
Great-Grandfather of
Harriette Isabella Gray

Unknown
Great-Grandmother of
Harriette Isabella Gray

Parents of Harriette Isabella Gray Bouschor

2.   David Gray

Born: Approximately 1796 in Nova Scotia Colony (Nova Scotia, Canada)
Died: 15 May 1880 in Fairbanks, Delta County, Michigan (Garden Township, Delta County, Michigan)

3.   Isabella Kinread

Born: Approximately 1806 in England
Died: 2 August 1884 in Garden, Delta County, Michigan

David Gray was born in 1796 in Nova Scotia, Canada. Virtually nothing is known of his childhood or early adult life until his marriage at the age of nearly forty. David married Isabella Kinread, possibly in Annapolis Royal, Nova Scotia, Canada. Although some sources have listed the marriage date as 1835, given that they had four children by this time it is highly likely they married several years earlier.

Isabella Kinread, the daughter of George Henry and Ann (Ford) Kinread, was born in approximately 1806 or 1807. Although some sources list her birthplace in Cornwall, England, given that the siblings immediately preceding and following her were both born in Whitehaven, England, it is more likely she was born there. It's also possible the family was in Cornwall related to George Henry Kinread's service in the Royal Navy. In any case, on 12 March 1808, she was christened at Holy Trinity Church in Whitehaven, England, a community in Cumberland County's Cumbria region across the Irish Sea from her parents' Isle of Man homeland.[1]

Although Isabella was born in England and spent at least part of her childhood in Cumberland, legend has it that her parents sent her to Nova Scotia because they disapproved of her and David's plan to marry. He followed her from England, and they married in Nova Scotia.[2] However, it's more likely she moved with her parents and siblings from Whitehaven to present-day Richibucto Parish, Kent County, New Brunswick, in 1820 when she was around twelve years old.

David and Isabella had seven children, all of whom lived to adulthood:

i.   **Anne Gray**, b. Nova Scotia Colony, approximately 1827; m. John Maxwell, unknown datae and location; d. Thompson, Schoolcraft County, Michigan, 13 May 1898[3]

ii.   **John Kinread Gray**, b. Richibucto, Kent County, New Brunswick Colony, 29 March 1828; m. Elizabeth Jane Trueblood, approximately 1853; d. South Bend, St. Joseph's County, Indiana, 15 May 1907[4]

iii.   **George K. Gray**, b. Nova Scotia Colony, approximately 1831; m. Rebecca Ruth Trueblood, unknown date and location; d. Approximately 1872[5]

iv.   **Mary Jane Gray**, b. Nova Scotia Colony, 20 August 1834; m. Reuben Cyrus Clark, unknown date and location; d. Manistique, Schoolcraft County, Michigan, 16 September 1913[6]

v.   **Margaret Elizabeth Gray**, Nova Scotia Colony, approximately 1836; m. Reuben S. Allen, Rochester, Monroe County, New York, 1851; d. Manitowoc, Manitowoc County, Wisconsin, 26 February 1903[7]

vi.   **Harriette Isabella Gray**, b. Hartford, Hartford County, Connecticut, 9 December 1839; m. Simon Bouschor, Washington Island, Door County, Wisconsin, 6 July 1854; d. Manistique, Schoolcraft County, Michigan, 18 December 1906[8]

vii.   **Charles Wesley Gray**, b. Rochester, Monroe County, New York, 1842; m. Mariah J. Trueblood, unknown location, 16 August 1866; d. Garden, Delta County, Michigan, 16 August 1872[9]

Life on the East Coast and Move to the Garden Peninsula

David and Isabella evidently lived in Nova Scotia and New Brunswick for several years, as their first five children—Anne, John Kinread, George K., Mary Jane, and Margaret—are all referenced as being born in Nova Scotia or Kent County, New Brunswick, where Isabella's family settled after leaving England.

Isabella Kinread Gray

David and Isabella immigrated to the United States sometime between the birth of their daughter Margaret in 1836 and the birth of their daughter Harriette in 1839. By 1842, they lived in Rochester, New York, as their youngest child, Charles Wesley Gray, was born there that year. The family moved frequently during their time in upstate New York. An 1844 directory for the city of Rochester lists David as working as a laborer and living on Meigs Street near Main Street. The following year, the directory lists David as still working as a laborer but living in the Asylum Building on Scio Street. Two years later, in 1847, the Rochester city directory records David as working as a mason but now living on Union Street south of Court. Finally, in 1849, the family lived at 120 Monroe Street while David again worked as a laborer.[10]

The 1850 U.S. Census lists the Gray family as living in Rochester, New York, where David worked at the age of forty-five as a teamster, reportedly participating in the operation of the Erie Canal. At this time, David and Isabella lived with six of their seven children—all but their eldest daughter, Anne—as well as David's mother, Esther Gray.[11] The Gray family appears one more time in the Rochester city directory—in 1851, when they are listed as residing on Pearl Street two streets east of the Erie Canal, while David worked as a teamster and jobber—but they are absent from the city directories thereafter.[12] Presumably, they left upstate New York to go west soon after the early 1850s. The family next moved to South Bend, Indiana, where David traveled around the region and worked as a timber scout.[13]

Establishment of Gray Family Farm

In 1856, David purchased land on the southern shore of Garden Bay—just over sixteen acres—which would form the core of the Gray family farm.[14] Legend has it that he walked over one hundred miles to Marquette, Michigan, to obtain the proper deeds to the new homestead on Garden Bay.[15] Soon thereafter, the family began their lives in the Upper Peninsula. They may have initially stayed on one of the Potawatomi Islands scattered between Wisconsin's Door Peninsula and Michigan's

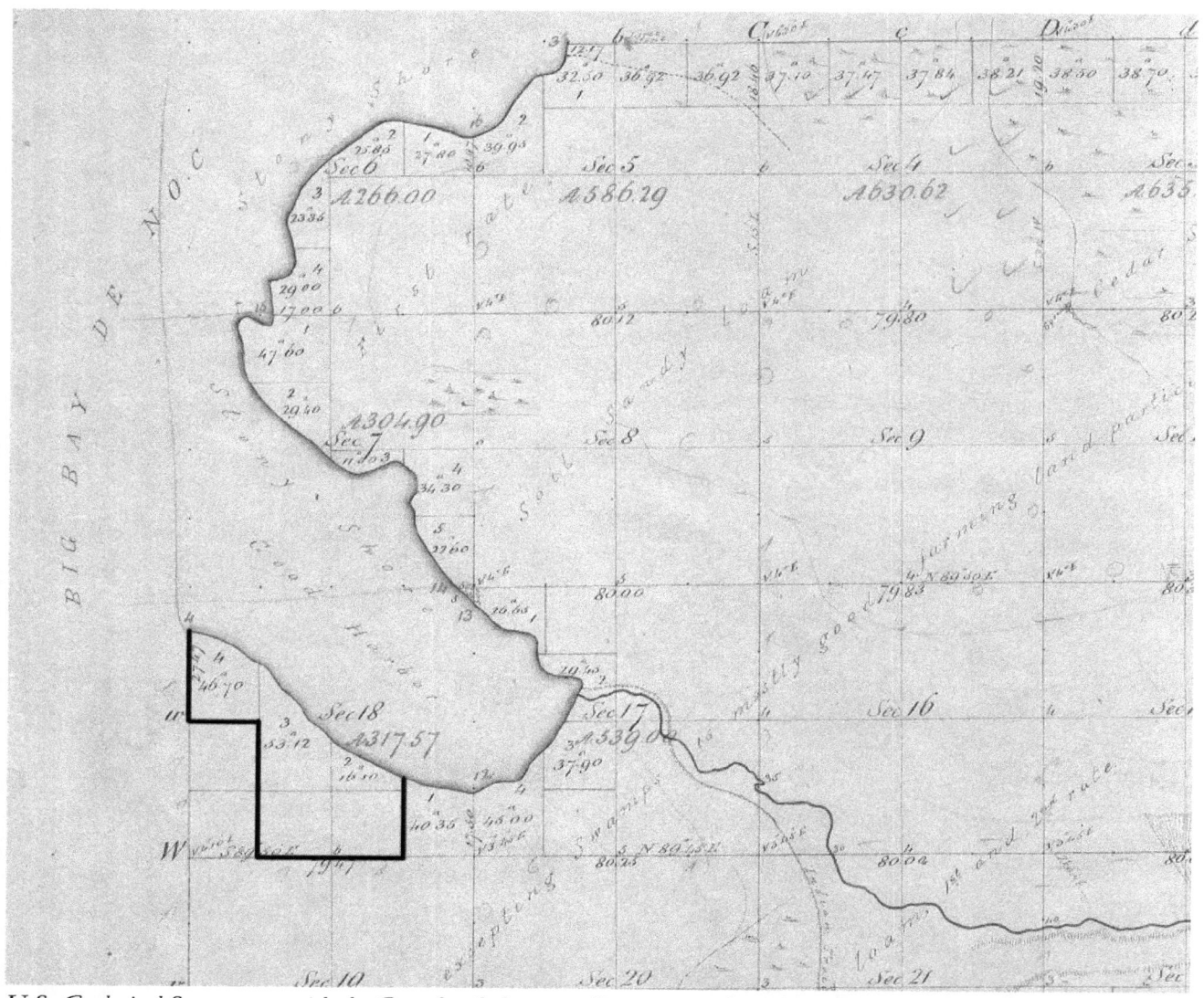

U.S. Geological Survey map with the Gray family homestead's maximum boundaries outlined with the darker line

Garden Peninsula, given that Harriette married Simon on Wisconsin's Washington Island in July 1854, two years before the purchase of the Gray family farm. Many early settlers to Delta County spent time on St. Martin Island, Big Summer Island, or one of the smaller islands before relocating to the mainland.[16] David and Isabella were soon joined by the family of their daughter and son-in-law, Margaret (Gray) and Reuben Allen, who had relocated from Chicago.[17]

The Garden Bay homestead steadily grew over a fifteen-year period from 1856 to 1874. The initial parcel that David walked to Marquette on 10 June 1856 to obtain consisted of Lot 2 in Section 18, Township 39 North, Range 18 West, comprising 16.10 acres.[18] Two further grants—both in Section 18 of Township 39 North, Range 18 West—expanded the Gray homestead. First, a 1 October 1860 cash entry sale grant to Isabella Gray conveyed title to Lot 4 in Section 18, comprising 46.70 acres.[19] Second, a 20 June 1870 homestead grant to David Gray added Lot 3, the southeast quarter of the southwest quarter, and the southwest quarter of the southeast quarter of Section 18, comprising 133.12 acres.[20] In total, the Gray homestead on Garden Bay comprised 195.92 acres. In addition, Isabella Gray obtained title via a 10 November 1874 grant to the northeast quarter of the northeast quarter of Section 28 in Township 40 North, Range 18 West comprising forty acres.[21] David and Isabella would remain on the Garden Peninsula the

192

rest of their lives.

David and Isabella built a homestead house that stood for many years on the southern shore of Garden Bay. In the early 1960s, Anne Wilson Gray described it as "a log house covered with shingles. It was 89 years old in 1960. The lumber cost $8.00 a thousand at Van's Harbor Lumber co. at Vans Harbor just a short distance west and north of Garden village."[22] A road known as the "Mackinaw Trail" was surveyed and realigned in 1870 such that the road no longer split the Gray family farm and they could consolidate their land holdings.[23]

The Gray family farm and homestead remained in the family's hands for well over a hundred years. It was declared a Michigan Centennial Farm in 1964, and the Michigan Historical Commission presented descendant Frank Gray with a Michigan Centennial Farm plaque on 16 August 1968 at the U.P. State Fair in Escanaba.[24]

The Gray Family in the 1860s and 1880s

The 1860 U.S. Census enumerated on 10 July 1860 lists David and Isabella as living in Delta Township. Living with them were their youngest son, Charles Wesley Gray, and a seven-year-old girl named Elizabeth Allen, likely the daughter of Margaret Gray and her husband, Reuben S. Allen.[25] Elizabeth was purported to be the first white child to live in Garden Bay, and she later led a storied life carrying the mail from Garden to Manistique on horseback at the age of sixteen; the local Indians honored her with the name "the white queen." Her 6 September 1934 obituary in the *Escanaba Daily Press* documents how she assisted her father, Reuben, with catching fish while wearing cork-soled shoes to prevent slipping off the deck, and that she would accompany him on trips around the Lake Michigan shore, including to Garden, Sac Bay, Mackinaw City, Escanaba, Beaver Island, and Washington Harbor.[26]

The 1860 U.S. Agricultural Census for Delta County paints a broader picture of life on the Gray homestead in its early years. The 13 July 1860 record reflects the homestead as comprising 25 acres of improved land alongside 122 acres of unimproved land, with the land valued at $300 and a $10 value assigned to the collected farming implements and machinery. The Gray family farm numbered two milch cows, four working oxen, and four other cattle, as well as three swine, with a total value of $300 for all the livestock and $40 worth of animals slaughtered in the preceding year. In addition, for the year ending 1 June 1860, the farm produced forty bushels of Indian corn, twenty bushels of oats, one bushel of peas and beans, five hundred bushels of Irish potatoes, one hundred sixty pounds of butter, four hundred pounds of maple syrup, and fifteen pounds of molasses.[27]

In 1867, David Gray conveyed a half-acre portion of their 16.10-acre Lot 2 of the homestead to School District No. 4. The half-acre was located on the northside of the old highway that bisected the Gray farm between Lot 2 and the southwest quarter of the southwest quarter of Section 18, until realignment of the highway in 1870. David appeared before Delta County Justice of the Peace A. G. Bailey on 31 August 1867 and made his mark on the deed instrument conveying the half-acre to the School District.[28]

Owing to David's land conveyance, the Gray family farm was the site of the first school in the Garden area, established in the 1870s. At least two structures on the homestead served as a school. The children of the families on the southside of the bay comprised nearly the entirety of the pupils, with the teacher's salary paid by the parents. The Gray family school lasted through the 1882–83 school term, with Mattie Gibbs serving as the final instructor.[29] Garden Peninsula historian Jacqueline Tatrow observed that schools in those days were very primitive, with desks often being planks pegged into walls. Due to a scarcity of books and paper, lessons were delivered orally by the teacher, and students used slates for writing and mathematics. School only took place for a handful of months during the year given that most students lived on farms and were needed to assist with farm labor, and attendance was far from compulsory and all but unenforced.[30]

The family of Reuben Cyrus Clark (seated far-left) and Mary Jane Gray Clark (seated far-right), the fourth child and second daughter of David and Isabella Gray – Reuben and Mary Jane married in Rochester, New York, before moving to Saginaw County on the Lower Peninsula – Mary Jane died in Manistique in 1913

David and Isabella continued to live in Delta Township ten years later. The 1870 U.S. Census lists the sixty-five-year-old David working as a farmer and holding $462 in real estate value and $440 in personal property. Their youngest son, Charles Wesley, his wife, Maria Trueblood Gray, and their two young children, David and John Wesley, and an eight-year-old girl named Martha Gray also lived with them on the farm.[31] In 1871, likely for estate planning reasons, David conveyed his interest in the 133.12 acres comprising Lot 3, the southeast quarter of the southwest quarter, and the southwest quarter of the southeast quarter of Section 18 to his son Charles Wesley Gray via a deed dated 20 November 1871. That same day, Charles Wesley

conveyed his interest in the same land via warranty deed to David and Isabella Gray. Both deeds were recorded with Delta County on 11 March 1872, just months before Charles Wesley's death.[32]

The Gray family farm served as a stagecoach stop as well in the late 1800s. In 1877, Peter Plante's stagecoach from Fayette to Manistique via Garden Bay ran four times per week and would call at the Gray homestead.[33] In 1876, Elizabeth Trueblood—mother of three daughters, Maria, Rebecca, and Jane Trueblood, who each married sons of David and Isabella Gray—paid a visit to her daughters in Garden and brought red, white, and pink peony plants that were planted at the Gray's home and remained for many years. Several Indians lived nearby on Puffy Creek in a settlement known as "Indian Town," and one Indian woman camped along the shoreline on the Gray family farm and made bark baskets. They wove these basswood baskets by peeling off the outer bark and harvesting the inner bark in strips. The Indians would then sell or trade the completed baskets to settlers.[34] On 4 July 1876, the Gray family hosted a celebration in honor of the United States' hundredth birthday in a pasture field near the Gray home.[35]

The Gray family's neighbors included the Farley family on the farm just to the east, whose eldest son, Tellas Farley, would go on to marry Simon and Harriette Bouschor's eldest daughter, Ida Isabelle Bouchard, in 1877. Originally from Quebec, the Farleys first settled on Mackinac Island in 1850, where they lived for fourteen years before relocating to Garden Bay. It's said when they left Mackinac Island, they took a ship to St. Ignace before making their way to Garden by ox cart. There they built a log house and, later, two large barns.[36] Also living nearby was David and Isabella's eldest daughter, Anne Gray Maxwell, along with her two children.[37] It's possible Ann moved to Delta County after the death of her husband, John, in New York.

The Jonathon Trueblood family also lived near the Grays. Originally from North Carolina, Jonathon came to the Upper Peninsula and settled on the islands with his wife, Catherine, in 1852 before moving to the mainland. Another branch of the Trueblood family was that of the South Bend Truebloods, three of whom—Elizabeth, Rebecca, and Marie—married sons of David and Isabella Gray.[38]

Another Garden Bay neighbor and relation was the Reuben Allen family. Reuben Allen came from Franklin County, New York, and married David and Isabella's daughter Margaret Gray in 1851, likely in Rochester. They later moved to the Garden Peninsula in approximately 1855 and built a home on the lakeshore near the Gray family farm. Reuben engaged in lumbering but also built and operated a trading vessel. In later years, the family lived on St. Martin Island managing a fish business before

Sisters Anne Gray Maxwell (seated) and Margaret Gray Allen

spending their final years in Sturgeon Bay on the Door Peninsula in Wisconsin.[39]

Despite no formal medical training, Isabella served as the community's de facto doctor. Known as "Grandma Gray," she traveled across the peninsula to minister to those in need of care. During an outbreak of diphtheria in 1881, Grandma Gray saved lives by traveling from family to family throughout the Garden Peninsula to administer treatment. She instructed parents of stricken children to apply sulfur in the children's throats to combat the disease. She didn't allow adverse weather to interfere with her duties. Once, during stormy weather, Grandma Gray traveled with John Sexton to Nahma across the Big Bay de Noc in a sailboat. "Are you afraid, Grandma Gray?" Sexton asked. "No," she quickly replied. "I know you wouldn't drown yourself,

John, for the sake of drowning me."[40]

Mrs. Gray was also a customer of Donald A. Wells' store in Sac Bay (also known as Sack Bay), a community founded in approximately 1854 and located south of Garden between Fayette and Fairport.[41]

Final Years

David died at home in Garden Bay on 15 May 1880.[42] David's obituary in Manistique's *Pioneer* included the following:

> In the death of Mr. Gray, one of the old landmarks has been removed--he being the oldest white settler of Garden Bay having come here 29 years ago, of the toils and privations incident to a life here at that time. It is unnecessary for us to speak, but being a man possessed in an imment [sic] degree of energy and perseverance he surmounted every difficulty and was successful in securing a modest competence, enough to support his declining years in peace and plenty. As a faithful friend, a kind and obliging neighbor and a man upright in all his dealings with his fellow man, David Gray will be remembered. Peace to his ashes.[43]

It is likely Isabella continued to live on the Gray family farm following David's death. The 1880 U.S. Census enumerated on 16 June 1880—two months after David's passing—shows her living in the same household as daughter-in-law Maria Trueblood Gray Tracy* and Maria's second husband, Thomas Joseph Tracy, as well as several of Isabella's grandchildren.[44] The Tracys took over operation of the Gray family farm after David's death. By a quitclaim deed dated 28 July 1882 and recorded with Delta County on 15 August 1882, Isabella Gray conveyed her interest in Lot 3, the southeast quarter of the southwest quarter, and the southwest quarter of the southeast quarter of Section 18 to her daughter-in-law Maria Tracy. Via a warranty deed recorded the same day, Maria Tracy conveyed her interest in the same land to her husband, Thomas Tracy.[45]

The 1880 U.S. Agricultural Census for Fairbanks Township in Delta County gives a detailed view of the Gray homestead The combined estate now comprised 120 acres of tilled land, 40 acres of "permanent meadows, permanent pastures, orchards, vineyards," and 240 acres of woodland and forests with an aggregate valuation of $6,000, along with $150 of farming implements and machinery, and $600 in livestock. In 1879, the farm paid out $200 in wages for farm labor and realized $1,400 for all yield produced on the farm. In terms of livestock, the Gray family farm had six working oxen, seven milch cows, and twelve other heads of livestock, along with twelve swine and forty-eight chickens that produced four hundred eggs. Four calves had dropped the previous year, one cow was slaughtered, and two died or went missing. The farm produced 600 pounds of butter in 1879 as well. In terms of crops, they had one acre of Indian corn under cultivation in 1879 that produced fifty bushels, nine acres of oats that produced two hun-

Thomas Tracy, owner and operator of the Gray family homestead farm after Isabella Gray's death

---

*   Maria was the widow of David and Isabella's youngest son, Charles Wesley Gray, who died in 1872.

dred twenty-five bushels, forty acres of wheat that produced seven hundred acres, and ten bushels of Canada peas.[46]

Four years after David's death, Isabella passed away on 2 August 1884 near Kates Bay in Garden, Delta County, Michigan, at the residence of her daughter Anne Gray Maxwell.[47] Kates Bay is located just north of Garden village and was named after a half-Indian woman named Kate Van Auckin who originally settled in the area in 1839.[48] Isabella's obituary, published in the 6 August 1884 edition of the *Schoolcraft County Pioneer*, included the following:

> Mrs. G. was one of the pioneers of this peninsula, having lived near Garden creek for 24 years. She lived to see that wilderness opened up into one of the finest agricultural districts in the northwest; to see villages, churches and school houses spring up and flourish all around her. Mrs. G leaves quite a family of grown up children, who are married and settled in the immediate neighborhood, to mourn her loss. Mother Gray was a good woman with no enemies, but hosts of friends. Her loss will be deeply felt by her many friends and relatives on the peninsula. A kind mother and friend has gone to rest. Her funeral took place on Sunday last and was attended by a large concourse of citizens. Rev. Mr. Williams of this village attended and preached a splendid discourse. Mrs. Gray was the oldest settler on the Bay shore. One by one the old pioneers are called from labor to reward.[49]

Both David and Isabella were initially buried in the Gray Family Cemetery located on the family's homestead. However, in 1914, family transferred their remains from the homestead to the Kates Bay Cemetery, where they were reinterred in the Thomas Tracy lot.[50] They remain buried in Kates Bay Cemetery just north of Garden.[51]

The homestead established by David and Isabella in the 1850s remained in the Gray family for over one hundred years. After their passing, different sections of the land were owned and worked by Thomas and Maria Tracy and three of her children: David Ephraim Gray, John Wesley Gray, and Margaret Isabella Gray Mellon, wife of Alexander Mellon. As a result of a series of conveyances recorded 8 April 1898, the core 133.12-acre homestead was divided three ways: Lot No. 3 of Section 18 (53.12 acres) to John Wesley Gray, the southwest quarter of the southwest quarter of Section 18 (40 acres) to David Ephraim Gray, and the southeast quarter of the southwest quarter of Section 18 (40 acres) to Margaret Isabella Mellon.[52] This division occurred after a probate court determined each was entitled to a one-third interest in the estate of their father, Charles Wesley Gray, who died on 16 August 1872, possibly resulting from the conveyances between him and his parents in 1871 shortly before his death.[53] A 1913 atlas of Delta County shows that John Wesley Gray also held title to Lot 4 of Section 18, while David Ephraim Gray held title to Lot 2 of Section 18—the original 16.10-acre parcel acquired by David Gray in 1856.[54]

Much like the Bouschor family homestead in neighboring Schoolcraft County, the Gray family farm became the first Michigan Centennial Farm to be recognized in Delta County. On Sunday, 12 July 1964, the Michigan Historical Society presented the farm's then owner, Frank W. Gray, with a Centennial Farm certificate recognizing ownership by the Gray family for over one hundred years. The Historical Society of Delta County and friends of Schoolcraft County helped organize the ceremony held on the Garden School grounds. The *Escanaba Daily Press* noted the Gray family's possession of the land since its purchase by David Gray in 1856 and that it had subsequently been owned by Charles, John, and Frank Wesley Gray. At a ceremony held on 12 September 1964, Frank Gray reported on Garden Township's history, and others in attendance shared memories as well.[55]

The Gray family homestead is no longer owned by any member of the Gray family, and its land has been subdivided and ownership passed to numerous individuals.

Grandparents of Harriette Isabella Gray Bouschor

4.   Unknown Gray

Born: Unknown
Died: Unknown

5.   Esther Gray

Born: Approximately 1778 in Nova Scotia Colony (Nova Scotia, Canada)
Died: Unknown

The author was unable to locate any information on David Gray's father or any of his paternal ancestors. His mother's name was Esther Gray, and she was born in approximately 1778 in Nova Scotia, Canada, possibly in Annapolis Royal.[56] David Gray's father and Esther Gray had at least one child:

 i. **David Gray**, b. Nova Scotia Colony, approximately 1796; m. Isabella Kinread, Annapolis Royal, Nova Scotia Colony, before 1827; d. Fairbanks, Delta County, Michigan, 15 May 1880[57]

Little is known about David's parents' whereabouts after his birth. In 1850, Esther lived with her son and his family in Rochester, New York.[58] It is possible she died in Rochester or South Bend, Indiana, sometime between 1850 and 1860, as the author has been unable to locate any record of her in the 1860 U.S. Census, including the record showing David and Isabella living in Delta County, Michigan, at that time.

6.   George Henry Kinread

Born: Approximately 5 May 1782 in Malew Parish, Rushen Sheading, Isle of Man
Died: Approximately 1865 in Rexton, Kent County, New Brunswick Colony

7.   Ann Ford

Born: Approximately 1782 in England
Died: Approximately 1830 in Rexton, Kent County, New Brunswick Colony

George Henry Kinread, father of Isabella Kinread Gray, was born in approximately May 1782 on the Isle of Man. He was christened on 5 May 1782 at St. Mark's Church in Rushen Parish on the Isle of Man.[59] The Isle of Man is an approximately 220-square-mile island located in the Irish Sea between Ireland and Great Britain. At the time of George's birth, the British Crown owned the rights to the Isle of Man, though the isle had considerable powers of self-government, which the Manx people retain to this day.[60] St. Mark's Church was constructed as a chapel of ease approximately ten years prior to George's christening at a cost of just over £280, and the straightforward, whitewashed structure sits amidst a churchyard filled with weathered grave markers.[61] Nothing is known of George's early years or his life on the isle. Additional details on the Kinread family and life on the Isle of Man will be discussed below in the section on George's parents, John and Isabel (Gawn) Kinread.

Marriage and Family

George evidently left the Isle of Man for good as a young man. According to a New Brunswick land petition filed in May 1820, George lived in Whitehaven, Cumberland County, England, located just east of the Isle of Man, for twenty-three years, meaning he settled there in approximately 1796 or 1797.[62] If this date is accurate, he likely left home when he was fourteen to fifteen years old.

George married Ann Ford in approximately 1805 or 1806 in the United Kingdom.[63] Ann was born in approximately 1782 in England. It is likely they met and married in or around the area of Whitehaven. George and Ann appear to have lived in Whitehaven for several years, and at least five of their children were born there.

George and Ann Kinread had the following children:[*]

i.   **Anne Kinread**, b. Whitehaven, Cumberland, England, 7 May 1806; m. Meracious Atkinson; d. New Brunswick, 8 July 1883[64]

ii.   **Isabella Kinread**, b. England, approximately 1806 to 1807; m. David Gray, Nova Scotia Colony, before 1827; d. Garden, Delta County, Michigan, 2 August 1884[65]

iii.   **John Kinread**, b. Whitehaven, Cumberland, England, 8 August 1810; m. Ann Peters, Richibucto, Kent County, New Brunswick Colony, 23 December 1838; d. Moncton, New Brunswick, 23 December 1886[66]

iv.   **Elizabeth Kinread**, b. Whitehaven, Cumberland, England, approximately 1812; m. Daniel Stuart Dougherty, Saint John, New Brunswick Colony, 12 July 1834; d. Saint John, New Brunswick, 1 October 1876[67]

v.   **Margaret Kinread**, b. Folkestone, Kent, England, approximately 1813; m. Henry Johnstone, Richibucto, Kent County, New Brunswick Colony, 26 March 1837; d. New Brunswick Colony, 9 August 1856[68]

vi.   **William Kinread**, b. Whitehaven, Cumberland, England, approximately 1818; m. (1) Margaret Lamb, Westmorland County, New Brunswick Colony, 27 March 1844; m. (2) Eleanor Simmons, New Brunswick, 1 December 1873; d. Richibucto, Kent County, New Brunswick, 5 January 1898[69]

vii.   **Thomas Kinread**, b. Richibucto, Kent County, New Brunswick, 22 December 1820; m. Hannah Elizabeth Tuttle, Moncton, Westmorland County, New Brunswick Colony, 26 January 1854; d. Moncton, Westmorland County, New Brunswick, 5 October 1892[70]

viii.   **Male Child Kinread**, b. Approximately 1823-24; d. Unknown[71]

ix.   **Martha Kinread**, b. Richibucto, Kent County, New Brunswick Colony, 4 December 1824; m. Stephen Peters, Kent County, New Brunswick Colony, 19 January 1844; d. Moncton, New Brunswick, 30 January 1890[72]

George served in the Royal Navy for several years until his discharge around 1820.[73] He may have also operated an apothecary shop in Cornwall, England, prior to relocating to New Brunswick.[74]

George, Ann, and their seven eldest children left Whitehaven in approximately 1820 following George's service with the Royal Navy. They relocated to New Brunswick, settling in present-day Upper Rexton, Richibucto Parish, Kent County, in 1820. According to a land petition filed months after their arrival, George and Ann had six living children.[75] At the time they arrived in 1820, the area was still part of Carleton Parish in what was then

---

[*]   Several online sources also reference George and Ann being parents to a George Kinread born in Whitehaven in 1815. As the author was unable to find any source records corroborating the existence of this child, I have omitted him from this list.

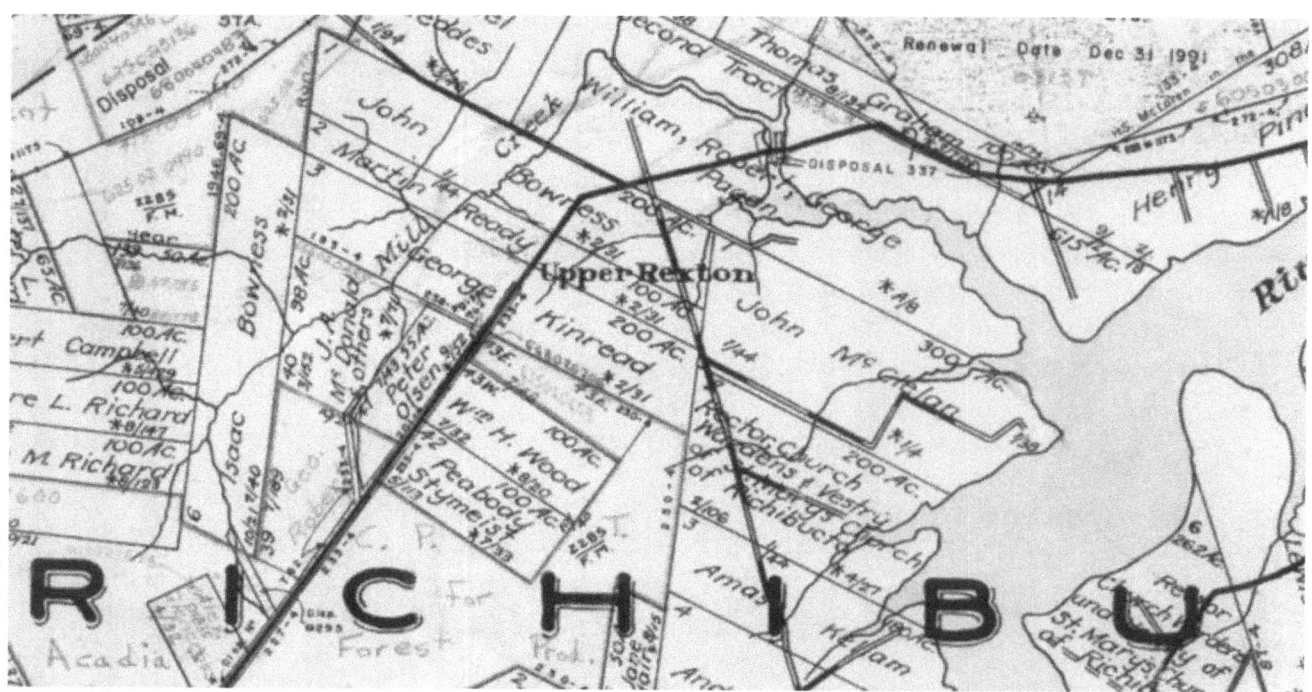

Map of Kent County, New Brunswick, depicting the 200-acre parcel granted to George Kinread in 1820

known as Northumberland County.[†] Their eighth child and youngest son, Thomas Kinread, was born in Richibucto Parish on 22 December 1820, likely in the village of Rexton where his parents settled. They had one more child, Martha, also born in Richibucto in 1824.

Life in New Brunswick and Land Deals

From his arrival in New Brunswick in 1820, George spent the next twenty-five years pursuing various land grants and transactions in Kent County. Months after arriving in New Brunswick, George filed a petition dated 27 May 1820 with the lieutenant governor of New Brunswick Colony seeking a grant of wilderness land for purposes of farming to support his family. The land in question had previously been the subject of a petition filed by Edmund Hudson, but George included a 21 May 1820 statement from Mr. Hudson granting his right and title in the land to George, as he was moving to Upper Canada and no longer needed the land.[76]

The 1820 petition resulted in a 200-acre land grant

in the Carleton Parish of what was then Northumberland County on 5 January 1826.[77] This parcel designated as Lot No. 3 and depicted above was situated inland to the east of a 200-acre parcel granted to St. Mary's Church of Richibucto and south of parcels granted to John Bowness and Martin Ready.

By his own admission, George chose poorly in selecting his parcel, for in February 1827 he submitted another petition to the lieutenant governor of New Brunswick claiming the land was "so unfit for tillageable purposes that he cannot maintain a large and young family thereon." He attributed his lack of knowledge to his life spent at sea and requested the lieutenant governor grant him either the parcel of land granted to John McClellan to the east fronting the Richibucto River or a separate parcel on the northside of the Molus River, a tributary of the Richibucto.[78]

George's petition was evidently to no avail, for on 13 October 1827 George and Ann conveyed their 200-acre parcel on the north side of the Richibucto River to one Silvester C. Hewes in exchange for

---

[†]   Kent County was split off from Northumberland County in 1826. Present-day Richibucto Parish was part of Carleton Parish until being split off as Liverpool Parish in 1827 and renamed Richibucto in 1832.

£150.[79] On 24 January 1839, George filed a land petition with the New Brunswick lieutenant governor seeking another royal land grant. George reemphasized his lack of agricultural knowledge upon coming to New Brunswick and his poor choice in selecting his original 200-acre parcel. He recounted that he had obtained a quitclaim deed on a neighboring parcel later determined to be owned by St. Mary's Church of Richibucto and—despite a lack of clarity over the lot's ownership—commenced improvements, including clearing thirty acres and erecting a "comfortable dwelling house." In light of George's efforts, he asked the lieutenant governor that he be granted one hundred acres. To add to his petition, George claimed he was "advanced in life" and owing to a severe rheumatic complaint, was incapacitated for labor, and that he had a fifteen-year-old son who would "remain entirely uncapable of assisting himself and will therefore require to be supported without his own exertions."[80]‡

A note affixed to George's land petition noted that the land in question had already been granted to St. Mary's Church of Richibucto in January 1838. Furthermore, Warden Layton of St. Mary's Church submitted a three-page response to George's petition on 2 February 1839 stating that George knew the church's land was reserved for a school and that there were no representations made by the church regarding a grant of the land. The warden observed that the land was granted to St. Mary's Church in 1836, and that George's neighbors even requested the church remove him from the lot so they could place their own schoolmaster on it. Warden Layton claimed he offered George a twenty-one-year lease of the land that the latter had improved at a rate of £5 per year and denied that George had received a notice to quit the land, or that there was any basis for George's statement that "he is now required at a moment's warning to be cast upon an unfriendly world for support." Warden Layton claimed George had cut every tree across the entire lot that would

make a mill log and even the land's firewood. Finally, the church disagreed with George's assertions regarding his infirmities and noted his two married daughters and two sons who operated a mill establishment.[81]

The matter dragged on for another decade, with George and family presumably remaining on the church's land during that time. On 30 March 1848, the New Brunswick Assembly passed legislation noting the church's title to said land by virtue of a 26 September 1838 land grant from the Crown and that "prior to the issuing of the Grant, [it] had been improved by George Kinread, who is now in the occupation thereof; and the said George Kinread hath agreed to purchase from the said Rector, Church Wardens, and Vestry, one hundred acres of the said land, to include improvements made by him . . . ." The legislation then authorized the church to sell the land in fee simple to George.[82] Thereafter, the rector, churchwarden, and vestry of Saint Mary's Anglican Church of Richibucto, with the approval of the lord bishop of the diocese, entered into an agreement dated 15 August 1849 to sell the one-hundred-acre parcel of land located on the north side of the Richibucto River to George for £30. The deed conveying the land from the church to George was recorded on 18 September 1849.[83] The same day as the conveyance from the church, George recorded a mortgage from him and Ann to John W. Weldon in consideration of £125 to be repaid in installments over a five-year period.[84]

Nearly ten years later, George went on another spree of transactions. On 30 March 1857, he convened the hundred-acre Kinread farm to his son William Kinread for £300.[85] To confuse matters, William then reconveyed the farm back to George only three months later on 25 June 1857 for £300. Two days later, George recorded a mortgage that granted William a security interest in the land in exchange for £100. A 23 September 1857 note ap-

‡   It's unclear which child George's petition is referring to as the only known child around fifteen years old at this time was his and Ann's youngest child and daughter, Martha Kinread, born in December 1824. Their next oldest known child was Thomas Kinread, born in December 1820 and approximately eighteen years old at the time of George's 1839 land petition. It's possible the family had another child whose identity was not recorded.

pended to the mortgage reflects that George fully paid and satisfied the mortgage.[86] George then conveyed the Kinread farm to a Richibucto merchant named David Wark on 23 July 1857 for £100.[87] Wark then reconveyed it back to George on 23 September 1857, again for £100. Recorded the same day were three mortgages executed by George for the benefit of David Wark, Robert Hutchinson, and William Kinread in the amounts of £100, £50, and £150, respectively. Notes appended to later mortgages reflect satisfaction and release of the Wark and Hutchinson mortgages.[88]

The reason for the multitude of conveyances to and from George is unclear but it likely had to do with the land serving as collateral for various loans. This suggests possible financial challenges with running and maintaining the Kinread farm.

Final Years and Death

The 1861 Census of Canada reflects that eighty-year-old George lived with his son William, the latter's family, and a twenty-year-old housekeeper named Isabella Burns, presumably on the one-hundred-acre parcel that was subject to the multitude of conveyances. The associated agricultural census for 1861 lists the Kinread farm as comprising forty acres of improved land and sixty acres of unimproved land with a cash value of £900, with £100 assigned to implements and machinery. The agricultural census further states that they owned two horses, four milch cows, one additional cattle, five sheep, and ten swine, and had slaughtered 600 pounds of pork.[89]

Ann Ford Kinread passed away sometime after September 1849 as she and George executed a mortgage that month. She was not a party of any of the land transactions George entered into in 1857, so she likely passed away sometime between late 1849 and 1857.

George Henry Kinread died in 1865 in Rexton, New Brunswick, Canada. George is believed to have been buried in the Methodist Point Cemetery, though much of the cemetery was lost to a flood and his headstone is no longer extant.[90]

Great-Grandparents of Harriette Isabella Gray Bouschor

8.   **Unknown (Paternal great-grandfather of Harriette Isabella Gray Bouschor)**

9.   **Unknown (Paternal great-grandmother of Harriette Isabella Gray Bouschor)**

10.   **Unknown (Paternal great-grandfather of Harriette Isabella Gray Bouschor)**

11.   **Unknown (Paternal great-grandmother of Harriette Isabella Gray Bouschor)**

12.   **John Kinread**

Born: Approximately 30 November 1760 in Braddan Parish, Middle Sheading, Isle of Man
Died: Approximately 23 November 1837 in Braddan Parish, Middle Sheading, Isle of Man

13.   **Isabel Gawn**

Born: Approximately 16 January 1756 in Rushen Parish, Rushen Sheading, Isle of Man
Died: Unknown

John Kinread, the son of John Kinread and Anne Cowin, was born around 30 November 1760 in Braddan Parish, Middle Sheading, on the Isle of Man, as he was baptized that day.[91] He was also known as John Kinrade. The Isle of Man was historically divided into six sheadings, which were historically administrative units on the isle analogous to counties in other countries. The six sheadings were in turn divided into a total of seventeen parishes. Middle sheading comprises the southeast portion of the Isle of Man with four parishes including Braddan Parish, which snakes north to south from the center of the isle to its capital, Douglas, on the southeast coast. Approximately three years prior to John's birth, Braddan Parish's total population numbered 1,121 inhabitants, excluding the town of Douglas, while the entire isle had fewer than 20,000 residents.[92] John's baptism took place in Old Kirk Braddan, a church located on the western outskirts of Douglas town and named such to distinguish it from a newer church a short walk away that bears the same name. Built in the 1700s, it was rebuilt in 1773 but was ultimately replaced by the present-day Kirk Braddan in 1876.[93]

John Kinread and Isabel Gawn married on 1 July 1781 in the Malew Parish Church (Kirk Malew) in Rushen Sheading, Isle of Man, in a ceremony officiated by Malew Vicar William Clucas and witnessed by Basil Quayle and John Birdson. They were both living in Castletown at the time of their marriage.[94] A visitor to the area arriving a little more than a decade after John and Isabel's marriage described Kirk Malew as "a gloomy and venerable building, as the Manks [sic] churches generally are, in a romantic solitude." The traveler, David Robertson, went on to note "the various monuments in the churchyard gave us another opportunity of admiring the pious veneration of the natives for their deceased friends."[95] The Parish of Malew is one of three parishes within Rushen Sheading and is located in the south end of the isle. In 1784, three years after John and Isabel's marriage, 1,861 individuals lived in Malew Parish. Castletown—the primary town in Malew Parish—numbered 1,318 inhabitants that year.[96]

Isabel Gawn was likely born around 16 January 1756, as baptismal records reflect that an Isabel Gawn, daughter of Thomas Gawn and Mary Nelson, was baptized at the Rushen Parish Church in Rushen Sheading that day.[97] It's also possible she was the Isabel Gawn baptized on 9 April 1758, one of twin daughters of Henry Gawn and Isabel Tay-

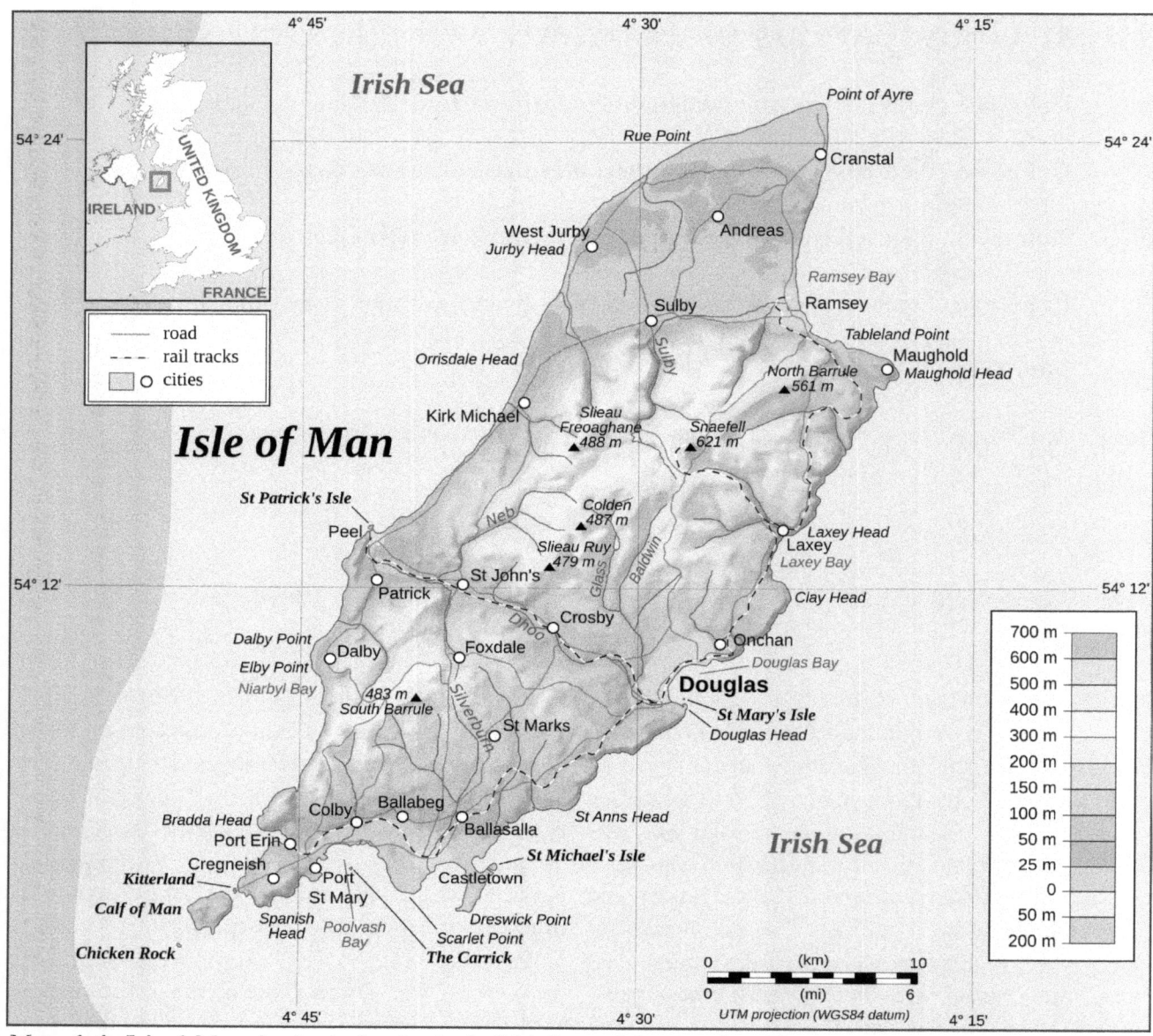

Map of the Isle of Man showing its location in the Irish Sea and denoting the isle's primary communities

lor.[98] Rushen Sheading covers the southwest corner of the Isle of Man with Rushen Parish being the most southwesterly parish in the isle. The Rushen Parish Church, also known as Kirk Christ, sits just east of the town of Port Erin and northwest of Port St. Mary. The present church occupies an ancient site that has undergone expansion and renovation over the centuries, while the present Manx-style whitewashed structure dates primarily from 1775.[99] Around the time of Isabel's birth, 1,007 residents called Rushern Parish home.[100]

John and Isabel Kinread are known to have been parents to at least one child:

i. **George Henry Kinread**, b. Malew Parish, Rushen Sheading, Isle of Man, 5 May 1782; m. Ann Ford, United Kingdom, approximately 1806; d. Rexton, Kent County, New Brunswick Colony, approximately 1865

John and Isabel lived in Castletown at the time of their marriage, and their only known child, George Henry, was born there a year later. Nothing is known about their lives in Castletown or where they lived

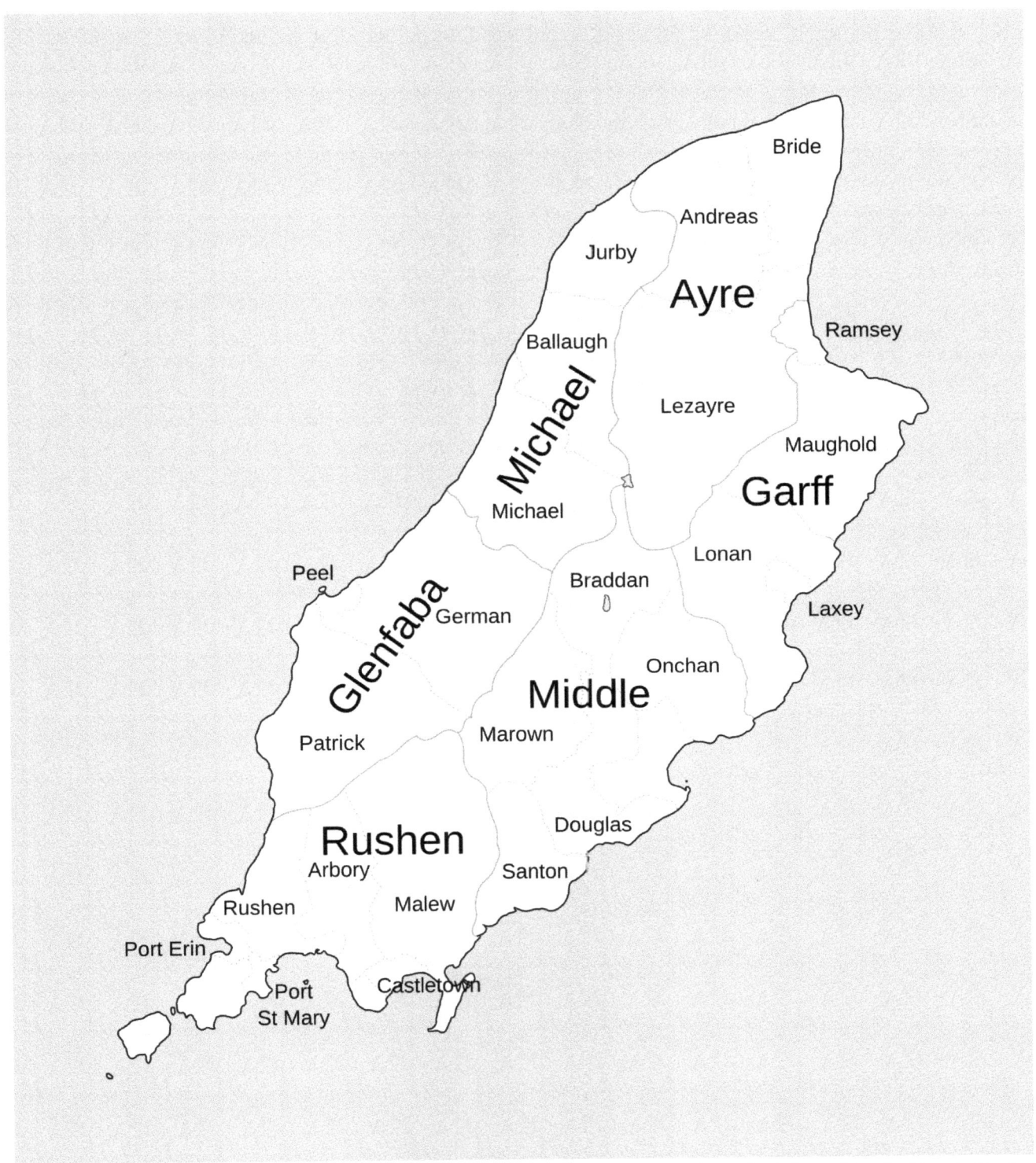

Map of Isle of Man parishes and sheadings — Malew Parish and Rushen Parish are both located in the historic Rushen Sheading in the isle's southern-most region

in town. In the 1780s, Castletown was the capital of the Isle of Man and hosted the Isle's legislative body, the House of Keys, until 1874 when it moved to Douglas.[101] On a visit in 1794, David Robertson described Castletown as "an airy and pleasant town," and in comparing it to the larger town of Douglas, noted it "surpasses the other in neatness; the houses being more uniformly elegant, and the streets more spacious and regular."[102] Another who visited Castletown three years later, John Feltham, observed that the town contained 500 houses and "is divided by a small creek, which opens into a rocky and dangerous bay. The difficulty of entering its harbour, in some degree injures its commerce. A considerable quantity of grain is annually exported hence, and a variety of merchandise imported; but rum, wine, sugar, tobacco, &c. are admissible only into the port of Douglas, from whence other towns are supplied."[103]

John Kinread lived to the age of seventy-seven and died on 21 November 1837 at Mount Rule in Braddan Parish, Middle Sheading.[104] He was buried two days later on Thursday, 23 December, in the Old Kirk Braddan churchyard surrounding the church where he was baptized nearly seventy-seven years earlier.[105] His possible cause of death was an outbreak of smallpox that ravaged the Douglas area in late 1837 ("the small pox made great havoc in Douglas, and yet the majority of the inhabitants rejected with scorn the 'genuine variola,' even when gratuitously offered by all the humane practitioners in medicine").[106] John Kinread's funeral undoubtedly followed many of the customs and traditions described earlier in this section.

It's unknown when Isabel Gawn Kinread passed away. Some online sources reference her date of death and burial as being 25 February 1784 in Lezayre Parish on the Isle of Man, but an examination of the parish burial records reveals that the Isabel who was buried that day was the widow of one Gilbert Kinread who had himself been buried several days earlier, on 19 February, in Lezayre Parish.[107] As such, we do not have a definitive record of Isabel's place or date of death.

14.   Unknown (Maternal Great-Grandfather of Harriette Isabella Gray Bouschor)

15.   Unknown (Maternal Great-Grandmother of Harriette Isabella Gray Bouschor)

Notes

ABBREVIATIONS

AC. Ancestry.com, https://www.ancestry.com/

BLM GLO. Bureau of Land Management, General Land Records Office, https://glorecords.blm.gov/

EPL. Escanaba Public Library, http://www.archiveol.com/escanaba/home

FS. FamilySearch, https://www.familysearch.org/en/united-states/

GB. Google Books, https://books.google.com/

MSPL. Manistique School & Public Library

NA. NewspaperArchive, https://newspaperarchive.com

RPL. Rochester Public Library, https://roccitylibrary.org/

UPDN. Upper Peninsula Digital Network, https://uplink.nmu.edu/

1   Isabella Kinread Christening Record, 12 March 1808, England Births and Christenings, 1538-1975, FS.

2   *The David Gray Family*, Undated, Garden Peninsula Historical Society, Unpublished Manuscript; *Gray Family*, Undated, Garden Peninsula Historical Society, Unpublished Manuscript.

3   Certificate and Record of Death for Mrs. Anna Maxwell, Filed 8 July 1898, State of Michigan, Michigan Department of State - Division of Vital Statistics, Michiganology.org; "Thompson," *Manistique Pioneer-Tribune*, 20 May 1898, UPDN.

4   Certificate of Death for John Kinread Gray, Filed 31 May 1907, Reg. No. 253-4, State of Indiana, Indiana Board of Health, AC.

5   1870 U.S. Census, St. Martin Island, Delta County, Michigan, population schedule, p. 2, dwelling 11, family 11, line 8, George Gray, AC.

6   Certificate of Death for Mary G. Clark, Filed 16 September 1913, Reg. No. 42, State of Michigan, Michigan Department of State - Division of Vital Statistics, AC; "Passed Away." *Manistique Pioneer-Tribune*, 19 September 1913, UPDN.

7   1870 U.S. Census, St. Martin Island, Delta County, Michigan, population schedule, p. 2, dwelling 10, family 10, line 2, Margaret Allen, AC; "Local News," *The Advocate* (Surgeon Bay, WI), 7 March 1903, Door County (WI) Library.

8   Certificate of Death for Mrs. Simon Bouschor, Filed 22 December 1906, Reg. No. 58, State of Michigan, Michigan Department of State – Division of Vital Statistics, AC; "A Pioneer Dies," *Manistique Pioneer-Tribune*, 21 December 1906, MSPL.

9   1870 U.S. Census, Delton Township, Delta County, Michigan, population schedule, p. 2, dwelling 12, family 12, line 29, Wesley Gray, AC; Aaron N. Bouschor, *Wesley Gray Headstone*, 4 September 2017, photograph, personal collection; "Charles Wesley Gray (1842 - 1872)," FindaGrave, Memorial No. 20981607, accessed 25 June 2024, https://www.findagrave.com/memorial/20981607/charles_wesley_gray.

10   James L. Elwood and Dellon M. Dewey, *A Directory and Gazetteer for the City of Rochester for 1844* (Rochester: Canfield & Warren, 1844), 166, RPL; *Canfield & Warren's Directory of the City of Rochester for 1845-46* (Rochester: Canfield & Warren, 1845), 85, RPL; *Daily American Directory of the City of Rochester for 1847-48* (Rochester: Jerome & Brother, 1847), 120, RPL; *Daily American Directory of the City of Rochester for 1849-50* (Rochester: Jerome & Brother, 1849), 126, RPL.

11   1850 U.S. Census, Rochester, Monroe County, New York, population schedule, p. 332, dwelling 253, family 284, line 20-21, David & Isabella Gray, AC; *David Gray Family*, Garden Peninsula Historical Society; Garden Peninsula Historical Society, "The David Gray Family," in *Our Heritage: Garden Peninsula, Delta County, Michigan 1840-1980* (Michigan: Garden Peninsula Historical Society, 1982), 226.

12   *Daily American Directory of the City of Rochester for 1851-2* (Rochester: Lee, Mann & Co., 1851), 138, RPL.

13   *The David Gray Family*, Garden Peninsula Historical Society; *Gray Family*, Garden Peninsula Historical Society.

14   *The David Gray Family*, Garden Peninsula Historical Society.

15   *The David Gray Family*, Garden Peninsula Historical Society; *Gray Family*, Garden Peninsula Historical Society.

16   Margaret Coppess, "Islands of Delta County," in *Our Heritage: Garden Peninsula, Delta County, Michigan 1840-1980*

(Michigan: Garden Peninsula Historical Society, 1982), 10.

17 Larry Peterson, *The Hiawatha Anthology: Stories from Upper Michigan's Pioneer Past* (Self-published, 2020), 85.

18 David Gray Land Patent, Homestead Certificate No. 961, 10 June 1856, BLM GLO.

19 Isabella Gray Land Patent, Homestead Certificate No. 1973, 1 October 1860, BLM GLO.

20 David Gray Land Patent, Homestead Certificate No. 3, Application No. 13, 20 June 1870, BLM GLO.

21 Isabella Gray Land Patent, Homestead Certificate No. 9454, 10 November 1874, BLM GLO.

22 *Notes on the Gray Family*, Undated, Garden Peninsula Historical Society, Unpublished Manuscript.

23 *Notes on the Gray Family*, Garden Peninsula Historical Society.

24 "Centennial Farms: Special Program of Recognition Planned at Fair," *Escanaba Daily Press*, 6 August 1968, 2019, NA.

25 1860 U.S. Census, Delta Township, Delta County, Michigan, population schedule, p. 1033, dwelling 1135, family 721, lines 23-26, David & Isabella Gray, AC. Notably, Margaret E. Allen, the seven-year-old daughter of Reuben and Margaret Gray Allen, is also listed on the 1860 census record taken two days earlier, 8 July 1860, showing her living with her parents and siblings in Delta Township as well. It's possible she was visiting her grandparents, or is a different Elizabeth Allen yet to be identified.

26 "Rights Held for Local Pioneer," *Escanaba Daily Press*, 6 September 1934, NA.

27 1860 U.S. Census, Delta County, Non-Population Schedule 4, Agricultural Census, p. 19-20, Farm 2, David Gray.

28 Delta County, Michigan, Deed Book B: 40 (David Gray to School District No. 4, 31 August 1867), FS.

29 Jacqueline Tatrow, "The Settling of the Village of Garden," in *Our Heritage: Garden Peninsula, Delta County, Michigan 1840-1980* (Michigan: Garden Peninsula Historical Society, 1982), 127.

30 Jacqueline Tatrow, "The Settling of the Village of Garden," in *Our Heritage: Garden Peninsula, Delta County, Michigan 1840-1980* (Michigan: Garden Peninsula Historical Society, 1982), 132.

31 1870 U.S. Census, Delton Township, Delta County, Michigan, population schedule, p. 2, dwelling 12, family 12, lines 27-33, David & Isabella Gray, AC.

32 Delta County, Michigan, Deed Book C:24 (David Gray to C. Wesley Gray, 20 November 1871; Delta County, Michigan, Deed Book C:25 (C. Wesley Gray to David and Isabella Gray, 20 November 1871), FS.

33 Margaret Coppess, "The Old Plante Place," in *Our Heritage: Garden Peninsula, Delta County, Michigan 1840-1980* (Michigan: Garden Peninsula Historical Society, 1982), 165.

34 *Notes on the Gray Family*, Garden Peninsula Historical Society; Jacqueline Tatrow, "Indians of the Garden Peninsula Wey-Oh-Qua-Touk or Bays de Nocquette," in *Our Heritage: Garden Peninsula, Delta County, Michigan 1840-1980* (Michigan: Garden Peninsula Historical Society, 1982), 119.

35 *Notes on the Gray Family*, Garden Peninsula Historical Society, Unpublished Manuscript.

36 Garden Peninsula Historical Society, "The David Farley Family," in *Our Heritage: Garden Peninsula, Delta County, Michigan 1840-1980* (Michigan: Garden Peninsula Historical Society, 1982), 221.

37 1870 U.S. Census, Delton Township, Delta County, Michigan, population schedule, p. 2, dwelling 12, family 13, line 34, Ann Maxwell.

38 Garden Peninsula Historical Society, "The Jonathon Trueblood Family," in *Our Heritage: Garden Peninsula, Delta County, Michigan 1840-1980* (Michigan: Garden Peninsula Historical Society, 1982), 270.

39 Garden Peninsula Historical Society, "The Reuben Allen Family," in *Our Heritage: Garden Peninsula, Delta County, Michigan 1840-1980* (Michigan: Garden Peninsula Historical Society, 1982), 194.

40 "Served Community for Years," *Escanaba Daily Press*, 2 September 1950, Garden Peninsula Historical Society.

41 Grace Stern, "Sack Bay" in *Our Heritage: Garden Peninsula, Delta County, Michigan 1840-1980* (Michigan: Garden Peninsula Historical Society, 1982), 21.

42 Record of Death for David Gray, Federal Non-Population Census Schedules, Schedule 5 - Persons Who Died During the Year Ending May 31, 1880, Enumeration No. 86, Page 2, Line 9, David Gray; "Died at his residence at Garden Bay on Monday, May 17, David Gray age 75 years," *Schoolcraft County Pioneer*, 27 May 1880, Garden Peninsula Historical Society.

43 "Died at his residence at Garden Bay on Monday, May 17, David Gray age 75 years," *Schoolcraft County Pioneer*, 27 May 1880.

44 1880 U.S. Census, Fairbanks Township, Delta County, Michigan, population schedule, enumeration district 86, p. 591, dwelling 79, family 80, line 20, Isabella Gray, AC.

45 Delta County, Michigan, Deed Book G:8 (Isabella Gray to Maria Tracy, 28 July 1882); Delta County, Michigan, Deed Book G:9 (Maria Tracy to Thomas Tracy, 28 July 1882), FS.

46 1880 U.S. Census, Delta County, Non-Population Schedule 2, Agricultural Census, enumeration district 36, page no. 6, Farm 3, Thomas Tracy, AC.

47 "Gray, Isabella," *Schoolcraft County Pioneer* (Manistique, MI), 6 August 1884, http://genealogytrails.com/mich/schoolcraft/obit.html; "Manistique News," *Iron Port* (Escanaba, MI), 16 August 1884.

48 Jacqueline Tatrow, "Kate's Bay History," in *Our Heritage: Garden Peninsula, Delta County, Michigan 1840-1980* (Michigan:

Garden Peninsula Historical Society, 1982), 33.

49   "Gray, Isabella," *Schoolcraft County Pioneer* (Manistique, MI), 6 August 1884, http://genealogytrails.com/mich/schoolcraft/obit.html.

50   George Leslie Bouschor, Notes on the David Gray and Isabella Kinread Gray Family, Courtesy of Robert Leslie Bouschor, collection of Aaron N. Bouschor.

51   Aaron N. Bouschor, *David Gray Headstone*, photograph, 4 September 2017, personal collection; Aaron N. Bouschor, *Isabella Gray Headstone*, photograph, 4 September 2017, personal collection.

52   Delta County, Michigan, Deed Book 8:164 (David Gray et al to John Wesley Gray, 8 April 1898); Delta County, Michigan, Deed Book 8:165 (John Wesley Gray et al to David Gray, 8 April 1898), FS; Delta County, Michigan, Deed Book 8:166 (John Wesley Gray et al to Margarette I. Mellon, 8 April 1898), FS.

53   Delta County, Michigan, Deed Book 9:523-24 (Estate of Charles Wesley Gray, Deceased, 1 February 1898), FS.

54   Geo. A. Ogle & Co., *Standard atlas of Delta County, Michigan* (Chicago: Geo. A. Ogle & Co., 1913), 58, University of Michigan Library Digital Collections.

55   "Farm At Garden Has Centennial," *Escanaba Daily Press*, 10 September 1964, Newspapers.com; "Review History of Garden Area," *Escanaba Daily Press*, 14 July 1964, Newspapers.com.

56   1850 U.S. Census, Rochester, Monroe County, New York, population schedule, p. 332, dwelling 253, family 284, line 28, Esther Gray, AC.

57   Record of Death for David Gray, Federal Non-Population Census Schedules, Schedule 5 - Persons Who Died During the Year Ending May 31, 1880, Enumeration No. 86, Page 2, Line 9, David Gray, AC; "Died at his residence at Garden Bay on Monday, May 17, David Gray age 75 years," *Schoolcraft County Pioneer*, 27 May 1880, Garden Peninsula Historical Society.

58   1850 U.S. Census, Rochester Monroe County, New York, population schedule, p. 332, dwelling 253, family 284, line 28, Esther Gray, AC.

59   Baptismal Record for George Kinread, 5 May 1782, Malew Baptisms 1782, Isle of Man Parish Registers, 1598-2009, Manx Museum and National Trust, FS.

60   Editors of Encyclopaedia Britannica, "Isle of Man." Encyclopedia Britannica, accessed 9 August 2024, https://www.britannica.com/place/Isle-of-Man.

61   "St. Marks," The Parish of Malew and Santan, accessed 27 June 2021, https://malewandsantan.wordpress.com/st-marks/.

62   New Brunswick, Crown Land Office, Land Petitions, Land Petition of George Kinread, 27 May 1820, FS.

63   "George Henry Kinread (1782-1865)," Find A Grave, Memorial No. 173479472, accessed 27 January 2019, https://www.findagrave.com/memorial/173479472/.

64   *Ann Kinread Atkinson Headstone*, "Ann Kinread Atkinson (1806-1883)," Find A Grave, Memorial No. 143249232, accessed 8 August 2024, https://www.findagrave.com/memorial/143249232; WikiTree contributors, "Ann (Kinread) Atkinson (1806-1883)," WikiTree: The Free Family Tree, last modified 2 February 2024, https://www.wikitree.com/wiki/Kinread-23.

65   "Gray, Isabella," *Schoolcraft County Pioneer* (Manistique, MI), 6 August 1884; "Manistique News," *Iron Port* (Escanaba, MI), 16 August 1884, EPL.

66   *John Kinread Headstone*, "John Kinread (1810-1886)," Find A Grave, Memorial No. 115016010, accessed 8 August 2024, https://www.findagrave.com/memorial/115016010; WikiTree contributors, "John W. Kinread (1810-1886)," WikiTree: The Free Family Tree, last modified 7 March 2023, https://www.wikitree.com/wiki/Kinread-2.

67   "Married," *Courier* (St. John, New Brunswick), 19 July 1834, New Brunswick Historical Newspapers Project; WikiTree contributors, "Elizabeth (Kinread) Dougherty (1812-1876)," WikiTree: The Free Family Tree, last modified 16 February 2024, https://www.wikitree.com/wiki/Kinread-25.

68   "Marriages," Gleaner and Northumberland, Kent and Gloucester Schediasma (Chatham, New Brunswick), 11 April 1837, Google News; *Margaret Johnson Headstone*, "Margaret Kinread Johnson (1813-1856)," Find A Grave, Memorial No. 144026396, accessed 8 August 2024, https://www.findagrave.com/memorial/144026396; WikiTree contributors, "Margaret (Kinread) Johnston (1813-1856)," WikiTree: The Free Family Tree, last modified 9 November 2023, https://www.wikitree.com/wiki/Kinread-26.

69   Marriage Record for William Kinread and Margaret Lamb, Registered 29 August 1845, Reg. No. 2551, Westmorland County Marriage Registers Vol. B, Westmorland County, New Brunswick, FS; Marriage Record for William Kinread and Eleanor Simmons, Registered 27 December 1873, Reg. No. 4650, Kent County Marriage Registers Vol. A, Kent County, New Brunswick, FS; Record of Death for William Kinread, 5 January 1898, Record No. 002284, Kent County, New Brunswick, Registration Division of Kent County, Provincial Archives of New Brunswick; WikiTree contributors, "William Kinread (1818-1898)," WikiTree: The Free Family Tree, last modified 20 November 2023, https://www.wikitree.com/wiki/Kinread-28.

70   Marriage Record for Thomas Kinread and Hannah E. Tuttle, Registered 1 May 1854, Reg. No. 3490, Westmorland

County Marriage Registers, Westmorland County, New Brunswick, FS; Record of Death for Thomas Kinread, 5 October 1892, Record No. 092283, New Brunswick Provincial Deaths, 1815-1938, FS; *Thomas Kinread Headstone*, "Thomas Kinread (1820-1892)," Find a Grave, Memorial No. 173621328 accessed 9 August 2024, https://www.findagrave.com/memorial/173621328; WikiTree contributors, "Thomas Kinread (1820-1892)," WikiTree: The Free Family Tree, last modified 22 November 2023, https://www.wikitree.com/wiki/Kinread-29.

71   New Brunswick, Crown Land Office, Land Petitions, Land Petition of George Kinread, 24 January 1839, https://www.familysearch.org/ark:/61903/3:1:3Q9M-C3HC-59H2-3?view=explore&groupId=TH-909-88494-33213-22. Note: George Kinread's 1839 land petition references a fifteen-year-old son who would "remain entirely uncapable of assisting himself and will therefore require to be supported without his own exertions."

72   Marriage Record for Stephen Peters and Martha Kinread, Registered 21 January 1847, Reg. No. 982, Kent County Marriage Registers Vol. A, Kent County, New Brunswick, FS; 1881 Census of Canada, Moncton, Westmorland County, New Brunswick, Schedule I - Population, page 17, line 9, Martha Peters, FS; WikiTree contributors, "Martha L. (Kinread) Peters (1824-1890)," WikiTree: The Free Family Tree, last modified 6 November 2022, https://www.wikitree.com/wiki/Kinread-8.

73   New Brunswick, Crown Land Office, Land Petitions, Land Petition of George Kinread, 24 January 1839, FS.

74   Joseph William Bouschor, Notes on the David Gray and Isabella Kinread Gray Family, Collection of Aaron N. Bouschor.

75   New Brunswick, Crown Land Office, Land Petitions, Land Petition of George Kinread, 27 May 1820, FS; New Brunswick, Crown Land Office, Land Petitions, Land Petition of George Kinread, 12 February 1827, FS.

76   New Brunswick, Crown Land Office, Land Petitions, Land Petition of George Kinread, 27 May 1820, FS.

77   New Brunswick, Crown Land Office, Land Petitions, Land Petition of George Kinread, 24 January 1839, FS.

78   New Brunswick, Crown Land Office, Land Petitions, Land Petition of George Kinread, 12 February 1827, FS.

79   Kent County, New Brunswick, Registar of Deeds, Deed Volume A:142-44 (George and Ann Kinread to S. C. Herves, FS.

80   New Brunswick, Crown Land Office, Land Petitions, Land Petition of George Kinread, 24 January 1839, FS.

81   New Brunswick, Crown Land Office, Land Petitions, Response of Warden of St. Mary's Church of Richibucto to Land Petition of George Kinread, 2 February 1839, FS.

82   New Brunswick Legislature, *The Local and Private Statutes of New Brunswick Vol. III* (Fredericton, NB: J. Simpson, 1855), 352, GB.

83   Kent County, New Brunswick, Registrar of Deeds, Deed Volume I:575-77 (Rector, Church Wardens and Vestry of Saint Mary's Church Richibucto to George Kinread, Registered 17 September 1849), FS.

84   Kent County, New Brunswick, Registrar of Deeds, Deed Volume J, Record No. 2742 (George Kinread and Wife, Mortgage, to John W. Weldon, Registered 18 September 1849), FS.

85   Kent County, New Brunswick, Registrar of Deeds, Deed Volume M, Record No. 4548 (George Kinread to William Kinread, Registered 30 March 1857), FS.

86   Kent County, New Brunswick, Registrar of Deeds, Deed Volume M, Record No. 4604 (William Kinread to George Kinread, Registered 25 June 1857), FS; Kent County, New Brunswick, Registrar of Deeds, Deed Volume M, Record No. 4605 (George Kinread, Mortgage, to William Kinread, Registered 27 June 1857), FS.

87   Kent County, New Brunswick, Registrar of Deeds, Deed Volume M, Record No. 4620 (George Kinread to David Wark, Registered 23 July 1857), FS.

88   Kent County, New Brunswick, Registrar of Deeds, Deed Volume N, Record No. 4677 (David Wark to George Kinread, Registered 23 September 1857), FS; Kent County, New Brunswick, Registrar of Deeds, Deed Volume N, Record No. 4678 (George Kinread, Mortgage, to David Wark, Registered 23 September 1857), FS; Kent County, New Brunswick, Registrar of Deeds, Deed Volume N, Record No. 4679 (George Kinread, Mortgage, to Robert Hutchinson, Registered 23 September 1857), FS; Kent County, New Brunswick, Registrar of Deeds, Deed Volume N, Record No. 4680 (George Kinread, Mortgage, to William Kinread, Registered 23 September 1857), FS.

89   1861 Census of Canada, New Brunswick, Kent County, Richibucto, Schedule I - Population, sheet 47, line 6, George Kinred, Library and Archives of Canada; 1861 Census of Canada, New Brunswick, Kent County, Richibucto, Schedule III - Agriculture, sheet 5, line 6, William Kinred, Library and Archives of Canada.

90   "George Henry Kinread (1782-1865)," Find A Grave, Memorial No. 173479472, accessed 27 January 2019, https://www.findagrave.com/memorial/173479472/.

91   Baptismal Record for John Kinread, 30 November 1760, Braddan Baptisms 1760, "Isle of Man Parish Registers, 1598-2009," Manx Museum and National Trust, FS.

92   "Total Population for the Island 1726-1891," A Manx Note Book, accessed 27 June 2021, http://www.isle-of-man.com/manxnotebook/history/pop.htm; Arthur William Moore, *Story of the Isle of Man: An Historical Reader for the Manx Schools* (United Kingdom: Unwin, 1901), 109, GB.

93   "Old Kirk Braddan," Isle of Man Guide, accessed 27 June 2021, https://www.iomguide.com/kirkbraddan.php.

94   Record of Marriage for John Kinread and Isabel Gawn, 1 July 1781, Malew Parish Marriage Register, "Isle of Man Parish Registers, 1598-2009," Manx Museum and National Trust, FS.

95   David Robertson, *A Tour Through the Isle of Man: To which is Subjoined a Review of the Manks History* (United Kingdom: author), 1794, 74, GB.

96   "Total Population for the Island 1726-1891," A Manx Note Book, accessed 27 June 2021, http://www.isle-of-man.com/manxnotebook/history/pop.htm.

97   Baptismal Record for Isabel Gawn, 16 January 1756, Rushen Parish Baptism Register 1709-1820, "Isle of Man Parish Registers, 1598-2009," Manx Museum and National Trust, FS.

98   Baptismal Record for Isabel Gawn, 9 April 1758, Rushen Parish Baptism Register 1709-1820, "Isle of Man Parish Registers, 1598-2009," Manx Museum and National Trust, FS.

99   John Duffield, *A History of Kirk Christ Rushen Isle of Man* (Port Erin, Isle of Man: Quine & Cubbon, Printers), 1935, Rushen Parish.

100   "Total Population for the Island 1726-1891," A Manx Note Book, accessed 27 June 2021, http://www.isle-of-man.com/manxnotebook/history/pop.htm.

101   "Old House of Keys," Isle of Man Guide, accessed 17 August 2024, https://www.iomguide.com/oldhouseofkeys.php.

102   Robertson, *A Tour Through the Isle of Man*, 63.

103   John Feltham, *A tour through the island of Mann, in 1797 and 1798* (United Kingdom: R. Cruttwell, 1798), 266, GB.

104   "Died," *Manx Liberal* (Douglas, Isle of Man), 2 December 1837, Manx National Heritage Library and Archives.

105   John Kinread Burial Record, 23 December 1837, Kirk-Braddan Burial Register 1796-1849, "Isle of Man Parish Registers, 1598-2009," Manx Museum and National Trust, FS.

106   Joseph Train, *An Historical and Statistical Account of the Isle of Man, from the Earliest Times to the Present Date: With a View of Its Ancient Laws, Peculiar Customs, and Popular Superstitions* (United Kingdom: M. A. Quiggin), 1845, 370, GB. This quotation references the reluctance of the population to embrace an early form of smallpox inoculation that met with great success relative to the normal mortality rates presented by smallpox, suggesting vaccine skepticism is far from a new phenomenon.

107   For the burial record of Isabel Kinread, widow of Gilbert Kinread, see Burial Record for Isabel Kinread, 25 February 1784, Lezayre Parish Burials 1696-1849, "Isle of Man Parish Registers, 1598-2009," Manx Museum and National Trust, FS.

Bibliography

Note: For printed sources maintained on an online database like Ancestry.com, FamilySearch.org, Google Books, HathiTrust.org, or Newspapers.com, I have provided the name of the database but omitted the URLs, access dates, and similar information for the sake of brevity. Readers who desire more information about a particular source are encouraged to contact the author. Electronic sources retain the URL and date of last modification or access. Individual census records, newspaper articles, vital records and recorded documents, webpages, or unpublished letters and manuscripts are listed in the notes sections for each chapter but omitted herein.

ABBREVIATIONS

GB. Google Books, https://books.google.com/

HT. HathiTrust Digital Library, https://www.hathitrust.org/

IA. Internet Archive, https://archive.org/details/texts.

LC. Library of Congress, https://www.loc.gov/

NARA. U.S. National Archives and Records Administration. https://www.archives.gov/

Books and Pamphlets

Bacqueville de la Potherie. "History of the Savage Peoples Who Are Allies of New France." In *The Indian Tribes of the Upper Mississippi Valley and Region of the Great Lakes*, edited by Emma Helen Blair. Cleveland: Arthur H. Clark Company, 1911, LC.

Bamford, Don. *Freshwater Heritage: A History of Sail on the Great Lakes, 1670-1918*. Toronto: Natural Heritage Books, 2007.

Barry, Gerald J. *The Sailors' Snug Harbor: A History*. New York City: Fordham University Press, 2000.

Beeson, Harvey C. *Beeson's Marine Directory of the Northwestern Lakes*. Harvey C. Beeson, Chicago, IL, 1911.

Bouchette, Joseph. *A Topographical Dictionary of the Province of Lower Canada*. London: Longman, Rees, Orme, Brown, Green, and Longman, 1832, GB.

Bryant, William Cullen. *Letters of a Traveller; or, Notes of Things Seen in Europe and America*. London: Richard Bentley, 1850, GB.

Canada Wildlife Service. *Cap Tourmente National Wildlife Area: Between Two Worlds*. Environment Canada, 1987, Government of Canada Publications.

Cleland, Charles E. *Rites of Conquest: The History and Culture of Michigan's Native Americans*. Ann Arbor: The University of Michigan Press, 1992.

Dickins, Asbury and John W. Forney, Eds. *American State Papers: Documents, Legislative and Executive, of the Congress of the United States.* Vol. 5. Washington, D.C.: Gales & Seaton, 1860, GB.

Duffield, John. *A History of Kirk Christ Rushen Isle of Man.* Port Erin, Isle of Man: Quine & Cubbon, Printers, 1935, Rushen Parish.

Dunbar, Willis F. and George S. May. *Michigan: A History of the Wolverine State.* 3rd Ed. Grand Rapids: Wm. B. Eerdmans Publishing Co., 1995.

Dunnigan, Brian Leigh. *A Picturesque Situation: Mackinac before Photography, 1615-1860.* Detroit: Wayne State University Press, 2008.

Faragher, John Mack. *A Great and Noble Scheme: The Tragic Story of the Expulsion of the French Acadians from their American Homeland.* New York: W.W. Norton & Company, Inc., 2005.

Feltham, John. *A tour through the island of Mann, in 1797 and 1798.* United Kingdom: R. Cruttwell, 1798, GB.

Freedman, Eric. *Michigan Free: Your Comprehensive Guide to Free Travel, Recreation, & Entertainment Opportunities.* Ann Arbor: University of Michigan Press, 1993, GB.

Garden Peninsula Historical Society. *Our Heritage: Garden Peninsula, Delta County, Michigan 1840–1980.* Michigan: Garden Peninsula Historical Society, 1982.

Harvey, Miles. *The King of Confidence.* New York: Little, Brown and Company, 2020.

Hornstein, Hugh A. *The Haywire: A Brief History of the Manistique and Lake Superior Railroad.* East Lansing, MI: Michigan State University Press, 2005.

Hyde, Anne F. *Born of Lakes and Plains: Mixed-Descent Peoples and the Making of the American West.* New York: W.W. Norton & Co., 2022.

Jameson, Anna. *Winter Studies and Summer Rambles in Canada.* Vol. 2. New York: Wiley and Putnam, 1839, GB.

Jensen, Trygvie. *Wooden Boats and Iron Men: History of Commercial Fishing in Northern Lake Michigan & Door County 1850 – 2005.* De Pere, WI: Paisa (Alt) Publishing Co., 2007.

Kappler, Charles J., ed. *Indian Affairs: Laws and Treaties.* Vol. 2. Washington, D.C.: Government Printing Office, 1904, GB.

Karamanski, Theodore J. *Deep Woods Frontier: A History of Logging in Northern Michigan.* Detroit: Wayne State University Press, 1989.
———. *Schooner Passage: Sailing Ships and the Lake Michigan Frontier.* Detroit: Wayne State University Press, 2000.

Laforest, Thomas J. *Our French-Canadian Ancestors.* Vol. 3. Palm Harbor, FL: LISI Press, 1985.
———. *Our French-Canadian Ancestors.* Vol. 12. Madison, WI: LISI Press, 1983.

LaFrombois, Pauline. *A Glimpse into the Past: A History of the Town of Scott*. New Franken, WI: John Grall Publishing, 2007, Archive.org.

LeDuc, M. Vonciel. *Manistique*. Charleston, SC: Arcadia Publishing, 2009.

Longfellow, Henry Wadsworth. "Evangeline." In *English Poetry III: From Tennyson to Whitman*. Vol. XLII. The Harvard Classics. New York: P.F. Collier & Son, 1910, GB.

Lowrie, Walter and Matthew St. Clair Clarke, Eds. *Documents, Legislative and Executive, of the Congress of the United States*. Vol. 8. Washington, D.C.: Gales and Seaton, 1832, HT.

Magnaghi, Russell M. *Understanding Two Centuries of Census Data of Michigan's Upper Peninsula*. Marquette, MI: Belle Fontaine Press, 2007, Northern Michigan University.

Manistique Centennial Inc. *Manistique Centennial Official Souvenir Book*. Manistique, MI: Manistique Centennial Inc., 1960.

Manistique Commercial Club. *Manistique: The Live Wire City of Upper Michigan*. Manistique, MI: Manistique Commercial Club, 1913.

Manistique Harold, *A Souvenir of Manistique Michigan*. Manistique, MI: Manistique Harold, 1901. Reprint, Manistique, MI: Schoolcraft County Historical Society, 2005.

Mansfield, J.B., ed. *History of the Great Lakes*. Vol 3. Chicago: J. H. Beers & Co., 1899.

Meron, Florence. *A History of the Township Village and People of Thompson Michigan*. Manistique School and Public Library. Unpublished Manuscript, 2003.

Milner, James W. "Report on the Fisheries of the Great Lakes; and the Result of Inquiries Prosecuted in 1871 and 1872." In *Report of the Commissioner for 1872 and 1873*. Washington, D.C.: Government Printing Office, 1874, GB.

Moore, Arthur William. *Story of the Isle of Man: An Historical Reader for the Manx Schools*. United Kingdom: Unwin, 1901, GB

Neville, Ella Hoes, Sarah Greene Martin, and Deborah Beaumont Martin. *Historic Green Bay*. Self Published: Green Bay, WI, 1893, LC.

New Brunswick Legislature. *The Local and Private Statutes of New Brunswick*. Vol. III. Fredericton, NB: J. Simpson, 1855, GB.

Orr, Jack. *Lumberjacks & River Pearls: Memories of Manistique*. Manistique: Pioneer-Tribune, 1979.

Osterhout, Mrs. Hasell. *Religious Heritage of Thompson, Michigan*. Self-published, 1970, Courtesy of Mary Bouschor.

Parkman, Francis. *France and England in North America*. Vol. 2, *Count Frontenac and New France under Louis*

XIV, A Half-Century of Conflict, Montcalm and Wolfe. New York: Library of America, 1983.

Peterson, Larry. *The Hiawatha Anthology: Stories from Upper Michigan's Pioneer Past.* Self-published, 2020.

Pioneer Society of the State of Michigan. *Report of the Pioneer Society of the State of Michigan.* Vol. 6. Lansing: W. S. George & Co., 1884, GB.

Powers, Perry F. *A History of Northern Michigan and Its People.* Vol. 3. Chicago: Lewis Publishing Company, 1912.

Reimann, Lewis C. *When Pine Was King.* Ann Arbor: Edwards Brothers, Inc., 1952.

Rentmeester, Les and Jeanne. *The Wisconsin Fur-Trade People.* Green Bay: Howard-Suamico Historical Society, Inc., 2009, 168, http://wi-research.info/wisconsin-history/The%20Wisconsin%20Fur%20Trade%20People.pdf.

R. L. Polk & Co., Comp. *Polk's Michigan State Gazetteer and Business Directory.* Detroit: The Tribune Printing Company, 1875, HT.

Robertson, David. *A Tour Through the Isle of Man: To which is Subjoined a Review of the Manks History.* United Kingdom: author, GB.

Saint Francis de Sales Church. *Triple Jubilee celebration: 1833, 1883, 1933.* Manistique, MI: St. Francis de Sales Church, 1958, HT.

Schoolcraft County Historical Society. *Historic Tour of Manistique.* Manistique, MI: Schoolcraft County Historical Society, n.d.

Schoolcraft, Henry R. *Personal Memoirs of a Residence of Thirty Years with the Indian Tribes on the American Frontiers.* Philadelphia: Lippincott, Grambo and Co., 1851, GB.

Scott, Gene. *Michigan Shadow Towns: A Study of Vanishing and Vibrant Villages.* Self-published, 2005.

Shepherd, Barnett. *Sailors' Snug Harbor, 1801-1976.* New York City: Snug Harbor Cultural Center, 1979.

Smith, Hugh M. and Merwin-Marie Snell, comps. *Review of the Fisheries of the Great Lakes in 1885.* Washington, D.C.: Government Printing Office, 1890, GB.

State Historical Society of Wisconsin. *Mackinac Register of Baptisms and Internments, 1695-1821.* Madison: State Historical Society of Wisconsin, 1910, LC.

Sulte, Benjamin. *Histoire des Canadiens-Français 1608-1880.* Vol. 4. Montréal: Wilson & Cie, 1882, HT.

Thwaites, Reuben Gold, Ed. *Collections of the State Historical Society of Wisconsin.* Vol. 19. Madison: Wisconsin Historical Society, 1910, HT.

————. *Collections of the State Historical Society of Wisconsin.* Madison: Wisconsin Historical Society, 1908, HT.

———. *The Jesuit Relations and Allied Documents: Travels and Explorations of the Jesuit Missionaries in New France 1610–1791*. Cleveland: Burrows Brothers Company, 1899, HT.

de Tocqueville, Alexis. *Democracy in America*. New York: Library of America, 2004, GB.

Train, Joseph. *An Historical and Statistical Account of the Isle of Man, from the Earliest Times to the Present Date: With a View of Its Ancient Laws, Peculiar Customs, and Popular Superstitions*. United Kingdom: M. A. Quiggin, 1845, GB.

Turner, George H., comp., *Record of Service of Michigan Volunteers in the Civil War, 1861–1865*. Vol. 37. Kalamazoo: Ihling Bros. & Everard, 1909, HT.

United States Army Signal Corps. *Annual Report of the Chief Signal-Office to the Secretary of War for the Year 1876*. Washington, D.C.: Government Printing Office, 1876, GB.

Van Fleet, James Alvin. *Old and New Mackinac*. Ann Arbor: Courier Steam Printing House, 1870, GB.

Vogel, Virgil J. *Indian Names in Michigan*. Ann Arbor: The University of Michigan Press, 1986.

W. Weeks & Co. *Annual City Directory of the Inhabitants, Business Firms, Incorporated Companies, etc., of Detroit for 1873–4*. Detroit: J. W. Weeks & Co., 1873, HT.

Welch, Richard W. *County Evolution in Michigan 1790–1897*. Lansing, MI: Michigan Department of Education, 1972, FS.

Wermuth, Mary L. *Michigan's Centennial Family Farm Heritage*. Hillsdale, MI: Ferguson Communications, 1986.

Western Historical Company. *History of the Upper Peninsula of Michigan*. Chicago: Western Historical Company, 1883, HT.

White, Stephen A. *Dictionnaire Généalogique Des Familles Acadiennes*. Moncton, N.B.: Centre D'études Acadiennes, Université De Moncton, 1999.

Widder, Keith R. *Battle for the Soul: Métis Children Encounter Evangelical Protestants at Mackinaw Mission, 1823–1837*. East Lansing: Michigan State University Press, GB.

Wood, Edwin Orr. *Historic Mackinac*. Vol. 1. New York: Macmillan Company, 1918, GB.

Journals and Periodicals

Bagger, Louis. "The Sailors' Snug Harbor." *Harper's New Monthly Magazine*. Vol. XLVI (December 1872 to May 1873), Archive.org.

Chamberlain, Alexander F. "Algonkian Words in American English." *Journal of American Folklore* 15 (October–December 1902).

Gagnieur, Rev. William F., S.J. "Indian Place Names in the Upper Peninsula and Their Interpretation." *Michigan History Magazine* 2, no. 3 (July 1918), GB.

Hodson, Christopher. "Exile on Spruce Street: An Acadian History." *The William and Mary Quarterly* 67, no. 2 (2010). https://doi.org/10.5309/willmaryquar.67.2.249.

Last, Fannie C. "The Astor House." *Green Bay Historical Bulletin* 3.6 (November–December 1927), GB.

Patrimoine du Vairais. "Bouchard Claude dit Le Petit Claude (vers 1626–1699)." *Les Carnets du Vairais* (7 September 2016), https://www.patrimoineduvairais.fr/app/download/22512070/Revue+n%C2%B07.pdf

Widder, Keith R. "After the Conquest: Michilimackinac, a Borderland in Transition, 1760–1763." *Michigan Historical Review* 34, no. 1 (Spring 2008), https://www.jstor.org/stable/20174257.
———. "Magdelaine LaFramboise: The First Lady of Mackinac Island." *Mackinac History* IV, No. 1 (2007).

Maps

Colton, G. W. "Lake Superior and the Northern Part of Michigan." *Colton's Atlas of the World.* New York: J.H. Colton. 1856. David Rumsey Map Collection, David Rumsey Map Center, Stanford Libraries.

Geo. A. Ogle & Co. *Standard atlas of Delta County, Michigan.* Chicago: Geo. A. Ogle & Co. 1913. University of Michigan Library Digital Collections.

Greeley, Aaron. *Plan of the Town and Harbor of Michilimacinac, Mackinac Island.* 15 July 1848. Records of the Bureau of Land Management, NAID: 301095564, NARA.

United States Geological Survey. "Point Aux Barques Quadrangle Map." United States Geological Survey. 2019. https://ngmdb.usgs.gov/ht-bin/tv_browse.pl?id=23b2c4e13c503448332bd9d5e483e714.

United States Lake Survey. *North End of Green Bay the Islands at the Entrance and N.W. Shore of Lake Michigan.* 1863. University of Wisconsin Digitalized Collections.

"Claim No. 2 Simon Champaigne." *Survey of Mackinac Islands and Private Claims, also Private Claims at Point St. Ignace.* Michigan Department of Natural Resources, Real estate Division Survey Notes, Michiganology.org.

Newspapers

Advocate (Sturgeon Bay, WI)
Assumption Pioneer (Napoleonville, LA)
Battle Creek Enquirer (Battle Creek, MI)
Bayfield County Press (Bayfield, MI)
Cheboygan Democrat (Cheboygan, MI)
Daily Advertiser (Lafayette, LA)
Daily Mining Journal (Marquette, MI)
Delta (Escanaba, MI)

Detroit Free Press (Detroit, MI)
Escanaba Daily Press (Escanaba, MI)
Evening News (Sault Ste. Marie, MI)
Grand Haven Times (Grand Haven, MI)
Grand Traverse Herald (Traverse City, MI)
Green Bay Press-Gazette (Green Bay, WI)
Green Bay Republican (Green Bay, WI)
Iowa County Democrat (Mineral Point, IA)
Iron Port (Escanaba, MI)
Lansing State Journal (Lansing, MI)
Leelanau Enterprise (Leland, MI)
Lowell Ledger (Lowell, MI)
Manistique Pioneer-Tribune (Manistique, MI)
Manistique Semi-Weekly Pioneer (Manistique (MI)
Port Angeles Evening News (Port Angeles, WA)
Proctor Journal (Proctor, MN)
Schoolcraft County Pioneer (Manistique, MI)
Semi-Weekly Pioneer (Manistique, MI)
Staten Island Advance (Staten Island, NY)
Washburn Times (Washburn, WI)
Wisconsin Enquirer (Madison, WI)

Illustration Credits

ABBREVIATIONS

DRMC. David Rumsey Map Collection, David Rumsey Map Center, Stanford Libraries, https://www.davidrumsey.com/

IA. Internet Archive, https://archive.org/details/texts

NARA. U.S. National Archives and Records Administration

Introduction

Page 3: Tanner, Henry S. *A New Map Of Michigan with its Canals, Roads & Distances.* Map. Philadelphia: H.S. Tanner, 1836. DRMC.

Page 4: Colton, G.W. *Lake Superior And The Northern Part Of Michigan.* Map. New York: J.H. Colton & Co., 1856. DRMC.

Part One – The Bouschor Family and Michigan's Upper Peninsula

Page 12: Manning, Warren H. *Mackinac Island Michigan State Park and Private Claims.* Map. Mackinac Island State Park Commission. 1913. Mackinac State Historic Parks Collection, https://www.sunsetforest.org/_files/ugd/5cf9dc_b8bcbeb4513144dc998f39173e4c440c.pdf.

Page 14: Dillon, Richard & Hall, Thomas. *Michilimackinac, on Lake Huron : To his Excellency Sir George Prevost Bart. Governor General and Commander in Chief of all his Majesties Forces in British America. / This print is humbly Inscribed by his Excellency's most obedient humble servant Richard Dillon Junr. ; Drawn by Richard Dillon Junr. ; Engraved by Thomas Hall.* Engraving. William L. Clements Library, University of Michigan Library Digital Collections, https://quod.lib.umich.edu/w/wcl1ic/x-6707/wcl006773.

Page 15: Detroit Publishing Co., Publisher. *Mackinac Island, Mich.* United States Michigan Mackinac Island, None. [Between 1880 and 1899]. Photograph, https://www.loc.gov/item/2016798650/.

Page 17: Tanner, Henry S. *A New Map Of Michigan with its Canals, Roads & Distances.* Map. Philadelphia: H.S. Tanner. 1836. DRMC.

Page 18: Jameson, Anna Brownell. *Indian Lodges on the Beach of the Island of Mackinac.* Etching. 1837. Baldwin Collection of Canadiana, Toronto Public Library, https://digitalarchive.tpl.ca/objects/266438/indian-lodges-on-the-beach-of-the-island-of-mackinac?ctx=dfa347d9dede-a261b90d6dbc0743fad0f2d2bb3d&idx=0.

Page 19: Walling, H. F. *Upper Peninsula, scale six miles to an inch (Delta County).* Map. Detroit: R.M. & S.T. Tackabury. 1873. DRMC.

Page 20: Wikimedia Commons contributors. *Delta County, MI Census Map.* Image. 2019. *Wikimedia Commons*, https://w.wiki/C9MR.

Page 21: *Gray Family Homestead Farmhouse*. 1926. Courtesy of M.L. Zambrana, Garden Peninsula Historical Society Facebook Page, https://www.facebook.com/groups/437875659638098/permalink/2365381380220840/.

Page 23: Lyon, Lucius. *Township No. 39 N. Range No. 17 W. Mer. Mich.*. Map. Surveyor General's Office, General Land Office. 15 March 1849. U.S. Department of the Interior, Bureau of Land Management. https://glorecords.blm.gov/details/survey/default.aspx?dm_id=31664.

Page 25: McKenney, Thomas L. *White Fish of the Lakes*. Drawing. *Sketches of a Tour to the Lakes, of the Character and Customs of the Chippeway Indians, and of Incidents Connected with the Treaty of Fond Du Lac*. Baltimore: Fielding Lucas, Jr., 1827, 172, Google Books.

Page 26: *Mackinac, August 3, 1859*. Drawing. 1859. Detroit Institute of Arts, https://dia.org/collection/mackinac-august-3-1859-95302.

Page 27: United States Commission of Fish and Fisheries. *Gill Net of Lake Michigan*. Drawing. 1871–72. Report of Commissioner of Fish and Fisheries. Freshwater and Marine Image Bank, University of Washington Ditigal Collections, https://digitalcollections.lib.washington.edu/digital/collection/fishimages/id/33433/rec/7.

Page 28: *Barque Point Fishing Boat*. Photograph. Undated. Courtesy of Robert Leslie Bouschor, collection of Aaron N. Bouschor.

Page 29: *Horses at Barque Point*. Photograph. Undated. Collection of G. Leslie Bouschor, Schoolcraft County Historical Society.

Page 31: *Barque Point Homestead*. Photograph. Undated. Courtesy of Robert Leslie Bouschor, collection of Aaron N. Bouschor.

Page 31: *Barque Point Homestead Fish Sheds*. Photograph. 1923. Courtesy of Mary Bouschor.

Page 31: *Barque Point Homestead*. Photograph. Undated. Courtesy of Robert Leslie Bouschor, collection of Aaron N. Bouschor.

Page 33: *Barque Point Homestead*. Photograph. Undated. Courtesy of Robert Leslie Bouschor, collection of Aaron N. Bouschor.

Page 34: Aaron N. Bouschor. *Bouschor Family Homestead Foundation Ruins*. Photograph. 14 May 2024. Collection of Aaron N. Bouschor.

Page 34: Aaron N. Bouschor. *Old Barque Point Trail*. Photograph. 17 May 2024. Collection of Aaron N. Bouschor.

Page 35: *Picnic at Little Harbor School*. Photograph. Undated [Before 1925]. Courtesy of Mary Bouschor.

Page 36: *Barque Point Picnic*. Photograph. Undated [Before 1925]. Collection of G. Leslie Bouschor, Schoolcraft County Historical Society.

Part Two – Simon Bouschor and Harriette Isabella Gray Bouschor

Page 62: Oliver Howard. *Harriette Isabella Gray Bouschor.* Photograph. Manistique: Howard Studio, Undated [Between 1888–1891]. Courtesy of Mary Bouschor.

Page 64: *Bouschor Family at Home.* Photograph [Before 1907]. Undated. Courtesy of Mary Bouschor.

Page 66: *Ida Isabelle Farley Bouschor, Mary Jane Clark Bouschor, and Simon Bouschor at Harriette Bouschor's Grave.* Photograph. Undated. Courtesy of Robert Leslie Bouschor, collection of Aaron N. Bouschor.

Page 66: *Simon Bouschor and Edward Albert Bouchard.* Photograph. Undated. Courtesy of Robert Leslie Bouschor, collection of Aaron N. Bouschor.

Page 67: *Memorial Card for Mrs. Simon Bouchard.* Reproduction. 18 December 1906. Ancestry.com.

Page 68: *Simon Bouschor at 701 Michigan Avenue, Manistique.* Photograph. Undated. Courtesy of Robert Leslie Bouschor, collection of Aaron N. Bouschor.

Part Three – Ancestors of Simon Bouschor

Page 82: Wikimedia Commons contributors. *Hudson's Bay company headquarters at York Factory, Manitoba.* Coloured lithograph. 1853. "File:HS34 1.jpg." Wikimedia Commons, https://w.wiki/C9MV.

Page 83: Hudson Bay Servant's Contract for Elie Bouchard. Document. 15 July 1824. Hudson Bay Company Archives, Archives of Manitoba.

Page 86: Detroit Publishing Co., Publisher. *Old time cavalier, the Great Lakes, Detroit, Mich.* Photograph. Undated [Between 1905 and 1915]. Library of Congress, https://www.loc.gov/item/2016811179/.

Page 89: Smithsonian Institute, Bureau of American Enthology. *Michigan 1.* Map. 1896–97. LC, https://lccn.loc.gov/13023487.

Page 92: *Captain E. A. Bouchard.* Photograph. Undated. Find a Grave Memorial No. 74242425, Capt Edward Albert Bouchard, https://www.findagrave.com/memorial/74242425/edward-albert-bouchard.

Page 94: *Remi Bouchard and Simon Bouschor.* Photograph. Undated. Collection of G. Leslie Bouschor, Schoolcraft County Historical Society. My thanks to Mary Bouschor for her identification of the man on the left as being Simon's younger brother, Remi Bouchard.

Page 95: Greeley, Aaron. *Plan of the Town and Harbour of Michilimacinac, Mackinac Island.* Map. Records of the Bureau of Land Management, 15 July 1848. NARA, https://catalog.archives.gov/id/301095564.

Page 97: *Admission of an Old Sailor to the Harbor.* Engraving. January 1873. Louis Bagger. "The Sailors' Snug Harbor." *Harper's Monthly,* January 1873. IA, https://archive.org/details/harpers-1873-vol-46/page/189/mode/2up.

Page 97: *One of the Sleeping-Rooms.* Engraving. January 1873. Louis Bagger. "The Sailors' Snug Harbor."

Harper's Monthly, January 1873. IA, https://archive.org/details/harpers-1873-vol-46/page/191/mode/2up.

Page 107: *La vieille église et le presbytère*. Photograph. Undated. Collection of Jean-Denis Beauchamp, Municipalité de Saint-Roch-de-l'Achigan, https://sra.quebec/histoire-de-la-riviere-de-lachigan.

Page 107: *La rue Principale en 1922*. Photograph. 1922. Collection of Rita Lamarche Perreault, Municipalité de Saint-Roch-de-l'Achigan, https://sra.quebec/histoire-de-la-riviere-de-lachigan.

Page 110: Greeley, Aaron. *Plan of the Island of Michilimackinac [Mackinac] shewing the Military Reservation upon that island*. Map. 1810. NARA, https://s3.amazonaws.com/NARAprodstorage/lz/cartographic/rg-075/305482/Batch0002B/305482_00754_01.jpg.

Page 110: Mullett, John. *Private Claims at Michilimackinac, Surveyed in October and November 1828*. Map. Washington, D.C.: General Land Office, 1847. University of Michigan Clark Library, UM Clark Library Maps, https://quod.lib.umich.edu/c/clark1ic/x-003538359/39015091881287.

Page 113: The Miriam and Ira D. Wallach Division of Art, Prints and Photographs: Art & Architecture Collection, The New York Public Library. *Habit of an Ottawa an Indian Nation of North America. Indien de la Nation Ottawa dans L'Amerique septentrional*. New York Public Library Digital Collections, https://digitalcollections.nypl.org/items/510d47e4-81bf-a3d9-e040-e00a18064a99.

Page 115: *Village Ottowa, Ile de Michilimakinac*. Black and white lithograph of Native American Village on Mackinac Island. Circa 1842. In the digital collection *Bentley Historical Library: Bentley Image Bank* University of Michigan Library Digital Collections, https://quod.lib.umich.edu/b/bhl/x-hs9911/hs9911.

Page 129: Bouchette, Joseph. *This topographical map of the Districts of Quebec, Three Rivers, St. Francis and Gaspe, Lower Canada* [Detail]. Map. London: James Wyld, 1831. DRMC.

Page 132: Brown, Emanuel. *A new & accurate map of the islands of Newfoundland, Cape Briton, St. John and Anticosta; together with the neighbouring countries of Nova Scotia, Canada* [Detail]. Map. London: William Innys et al., 1747. DRMC.

Page 141: Bouchette, Joseph. *Map of the Provinces of Lower & Upper Canada* [Detail]. London: James Wyld, 1831. DRMC.

Page 146: Montresor, John. *Map of Nova Scotia or Acadia with the Islands of Cape Breton and St. John's* [Detail]. Map. London: A. Bury, 1768. DRMC.

Page 147: Craig, George. *Deportation of the Acadians*. Painting. 1893. Wikimedia Commons, https://w.wiki/C9MW.

Page 159: de Champlain, Samuel. *Le Canada faict par le Sr de Champlain, ou sont la Nouvelle France la Nouvelle Angleterre la Nouvelle Hollande la Nouvelle Suede la Virginie &c avec les nations voisines et autres terres nouvellement découvertes suivant les mémoires de P. Du Val géographe du Roy*. Map. 1615. In the digital collection William L. Clements Library Image Bank. William L. Clements Library, University of Michigan

Library Digital Collections, https://quod.lib.umich.edu/w/wcl1ic/x-8963/wcl009038.

Page 160: Wikimedia Commons contributors. *Plan de la Seigneurie de Beau-Pre - 2e feuillet*. Map. 1751. Wikimedia Commons, https://w.wiki/C9MX.

Page 166: Wikimedia Commons contributors. *Baie Saint-Paul vu du nord*. Photograph. 30 July 2007. Wikimedia Commons, https://w.wiki/C9MY.

Page 168: Wikimedia Commons contributors. *Plan du Fort du Port Royal a la Acadie*. Map. 1702. Wikimedia Commons, https://w.wiki/C9MZ.

Page 176: Bouchette, Joseph. *This topographical map of the Districts of Quebec, Three Rivers, St. Francis and Gaspe, Lower Canada* [Detail]. Map. London: James Wyld, 1831. DRMC.

Part Four – Ancestors of Harriette Isabella Gray Bouschor

Page 191: *Isabella Kinread Gray*. Photograph. Undated. Courtesy of the Garden Peninsula Historical Society.

Page 192: Lyon, Lucius. *Township No. 39 N. Range No. 18 W. Mer. Mich*. Map. 19 April 1849. Surveyor General's Office, General Land Office, U.S. Department of the Interior, Bureau of Land Management, https://glorecords.blm.gov/details/survey/default.aspx?dm_id=31667.

Page 194: *Reuben Cyrus and Mary Jane Clark Family*. Photograph. Undated. Courtesy of Robert Leslie Bouschor, collection of Aaron N. Bouschor.

Page 195: *Anne Gray Maxwell and Margaret Gray Allen*. Photograph. Undated. Courtesy of the Garden Peninsula Historical Society.

Page 196: Van Sickle, Adolphus. *Thomas Tracy*. Photograph. Escanaba & Ishpeming: Van Sickle Studio, Undated (between 1890–1891). Courtesy of the Garden Peninsula Historical Society.

Page 200: New Brunswick Grant Reference Plan No. 89 [Detail]. Map. Undated. New Brunswick Department of Lands & Mines. Provincial Archives of New Brunswick, https://archives.gnb.ca/Exhibits/Communities/Details.aspx?culture=en-CA&community=4200.

Page 204: Gaba, Eric – Wikimedia Commons user: Sting. *Isle of Man topographic map-en.svg*. Map. 4 September 2008. Wikimedia Commons, https://w.wiki/C9Ma.

Page 205: Wikimedia Commons contributors. *Sheadings and parishes - Isle of Man.svg*. Map. 15 February 2018. Wikimedia Commons, https://w.wiki/C9Mb.

Index

Index

Index

About the Author

Aaron N. Bouschor is an attorney and former higher education administrator. He lives in southern Arizona with his wife and Siamese cat. He is the author of the novel *The Blue Flame* and the forthcoming *The New King* under the pen name Nathan Shore.